Chronic inflation in an industrialising economy: the Brazilian experience

Chronic inflation in an industrialising economy: the Brazilian experience

Vincent Parkin

CAMBRIDGE UNIVERSITY PRESS
Cambridge
New York Port Chester
Melbourne Sydney

CAMBRIDGE UNIVERSITY PRESS
Cambridge, New York, Melbourne, Madrid, Cape Town, Singapore,
São Paulo, Delhi, Dubai, Tokyo

Cambridge University Press
The Edinburgh Building, Cambridge CB2 8RU, UK

Published in the United States of America by Cambridge University Press, New York

www.cambridge.org
Information on this title: www.cambridge.org/9780521134125

First published 1991
This digitally printed version 2010

A catalogue record for this publication is available from the British Library

Library of Congress Cataloguing in Publication data
Parkin, Vincent
Chronic inflation in an industrialising economy: the Brazilian experience / Vincent Parkin.
p. cm.
Based on the author's thesis (Ph. D.) – University of Cambridge.
Includes bibliographical references and index.
ISBN 0–521–37540–1
1. Inflation (Finance) – Brazil. 2. Prices – Brazil. 3. Wages – Brazil. 4. Inflation (Finance) – Brazil – Econometric models.
I. Title.
HG835.P37 1990
332.4′1′0981 – dc20 90–41079 CIP

ISBN 978-0-521-37540-5 Hardback
ISBN 978-0-521-13412-5 Paperback

Contents

Preface

This book grew out of a Ph.D. thesis presented in the Faculty of Economics and Politics of the University of Cambridge. Besides doing away with a most unwieldy title, revising some of the econometric work in chapters 3 and 4 and, making a series of minor revisions throughout, the primary change made has been to rewrite chapter 1 in collaboration with T. G. Srinivasan of the University of Glasgow and the Indian Economic Service and Professor David Vines of the University of Glasgow. In its new form, chapter 1 offers a rigorous theoretical analysis of structural inflation and its interactions with money and finance. A new section has also been added to chapter 2 on Brazil's recent experience with inflation and stabilisation.

A great debt of thanks is due to Professor David Vines for his encouragement, guidance and enthusiasm not only during his time as my thesis supervisor at Cambridge but also in the run up to publication of this book. I am also grateful to Mr Ken Coutts of the Department of Applied Economics at Cambridge for his helpful assistance and for allowing me to make use of the Cambridge Economic Policy Group's *Model Processing System* to carry out the simulation exercises in this book.

As a research student at Cambridge I benefited greatly at various stages from the financial support of the Commonwealth Scholarship Commission in the United Kingdom, the Social Sciences and Humanities Research Council of Canada, as well as the European University Institute in San Domenico di Fiesole, Tuscany, where I spent a fruitful and stimulating period.

My Brazilian colleagues at Cambridge, Roberto Viana Batista and Maria de Lourdes de Medeiros Kain both went out of their way to assist a non-native embarking upon a study of their country's economy. For this and for their friendship I am grateful. During our time together as research students, Sveinbjörn Blöndal became a valued colleague and friend.

To Helen Dunkley I owe my thanks for her moral support as well as her invaluable assistance in preparing the original manuscript.

Naturally the usual disclaimers apply.

Introduction

This study seeks to shed light upon the nature of the chronic price inflation that today afflicts many of the world's developing economies, as it has done for decades. Chronic inflation, measured in increases in the price level of tens and sometimes hundreds of per cent per year, profoundly affects the pattern of a country's economic growth and development, its political and social fabric and the wellbeing of its citizens.

The specific focus of this study is the Brazilian inflation in the period from the military *coup d'état* of 1964 up to the mid-1980s – its root causes, the processes by which it became self-perpetuating and its interactions with government's macro- and microeconomic policies.

While the focus is on Brazil, both the conceptual framework applied to the problem and the lessons to be learned from the empirical analysis should be of general interest for other high inflation industrialising economies – especially those in Latin America.

Attempts to explain the causes of high and volatile rates of inflation in Latin America, as well as the policy prescriptions that flow from these explanations, have tended to fall into one of two categories – monetarist or a combination of structuralist and cost-push.

The monetarist perspective on inflation is now well known both in the industrialised and in the developing world. The roots of inflation, according to this school of thought, reside in an overly expansionary rate of increase in money and credit. Government's inability or unwillingness to tailor its expenditure to levels commensurate with available revenues is often cited as a cause of excessive monetary growth. Fiscal deficits that are not amenable to financing through the capital markets, given the thinness of these, are covered instead by borrowing from the central bank; in other words through monetary expansion.

The simple logic of the monetarist explanation and the apparently straightforward policy prescriptions that it throws up have proved persuasive to many especially where, as in the high inflation economies of

Latin America, rising price levels are indeed often accompanied by large fiscal deficits, financed through money creation. Yet the limitations of the approach are now also widely recognised and include such problems as the definition of 'money', the difficulty of sustaining the assumption of a clear 'one way' chain of causation between money and prices and, of particular relevance in the context of developing economies, a high degree of abstraction from a given institutional, political and historical context.

Those who have rejected narrowly based monetary explanations for the chronic Latin American inflations have tended instead to look, to varying degrees, at rigidities in the structures of production, trade and distribution as ultimate causes of inflation. The viability of 'structuralism' as an alternative basis to monetarism around which to organise economic policy has been hampered by difficulties in extracting simple policy prescriptions – particularly for the short term, a lack of attention to the financial side of the economy and, generally, to the absence of a widely accepted and clearly articulated framework for policy orientated analysis and planning.

The jumping off point for this study is the now widespread recognition that inflation in the industrialising economies of Latin America is typically a complex process of which neither a monetarist nor a naive structuralist cum cost-push diagnosis provides an adequate characterisation. Notwithstanding the above, the present study starts from the premise that the Latin American structuralist tradition provides a much richer and more promising basis than monetarism upon which to build a more general framework for the analysis.

A macroeconomic model developed here for the study of inflation provides a framework that allows for an explicit consideration of important interactions between structural and cost-push inflations on the one hand, and demand and financial factors on the other. In this way a bridge is formed between explanations for inflation centred upon the interaction of prices and wages with the 'real' economy, and predominantly monetary explanations for the same phenomenon.

On the level of economic policy-making, it is hoped that the present study, by helping advance the process of integrating the key tenets of structuralism into a more general macroeconomic framework, makes a contribution towards creating an improved basis for policy orientated analysis and planning in economies afflicted by chronic structural inflation.

Econometric techniques are used extensively in this study both to analyse the sectoral price formation process and also to estimate many parameters of the 'real' sector equations of the structural macromodel. This statistical method lends itself to the identification of multipliers and elasticities inherent in relationships between variables that are often too complex to be gleaned from simpler statistical or graphical forms of analysis. By estimating a simultaneous system of equations, one is able tentatively to identify causal links and interdependencies between variables in a way that is not possible using reduced form models. Prices and inflation rates are so highly interdependent that it can prove even more difficult otherwise to sort out cause and effect. The aim has been to build with care a structural model of wage and price determination in order to impart a more solid foundation to the subsequent simulation and policy experiments. A brief note on the specific research methodology employed is presented in appendix 2.

Outline of the chapters

Part I introduces a proposed theoretical framework for the study of inflation as well as the specific problem to be analysed, namely inflation in Brazil. Chapter 1 begins with a brief review of the Latin American structuralist, and the more recent neo-structuralist, approaches to inflation. A formal model that captures the key tenets of the structuralist approach is developed and its properties are analysed qualitatively and graphically. A second version of the model is then presented which retains its structuralist character while also including an explicit role for stocks and flows of financial assets.

Chapter 2 is devoted to an overview of Brazilian inflation from the mid-1960s through to the present and to a review of existing interpretations placed upon this phenomenon. The concentration is on the period following the military *coup d'état* of 1964 up to the end of 1984. The choice of 1984 as the initial cut off point coincides with the end period used in the econometric analysis of later chapters. This in turn reflected the availability of data at the time the modelling exercise was begun.

The conclusion to emerge from this review is that many elements in the inflationary process have yet to be adequately explained in the literature. This is particularly true of the interaction between 'real' and 'financial' sectors and of the contribution of the food market to overall inflation.

In a final section of chapter 2, Brazil's experience with inflation since 1984 is looked at in brief. It is argued that the economic structure which is the focus of this analysis is not so different today relative to the early 1980s as to make the analytical content of this study of purely historical interest. On the contrary, the insights gained into the roots of inflation, the means by which it is propagated and becomes self-sustaining and the feedbacks between public policy and inflation remain very relevant to today's problems.

Part II comprises four chapters devoted to the microeconomics of pricing in the context of a developing economy. Each chapter is devoted to the specification and estimation of models to explain particular prices. In each instance the principal relevant theories of pricing are reviewed with special emphasis upon the applicability of each in light of certain particular features of a developing economy. Also examined is the literature on the empirical testing of pricing hypotheses, with a view to identifying the 'best practice' modelling techniques. Despite a Brazilian bias, most of part II will be found to be applicable to the modelling of prices in developing countries in general.

Part II is sub-divided as follows: chapter 3 is concerned with price formation in manufacturing industry; chapter 4 with changes in average earnings in manufacturing; chapter 5 with price and output determination in the market for domestic foodstuffs; and chapter 6 with the cruzeiro/U.S. dollar exchange rate along with various aggregate price indices.

In part III a macroeconomic model comprising fifty-two definitional and stochastic equations is set out, validated and used in simulation exercises in an effort to identify the impact upon the economy of certain inflationary shocks and policy responses. The simulation period is 1966–83. Chapter 7 is devoted to an exposition of the model which is built around the core wage and price relationships identified in part II. An historical simulation of the complete model is performed in chapter 8 and its 'tracking' properties are evaluated. Multiplier analysis is then used to enquire further into the nature of the model, specifically as regards its stability. The counterfactual shock experiments performed also afford an initial look at how the model economy responds to inflationary stimuli from different sources. In chapter 9, we use the model to consider again some of the issues and processes discussed initially in part I. Policy experiments are performed to assess:

(a) the implications of changes in wage and exchange rate indexation regimes upon the response of the model to a foreign price shock, and
(b) the impact of a negative food production shock under three different assumptions about the reaction of policy-makers.

The study ends with a series of broad conclusions and suggestions for further research in chapter 10. It is here that we draw out the implications of the simulation exercises for an understanding of Brazil's inflation and, more generally, argue in favour of the relevance of an expanded structuralist approach for the study of inflation.

Caveats

The study covers a broad and complex topic and approaches it from more than one angle. At the same time, it is concerned with an investigation of a series of hypotheses about pricing at the level of individual markets and with the nature of the overall inflationary process. Of necessity, the approach taken has required the exercise of considerable selectivity in the choice of issues and in the amount of detail with which each is treated. Compromises have had to be made.

Detailed limitations of coverage and analysis are pointed out at relevant junctures in the main body of the study. Here the principal limitations can conveniently be discussed under two headings:
(a) limitations in the investigation of wage and price determination, and
(b) limitations inherent in the empirical macroeconomic model.

As regards (a), the focus in part II is upon a few key prices. Determinants of other important prices, particularly those of raw materials and services, are not investigated. The degree of sophistication applied to the analysis of those prices considered is limited. The main reason, in both cases, stems from a lack of adequate data. Appropriate data series, as suggested by theoretical considerations or by 'best practice' modelling techniques, were in many cases unavailable and had either to be proxied by other series or left out of the analysis. The problem was found to be particularly acute in the formulation and estimation of food sector models. In other cases, the only data available were of questionable quality. These deficiencies limited the range of hypotheses that could be confronted properly with the data.

A further constraint upon the empirical analysis arose out of the relatively short number of observations available for important data series. This limited the generality of hypotheses that could feasibly be tested and imposed constraints upon the assessment of the statistical quality of the estimation results obtained. The study had to be carried out using annual data as no quarterly series were available for a range of key statistics; in particular, for national accounts aggregates.

Notable omissions from the wage and price relationships of the empirical model are explicit expectations variables. This is justified further on by reference to the pervasive nature of indexation in the economy which, to a large measure at least, replaced the role normally ascribed to independently formed expectations. This was particularly true in the wage determination process. Nonetheless, expectations of future prices, formed independently of known indexation plans, almost certainly had a role in price and wage formation that is not accounted for in our model. This comment applies most forcefully to the period beginning in 1986 when continuous, institutionalised indexation was abolished.

The second major set of limitations, referred to in (b) above, relates to the construction and use of the empirical macromodel. Constraints of time and space meant it was not feasible to construct a complete macromodel without drawing heavily upon the existing modelling literature for Brazil as a source for most of the non-price stochastic relationships. While in principle it represents good practice to build on the previous work of others, the approach adopted did pose certain problems. Some relationships were clearly consistent with theory and institutional concerns as well as being statistically significant and robust. Others, however, left something to be desired in these same respects.

The model could benefit greatly from extension in two major directions. First, a much fuller modelling of the financial side of the economy would enrich the analysis of the financial implications of, and contributions to, the inflationary process by allowing interest rates, foreign capital inflows and credit variables, among others, to be endogenised. Secondly, if the serious data deficiencies in this area could be overcome, a disaggregation of income and expenditure flows for main social groupings – i.e. workers, capitalists and farmers – would permit explicit consideration of the important interactions between inflation and distributional issues.

A constraint imposed by the length of the study precluded more policy and counterfactual experiments from being performed with the model. While the analysis of chapters 8 and 9 gives a good indication of the model's characteristics and allows for explicit consideration of a number of issues, clearly many more experiments could have been performed to shed additional light upon the Brazilian inflation. In this vein, it is hoped that the study may form the basis for a future research agenda.

PART I
THEORY AND EMPIRICAL BACKGROUND

1 A theoretical framework for the study of inflation rooted in the Latin American structuralist approach

1.1 Introduction

Section 1.2 of this chapter is devoted to a review of Latin American structuralist views on inflation as first formulated in the 1950s and 1960s. Certain weak links in the analytical framework that emerged are highlighted along with general criticisms made of the structuralist approach. Key points of contrast with the monetarist viewpoint – this being the established orthodoxy confronting the new school – are noted although no attempt is made to review the extensive Latin American monetarist/structuralist debate.[1]

Section 1.2 ends with a note on a body of literature that appeared in the late 1970s and 1980s, very much rooted in the structuralist tradition but which represents a certain evolution in thinking, emphasis and presentation that justifies the use of the term 'neo-structuralist'.

A neo-structuralist type model forms the starting point for the derivation of a formal model in section 1.3 which encompasses the insights of the structuralist school while also including stocks and flows of financial assets. It is this construct that underpins the analysis carried out in subsequent chapters.

1.2 Latin American structuralism and the inflationary process

1.2.1 *The 'classic' literature*

A distinct Latin American structuralist school emerged during the 1950s out of the work of a group of economists, many of whom had associations with the United Nations Economic Commission for Latin America (CEPAL or ECLA), based in Santiago, Chile.[2] A central issue addressed by this school was the nature of a price inflation in middle-income developing countries.

Structuralism is best thought of as denoting an approach to, or method of analysis of macroeconomic issues rather than a specific theory. Structuralists considered that the fundamental explanation for chronic inflation in many parts of Latin America was to be found in the rigid and relatively unadaptable economic structures present in these countries. The perspective adopted was very much rooted in a particular Latin American historical and temporal context (Sunkel, 1958) and, as such, contrasted sharply with monetarism which tends to abstract from particular characteristics – be they institutional, historical or geographical – that may differentiate one economy from another. By virtue of the emphasis on economic structures, structuralism is ultimately concerned with longer-term phenomena and not with the short run. In this way, as well, there is a juxtaposition between structuralism and monetarism. As we note further on, an important characteristic of the more recent neo-structuralist work has been precisely to apply structuralist methods to an analysis of short-run problems.

Structuralists sought to explain the pervasive nature of inflation that characterised Latin America in the post-World War II period. Development was characterised by widespread import-substituting industrialisation and urbanisation that put great strains upon economic structures, particularly the structures of production and trade. Olivera (1964) has argued that countries going through this 'intermediate' stage of economic evolution – i.e. countries that are neither pre-industrial nor fully developed – are the most susceptible to structural inflation.

Underlying the structuralist position is the concept of 'required or acceptable growth' (Seers, 1962). Taken as given was the need to ensure adequate growth in national income, output and employment to meet the challenge posed by a growing population with rising economic aspirations, large portions of which had very low absolute standards of living. It was recognised that the existence of enormous political and social pressures compelled policy-makers to pursue growth. This point, while apparently obvious, is an important one because in some sense – although, for reasons to be illustrated further on, a largely irrelevant one – structural inflation can be 'cured' by accepting a permanent reduction in growth and developmental objectives – the main obstacle to this course of action being relentless population expansion.[3]

Structuralist reasoning started from the observation that as a by-product of development, great disparities arise between the growth of demand and supply in different markets, as the economic structure is insufficiently elastic to adapt continuously to match changing patterns of demand to supply (Pinto, 1968). For reasons connected with a country's historically given position in world trade or with backward economic structures in certain productive sectors, the supply of key goods may be very inflexible and also subject to great volatility. Downward inflexibility of key relative prices and immobility of productive resources means that the price system alone cannot fulfil the role of ensuring that sectoral imbalances in demands lead only to relative price adjustments without influencing the general price level or its rate of change, as economic orthodoxy suggests they should. Rather, with a degree of downward inflexibility in important prices such as those of industrial goods and labour, bottle-necks in the supply of key goods can result in continuous inflationary pressures even in the presence of excess supply in other sectors. The result is that inflation may occur in the presence of overall excess supply.[4] This is the essence of a structural inflation and it is this that distinguishes it from an aggregate demand or 'demand-pull' inflation. The recurrent and endogenous nature of the inflationary pressure also sets apart structural from cost-push inflation. The latter is usually thought of as resulting from an autonomous rise in a key relative price due for instance to a foreign price rise or to an increase in real wages brought on by the exercise of market power by a particular social group.

An important distinction is made in structuralist thought between sources of 'basic inflationary pressures' and 'mechanisms of propagation' (Noyola, 1956). Confusion can arise when this distinction is not made, yet, in practice, it is often hard to sort out basic from propagating influences in the inflationary process.

1.2.2 *Basic pressures*

As alluded to above, basic inflationary pressures were argued to emanate from deficiencies in the structures of production and trade. The most often identified sources of such pressures were: first, stagnation or slow growth in the supply of food; and, secondly, an inability to expand and diversify exports – and to increase the purchasing power of these – at a pace sufficient to finance required imports.[5]

It was argued that the traditional pattern of land tenure characteristic of much of Latin America – whereby large and often unproductive estates belonging to the rural oligarchy dominated – served as an impediment to the expansion of output and productivity in agriculture.[6] Moreover, traditional food crops and animal by-products for domestic consumption suffered disproportionately as the more modern subsectors of agriculture tended to be engaged in export orientated production. The relative rigidity in food production has important consequences for prices and inflation.

Agricultural markets tend to adjust to disequilibria between supply and demand through price changes whereas industrial markets are more likely to adjust through variations in output. Over the medium term, rising aggregate demand may tend therefore to cause food prices to rise relative to industrial prices. The upward movement in relative food prices will be more pronounced, the higher the income elasticity of demand for food and the lower the rate of technological change and capital accumulation in the food sector. Over the shorter run, the generally underdeveloped structure of production and marketing in the traditional agricultural sector means that production is prone to volatility and there are little in the way of stockpiles to act as a buffer when supply and demand imbalances emerge: as a result, price elasticity of supply is low and prices are susceptible to erratic and pronounced movements.

In low- to middle-income countries where food is an important component of the average consumption basket, a change in its relative price has a direct and particularly significant impact upon real purchasing power of average wages and salaries. Given a rise in relative food prices, workers will seek compensatory changes in nominal wages and salaries which, assuming mark-up pricing in industry, cause the basic inflationary pressures in the food market to be transmitted to product prices, with the result that a wage-price spiral may ensue.

As regards the pattern of foreign trade, structuralists emphasised that a country's capacity to import, ultimately determined by growth in the value of exports, was an important determinant of inflation. There are various strands to this argument. Firstly, industrialisation, as is well known, brings with it significant requirements for imports, initially mainly of capital goods and later on of non-substitutable intermediate inputs into domestic production. The latter tend to have a high income elasticity. A long-run tendency for slow growth in the capacity to import and/or a tendency for this to undergo significant short-term variations can, given a desired real growth in industry or in output generally, lead to chronic shortages of imports. To the extent that demand for these imports exceeds supply, relative prices may be bid up and inflationary consequences can ensue directly. Secondly, a persistent imbalance in trade will eventually necessitate real exchange devaluation, which likewise brings with it potent cost-push inflationary pressures. Thirdly, the trade balance offers a potentially very important safety valve through which temporary shortages of domestic consumer goods – such as might arise in the case of a poor harvest – can be alleviated with a concomitant stabilising effect upon inflation. If the capacity to import is already strained there can exist little flexibility and the safety valve is effectively closed.

Explanations for a long-run tendency towards slow growth in the capacity to import generally revolved around the predominance of primary product exports in the total for most Latin American countries in the decades before and after World War II. Prebisch (1964) was the best known exponent of the view that there existed a tendency for the terms of trade of primary producers to suffer secular deterioration. Declining terms of trade and/or a generally low income elasticity of primary exports relative to industrial imports tended, it was argued, to create recurring foreign exchange bottle-necks.

1.2.3 *Propagation mechanisms*

For a basic inflationary pressure, which manifests itself in a relative price rise, to lead to an on-going inflation of the general price level, the initial pressure must be propagated throughout the system and be underpinned by the means to finance ever increasing levels of nominal national income. Sunkel (1958) succinctly categorised the propagation mechanism as the result of society's inability to solve two major struggles of economic interests. The first revolves around the distribution of income among social groups and the second around the conflict between the public and private sectors over the distribution of productive resources.

As regards the income share conflict, a relative price rise implies necessarily a reduction in the real income share of one group in favour of another, either at home or overseas. Continuous inflation is the outcome of a process by which social groups seek – ultimately unsuccessfully – to protect their real income shares by nominal wage or price adjustments.[7] Paradoxically the income share conflict makes relative price adjustments, which may go some way towards correcting sectoral imbalances between supply and demand and thus alleviating 'basic' inflationary pressures, very hard to bring about.

As shown analytically later in this chapter and in the simulation exercises of chapter 9, attempts to 'resolve' the income conflict and effect the required relative price changes may only be achieved at the cost of very high rates of inflation. Moreover, unless at least one social group ultimately loses out because it is unable to avoid a shrinkage in its real income relative to other groups, an uncontrolled spiral leading to hyperinflation may ensue.

Sunkel's second conflict between public and private sectors arises out of the former's determination to increase or to maintain a given share in national expenditure in spite of an inability to compel the requisite transfer of real income from the private sector. The traditional structuralist argument was that state expenditures and transfers tended to be downwardly inflexible in real terms, particularly as public spending was often directly linked to high priority developmental goals. On the other hand, rigid and regressive tax systems – characterised by high reliance on indirect taxation and by narrowly based income taxation with low marginal rates –

meant that taxes were typically inelastic with respect to nominal income. If the marginal ratio of government receipts to national income was lower than the average ratio, a budget deficit would be opened up as nominal national income grew. Quite apart from more deep-seated rigidities and inelasticities in the tax system, the mere existence of lags in the collection of taxes and less than full indexation of tax arrears created a deficit-inducing bias. Olivera (1967b) demonstrated how inflation leads to a deficit (assuming public expenditure is constant in real terms) as it reduces the real value of actual tax receipts. Taxpayers enjoy an increasing incentive to delay payment as this reduces their real tax bill. Conversely, the greater the use of specific taxes and of withholding of tax at source, the less important is this effect.

Structuralists therefore often viewed the large government deficits that typically characterised the high inflation economies more as a by-product of inflationary growth than as a primary cause. Government deficits acted as the main mechanism through which financial assets were created to make possible a continuous inflation. On this point the structuralists' viewpoint contrasts sharply with that of the monetarists', who argued that deficits, financed by central bank credit to government, were largely a cause rather than an effect of inflation. Structuralists retorted that, in the absence of the political will to implement broadly based tax reform, drastic cuts in fiscal expenditures had strongly negative impacts upon output and employment, while being largely ineffectual in combating inflation.

Paradoxically, Sunkel's reasoning leads to the view that the state, by allowing inflation to reduce its share in national income, actually attenuates the income share conflict. A constant or rising tax share would tend to exacerbate the conflict over income shares and, in this way, make inflation temporarily worse.

In addition to the two main propagating mechanisms that he identifies, Sunkel also explicitly acknowledges the importance of so-called cumulative factors. These are inflationary pressures induced by inflation itself. Many of these are the result of ill thought out policy responses by the authorities to initial inflationary pressures. Price controls and subsidies intended to dampen inflation in the short run and/or to stimulate the elimination of bottle-necks over the longer run, if not applied judiciously, may, in the case of controls, cause distortions to the price system that further cripple its ability to stimulate necessary restructuring. Subsidies may lead to expanded government deficits that stimulate aggregate and sectoral demand pressures – bringing about further inflation.

1.2.4 *Weaknesses in the structuralist approach*

A fundamental criticism of structuralism is directed at the suggested inevitability and insurmountability of structural bottle-necks. Lewis (1964), for instance, questioned how long-run structural inflation could persist while accepting that it may well be a problem in the shorter term as a developing economy is adjusting through changing propensities to import and to export, raising productivity in traditional agriculture and attaining a generally increased degree of economic flexibility. Ultimately Lewis is correct. However fundamental adjustment takes time and, in the interim, severe and persistent inflations can arise. Moreover, inflation may in turn hamper the process of structural change. Even if we discard the idea of immutable bottle-necks, short-run imbalances can set off inflationary processes that become very hard to reverse even after the original cause has vanished.

The weakest specific points in the structuralist interpretation of inflation concern the interrelationship between a structural inflation and the other types of inflation, principally demand-pull, lack of attention to the monetary and financial aspects of inflation and the relative dearth of policy prescriptions for the short run.

The very real probability that what begins as a structural inflation may precipitate, or be accompanied by, a problem of aggregate demand inflation is seldom considered explicitly. Olivera, conscious of the fact that LDCs have a strong proclivity to demand-pull inflations, warns that, 'One thing is structural inflation and another structural proneness to inflation' (Olivera, 1964, p. 332).

Partly for the sake of analytical clarity and partly as a reaction to the monetarist position, structuralist treatises on the causes of inflation tended not to focus upon the monetary and financial implications of the process. Often it was simply assumed that money was passive and necessarily accommodating. Discussion of specific methods of accommodation was generally restricted to the inelastic tax/budget deficit argument. While this may be an important phenomenon it is also necessary to examine other interactions between the deficit and inflation, specifically between the financial consequences of short-run anti-inflationary policies and long-run inflation. Other endogenous mechanisms of financial asset accumulation, e.g. via the balance of payments, require explicit consideration as well. Most importantly, it is necessary to abandon the assumption that money is always an accommodating and never a contributory factor in inflation.

Early structuralists were very clear about the need to view inflation in Latin America not as being due to short-term financial mismanagement but rather as a chronic long-term phenomenon (Sunkel, 1958). However, the recognition of the deep rooted nature of inflation did not offer much comfort to policy-makers in countries facing very high and volatile inflation in the short run with the concomitant noxious effects upon the financial system, the price system, the balance of payments and income distribution.

Structuralism has also suffered from a perceived lack of rigour and formalisation. Much of the writing in the structuralist tradition has tended to be descriptive and at times even discursive. Because of the emphasis on specific institutional and historical factors there has been a reluctance, perhaps understandable, to posit neat and abstract algebraic models. Even early on, however, rigorous exposition of the key propositions of structuralism were advanced by Olivera (1964, 1967a) and to a lesser extent by Seers (1962). Still, only recently have structuralist precepts come to be incorporated into empirical models that can form the basis for analysis of actual inflationary experiences and policy responses.

1.2.5 *Recent work in the structuralist tradition*

From the late 1970s onwards, the Latin American structuralist school has inspired a body of literature, much of it emanating from the industrialised world, that has considerably broadened interest in, understanding of, and possibly also acceptance of, the key tenets of the approach.[8] The literature is characterised by a strong emphasis upon formalisation of structuralist concepts through the use of mathematical models as well as by an attempt to bring structuralism into the short run – combining it with cost-push elements – to create a framework in which to analyse inflation and stabilisation policy.

Formalisation has enabled unambiguous statements to be made both on how sectoral excess demand can cause inflation in the absence of generalised excess demand and also on the dynamics of continuous inflation resulting from the income share conflict.[9] While implicit in much of the analysis, the emphasis on long-run secular impediments to supply, particularly to the supply of foreign exchange, is muted. In trying to make structuralism relevant for short-term analysis and policy prescription, considerable emphasis has been placed upon understanding the response of an economic system – characterised by the type of rigidities brought to the fore by the early structuralists – to supply 'shocks', i.e. to one-off changes in key relative price or quantity variables. In this way inflationary pressures that may have structural roots tend to be treated as short-run phenomenon and, therefore, the models proposed are closely linked to cost-push models of inflation. This helps to make the analytical treatment of the issues more tractable but can at times obscure the fact that recurrent shocks may not represent a string of independent events but rather result from pressures inherent in the economic system.

One strand in the neo-structuralist literature has laid particular emphasis upon the relative rigidity of inflation – given 'backward looking' or lagged indexation of wages at fixed intervals – in the absence of shocks.[10] This literature is considered at various points throughout this study.

1.3 A formal model of structural inflation

In this section we outline a theoretical framework for the study of recent inflation and anti-inflation policy in Brazil. The model, developed by the present author in collaboration with colleagues (Srinivasan, Parkin and Vines, 1989), draws upon a formalisation of the structuralist approach to inflation presented in Cardoso (1981). The dynamics of inflation are modelled under the assumption of lagged adjustment of nominal wages to changes in the price level. This ensures that a change in the rate of inflation will cause some adjustment to occur in the level of the real wage. Although not reproduced here, Srinivasan, Parkin and Vines (1989) relax this assumption to consider, as well, the dynamics of inflation given instantaneous adjustment of nominal wages to changes in the price level.

The basic model, excluding financial assets, is set out and solved in sections 1.3.1 to 1.3.3. Comparative statics are applied in section 1.3.4 to analyse qualitatively the impact of changes in agricultural output, real government spending and the rate of food consumption subsidy upon industrial output, the relative prices of food and the rate of inflation.

Extensions to the basic model are examined briefly in section 1.3.5. The impact of demand upon industrial wages is considered along with the consequences of endogenous agricultural output and of the addition of a foreign sector. These extensions are not incorporated formally into the basic model nor are algebraic solutions obtained. Simulation techniques are used in the last chapters of this study to examine the properties of an empirical model, estimated for the Brazilian economy, that incorporates the features of the basic model as well as the proposed modifications.

In sections 1.3.6 to 1.3.8 a rudimentary mechanism of asset accumulation is added to the model of section 1.3.1 and a new solution obtained. By embedding the structuralist model within a framework that includes stocks and flows of financial assets, we seek here to overcome a common limitation of much of the work in the structuralist tradition. Using the example of a food consumption subsidy, it becomes possible to address the issue of the inflationary consequences of deficit financing – an issue central to monetarist explanations of inflation in developing countries. The result is to create a bridge between, on the one hand, explanations for inflation centred upon the interaction of prices and wages with the real economy and, on the other, predominantly monetary explanations for inflation.

The same set of comparative static exercises performed in section 1.3.4 are carried out again in section 1.3.9 using the fuller model; differences in results are noted.

1.3.1 *The basic model*

Production is disaggregated into two sectors: agriculture (also referred to as food) with output level (Q_A) and industry with output (Q_I). Prices of the goods are (P_A) and (P_I) respectively. The economy is closed. Output of industrial goods is determined endogenously with the market clearing via the 'Keynesian' mechanism of changes in quantity produced. Agricultural output is exogenous and this market clears by the 'classical' mechanism of changes in the relative prices of agricultural goods.

Letting $(\theta = P_A/P_I)$, then $(\theta\bar{Q}_A + Q_I)$ is total income in the economy expressed in terms of industrial goods. Income is both consumed and saved with the propensity to consume equal to (c). A constant proportion of expenditure (α) is directed towards the industrial good, with $(1-\alpha)$ spent on food. We are assuming, therefore, a unit income elasticity of consumption and a unit elasticity of substitution in consumption between food and the industrial good. The basic insights are not altered by using the constant elasticity model instead of a more general specification. This offers the advantage of making the exposition clear and the extensions to the basic model more tractable.

Letting (s) be the rate of subsidy on consumption of agricultural goods, $0<s<1$, then in nominal terms food market equilibrium requires that

$$(1-s)P_A\bar{Q}_A = (1-\alpha)c(P_A\bar{Q}_A + P_IQ_I) \tag{1.1}$$

Expressed in terms of industrial goods, the agricultural market clearing condition becomes

$$(1-s)\theta\bar{Q}_A = (1-\alpha)c(\theta\bar{Q}_A + Q_I) \tag{1.2}$$

The value of demand for agricultural goods expressed in units of industrial goods is represented by the right-hand side of equation (1.2). The left-hand side equals the post-subsidy value of supply of agricultural goods also expressed in units of industrial goods. Equation (1.2) can be rewritten to solve for market clearing relative prices

$$\theta = \frac{(1-\alpha)cQ_I}{[1-s-(1-\alpha)c]\bar{Q}_A} \tag{1.3}$$

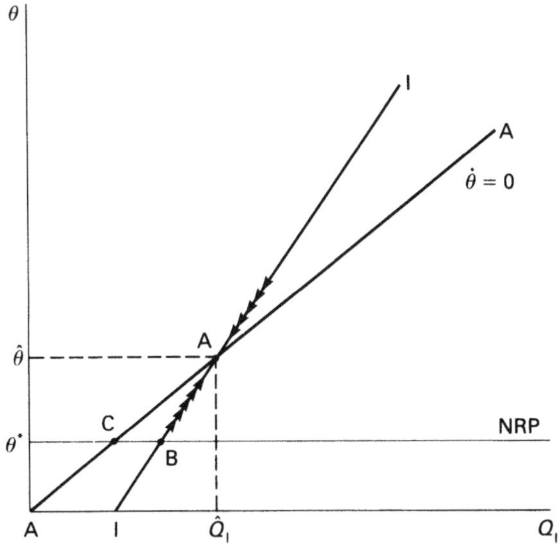

Figure 1.1 Equilibrium relative price in a model without asset effects

An increase in industrial output (Q_I) increases the demand for food and thus its market clearing price providing that

$$(1-\alpha)c<(1-s)$$

The effect of this condition is to ensure that, given (Q_I), a rise in the relative prices of food reduces the gap between the demand for food $[(1-\alpha)c\theta\, Q_A]$ and its cost $[(1-s)\theta Q_A]$. We assume that the rate of subsidy never reaches a level high enough to prevent this.

Equation (1.3) is plotted as line AA in figure 1.1. We assume below that relative food prices adjust slowly with the result that the economy need not always be on the AA line.

Industrial output is demand determined; demand emanating from consumers and government. Quantity rather than price adjusts to clear the market. In equilibrium the following condition holds

$$P_I Q_I = \alpha c(P_A \bar{Q}_A + P_I Q_I) + P_I \bar{g} \tag{1.4}$$

where $\bar{g}$ = exogenously determined real government expenditure on industrial goods and (α) and (c) are as defined above. In real terms, dividing through by (P_I)

$$Q_I = \alpha c(\theta \bar{Q}_A + Q_I) + \bar{g} \tag{1.5}$$

This industrial market equilibrium condition can be rewritten to solve explicitly for market clearing output

$$Q_I = \frac{\alpha c \bar{Q}_A \theta}{(1-\alpha c)} + \frac{\bar{g}}{(1-\alpha c)} \tag{1.6}$$

Equation (1.6) shows that equilibrium industrial output depends positively on agricultural real incomes ($\bar{Q}_A\theta$) and real government expenditure (g). The expression $[1/(1-\alpha c)]$ is a Keynesian type multiplier which is positive provided that the propensity to spend on industrial goods (αc) is less than unity. We assume this to be the case. Equation (1.6) is plotted as line II in figure 1.1. By adopting the assumption that the multiplier process is instantaneous, we ensure that the economy is always on the II line.

With (Q_A) fixed, equations (1.3) and (1.6) represent the combinations of (θ) and (Q_I) that ensure market clearing for industrial goods and food. Graphically, overall goods market equilibrium prevails at ($\hat{\theta}$) and ($\hat{Q}_I$) in figure 1.1, point (A).

The consumer price level (P_C) is defined as

$$P_C = [(1-s)P_A]^{(1-\alpha)} P_I^{\alpha} \tag{1.7}$$

Industrial prices are set as a fixed mark-up over the nominal wage rate per unit output

$$P_I = (1+u)\beta W \tag{1.8}$$

where u is the mark-up,
 W is the nominal wage rate, and
 β is the unit labour requirement for industrial output
 (the inverse of labour productivity).

The desired nominal wage rate (W^*) is given by

$$W^* = wP_C \tag{1.9}$$

where (w) is the target real wage.

The first step in deriving the inflation mechanism in the model is to note that the combination of mark-up pricing and real wage resistance determines a price for food relative to the industrial good, on the supply side of the economy, that is compatible with price stability – i.e. a non-inflationary relative price (θ^*). Setting (W) equal to (W^*), substituting equation (1.7) into (1.9) and solving for (θ) using equation (1.8) gives

$$\theta^* = \frac{[(1+u)\beta w]^{-1/(1-\alpha)}}{(1-s)} \tag{1.10}$$

The non-inflationary relative price (θ^*), plotted as NRP in figure 1.1, will be lower, the higher the unit labour requirement and the higher the target real wage and/or the mark-up. The higher the rate of food subsidy the higher will be the non-inflationary relative price.

We now have two relative prices ($\hat{\theta}$) and (θ^*). If they coincide, a non-inflationary equilibrium in food and industrial goods markets prevails. If however, as in figure 1.1, the economy is at point (A), where goods markets clear but the prevailing real wage is too low to satisfy workers' aspirations (θ too high), a price inflation will be sparked off. The dynamics of the inflationary process will determine the outcome of the ensuing struggle over real income shares. For the moment, we assume a completely passive financial system that ensures financial accommodation of any increase in nominal income.

The assumption underlying the model's inflation mechanism is that nominal wages adjust slowly to the gap between the target wage (W^*) and the actual wage (W). This may represent the outcome of a formal lagged wage indexation scheme with fixed period adjustment or of a process by which nominal wage adjustments are agreed by workers and capitalists without taking expected inflation into account.[11] An important property of this mechanism is that a change in the rate of inflation will cause some adjustment to occur in the level of the real wage. Although not reproduced here Srinivasan, Parkin and Vines (1989) relax this assumption to consider, as well, the dynamics of inflation given instantaneous adjustment of nominal wages to changes in the price level.

The second stage in the derivation of the inflation model follows directly from the assumption of a gradual adjustment of wages to the gap between the target and actual wage rates. Through a process of simple substitution, this adjustment process can also be represented by

$$\dot{W}/W = h(\theta/\theta^* - 1) \tag{1.11}$$

In equation (1.11) above and in other equations that follow, a dot over a variable indicates its time derivative.

Industrial price inflation adjusts instantaneously to changes in costs. Therefore, assuming that the mark-up and unit labour requirement remain constant

$$\dot{P}_I/P_I = \dot{W}/W \tag{1.12}$$

To complete the specification of our model, an adjustment process for the relative prices of agricultural goods is required. Since we have assumed that industrial output (Q_I) adjusts instantaneously to clear the market for industrial goods, no adjustment equation for this market is required. We postulate that the relative prices of agricultural goods adjust gradually in response to excess demand in the food market

$$\dot{\theta}/\theta=\lambda\left[\frac{(1-\alpha)(Q_I\theta^{-1}+\bar{Q}_A)-\bar{Q}_A(1-s)}{(1-s)}\right] \tag{1.13}$$

It can be seen from equation (1.3) that ($\dot{\theta}=0$) when the economy is on the AA line in figure 1.1. At points above the AA line there exists excess supply of the agricultural good and (θ) falls, providing only that the condition beneath equation (1.3) holds. At points below AA excess demand drives (θ) up. This is the key to the inflationary dynamics in the model. As long as the rate of relative price change is non-zero, the rate of inflation is accelerating or decelerating, driven by a changing rate of wage inflation (equation (1.11)). Since, $\dot{\theta}/\theta=\dot{P}_A/P_A-\dot{P}_I/P_I$, it follows that $\dot{P}_A/P_A=\dot{\theta}/\theta+\dot{P}_I/P_I$.

To illustrate the model's dynamics, assume that the economy is at point (B) in figure 1.1. There is excess demand for food that pushes relative food prices up. Rising (θ) causes real agricultural incomes to increase and the resultant boost to demand brings forth a rise in (Q_I). The economy starts to move up the II line towards point (A) with inflation accelerating continuously as real wages fall; ($\dot{\theta}/\theta$) increases. Once point (A) is reached a short-run inflationary equilibrium is attained at which[12]

$$\dot{P}_A/P_A=\dot{P}_I/P_I=\dot{W}/W=\dot{P}/P$$

The on-going but failed attempt to re-establish the target real wage lies at the root of the inflationary dynamics outlined.

A typically structuralist dilemma prevails at point (A) due to the fact that the maintenance of industrial output level ($\hat{Q}_I$) can only be achieved with inflation because of a production bottle-neck in the food sector. If policy-makers were determined to eliminate inflation without altering either the social production relationships in industry or the parameters of the food market, including finding a means to boost food supply, this would require shifting the II schedule to the left – through deflationary policy – until a non-inflationary equilibrium prevailed at point (C).

It is instructive to consider how changes to key parameters of the model would affect the nature of the adjustment process. Assuming that the economy is at point (A) in figure 1.1, from equation (1.11) it is apparent that an increase in the wage adjustment coefficient (h), due for instance to more frequent nominal wage adjustments, will increase the rate of wage inflation and, therefore, of overall inflation. Conversely, less frequent wage adjustments (lower (h)) would mean lower inflation although at the cost of a reduced real wage. Looking at the parameters of the food market, an increase in the speed with which relative food prices adjust (λ) in the face of disequilibrium would cause a new inflationary equilibrium to be re-established more rapidly following a shock.

1.3.2 *Stability*

Given that the market for industrial goods is continuously in equilibrium, we may substitute for (Q_{I}) from equation (1.6) into equation (1.13) and rearrange to get a first-order differential equation in (θ)

$$\dot{\theta}=\left(\frac{\bar{g}\lambda(1-\alpha)c}{(1-s)(1-\alpha c)}\right)-\left(\frac{\lambda[1-c-s(1-\alpha c)]}{(1-s)(1-\alpha c)}\right)\bar{Q}_{\mathrm{A}}\theta \qquad (1.14)$$

Stability requires that

$$(1-\alpha)\frac{c}{(1-\alpha c)}<(1-s) \qquad (1.15)$$

Simple substitution shows that this is equivalent to a requirement that the II line be steeper than the AA line. This stability condition is stronger than the condition given beneath equation (1.3) which showed that, for a given (Q_{I}), a rise in (θ) reduces the excess demand for food providing only that $[(1-\alpha)c<(1-s)]$. However, through the multiplier, this rise in (θ) causes (Q_{I}) to increase and this in turn again stimulates the demand for food. It is important that this effect not be so strong as to create instability. In figure 1.1 the phase arrows point towards the AA line provided only that $[(1-\alpha)c<(1-s)]$. Yet, since we have assumed that the economy is always on II, there will still be instability unless AA is also flatter than II. We assume from now on that the rate of food subsidy is never large enough for such instability to arise.

1.3.3 *Equilibrium*

Equilibrium obtains when both the industrial and the agricultural markets clear. To obtain the equilibrium for relative prices, we set $\dot{\theta}=0$ in equation (1.14) and solve for (θ). This gives

$$\hat{\theta}=\frac{(1-\alpha)c\bar{g}}{[1-c-s(1-\alpha c)]\bar{Q}_{\mathrm{A}}} \qquad (1.16)$$

Substituting the equilibrium relative price $(\hat{\theta})$ into equation (1.6) yields the equilibrium industrial output

$$\hat{Q}_{\mathrm{I}}=\frac{[1-s-(1-\alpha)c]\bar{g}}{[1-c-s(1-\alpha)c]} \qquad (1.17)$$

This expression is unambiguously positive if condition (1.15) holds. When equilibrium is reached and relative prices have stopped adjusting, overall

Table 1.1. *Comparative statics for the model without asset effects*

	Increase in		
Effects on	Q_A	g	s
Q_I	0	+	+
θ	−	+	+
π	−	+	+

inflation (π) equals the rate of change of both agricultural and industrial prices. Therefore, using equations (1.11) and (1.12), we can solve for inflation

$$\hat{\pi}=h\left(\frac{(1-\alpha)c\bar{g}}{[1-c-s(1-\alpha c)]\bar{Q}_A\theta^*}\right)-1 \tag{1.18}$$

1.3.4 *Comparative statics*

In this section we use comparative statics to examine the workings of the model and specifically to analyse the impact upon industrial output, relative prices and inflation of an increase in agricultural output, real government expenditure and the rate of subsidy to food consumption. These results, derived from equations (1.14), (1.15) and (1.18), are equilibrium solutions that hold once relative prices have adjusted fully in the wake of a change. They are summarised in table 1.1 with full derivations appearing in appendix 1.

An increase in real government expenditure (g) causes a rise in industrial output (Q_I), relative prices (θ) and overall inflation (π). The mechanisms at work here are straightforward and correspond to an outward shift in the II schedule: a rise in (g) increases aggregate demand causing not only (Q_I) and (θ) to rise but also, because the gap between (θ) and (θ^*) is now wider, real wages to fall further below target and therefore inflation to increase.

The impact of an increase in agricultural output (Q_A) is shown diagrammatically in figure 1.2 by a downward rotation in the AA line and a shift to the right of the II line. The lower relative price achieved at point (E) results in lower inflation. Industrial output remains unchanged as agricultural income is unaffected by the increase in output. The Cobb-Douglas form of our demand system ensures that the fall in (θ) is equiproportional to the rise in (Q_A).

A rise in the rate of subsidy has the effect of stimulating consumer real

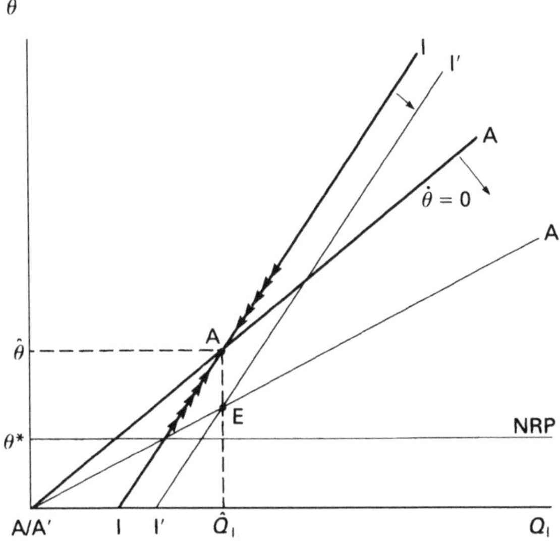

Figure 1.2 Impact of an increase in agricultural output in a model without asset effects

incomes and increasing demand; as a consequence both (Q_I) and (θ) rise. At the same time, the non-inflationary relative prices of agricultural goods (θ^*) increase as the purchasing power of industrial workers is now higher due to the subsidy (see equation (1.10)). In our model, the increase in the market clearing relative price (θ) dominates the effect of a rise in (θ^*) and therefore inflation rises.

Diagrammatically the impact of a higher subsidy rate is shown in figure 1.3. The AA line rotates upwards, the II line is unaffected and there occurs an upwards shift in the (θ^*) schedule. A new equilibrium is established at (E_1) at which both (θ) and (Q_I) are higher than at (E_0). As illustrated in appendix 1, the gap between (θ_1) and (θ_1^*) is greater than that between (θ_0) and (θ_0^*) with the result that inflation accelerates.

A useful insight into the working of the model is attained by examining the transition towards a new equilibrium following a rise in the subsidy rate (figure 1.3). The immediate impact of the change is to cause (θ_0^*) to rise to (θ_1^*), thereby reducing inflation as industrial workers experience a boost to their spending power and come closer to attaining their target level of real wages. Thus, subsidy increases have a cost-push dampening effect upon inflation (equations (1.10) and (1.11)). However, the second impact of the subsidy change is to set in motion a gradual rise in market clearing relative prices (θ) as excess demand for food builds up (equation (1.13)). The gap

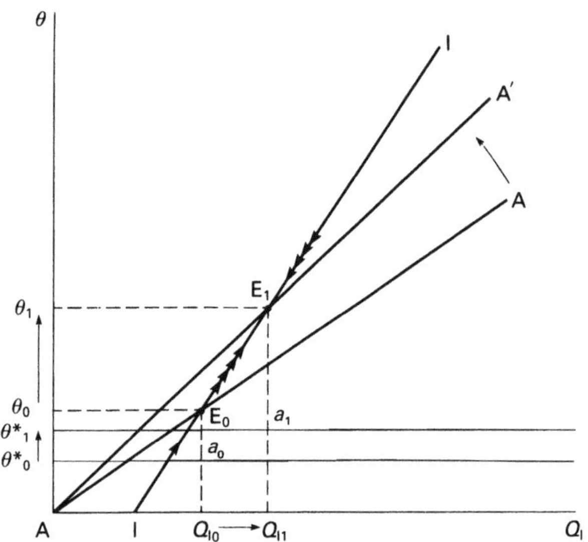

Figure 1.3 Impact of an increase in the rate of subsidy in a model without asset effects
(*Note*: initial 'inflation gap' a_0E_0, ultimate 'inflation gap' a_1E_1)

between (θ_1^*) and (θ_1) starts to rise, bringing with it, through a demand-increasing effect, renewed upward pressure on inflation.

The modelling of lags in the adjustment of relative food prices highlights how the divergent effects of food subsidies may operate over different time frames. From a policy perspective it is important to recognise that the demand-increasing effect may, in time, come to dominate the initial cost-reducing impact – as happens in the present model.

1.3.5 *Extensions to the basic model*

In the empirical chapters of this study the structure outlined above is generalised to allow for:
(a) endogenous agricultural supply,
(b) demand sensitivity of industrial wages and prices, and
(c) foreign trade.
Little is achieved by extending the formal model in these directions and to do so greatly increases the level of complexity and correspondingly lessens tractability. Nonetheless, it is useful to set out in brief some of the main implications of these changes to the model.

The more price elastic is agricultural supply, the less relative price (θ)

needs to adjust to restore equilibrium between demand and supply, given a shock to the system. This in turn means that, in the face of excess demand, inflation will be less than in the rigid supply case. Supply response lags, as well as the degree of elasticity, will be important determinants of the inflationary process. Since the level of industrial output is, in part, determined by agricultural incomes, elastic agricultural supply means that, for a given relative price, a higher (Q_I) will prevail compared with the fixed supply case.

To the extent that the target real wage (w^*) and the industrial mark-up (u) are functions of the level of excess demand for labour and industrial goods respectively and, that these demands are functions of (Q_I), the determination of the supply side equilibrium price (θ^*) will be affected. On the assumption that the above variables are positive functions of demand, the non-inflationary price schedule would be downward sloping instead of flat. *Ceteris paribus*, higher levels of (Q_I) now imply higher rates of inflation and conversely, lower industrial output means less inflation. The model economy now faces an additional constraint upon non-inflationary expansion – one that emanates from the industrial as opposed to the food sector. On the other hand, price stabilisation through demand deflation becomes more effective.

The introduction of foreign trade into the model brings with it a number of implications. From the point of view of price formation and inflation the most important direct consequence stems from the role of the exchange rate. If we assume that imports include inputs into industrial production then, under the pricing rules assumed, the prices of industrial goods will be set as a mark-up over unit labour costs and imported raw material prices. A real devaluation of the exchange rate or a rise in 'world' prices will cause imported input costs in domestic currency terms to increase, thereby putting upward pressure on (P_I) and inflation. Interactions between the real exchange rate, output and inflation are examined in detail in chapters 8 and 9.

1.3.6 *A model including a government sector and stocks and flows of financial assets*

In order to provide a more complete explanation of the inflationary process, particularly over the longer term, it is necessary to drop the assumption – implicit above and common to most structuralist models of inflation – of a passive and accommodating money supply. Instead, in the model developed below, we consider directly the process of financial asset creation and accumulation in the economy. The mechanism adopted is a simple one and its incorporation falls well short of the introduction of a complete financial sector. Nonetheless, it is adequate to allow direct examination of important interactions between prices and inflation on the one hand, and stocks and flows of financial assets on the other. The model does not explain the demand for financial assets nor their prices but concentrates instead upon the asset supply process and shows both how financial accommodation of inflation can have an important endogenous component – particularly in an indexed economy – and also how stocks of financial assets can themselves have an impact upon inflation.

The simple model of the financial system is based on the body of monetary theory, sometimes referred to as the asset or stock equilibrium approach, that explicitly models stocks and flows of financial assets – broadly defined – and the mechanisms whereby they influence expenditure, output and inflation.[13] While now quite standard in the modelling literature for the industrialised world, this approach is much less widely used in the LDC context where, when finance is considered, there is a tendency to adopt a more narrow and often monetarist, perspective.

When a very simple asset equilibrium model is integrated with the structuralist approach and adapted to capture key institutional features of the economy under study, a novel and useful framework emerges for the study of inflation in a middle-income industrialising country such as Brazil. Here the rudiments of such a model are considered formally.

There are two financial assets in private portfolios, high-powered money (H) and government bonds (B)

$$A = M + B \tag{1.19}$$

where (A) is the total nominal value of financial assets.

A surplus of private sector income over expenditure equals private sector net acquisition of financial assets. In a closed economy, which we assume here for simplicity, this must in turn be exactly matched by a government deficit. Government revenue consists of a proportional tax at rate (t) levied on both agricultural and industrial incomes. Its expenditure is made up of spending on industrial goods ($P_I g$) – fixed in real terms as in the basic model – food consumption subsidies ($sP_A Q_A$) and interest on bonds [$\rho(1-\delta)A$], where (ρ) is the nominal rate of interest net of income tax and (δ) is the share of non-interest bearing money in total assets. Government covers the difference between its expenditure and revenues by issuing bonds or money. Nominal asset accumulation is therefore

$$\dot{A} = \dot{M} + \dot{B} = P_I g - t(P_I Q_I + P_A \bar{Q}_A) + sP_A \bar{Q}_A + \rho(1-\delta)A \tag{1.20}$$

Defining real wealth as nominal financial wealth deflated by *industrial* prices

$$a = A/P_I \tag{1.21}$$

it follows that real asset accumulation is given by

$$\dot{a} = \dot{A}/P_{\mathrm{I}} - (A/P_{\mathrm{I}}) \cdot (\dot{P}_{\mathrm{I}}/P_{\mathrm{I}}) \tag{1.22}$$

Substituting equation (1.20) into (1.22) gives an expression for the rate of change of real wealth

$$\dot{a} = g - t(Q_{\mathrm{I}} + \bar{Q}_{\mathrm{A}}\theta) + s\bar{Q}_{\mathrm{A}}\theta + \rho(1-\delta)a - a\pi \tag{1.23}$$

where (π) is now used to denote not the rate of overall inflation but rather inflation of industrial prices only. Using a linear approximation for the inflation tax, where subscript (0) denotes initial values

$$a\pi \approx a_0\pi_0 + a_0\pi + \pi_0 a$$

and restricting ourselves to the case of $\delta = 1$, i.e. all financial wealth is non-interest bearing money, it becomes possible to express the rate of change of real assets, beginning for simplicity from zero initial inflation, as

$$\dot{a} = g - tQ_{\mathrm{I}} + (s-t)\bar{Q}_{\mathrm{A}}\theta - a_0\pi \tag{1.24}$$

Ignoring for the moment the final term in the equation ($a_0\pi$), this expression shows that when either real government spending on industrial goods exceeds real tax revenue from the same sector or real subsidy payments exceed real taxes upon agricultural income then, *ceteris paribus*, real assets will rise.

The last term in equation (1.24) captures the inflation tax; a positive rate of industrial price inflation, *ceteris paribus*, causes a decline in real assets. Since we have restricted ourselves to the case of one non-interest bearing asset only, a one for one inflation tax prevails. Equation (1.23) shows that we would also get a one for one inflation tax with bonds and money provided that the nominal interest rate was fixed – this is true irrespective of the share of money in total assets. On the other hand, in the two asset case, if we were to assume that the interest rate was indexed to inflation $\rho = \dot{P}_{\mathrm{I}}/P_{\mathrm{I}}$ and that $\delta = 0$ (i.e. all assets were bonds), the final expression ($a\pi$) would fall out of equation (1.23) and there would no longer be a stabilising inflation tax.

The introduction of taxes, interest income and wealth into the model necessitates certain changes in the private expenditure functions. Assuming that private spending on food and industrial goods depends upon private disposable income and wealth, we can rewrite the agricultural goods market equilibrium condition as

$$(1-s)\bar{Q}_{\mathrm{A}}\theta = (1-\alpha)c(1-t)(\bar{Q}_{\mathrm{A}}\theta + Q_{\mathrm{I}}) + (1-\alpha)\gamma a \tag{1.25}$$

where (γ) is the propensity to spend out of wealth and (c) is now the propensity to consume out of *disposable* income. We can rewrite equation (1.25) to solve explicitly for market clearing (θ)

$$\theta = \frac{(1-\alpha)\gamma a}{[1-s-(1-\alpha)c(1-t)]\bar{Q}_{\mathrm{A}}} + \frac{(1-\alpha)c(1-t)Q_{\mathrm{I}}}{[1-s-(1-\alpha)c(1-t)]\bar{Q}_{\mathrm{A}}} \tag{1.26}$$

Equation (1.26) shows that real assets and industrial output are positively related to market-clearing relative food prices, whereas, an increase in agricultural output reduces relative prices, providing that

$$(1-a)c(1-t) < (1-s)$$

This condition is identical to that given beneath equation (1.3) except that here we allow for income taxes.

Equilibrium in the industrial market obtains when

$$Q_{\mathrm{I}} = \alpha c(1-t)(\bar{Q}_{\mathrm{A}}\theta + Q_{\mathrm{I}}) + \alpha\gamma a + g \tag{1.27}$$

In order to highlight the positive impact of real government expenditure, real assets and real agricultural incomes upon market-clearing industrial output, equation (1.27) can be rewritten as

$$Q_{\mathrm{I}} = \frac{\alpha\gamma a}{[1-\alpha c(1-t)]} + \frac{\alpha c(1-t)\bar{Q}_{\mathrm{A}}}{[1-\alpha c(1-t)]}\theta + \frac{g}{[1-\alpha c(1-t)]} \tag{1.28}$$

The expression $\{1/[1-\alpha c(1-t)]\}$ is a Keynesian-type multiplier.

1.3.7 *'Short-run' equilibrium*

For simplicity of exposition here we drop the assumption of slow adjustment of relative prices to changes in demand and supply for agricultural goods. We assume instead that both the agricultural and industrial goods markets clear instantaneously. Under this assumption, substituting equation (1.26) into (1.28) and simplifying gives us a short-run equilibrium value for (Q_{I}) at any point in time when real assets are momentarily constant

$$Q_{\mathrm{I}} = \left[\frac{(1-s)\alpha\gamma}{\eta}\right]a + \left[\frac{[1-s-(1-\alpha)c(1-t)]}{\eta}\right]g \tag{1.29}$$

where $\eta = \{1-c(1-t)-s[1-\alpha c(1-t)]\}$.

We assume that $\eta > 0$; an assumption that corresponds exactly to the stability condition (equation (1.15)) of section 1.3.2. The positive impact upon industrial output of real government expenditure follows from $\eta > 0$ combined with the condition specified beneath equation (1.26) relating to the rate of income taxation and food subsidy. As in section 1.3.3, an increase in agricultural output has no effect upon industrial production.

We obtain a short-run equilibrium solution for the relative prices of agricultural goods by substituting equation (1.28) into (1.26) and rearranging

$$\theta = \left[\frac{(1-\alpha)\gamma}{\eta \bar{Q}_A}\right] a + \left[\frac{(1-\alpha)c(1-t)}{\eta \bar{Q}_A}\right] g \tag{1.30}$$

The equilibrium solutions for relative prices and industrial output represented by equations (1.29) and (1.30) are equivalent to those given by equations (1.6) and (1.3) in section 1.3.1, with the difference being that we now account explicitly for the influence of assets and income taxation.

1.3.8 *Local stability*

Since with instantaneous adjustment in the agricultural market $[\pi = h(\theta/\theta^* - 1)]$, we can restate the rate of change of real assets, by eliminating (π), as

$$\dot{a} = g - tQ_I + [(s-t)\bar{Q}_A - a_0 h/\theta^*]\theta + a_0 h \tag{1.31}$$

We can now proceed to linearise our three equation system (equations (1.29), (1.30) and (1.31) – around the initial equilibrium values – with respect to the endogenous variables (θ, Q_I and a) and the exogenous variables (g, Q_A and s). Dropping constants, the system becomes

$$Q_I = k_{11}a + k_{12}g + k_{14}s \tag{1.32}$$

$$\theta = k_{21}a + k_{22}g + k_{23}Q_A + k_{24}s \tag{1.33}$$

$$\dot{a} = g - tQ_I + k_{30}\theta + k_{33}Q_A + k_{34}s \tag{1.34}$$

where variables are measured as small deviations around initial values and the following definitions apply

$$k_{11} = \frac{(1-s_0)\alpha\gamma}{\eta_0} > 0$$

$$k_{12} = \frac{1 - s_0 - (1-\alpha)c(1-t)}{\eta_0} > 0$$

$$k_{14} = a_0 \frac{\partial k_{11}}{\partial s_0} + g_0 \frac{\partial k_{12}}{\partial s_0} > 0$$

$$k_{21} = \frac{(1-\alpha)\gamma}{\eta_0 Q_{A0}} > 0$$

$$k_{22} = \frac{(1-\alpha)c(1-t)}{\eta_0 Q_{A0}} > 0$$

$$k_{23} = a_0 \frac{\partial k_{21}}{\partial Q_{A0}} + g_0 \frac{\partial k_{22}}{\partial Q_{A0}} < 0$$

$$k_{24}=a_0\frac{\partial k_{21}}{\partial}s_0+g_0\frac{\partial k_{22}}{\partial s_0}>0$$

$$k_{30}=(s_0-t)Q_{A0}-\alpha_0 h/\theta_0^*>0$$

$$k_{33}=(s_0-t)>0$$

$$k_{34}=Q_{A0}+a_0 h/(1-s_0)>0$$

The local stability condition for asset accumulation is $\partial\dot{a}/\partial a<0$. From equations (1.32) and (1.34) a sufficient condition may be written as

$$\mathrm{d}\dot{a}/\mathrm{d}a=-t(\mathrm{d}Q_I/\mathrm{d}a)+(s_0-t)\bar{Q}_{A0}(\mathrm{d}\theta/\mathrm{d}a)<0$$

which is equivalent to

$$-tk_{11}+(s_0-t)\bar{Q}_{A0}k_{21}<0$$

and can be further simplified using the definitions of k_{11} and k_{21} to give

$$s<\frac{t}{[1-\alpha(1-t)]} \tag{1.35}$$

Given an absence of subsidies, a rise in real assets (a) would lead to an increase in both industrial output (Q_I) and agricultural incomes ($\theta\bar{Q}_A$), thereby increasing tax revenues and reducing asset creation. This is a process illustrated by Blinder and Solow (1973). However, in the presence of subsidy payments to consumers of agricultural goods, a rise in assets increases subsidy payments which in turn puts upward pressure on asset creation and leads to potential instability. Because in our model subsidies are paid only within the agricultural sector while taxes are levied on both agricultural and industrial incomes, stability is possible even if ($s<t$). Condition (1.35) places an upper boundary upon the rate of subsidy compatible with stability. In fact, even higher rates of subsidy may ensure stability since we have ignored the stabilising real balance effect of the term ($\alpha_0 h/\theta^*$) in the coefficient (k_{30}).

In order to render the expanded model amenable to graphical representation, we can reduce our system to two equations defining the two endogenous variables (θ) and (a). Equation (1.32) defines (θ) and by substituting for (Q_I) in equation (1.34) from equation (1.32) we can derive a new expression for ($\dot{a}$)

$$\dot{a}=k_{40}\theta+k_{41}a+k_{42}g+k_{43}Q_A+k_{44}s \tag{1.36}$$

where

$$k_{40}=k_{30}\gtrless 0$$

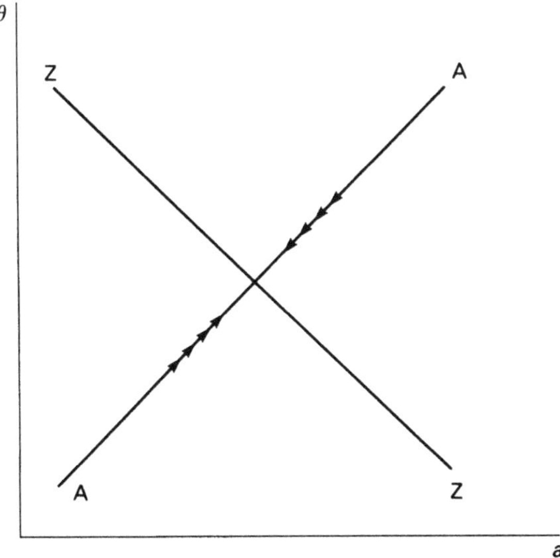

Figure 1.4 Long-run equilibrium in a model with asset effects

$$k_{41} = -k_{11}t < 0$$

$$k_{42} = (1 - k_{12}t) > 0$$

$$k_{43} = k_{33} \gtrless 0$$

$$k_{44} = k_{34} - tk_{14} \gtrless 0$$

When equilibrium prevails in the asset market, ($\dot{a} = 0$) and consequently we can rewrite equation (1.26) as

$$\theta = -\left(\frac{k_{41}}{k_{40}}\right)a - \left(\frac{k_{42}}{k_{40}}\right)g - \left(\frac{k_{43}}{k_{40}}\right)Q_A - \left(\frac{k_{44}}{k_{40}}\right)s \qquad (1.37)$$

Equations (1.33) and (1.36) appear as straight lines in the (θ, a) plane in figure 1.4. The former traces out a locus AA, along which points represent short-run equilibria. The upward slope of this schedule stems from the fact that, *ceteris paribus*, higher levels of real assets are compatible with, and imply, a higher relative price of food. By assumption, the economy always remains on this line. Equation (1.36) is represented by the locus ZZ. Points along this line represent asset market equilibria. As long as k_{30} is negative

Table 1.2. *Long-run comparative statistics for the model with asset effects*

	Increase in		
Effects on	Q_A	g	s
Q_I	+ if $s_0 < t$ and $k_{30} > 0$	+ if $k_{30} > 0$	+ if $k_{44} > 0$ and $k_{30} > 0$
θ	− if $s_0 < t$	+	+ if $k_{44} > 0$
π	− if $s_0 < t$	+	+ if $k_{44} > 0$ and $k_{30} > 0$

(positive) this line is downward (upward) sloping. The condition for local stability set out above implies either that the locus ZZ is downward sloping or, if upward sloping, that it is steeper than AA. For the purposes of figure 1.4 we have assumed that ZZ is downward sloping. At points above ZZ real assets are decreasing while the opposite is true at points below the line.

1.3.9 *Comparative statics*

The comparative statics of the model with financial assets are worked out in detail in appendix 1 and summarised in table 1.2. As in section 1.3.4 we examine the impact upon industrial output, relative prices and inflation of increases in agricultural output, real government expenditure and the rate of subsidy.

Looking first at the effects of an increase in government spending, in short-run equilibrium this causes a budget deficit to emerge. The process of asset accumulation set in motion by the deficit stimulates private sector expenditure and thereby causes both (θ) and (Q_I) to rise. A higher relative price in turn leads to an acceleration of inflation which, through the inflation tax effect, counteracts to some extent the stimulus given to real asset creation by the budget deficit. In fact, if the initial stock of assets (a_0) is large enough, then real asset creation will be negative in the short run and (Q_I) and (θ) will converge to lower levels in the long run compared with the short run.

The impact of a rise in (g) is illustrated in figure 1.5. Suppose that, initially, long-run equilibrium prevails at point (A). An increase in (g) immediately shifts the AA locus up and a short-run equilibrium will be

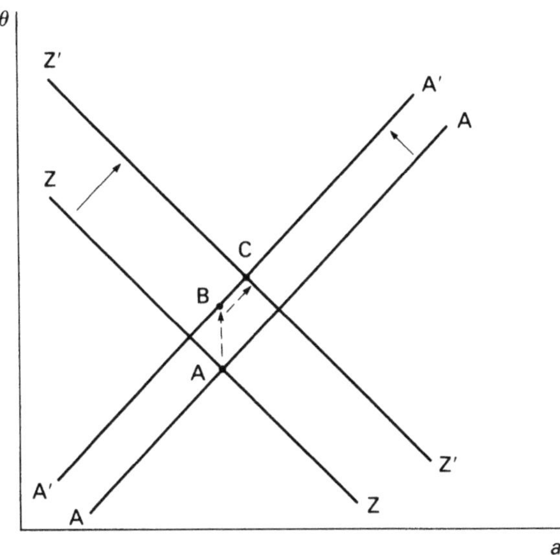

Figure 1.5 The impact of an increase in real government expenditure in a model with asset effects

established at a point such as (B). Using equation (1.31) and recalling that ($k_{30}<0$), it can be seen that a second impact of higher government spending is to shift the ZZ locus to the right. A new long-run equilibrium is achieved at point (C) where, because of the configuration of the curves, (θ) and (Q_{I}) are higher than at the short-run equilibrium point.

As shown previously, the short-run impact of an increase in agricultural output upon relative prices and inflation is negative, but positive for industrial production. In the long run the results are more ambiguous. If, prior to the rise in agricultural output, the farm sector was a net recipient of subsidies (i.e. $s_0>t$), as is often the case in developing economies, then subsidies payable on an increased level of agricultural output will lead to a process of asset creation. This process may be strong enough to reverse the short-term decline in the relative prices of food and in the rate of inflation through the stimulus to demand that it implies. Should the impact of higher subsidies (and a reduced inflation tax) upon asset creation dominate the expansion of tax revenues that also flows from a rise in agricultural output, then (Q_{I}) may also rise in the long run.

The long-run impacts of an increase in the rate of subsidy are also ambiguous and depend upon the sign of (k_{44}). The latter captures the three part effect of an increased subsidy rate upon asset creation which comprise: (a) an expansionary effect due to higher subsidy payments,

(b) an expansionary effect due to a short-term reduction in (θ) relative to (θ^*) – i.e. a lower inflation tax, and
(c) a contractionary effect stemming from the rise in tax revenues from the expanding industrial sector.

Either a small industrial base or a low tax rate is sufficient to ensure that the net effect of a higher rate of subsidy on asset creation is positive. This in turn would ensure that, in the long run, the relative prices of food would actually *rise* following an increase in subsidies to food consumption. Moreover, if the initial value of (s) is large enough to ensure that the effect of a rise in relative prices on asset creation is positive ($k_{30}>0$), then a rise in the subsidy rate would also result in higher inflation and industrial output.

We have shown, therefore, that, while far from inevitable, it is possible for increased use of consumption subsidies in agriculture actually to cause an acceleration in inflation in the longer term as demand-increasing effects come to outweigh the initial cost-reducing impact.

Because real demand for food depends upon the stock of real assets, a link has been established between stocks of money and bonds and the rate of inflation.[14] This change is important as the model now allows real and financial variables to affect the inflationary process and thereby greatly enriches its potential as an aid to understanding actual inflationary processes. Even in developing economies where inflationary bottle-necks exist, invariably at some point price inflation will be associated with an expansion of financial assets and this will not necessarily be of a purely accommodating nature. An understanding of the complex interrelationships between real and financial variables in the inflationary process is essential. The present framework is useful not only in understanding how the financial system may respond in the face of an initially structural inflation but also allows consideration of the mechanics of a more orthodox aggregate demand inflation – fuelled by expansionary fiscal and/or monetary policies – of the kind emphasised by monetarists.

In its present configuration, the model exhibits a new feature: a potentially stabilising real balance effect. There will be a tendency for rising real demand for food and industrial goods to be dampened by the impact of the resultant inflation upon the real value of financial assets.

Although not considered explicitly here, equation (1.23) showed that the existence of an operational government deficit and real interest payments on the public debt will put upward pressure on nominal assets. In an economy where interest rates are indexed to inflation and interest bearing assets are widely used, a large (and, as inflation rises, likely an increasing) share of financial wealth is protected from inflation – thereby reducing the strength of the real balance effect.

Mechanisms may even exist that cause inflation to stimulate real asset accumulation and thus imply a perverse real balance effect that is destabilising. Although not incorporated in this simple model, the most important such mechanism operating in Brazil during much of the 1970s and early 1980s resulted from the widespread use of official subsidised credit to the private sector. The mechanisms involved are discussed in chapter 2 (2.3.2) and share certain characteristics with those identified by Olivera (1967b) to illustrate the causal link between inflation and the public sector deficit created by lags in tax collection and imperfect indexation of tax arrears.

1.4 Conclusion

The framework delineated in the previous pages, while rooted in the structuralist approach to inflation, represents an integration of this with a more complete model of the macroeconomy. The proposed structure goes some way towards overcoming a number of the deficiencies – and filling some of the lacunae – often associated with the Latin American structuralist position on inflation. This is true particularly as regards the role both of financial variables and of demand pressures in the markets for industrial goods and labour.

The remaining chapters of this study are devoted to building, testing and experimenting with an empirical model based on the simple analytical framework proposed here.

2 Brazil's experience with inflation since 1960: the evidence and existing interpretations

2.1 Introduction

In presenting an overview of Brazilian inflation in recent decades the aim is to identify major issues that require further investigation and to review the main interpretations that have been advanced in the literature to explain the inflationary experience. To the extent possible, the theoretical framework set out in chapter 1 is used to give coherence to the presentation.

The focus of this study is the inflationary experience of Brazil in the two decades up to 1983–4. The choice of cut-off date was dictated by the availability of data at the time the empirical analysis carried out for this study was begun (mid–1986). Where available, data from 1960 onwards are presented in this chapter, although the modelling exercises use 1964–5 as a convenient starting point. There is considerable evidence to suggest that the wide-ranging institutional changes that occurred in Brazil after the military *coup d'état* of October 1964, altered important chacteristics of the wage and price system and especially of the mechanisms of inflationary propagation.[1] Brazilian inflation pre-1964, distinct in many respects from the more recent experience, has been widely analysed elsewhere (Baer and Kerstenetzky, 1964, A. Lara Resende, 1979, Rangel, 1981, Zottman, 1978 and Kahil, 1973).

Given the period chosen for the subsequent empirical analysis, the main body of this chapter concentrates on a review and initial appraisal of inflation through 1984. In a final section to this chapter we very briefly consider Brazil's more recent experience with inflation and stabilisation, in order to illustrate the fact that the major processes at work prior to 1984 continue to be present, and of relevance, today.

This chapter is organised in the following way. In section 2.2 the basic data on inflation are presented along with a range of key macroeconomic indicators, in order to set the stage for the discussion that follows in section 2.3. In this latter section, the main interpretations given to the Brazilian experience in the empirical literature on the subject are reviewed and the principal findings summarised.[2] This review of the literature is interspersed with a graphical and tabular presentation of additional data. An initial attempt is made to identify possible relationships between macroeconomic variables – whether prices or quantities – that have a bearing upon inflation. At this stage the treatment of many issues is somewhat impressionistic. From this review there emerges a set of hypotheses, some of which have already been adequately tested while others require further examination. Many of the latter are considered in greater analytical detail in later chapters. A brief description of the inflationary experience and failed attempts at stabilisation from 1984 through to 1989 are the subject of section 2.4. Section 2.5 is devoted to a summing-up.

2.2 An overview of inflation through 1984

Annual averages of aggregate inflation as measured by the broadest indicators – the GDP deflator and the general price index (GPI) – are presented in table 2.1.[3] Inflation as measured by the GPI averaged 58 per cent annually over the period 1960 to 1984, ranging from a low of 15 per cent in 1973 to a high of 221 per cent in 1984. The standard deviation of the GPI inflation series is 48 percentage points; attesting to a high degree of volatility in rates. GDP and sectoral rates of growth for industry and agriculture, the current account balance, an estimate of the public sector deficit, and the registered foreign debt are also included in table 2.1. For all the data series, five year annual averages are given; the choice of time periods is purely arbitrary but serves to highlight changing trends.

The time path of GPI inflation is charted in figure 2.1 along with the rate of real GDP growth. By way of a 'broad brush' description, inflation can be seen to have accelerated through 1964, while growth rates followed a sharp downward trend from a cyclical output peak in 1961. This coincided with a swing in the current account position from a deficit of over 3 per cent of GDP in 1960 to a surplus of 1.3 per cent in 1965. Inflation fell sharply in 1965–6 and began a period of further gentle deceleration that continued through 1973. Beginning in 1966, the economy moved first into a recovery phase and then into the extraordinary boom period known as the Brazilian 'miracle'. The current account deficit expanded to an average of just under 3 per cent of GDP in 1970–3. This was however easily financed by enormous capital inflows – as witnessed by the growth in foreign debt.

A notable change occurred in the pattern of inflation after 1973. With only two fairly minor exceptions (in 1978 and 1982) inflation never decelerated but instead ratcheted upwards from plateau to plateau. Notable changes in the plateau, or threshold, occurred in 1974, 1976, 1979, 1980, 1983 and 1984.

Table 2.1. *Assorted macroeconomic data*

Year	Percentage rates of change					As percentage of GDP				U.S.$ billions
	Real GDP	Real agricultural output	Real industrial output	GDP deflator	General price index (annual averages)	Current account of balance of payments	Public sector 'operational' surplus (−deficit)[a]		Net taxation burden	Gross foreign debt
1960	9.7	5.0	9.6	26.1	31.8	−3.1	—	—	19.1	—
1961	10.3	7.6	10.7	33.3	37.9	−1.6	—	—	15.8	—
1962	5.2	5.5	7.7	55.0	50.0	−2.2	—	—	13.5	—
1963	1.6	1.0	0.5	78.3	75.0	−0.8	—	—	14.9	—
1964	2.9	1.3	4.9	87.5	90.5	0.4	—	—	13.5	—
1965	2.7	13.8	−4.7	55.4	57.0	1.3	—	—	13.5	—
1966	3.8	−14.6	9.9	39.5	38.2	−0.1	—	—	16.0	—
1967	4.9	9.2	3.2	28.8	28.3	−0.9	—	—	13.4	3.3
1968	11.2	4.5	13.2	27.8	24.1	−1.6	—	—	15.7	3.8
1969	9.9	3.8	12.3	20.3	20.8	−0.9	—	—	16.6	4.4
1970	8.8	1.0	10.4	18.2	19.8	−2.0	−1.2	—	15.7	5.3
1971	11.4	10.2	11.8	19.3	20.4	−3.3	0.1	—	16.2	6.6
1972	12.0	4.0	14.2	19.9	17.0	−2.9	−0.3	—	16.7	9.5
1973	13.9	0.1	17.0	29.6	15.1	−2.6	0.3	—	16.1	12.6
1974	8.3	1.3	8.5	34.5	28.7	−6.9	0.5	—	15.8	17.2
1975	5.1	6.6	4.9	34.0	27.7	−5.4	−2.7	—	14.6	21.2
1976	10.2	2.2	11.7	41.4	41.3	−4.3	−1.7	—	15.0	26.0
1977	4.9	12.1	3.1	45.5	42.7	−2.9	−1.5	—	14.9	32.0
1978	4.9	−2.8	6.4	39.2	38.7	−3.5	−2.5	—	13.6	43.5

1979	6.8	4.8	6.8	54.4	53.9	−4.7	−0.9	—	12.8	49.9
1980	9.3	9.6	9.3	90.3	100.2	−5.4	−2.5	—	11.3	53.8
1981	−4.4	8.8	−8.8	103.1	109.9	−4.4	−2.9	−6.2	11.4	61.4
1982	0.6	−0.4	0.2	105.6	95.4	−5.7	−3.7	−7.3	10.8	69.7
1983	−3.5	−0.5	−5.9	141.4	154.5	−3.3	−4.1	−4.2	9.7	81.3
1984	5.1	3.0	6.4	215.0	220.6	0.0	—	−2.5	6.1	91.1
Annual averages[(b)]										
1960–4	5.9	4.0	6.6	54.2	55.5	−1.5	—	—	—	—
1965–9	6.4	2.9	6.5	33.9	33.1	−0.4	—	—	—	—
1970–4	10.9	3.3	12.3	24.1	20.1	−3.5	−0.1	—	16.1	10.2
1975–9	6.4	4.5	6.5	42.7	40.6	−4.2	−1.9	—	14.2	34.5
1980–4	1.3	4.0	−0.1	127.1	131.9	−3.8	—	—	9.9	71.5

Notes: [a] Series beginning 1981 from Banco Central do Brasil (includes state owned enterprises) while series beginning 1970 is from Fundação Getulio Vargas (excludes state owned enterprises) – see text.

[b] Compound annual growth rates for output and price series, simple averages in other cases.

Sources and definitions: see appendix 4 (A4.2).

Figure 2.1 Percentage rates of change of prices and real GDP
Sources and definitions: See appendix 4 (A4.2)

Growth rates fell in 1974–5 and never regained the levels of 1971–3. However, in the period 1976 to 1980, average annual growth of 7.1 per cent was maintained; a rate just above Brazil's post-war average of 6.7 per cent. A burgeoning of the current account deficit occurred in 1974, which was reversed over the years 1975–7. A further worsening of the external position began in 1978, culminating in average current account deficits of about 5 per cent of GDP in 1980–2. In 1981–3 a severe recession hit the economy and growth plummeted to an average of −2.4 per cent. Recovery began in 1984, at the same time as a remarkable turn around in the current account position.

Brazilian inflation over the last two and a half decades is notable for the fact that high and rising inflation has co-existed with a falling rate of growth while an unprecedented boom was accompanied by falling and, by post-war Brazilian standards, moderate rates of price increase. No simple correlation is evident between growth and inflation.

A very important distinguishing feature of the economy in the period under review was widespread use of indexation or 'monetary correction'. Between 1964 and 1966, *ex ante* or *ex post* indexation came to be applied to large categories of financial assets including government securities, public and private sector wages and salaries, balance sheet items such as fixed assets, working capital and depreciation allowances, rents as well as to income tax brackets and exemptions.[4] Indexation had a profound impact upon the economy, changing the nature of government finance, fuelling a remarkable increase in, and diversification of, financial assets and creating a means by which economic growth and development could co-exist with often very high rates of inflation. At the same time, for reasons to be illustrated further on, indexation to a large extent 'institutionalised' inflation.[5]

2.2.1 *A decomposition of changes in the inflation rate*

A simple but useful starting point in an analysis of aggregate inflation is to decompose mechanically a broad official price index with the aim of identifying the immediate contributors to inflation. This is purely an accounting exercise that is devoid of any causal or behavioural content. Still, it does help to identify 'engines of inflation' and thereby provides a focus for the subsequent behavioural analysis.[6]

Given high rates of average inflation it can be difficult to interpret a decomposition of these. Instead, in table 2.2, changes in the rate of inflation are decomposed, showing the immediate contributors to any acceleration or deceleration of overall inflation.

For the purposes of this exercise, GPI is broken down into six major constituent parts.[7] Five of these correspond to actual indices, these being: the wholesale prices of food, unprocessed raw materials and manufactured goods, the Rio de Janeiro consumer price of food and the Rio de Janeiro construction cost index. The sixth component, 'consumer miscellaneous' is a composite measure of six non-food constituents of the Rio de Janeiro consumer price index.[8] The acceleration of each component is weighted by its approximate corresponding share in the overall index.[9]

Certain salient points emerge from the data in table 2.2. The first is the all important contribution of changes in manufacturing price inflation. The latter was the dominant contributor in seven of the thirteen years in which inflation accelerated and in three of the twelve years marked by a fall in inflation. This would seem to confirm the view that this price is key to understanding Brazilian price setting practices and inflation generally.

A second point of interest concerns the immediate contribution of food price inflation. A change in the consumer food price inflation was the dominant factor in the overall change in one year only, namely 1975, a year in which inflation fell. Wholesale food prices had a much more active role in fuelling changes in prevailing inflation. In 1967, 1968, 1972 and 1973, changes in this constituent led the deceleration of inflation and also once

Table 2.2. *Decomposition of changes in the rate of aggregate inflation (in percentage points)*

Year	Changes in the rate of aggregate inflation	Made up of changes in inflation of the following prices					
		Wholesale food	Wholesale raw materials	Wholesale manufactured goods	Consumer food	Consumer miscellaneous	Construction cost
1960	−5.7	−1.2	−0.2	−6.3	−1.8	−1.6	7.7
1961	6.1	0.4	0.4	6.0	0.6	0.9	−5.5
1962	12.1	4.1	1.8	1.0	3.2	2.2	3.9
1963	25.0	2.4	1.1	11.4	0.5	5.1	1.9
1964	15.5	2.6	2.1	0.8	3.6	2.9	7.8
1965	−33.5	−7.3	−4.1	−7.4	−5.9	−0.7	−10.2
1966	−18.8	0.7	−0.8	−8.8	−1.0	−7.5	−4.3
1967	−9.9	−5.0	−1.5	−2.2	−1.9	−1.1	2.0
1968	−4.3	−1.7	−0.1	1.5	−1.2	−1.4	0.7
1969	−3.2	1.2	−0.3	−3.2	1.3	−1.5	−1.2
1970	−1.1	0.1	0.2	−1.1	0.2	0.0	−1.3
1971	0.6	1.0	−0.4	0.1	−0.3	−0.4	0.0
1972	−3.4	−1.7	−0.1	−0.3	−0.6	−0.6	0.0
1973	−1.9	−1.0	0.1	−0.1	−0.4	−0.8	0.6
1974	13.6	2.5	1.9	4.4	2.6	1.8	0.8
1975	−0.1	0.1	−0.4	−0.7	−1.4	1.9	−0.6
1976	13.6	3.8	0.3	2.9	2.0	1.7	2.2
1977	1.4	0.8	0.0	1.0	0.4	0.1	0.7
1978	−3.9	0.9	−0.5	−1.0	−0.7	−0.9	−1.5
1979	15.2	2.0	2.1	6.1	2.5	1.5	1.2
1980	46.3	11.0	4.8	13.8	3.1	6.0	4.8
1981	9.7	0.5	−0.7	2.9	2.9	3.8	0.5
1982	−14.5	−5.5	−1.2	−2.3	−2.1	0.3	−0.3
1983	59.1	24.7	4.6	13.0	9.2	2.3	2.2
1984	66.1	5.9	8.8	25.1	5.7	10.2	7.5

Sources and definitions: See appendix 4 (A4.2).

again in 1982. The wholesale price index appears to have been the primary engine of acceleration in inflation in only three years: 1962, 1976 and 1983 and an important secondary factor in the acceleration of 1980. In 1966, 1969, 1970, 1975, 1977 and 1978, wholesale food price inflation moved against the dominant downward trend. These rough and ready indicators point to the need for detailed examination of food price inflation; a topic, taken up again below, which has been largely ignored in the existing empirical literature on Brazil.

As regards the immediate contributions of other constituents, no clear trends are evidenced by the decomposition.

2.3 The empirical literature on Brazilian inflation and a graphical examination of certain macroeconomic relationships

While any attempt to categorise in a broad-brush fashion a wide cross-section of studies is bound to be somewhat arbitrary, it can be said that most explanations for Brazilian inflation have tended to be either monetarist, or of a neo-structuralist or cost-push variety. While in recent years one detects some movements towards cross fertilisation between monetarists and others, it cannot be said that a well-articulated general vision of the inflationary process has yet achieved widespread acceptance.[10]

2.3.1 *The monetarist view of short-run inflation*

Analyses of inflation within this paradigm have invariably adopted the construct of the accelerationist or 'natural rate' Phillips curve to explain short-run inflation.[11] While implicitly at least, the root causes of short-run inflation are sought in the labour market, the analyses are generalised to cover the commodity market with overall price inflation being used as the dependent variable. Making use of Okun's Law (Okun, 1962) that posits the existence of a reasonably stable relationship between the rate of unemployment and output over the trade cycle, assuming exogenous potential output, the GDP output gap is used in place of the unemployment rate as a proxy for demand pressure.[12] Short-run inflation is dependent only upon changes in demand and is not responsive to cost-push pressures. With a coefficient of unity on the expectations variable, once these adjust to match actual inflation, the short-run trade-off between inflation and demand is eliminated.

The credibility of the monetarist vision as an explanation for short-run inflation depends crucially upon the existence of a negative relationship between the output gap and the inflation rate; given expected inflation.

Table 2.3. *Estimates of 'commodity market' Phillips curve*

Author	Dependent variable	Period	N	Method	Estimated equations (t statistics)	R^2	DW	SEE
Lemgruber (1974)	$\dot{P}^{GDP}$	1953–73	21	OLS	$0.090 - 0.905GDPG + 0.951\dot{P}^{GDP}_{t-1}$ (-1.94) (6.73)	0.72	1.65	0.115
Contador (1977)	$GDPG$	1947–75	29	OLS	$0.037 - 0.160\dot{P}^{WG} + 0.337\dot{P}^{E}$ (2.87) (-3.04) (5.91)	0.59	0.94	0.037
Lemgruber (1980)	$INDG$	1950–79	30	OLS	$-0.183 - 0.198\Delta\dot{P}^{G} - 0.747INDG_{t-1}$ (-0.25) (1.96) (-6.88)	0.76	1.48	3.95
Lemgruber (1980)	$\dot{P}^{G}$	1950–79	30	OLS	$3.33 - 0.584INDG + 0.913\dot{P}^{G}_{t-1}$ (1.18) (-3.34) (9.09)	0.75	2.29	6.95
Contador (1982)	$\dot{P}^{WI}$	1950–79	30	OLS(?)	$0.012 - 0.700INDG + 0.828\dot{P}^{WI}_{t-1}$ (2.66) (-1.86) (5.99)	0.57	2.39	—
Lopes (1982)	$\dot{P}^{WG}$	1952–81	30	OLS	$0.103 - 1.025GD\dot{P}G + 1.065\dot{P}^{WG}_{t-1}$ (1.90) (-2.44) (8.74)	0.74	1.96	0.140
Lopes (1982)	$\dot{P}^{WG}$	1952–64	12	OLS	$-0.074 + 1.837GDPG + 0.889\dot{P}^{WG}_{t-1}$ (-0.69) (1.21) (3.68)	0.75	2.25	0.124
Lopes (1982)	$\dot{P}^{WG}$	1965–81	16	OLS	$0.118 - 1.205GDPG + 1.053\dot{P}^{WG}_{t-1}$ (1.56) (-2.60) (6.84)	0.77	1.46	0.148
Penha Cysne (1985)	$\dot{P}^{GDP1}$	1950–83	34	IV	$0.046 + 0.47INDG + 0.83\dot{P}^{GDP1}_{t-1} + 0.23D$ (1.32) (2.42) (7.04) (3.71)	0.84	—	—

Symbols used:

$\dot{P}^{GDP}$ – rate of inflation, implicit GDP deflator,
$\dot{P}^{GDP1}$ – rate of inflation ($\Delta\log$) implicit GDP deflator,
GDPG – GDP output gap,
$\dot{P}^{WG}$ – inflation rate, wholesale price index,
$\dot{P}^{E}$ – expected wholesale price inflation, generated by autoregressive model,
INDG – output gap in industry,
$\dot{P}^{G}$ – rate of inflation (measured as $100 \cdot \log(\dot{P}^{G}_{t}/\dot{P}^{G}_{t-1})$) general price index,
$\dot{P}^{WI}$ – rate of inflation, wholesale industrial price index,
D – dummy variable with value 1 in 1980–3 and 0 in other years.

Largely as a consequence of this fact, much of the debate on the causes of Brazilian inflation has revolved around the applicability of the Phillips curve in its commodity market version – i.e. where price rather than wage inflation becomes the dependent variable. Lemgruber (1974, 1980), Contador (1977, 1982) and Cysne (1985) are among the most important studies that have attempted to fit the model to Brazilian data.[13] Estimation results from these studies are summarised in table 2.3.

With the exception of Contador (1977), who uses a fourth-order adaptive expectations scheme, first-order adaptive expectations are assumed. The unlikely implication of this scheme is that agents are unable to forecast any change in inflation, despite the volatile inflationary climate. The estimated coefficients of the expectations variables are generally found to be insignificantly different from unity.[14] This has led to the common practice of imposing a coefficient of unity and estimating the models using the acceleration of inflation as the dependent variable.

In general, in Phillips curve studies applied to Brazil the regression results presented are minimal, with diagnostic statistics for misspecification limited in most cases to the Durbin-Watson test. This makes it difficult to assess the quality of the statistical findings but there is clear evidence of misspecification in many instances.[15] The most striking feature of the empirical results obtained is that the demand proxy is invariably of borderline significance or actually insignificant. Moreover, as Lopes (1982) has pointed out, the implied strength of the relationship between the unemployment rate and inflation seems rather high.[16] Even if the effect were as strong as is implied, there is an asymmetry between the impact of changes in demand at low rates of inflation compared with high rates. The Phillips curve results for Brazil imply that a massive 5 per cent rise in the rate of unemployment brings with it a 7.5 per cent to 12.5 per cent fall in the rate of inflation. This is very significant in the context of inflation of 10 per cent to 20 per cent but much less so when prices are inflating at 50 per cent to 100 per cent *per annum*. It follows that deflationary policies will prove much more effective as a stabilising measure in a low rather than a high inflation context.

A measure of capacity utilisation in manufacturing, derived and discussed in appendix 3, is plotted along with the acceleration of general price inflation in figure 2.2.[17] An unambiguous positive correlation between the variables is most clearly apparent in two subperiods, 1963–6 and 1980–2. In both 1961–3 and 1982–3, an acceleration of inflation is associated with a fall in capacity utilisation and not with a rise, as suggested by the commodity market Phillips curve. Lopes (1982) argues forcefully that the impression of a short-run trade-off between inflation and excess capacity is a statistical illusion due to the coincidence first, of external price

Figure 2.2 Changes in inflation and the level of demand
Sources and definitions: See appendix 4 (A4.2)

shocks with high levels of activity (in 1974, 1976, 1979 and 1980) and secondly, of the policy induced real wage compression of 1964–7 with low activity. In other words he concludes that an explanation of inflation based upon demand pressures which both ignores institutional arrangements as well as structural or cost-push factors is inadequate.

Contador (1985) attempts to revive the essentially demand-pull explanation of inflation by proposing a monetarist model with an augmented supply function that purportedly includes unanticipated supply shocks as well as fiscal and monetary induced demand shocks. The conclusion he reaches is that, in general, aggregate demand was responsible for short-run inflation, while cost pressures affected mainly output.[18]

In sum, the statistical evidence does not support the hypothesis that short-run inflation was essentially determined by aggregate demand pressures operating through the labour market. Rejection of this view does not imply a denial of a role for demand in inflation but it does suggest that the commodity market Phillips curve paradigm – based as it is upon a one

Table 2.4. *Prices, monetary aggregates and foreign assets of the monetary authorities (percentage rates of changes – December to December)*

Year	General price index	High-powered money	*M1*	*M3*	Foreign assets of the monetary authorities
1960	30.5	40.2	38.8	40.0	—
1961	47.7	60.4	52.5	57.1	—
1962	51.3	64.4	64.1	63.6	—
1963	81.3	70.1	64.6	61.1	—
1964	91.9	78.5	81.6	82.8	250.0
1965	34.5	72.7	79.5	75.5	114.3
1966	38.8	23.1	13.8	22.6	−6.7
1967	24.3	30.8	45.7	45.6	−21.4
1968	25.4	42.0	39.0	44.6	54.5
1969	20.2	29.1	32.5	32.5	152.9
1970	19.2	16.5	25.8	28.3	69.8
1971	19.8	36.3	32.3	11.0	56.2
1972	15.5	18.5	38.3	43.3	148.2
1973	15.7	47.1	47.0	45.0	52.3
1974	34.5	32.9	33.5	32.7	2.8
1975	29.4	36.4	42.8	44.5	0.2
1976	46.3	49.8	37.2	38.6	111.0
1977	38.8	50.7	37.5	45.0	41.6
1978	40.8	44.9	42.2	51.3	113.5
1979	77.2	84.4	73.6	71.9	61.0
1980	110.2	56.9	70.2	62.6	60.5
1981	95.2	69.8	87.6	86.8	83.3
1982	99.7	87.3	65.0	85.0	27.3
1983	211.0	96.3	95.0	136.0	380.1
1984	233.8	243.8	203.5	259.8	535.5
Compound annual growth rates					
1960–4	59.0	62.2	59.7	60.3	—
1965–9	28.5	38.5	40.5	43.1	43.8
1970–4	20.7	29.8	35.2	31.5	59.4
1975–9	45.7	52.4	46.1	49.8	59.4
1980–4	141.7	102.1	99.0	116.6	158.0

Sources and definitions: See appendix 4 (A4.2).

good, one pricing mechanism model of the economy – is an inappropriate conceptual framework in which to examine the causes of inflation in an industrialising economy with a heterogeneous market structure. The possibility of alternative forms of pricing behaviour in different sectors of the economy is ruled out *ex hypothesis* by the adoption of the commodity market Phillips curve construct, as is a role either for factors that impinge upon the competitive determination of wages and prices or for other non-labour costs. As argued at length in chapter 4, it is even doubtful whether, given the Brazilian institutional setting, the Phillips curve is an appropriate construct for the study of aggregate wage inflation.

2.3.2 *Money and the monetarist view of inflation in the long run*

Complete monetarist models of inflation make use of the Phillips curve plus the quantity theory of money to explain long-run inflation. Simonsen (1980), Lemgruber (1980) and Contador (1985) have advanced models of this type to explain Brazilian inflation in recent decades. They differ slightly, particularly as regards the exact form of the supply function, but the key properties are the same. The authors conclude that the empirical evidence supports the view that, in the long run, inflation becomes independent of the output gap, being determined solely by the rate of monetary expansion minus the rate of exogenous trend growth in real output. Lemgruber (1977), basing his analysis upon an IS/LM type Keynesian model, reaches basically the same conclusion. He maintains that his single equation estimates for the period 1952–73 show that inflation was caused by growth in narrow and high-powered money and by past inflation, with only a limited role for foreign prices and world trade.[19]

In table 2.4, December to December rates of change are shown for the GPI, credit money ($M1$ and $M3$), high-powered money (H) and foreign assets of the monetary authorities (in cruzeiro terms). Plotted in figure 2.3 are the rates of change of high-powered money and inflation. Monetary aggregates grew very rapidly in the 1967–73 period when inflation was decelerating, and at much slower rates from 1979–80 to 1983–4 when inflation was on an upward trend. On the other hand, two periods in which rates of monetary expansion well in excess of inflation and which were followed by a marked acceleration of inflation were 1960–2 and 1971–3. Both periods coincided with cyclical peaks (see figure 2.2) and there is a widely held view that monetary expansion did help to fuel aggregate demand inflations at these points in time. Overall, however, there is little indication of a clear and systematic causal relationship linking changes in money with changes in the price level.[20]

To an even larger extent, the degree of flexibility and adaptability in the

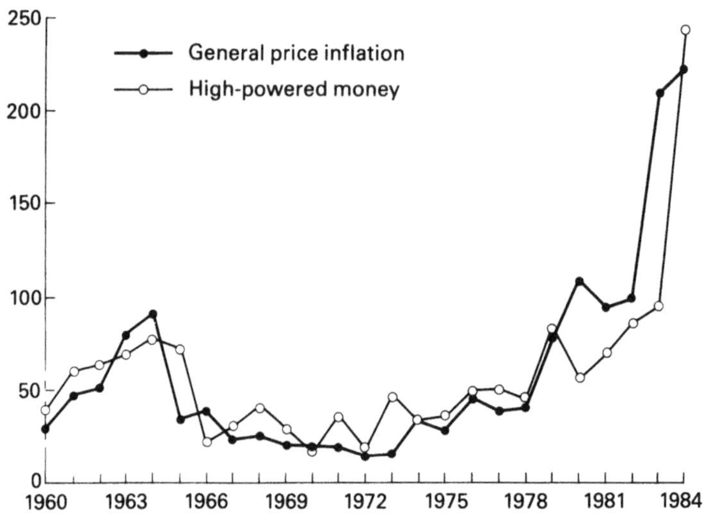

Figure 2.3 Percentage rates of change of prices and high-powered money
Sources and definitions: See appendix 4 (A4.2)

financial system increased after 1965, encouraging substitution between monetary and non-monetary assets.[21] This made control of any given financial asset increasingly ineffectual in controlling broad liquidity and helps to explain the divergent pattern of growth in different monetary aggregates that is apparent in table 2.4. The 'financial deepening' that occurred post-1965 casts doubts upon the usefulness of a paradigm that posits a stable causal relationship between narrowly defined money and the price level. It suggests instead that an approach which takes a broad view of the role of financial assets in the economic system – such as the asset equilibrium approach introduced in chapter 1 – is an appropriate one to adopt for a study of Brazil post-1965.

The asset equilibrium approach is also useful in that it identifies specific channels through which financial factors influence prices and inflation; the main ones being the effect upon private expenditure and demand of changes in private wealth and interest rates. Monetarist interpretations of the Brazilian inflation are generally less clear about the exact linkages proposed between money and prices. One common, if implicit, view is that money growth targets determine agents' expectations as to future inflation and these in turn influence current pricing decisions. However, there is little reason to believe that monetary targets rather than past inflation and indexation plans were significant determinants of expectations (Dornbusch, 1985). The fact that little credence was placed upon announced monetary policy meant that tight money had an impact upon inflation primarily through recession.

A number of studies have examined the issue of causality in Brazil between money and credit on the one hand, and inflation on the other, using the tests derived by Sims (1972) and Granger (1969). The weight of evidence points to two-way, or bidirectional, causality between money and prices, and between a major determinant of high-powered money – Bank of Brazil credits – and economic activity.[22] This casts further doubt upon the simple one-way causality suggested by monetarists and implies instead that money and credit were to a degree endogenous with respect to national income.

The money supply process, and more generally, the process of financial asset accumulation in Brazil is a complex one. It is beyond the scope of the present chapter to analyse this process in detail.[23] Here it is only possible to review in brief certain elements that are of particular importance in an explanation of the apparent tendency towards endogeneity. We focus first upon certain traits of public finances and then turn to the contribution of the overseas sector.

Measurement of the public sector deficit in Brazil is complicated by the dispersion of fiscal expenditures between both branches of the monetary authorities as well as the different levels of government (Horta, 1981). Two estimates of the deficit as a percentage of GDP are presented in table 2.1. The first represents an estimate of the consolidated public sector deficit (from Fundação Getulio Vargas) excluding the financing requirements of non-financial firms which are wholly or partly owned by the public sector and covers the period 1970–83. The second (from Banco Central do Brasil) covers the overall public sector and is computed from overall financing requirements rather than from the balance sheets of individual public institutions. This series covers 1981–8 (tables 2.1 and 2.7). Both estimates are inflation adjusted as they exclude monetary correction on the public debt as well as that portion of interest that corresponds to inflation. A rising trend is clearly evident in the first series, with the highest deficits, equal to 3.7 per cent and 4.1 per cent of GDP, being recorded in 1982 and 1983. In very broad terms, the principal factors behind the observed growth of the deficit were rising subsidies – notably consumption and some producer subsidies to wheat, sugar, coffee and petroleum derivatives – and current transfers which included real interest payments on the public debt. Direct subsidies represented, to an appreciable degree, the response of policy-makers to rising prices of key consumer or intermediate goods or, alternatively, they were designed to loosen potentially inflationary bottlenecks.

These increased outlays were not accompanied by a concomitant rise in tax revenues. In fact, the figures on net tax burden presented in table 2.1 show that total direct and indirect taxes, minus subsidies and transfers, fell very sharply as a percentage of GDP after 1972. This was due mainly to a marked fall in indirect tax receipts from 16.7 per cent of 1970 GDP to 10.2 per cent in 1984. It would appear that the fall in net taxation came about due to inefficiencies and rigidities that prevented growth in receipts at least proportional to growth in national income. In the way Sunkel (1958) foresaw, faced with enormous demands upon its resources to sustain growth and to bail out sectors adversely affected by changing patterns of growth and specific fiscal and economic policies, government was unable to command the requisite transfer of resources necessary to finance itself. To what extent inflation had a direct negative impact upon real tax receipts in the way analysed by Olivera (1967b) is unclear. Despite indexation of tax arrears and exemptions, there is some evidence that the system in place did not fully compensate for inflation.

Changes in net lending by the monetary authorities were an important 'use of funds' in the public sector deficit and therefore relevant to the determination of asset accumulation. Particularly after 1973, subsidised lending by the state was seen as a way to compensate specific sectors (mainly agriculture) for the adverse consequences of other non-financial measures taken to promote industrial expansion and/or to alleviate the balance of payments crisis associated with the oil shock.[24] Credits were often extended at fixed nominal rates of interest, with the result that as inflation rose the implicit interest rate subsidies grew and the charge on public sector financial resources intensified. Credit subsidies, while not the direct result of price pressures, tended to expand automatically with an acceleration of inflation. In this way an endogenous link was present between inflation and the real expansion of money and bonds, required to finance these subsidies. A model incorporating this feature is developed by Fraga Neto (1985). Unofficial estimates by the World Bank suggest that the value of the implicit credit subsidies equalled 5.5 per cent of GDP in each of the years 1977 and 1978.

Finally, as was shown in chapter 1 (1.3), even with an unchanging real deficit, to the extent that the inflation tax decreases because of a rising proportion of indexed assets in the financial system, there will be increased upward pressure on the real stock of assets. This phenomenon was important in Brazil during the 1970s and early 1980s as an increasing proportion of financial assets came to be indexed and the stock of high-powered money suffered a relative shrinkage.[25]

Technically the endogeneity of assets through the public sector budget constraint could have been broken by the exercise of firm control on the part of policy-makers. This topic is discussed at length by Simonsen (1980), himself a former Brazilian Finance Minister. He describes the near impossibility of controlling monetary and fiscal policy in Brazil during the 1970s.[26] One important factor that he highlights was the role of the Bank of Brazil and the 'conta do movimento' (described in note 22 above) that linked its lending to the money supply process. To attempt to control the virtually unlimited demand by the Bank of Brazil for free central bank credits, the assets and non-monetary liabilities of the monetary authorities were subject, at least officially, although not always in practice, to the constraint of a so-called monetary budget. High-powered money was then determined as a residual. The monetary budget was controlled separately from the various government budgets – by the National Monetary Council – despite the fact that many important *de facto* fiscal expenditures were included in it. The diffusion of control over the budgets coupled with the political and economic pressures for monetary and fiscal expansion, made effective control a near impossibility.

Another important channel through which endogenous asset creation occurred was the balance of payments. The rate of change of foreign assets of the monetary authorities (official foreign reserves), in cruzeiro terms, is shown in table 2.4. Large-scale accumulation of foreign assets took place in 1964–5, 1968–73 and again in 1983–4. Marques (1985) showed that, after lending by the monetary authorities to the financial and non-financial private sectors, the main determinant of changes in high-powered money during the 1970s was changes in foreign reserves. Sterilisation of reserve inflows through sales of government securities was not able to sever completely the linkage between reserves and high-powered money.

Ramos (1981), among others, has argued that sterilisation, by driving up domestic interest rates, actually fuelled inflation from the side of costs.[27] More generally, an asset equilibrium approach to finance shows that expansion of government bonds, by driving up private wealth and expenditure, puts upward pressure on demand. To the extent that this is not counterbalanced by the deflationary impact of higher interest rates, bond financing may be inflationary. The overemphasis placed by Brazilian policy-makers upon control of monetary aggregates seems to have obscured this implication of bond financing.[28]

2.3.3 *Neo-structuralist and cost-push explanations for Brazilian inflation*

These interpretations place primordial emphasis upon the role of costs in triggering inflationary spirals. As illustrated in chapter 1, official or *de facto* indexation of wages and prices tends to ensure that any incipient change in important relative prices, originating from a structural bottle-neck or an autonomous cost-push pressure, will lead to an increase in the rate of inflation.

Excess aggregate demand is not generally accorded a pivotal role in these explanations of inflation. There is more emphasis placed upon imbalances between supply and demand in particular sectors.

In the 1960s, non-monetarist explanations for Brazil's inflation were prompted by the observed pattern of changes in output and the price level that did not accord easily with monetarist orthodoxy. Morley (1971), Fishlow (1973), Bacha (1977) and A. Lara Resende (1982), among others, argued that the initial surge of inflation in 1963–4 and its subsequent fall to about 20 per cent in 1968–9 had to do principally with the behaviour of costs and not with demand factors. In fact, Fishlow (1973) and Morley (1971) present evidence which appears to show that prices rose less rapidly in faster growing sectors of industry. Faster productivity growth contributed to slower increases in, or even to falling, real unit labour costs, with a mitigating influence upon price inflation. We discuss this phenomenon further below.

These studies highlight the importance of the restrictive money and credit policies – followed in the period from 1964 to mid-1967 – in depressing growth in industrial output by starving firms of reasonably priced credit necessary to finance working capital while also driving up the cost of credit from alternative sources. These same policies were relatively ineffectual as anti-inflationary measures. In fact, Fishlow (1973) suggests that rising real interest rates resulting from tight money policies may have put upward pressure on inflation from the side of costs.

Data on effective borrowing costs in Brazil, especially during the 1960s, is scarce and often misleading.[29] However, an approximate indication of the evolution over time of short-term interest rates is given by data on the cost of consumer credit from finance companies (financeiras) and by the yield on bills of exchange.[30] Using general price inflation as a deflator, real rates are plotted in figure 2.4. The data show that real lending rates jumped in 1965–6 by almost 40 percentage points from a negative position in 1963–4. They averaged over 20 per cent between 1965 and 1977. When analysing industrial price formation in chapter 3, we consider further the hypothesis of 'interest rate-push'.

Related to Fishlow's point regarding financial costs, Morley (1971) argued that the inflation of 1963–6 was profit-push led, as firms were forced to generate funds to finance working capital internally due to the scarcity of credit.[31]

Another cause to which the surge in inflation of 1963–4 is attributed is 'corrective inflation', set off by the elimination of price controls and subsidies coupled with devaluation.[32] Fishlow (1973) maintains that the

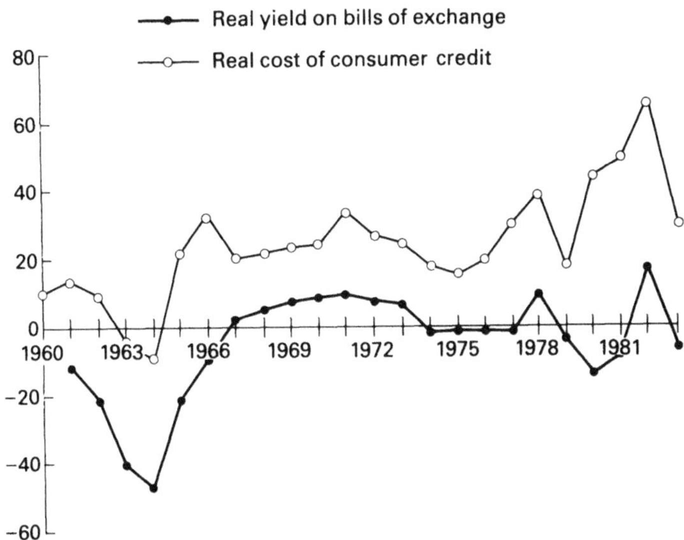

Figure 2.4 Average annual real interest rates in percentage points
Sources and definitions: See appendix 4 (A4.2)

cost pressures in 1965–7 were further aggravated by tax increases while Kafka (1967) credits the squeeze on imports that occurred in 1964–6 with hampering the fight against inflation by creating supply bottle-necks for certain vital wage goods.

Bacha (1980) and A. Lara Resende (1982) focus upon the role of the institutionalised wage fixing arrangements, introduced in 1964–5, in bringing about the reduction of inflation after 1964.[33] The consensus view is that a deliberate manipulation of the wage adjustment system led to a fall in the real wage that put downward pressure on price inflation.[34] Rates of change of annual averages of the following variables are set out in table 2.5: the urban minimum wage, mandatory official wage adjustments, earnings in manufacturing, the cost of living and unit labour costs in manufacturing.[35] Indices of the average minimum wage and of the wage implied by official adjustments – both deflated by the cost of living – are plotted in figure 2.5 along with an index of real unit labour costs in manufacturing.

After peaking in 1961, the real minimum wage fell sharply in 1962–3 and then declined, more gently, through to the early 1970s. Officially decreed wage adjustments followed a similar pattern over time. The real rate of change of official adjustments is plotted in figure 2.6 along with the rate of change of earnings in manufacturing.

Table 2.5. *Wages, earnings and unit labour costs: average annual observations (percentage rates of change)*

Year	Urban minimum wage	Official wage adjustments	Average manufacturing earnings	Cost of living	Unit labour cost in manufacturing
1960	10.0	—	—	28.6	30.4
1961	57.9	—	—	33.3	38.7
1962	29.2	—	—	52.8	43.2
1963	56.4	—	—	69.1	77.7
1964	83.2	—	77.7	92.5	87.2
1965	61.0	—	47.8	65.4	56.2
1966	30.7	30.1	52.9	41.2	33.4
1967	25.3	21.0	31.0	30.6	27.0
1968	21.6	23.4	30.8	22.3	18.8
1969	19.2	24.4	26.6	22.0	19.4
1970	20.1	24.1	26.6	22.7	15.0
1971	20.4	22.3	24.0	20.2	15.7
1972	19.5	21.4	25.8	16.4	15.8
1973	17.0	17.3	23.7	12.7	15.3
1974	25.2	25.0	30.6	27.7	30.6
1975	35.7	38.7	41.3	29.0	36.2
1976	37.0	41.3	46.9	41.8	36.2
1977	44.1	40.2	50.3	43.8	47.5
1978	41.7	40.4	50.4	38.7	43.6
1979	52.1	47.6	57.7	52.7	52.9
1980	87.5	87.2	92.4	82.8	84.1
1981	102.9	100.0	115.9	105.6	112.9
1982	99.6	112.9	115.0	98.0	101.5
1983	113.7	117.0	117.0	142.0	114.7
1984	176.5	184.9	195.0	196.7	172.3
Compound annual growth rates					
1960–4	45.1	—	61.6	53.5	53.8
1965–9	30.7	24.7[a]	37.5	35.4	30.3
1970–4	20.4	22.0	26.1	19.8	18.3
1975–9	42.0	41.6	49.2	41.0	43.1
1980–4	114.0	118.0	124.6	121.6	115.2

Note: [a] Average refers to 1966–9.
Sources and definitions: See appendix 4 (A4.2).

Figure 2.5 Real wage levels and real unit labour cost (indices with base 1970 = 1)
Sources and definitions: See appendix 4 (A4.2)

The data on earnings in manufacturing show that these fell sharply in real terms in 1964–5. From 1967 through 1981, a close correlation is evident between changes in official adjustments and average earnings, with the latter increasing by a reasonably consistent amount in excess of official adjustments.[36] In section 2.3.4 and again in more detail in chapter 4, we review evidence on the hypothesis that real wages were in part determined by the state of demand.

It is clear from figure 2.6 and table 2.5 that average manufacturing earnings grew in real terms in each year from 1966 to 1982. Assuming that industrialists followed mark-up pricing, what is important in assessing the direct impact of these changes upon industrial price inflation is the behaviour not of real earnings alone but rather of unit labour costs. As is apparent from table 2.5, average annual unit labour costs in manufacturing rose by less than the rate of inflation in each year from 1964 through 1972. An index of unit labour costs – deflated by manufacturing prices and graphed in figure 2.5 – shows this very clearly.

The foregoing discussion points to the importance of distinguishing between the impact of changes in demand and changes in output; even though the former may be proxied by the deviation in output from trend. Assuming mark-up pricing over actual unit costs in manufacturing, a cyclical rise in output, if accompanied by a slower rise in employment, will

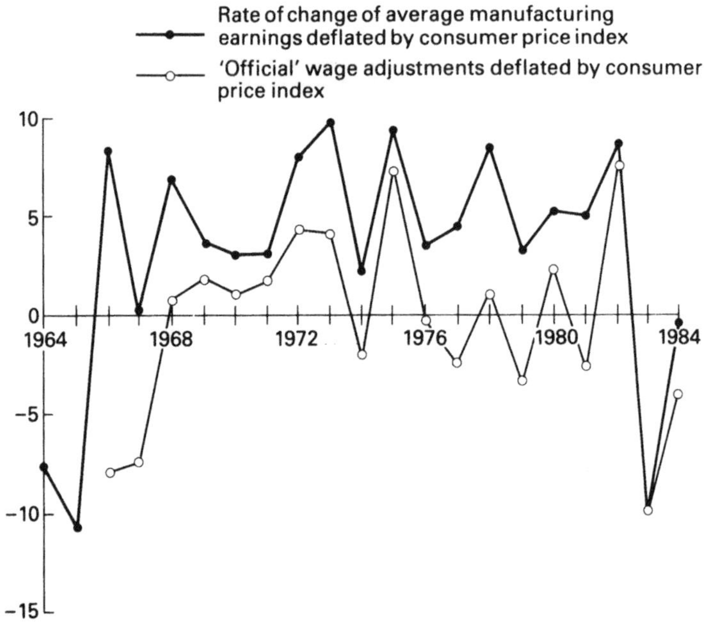

Figure 2.6 Percentage rates of change in real earnings and official wage adjustments
Sources and definitions: See appendix 4 (A4.2)

put downward pressure on price independently of a possible demand effect upon the mark-up.[37] It also follows that a credit squeeze, which causes a contraction of industrial output by making finance for working capital scarce and/or expensive, will tend to reduce productivity and thereby to increase actual unit labour costs – with a concomitant impact upon inflation. The pro-cyclical pattern of variation in productivity is attested to in figure 2.7 where a very high degree of positive correlation is evident. It would seem that a marked improvement in productivity, coupled with slow growth in average real earnings was important in the deceleration of inflation during the years of the 'miracle'.[38]

Indirectly, wages may have implications for inflation through the channel of demand for food. The relevant variable here is not so much average manufacturing earnings but rather the minimum wage to which wages paid to the bulk of unskilled and semi-skilled urban workers were closely linked (Correa do Lago *et al.*, 1984). The fact that the real minimum wage fell very markedly between 1961 and 1970 (see figure 2.5) must have put downward pressure on the demand for food and therefore also upon the

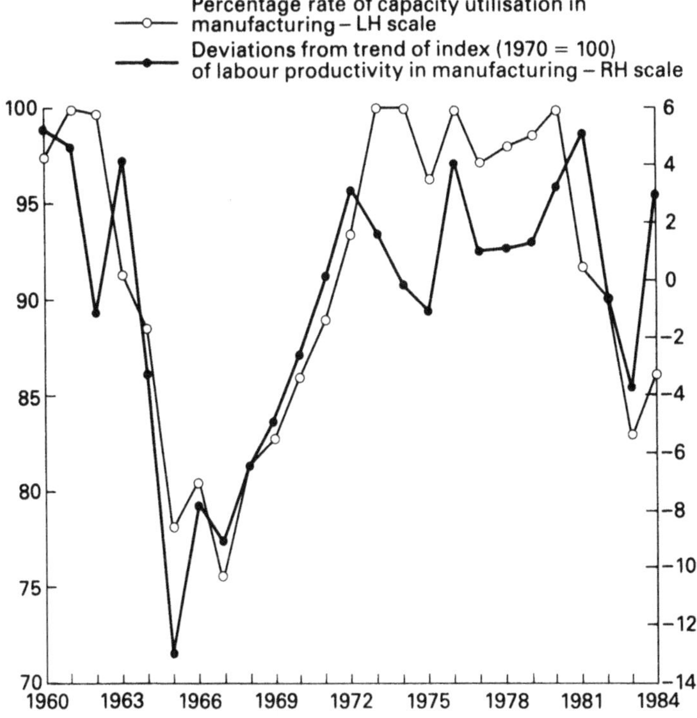

Figure 2.7 Capacity utilisation and productivity
Sources and definitions: See appendix 4 (A4.2)

rate of inflation. The very gentle rise in real terms between 1971 and 1980 is unlikely to have had a dramatic impact upon food demand.

Very little empirical analysis has been undertaken of the role, if any, of agricultural prices in the Brazilian inflation of recent decades. Various commentators have made passing reference to the impact of changes in food or agricultural prices upon the general level of prices or inflation in years in which large variations in production occurred. Alternating good and bad harvests during 1965–7 is an example from the pre-oil shock period while poor harvests in 1976 and 1978 have also been highlighted. The paucity of more analytically detailed work stems in part from inadequacies in agricultural production statistics that make the setting-up and testing of hypotheses difficult (see chapter 5 (5.2)). Because of the great diversity that characterises Brazilian agriculture – particularly as regards productivity, output and pricing practices in those subsectors producing for export *vis-à-vis* those engaged primarily in supplying the domestic

Table 2.6. *Compound annual growth rates of food crop production, total agricultural output and real GDP in per capita terms (percentage rates of change)*

Years	All agriculture	Food crops	Real GDP
1961–4	0.6	1.0	1.7
1965–9	0.2	2.1	3.7
1970–4	0.7	0.7	8.1
1975–9	2.1	−1.6	3.9
1980–4	1.7	−1.6	−1.0
1961–84	1.1	0.1	3.3
1961–9	0.4	1.6	2.8
1970–84	1.5	−0.8	3.6

Sources and definitions: See appendix 4 (A4.2).

market – it is generally misleading to try and draw conclusions from aggregate price and output data for all agriculture. It is also important to consider diverse price behaviour at different marketing levels, i.e. at the retail and wholesale levels.[39]

The structuralist framework suggests that, in a study of inflation, the key prices and quantities are those relating to food for domestic consumption as it is these that feed most directly into the cost of living and, thus into wage demands. However, in Brazil there is no readily available index of food production. An imprecise indication of the evolution of food output was obtained by constructing a fixed value weighted index from production data for eight important domestic food crops.[40] Various average annual *per capita* growth rates of this index are shown in table 2.6 along with similar statistics for all agricultural output (as measured in the National Accounts) and GDP.[41]

The slower average growth of food crops compared with total agricultural output is evident from the table, as is the opposing trend in the two series; downwards for food and upwards for all agriculture.[42] If we assume an income elasticity of demand for food in the range of 0.4–0.6 and use GDP as a proxy for private sector income, a 'back of the envelope' calculation suggests that average growth of food production (assuming no alternative sources of supply) of 1.3 per cent–2.0 per cent would have been required to avoid inflationary disequilibria in the food market.[43] In fact, over the period 1961–84, *per capita* food crop growth was close to zero. More interestingly, however, output growth was close to or equalled the 'required' rate in the 1960s and early 1970s but was actually negative in the more highly inflationary period post-1974.[44]

Relative consumer and wholesale prices of food are plotted in figure 2.8.

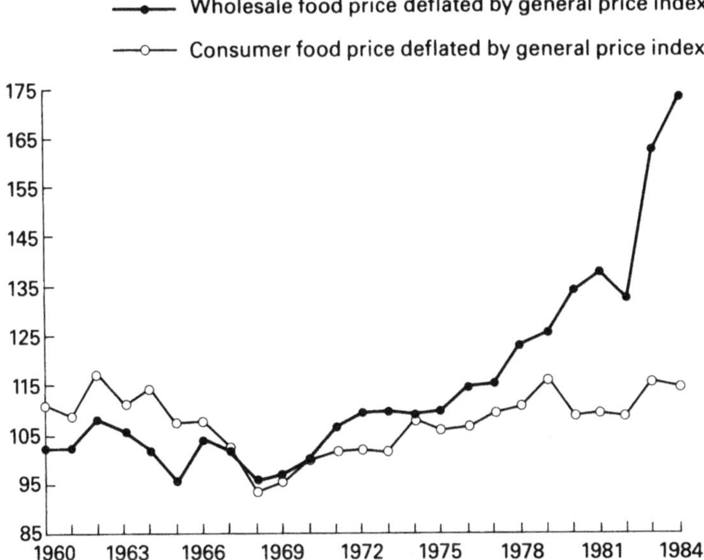

Figure 2.8 Relative food prices (indices with base 1970 = 100)
Sources and definitions: See appendix 4 (A4.2)

Retail and wholesale prices followed a downward trend in the period 1962–8; with a more pronounced fall in consumer prices. Post-1969 a rising trend in prices began, with wholesale prices moving much more sharply upwards than consumer prices. The increasing gulf between the two series, after 1974, is almost certainly explicable in large part by the growth of consumer subsidies and price controls.[45]

While the observed pattern of change in relative food prices and food output described above is compatible with the existence of a causal link between excess demand for food and inflation as posited in the model of chapter 1, the hypothesis requires testing before the existence of such a link can be claimed. This is the topic of chapter 5. What is clear is that, to the extent that the relentless rise in the relative prices of food after 1969 triggered a spiral in other prices or wages, it was a contributing factor in the upward movement in inflation that characterised most of the period. In Brazil the wholesale food price index is an important constituent of the aggregate wholesale price index that formed the basis for *de facto* indexation of the exchange rate and indexation of important financial assets and contracts. In this way food prices were propagated throughout the economy. Nevertheless, the most direct channel of propagation – namely via wage increases linked to consumer price changes – was

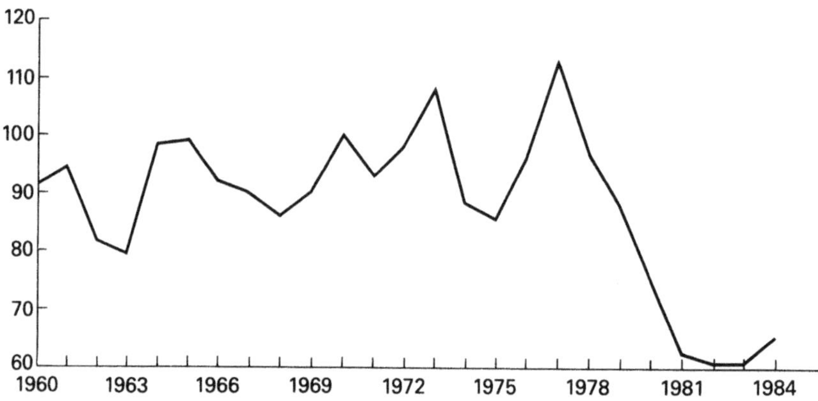

Figure 2.9 External terms of trade (indices with base 1970 = 1)
Sources and definitions: See appendix 4 (A4.2)

neutralised by the expanding use of subsidies and controls. An evaluation of the aggregate impact of a relative wholesale food price rise, given the subsidy policy, is made in chapter 9, using model simulations.

Neo-structuralists argue that the vigorous economic recovery that began in Brazil in 1967 was stimulated by accommodating money and credit policies pursued by the newly appointed finance minister Delfim Netto (Bacha, 1977 and A. Lara Resende, 1982). Rapid growth was made possible by the combination of extremely favourable external conditions and considerable excess capacity in the domestic industrial sector. Buoyant world trade stimulated demand for Brazil's exports as well as world export prices. At the same time vigorous export promotion and a competitive and stable real exchange rate policy at home stimulated exports from the supply side. Between 1967 and 1974, the constant dollar value of exports more than doubled while industrial exports alone rose 200 per cent. Brazil's external terms of trade, plotted in figure 2.9, fell from 1965 to 1968 but then followed a strong upward trend through 1973 as a result of the world commodity boom.

The fact that the country's capacity to import expanded phenomenally had anti-inflationary implications. The possibility of bottle-necks in the supply of essential imports was all but eliminated and a safety valve existed through which imbalances between demand and domestic supply of key wage and intermediate goods could be corrected. Moreover, the improving terms of trade and rapid export expansion coincided with favourable conditions in international capital markets which allowed Brazil to finance with ease substantial current account deficits and still to accumulate reserves. The cost of this policy was of course a growing level of external indebtedness (see data in tables 2.1 and 2.7). The ease with which short-falls on the current account could be financed obviated the need for real devaluation of the cruzeiro, thus avoiding potentially inflationary cost-push pressures from this source.

Neo-structuralist views on Brazil's post-1973 inflation emphasise the susceptibility to supply shocks and to shifts in patterns of demand of an economy characterised by an increasing degree of indexation, reduced flexibility in its balance of payments, very high initial rates of capacity utilisation and a commitment to continued rapid growth in output.[46] A series of such shocks during the 1970s and early 1980s drove the inflation threshold relentlessly upwards.

Both directly and indirectly the foreign sector contributed to rising inflation in the post-1973 period. The importance of direct price shocks emanating from the external sector can be seen in figures 2.10 and 2.11. The first figure shows: (a) an index of the real cruzeiro/U.S. dollar exchange rate (a rise denotes a real depreciation of the cruzeiro), (b) the dollar price of Brazil's raw material imports relative to the U.S. wholesale price index and (c) the dollar price of Brazil's raw material imports converted into cruzeiros using the average annual exchange rate and expressed relative to the Brazilian general price index (GPI). The last can be thought of as approximating what would have been the domestic relative price of imported raw materials in the absence of subsidies and taxes. The graph shows that, up to 1972–3, both dollar and cruzeiro relative prices of imported raw materials followed a gradual downward trend with a dampening effect upon inflation. The real exchange rate was quite volatile up until 1967 but was largely stable from 1968 through 1978 due to the informal purchasing power parity indexation rule that was followed.[47]

The economy suffered serious foreign price shocks in 1974 and in 1979–80 as prices of oil and other raw materials rose on world markets. The impact of the 1979–80 price rises was accentuated by a sharp real devaluation in late 1979 followed by a further real devaluation in 1983. Increases in real 'world' prices and in the real exchange rate reinforced one another during the 1970s to occasion a pronounced rise in the relative cruzeiro price of imported raw materials.

Following the logic of the model of chapter 1, a real devaluation, not accompanied by a reduction in the target real wage, drives up the relative food prices compatible with price stability and thereby unleashes a powerful wage-price spiral.

There exists a degree of controversy surrounding the direct contribution of the first oil price shock to the inflationary acceleration evidenced in Brazil during 1974.[48] This stems from the divergent behaviour of inter-

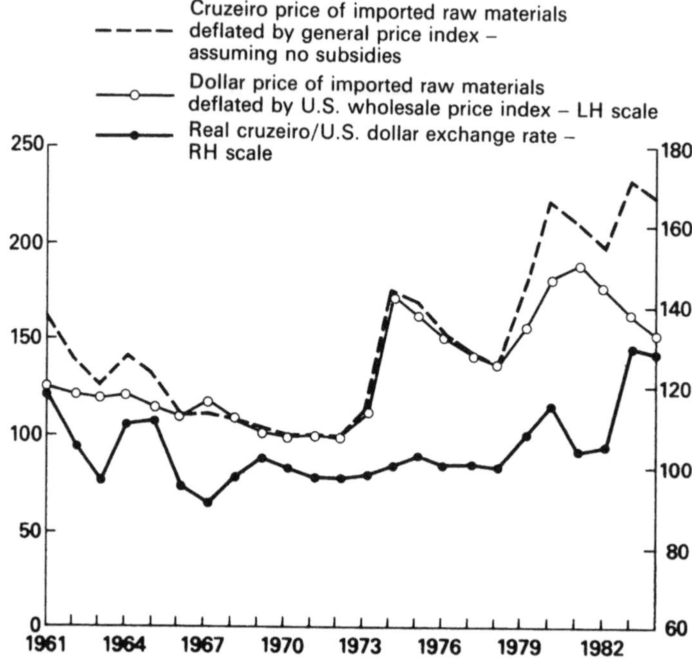

Figure 2.10 Relative raw material import prices and the real exchange rate (indices with base 1970 = 1)
Sources and definitions: See appendix 4 (A4.2)

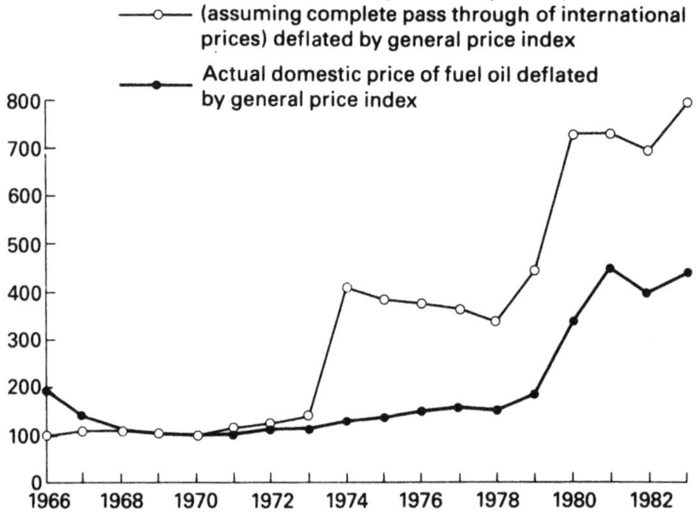

Figure 2.11 Relative domestic prices of petroleum products (indices with base 1970 = 1)
Sources and definitions: See appendix 4 (A4.2)

national and domestic Brazilian prices of petroleum and derivatives, coupled with the difficulty, discussed further below, of isolating the effects of the oil shock given a confluence of potentially inflationary phenomena at the time. The divergence in international and domestic prices is apparent from figure 2.11 which shows the time paths of the actual domestic relative price of fuel oils – heavily influenced by subsidies and price controls – and the corresponding 'notional' relative price in cruzeiros of imported oil, assuming no subsidies. The divergence is especially noticeable in 1974, when domestic prices hardly rose while border prices increased dramatically. The impact of the second oil shock was much more fully reflected in domestic prices.

As with food subsidies, subsidies to petroleum products mitigated the immediate impact upon inflation of price shocks but, to the extent that they were not financed by higher taxes, also helped validate existing inflation through an increased budget deficit and possibly added to demand-pull inflation in the longer run. It would seem that the direct contribution of the first oil shock to the spurt in inflation was not great although indirectly, through the impact upon domestically produced raw material prices, the public sector deficit and the balance of payments, the contribution was much more pronounced.

Bacha (1977) argues forcefully that the balance of payments constraint on growth that re-emerged after 1973–4, brought with it inflationary consequences. While the immediate catalyst was the unfavourable shift in the terms of trade caused by the oil price shock (see figure 2.9), he presents evidence to show that an unsustainable trend had been developing even before this event. His calculations suggest that the ratio of imports to exports required to sustain a given rate of capacity utilisation in the economy – particularly in industry – shifted markedly upwards in the post-1964 period of outward-looking expansion. This caused the trade-off between growth and the trade balance deficit to become more acute. In the mid-1970s, with a much less favourable environment for international trade and payments than in the pre-oil shock period, maintenance of vigorous growth in GDP brought with it accelerating inflation as the capacity to import was squeezed.

Cline (1981) attempted to quantify the impact upon inflation of the severe restrictions imposed upon imports after the first oil shock. He included an index of protection – constructed from data on the level of tariffs and other barriers to imports – in a reduced form equation to explain inflation in 1961–77. He found this variable to be a very significant determinant of inflation, particularly after 1974.

A pronounced fall was registered in Brazil's external terms of trade in the period 1979–81, with virtually no recovery through 1984 (figure 2.9). This was a key factor in the recession of 1981–2 and in the balance of payments crisis of 1982–3. Besides causing potentially inflationary import shortages, the balance of payments situation precipitated inflation indirectly via the large real devaluations of 1979–80 and 1983.

Outside the foreign sector, other processes were at work in the 1970s and early 1980s that contributed to inflation. There is a wide consensus that the foreign reserve build-up of the early 1970s – through its impact upon high-powered money and liquidity in general – stoked an aggregate demand inflation as industry reached very high levels of capacity utilisation (see figure 2.2).[49] Bacha (1980) maintains, moreover, that shortages of certain raw materials and skilled labour also developed in 1973–4. The pressures had been mounting prior to 1974 but only emerged then because of the lifting or relaxation of various price controls and subsidies by the new Geisel government.

Domestic raw material prices and their possible contribution to inflation have been largely ignored in the Brazilian literature. A plot of the rate of change of domestic wholesale raw material prices, relative to the GPI, and of capacity utilisation is presented in figure 2.12. Because demand is considered separately from supply and the likely influence of 'world' commodity prices is not captured, the graph only deals with one possible factor in the price determination process. Nonetheless, a positive correlation between the series is evident over the years 1960–74 and 1979–84. The surge in relative prices in 1973–4 is certainly compatible with Bacha's view that demand pressures drove up many raw material prices in this period but probably also reflects a spill-over effect of foreign commodity price increases to prices of domestically produced substitutes.

Added to the cost-push pressures that hit the economy in 1979–80 from import price rises and the exchange rate devaluation, many writers have pointed to the inflationary consequences of the switch from annual to semi-annual wage adjustments in 1979.[50] As shown in chapter 4 (4.2), this change is equivalent to an increase in the wage adjustment coefficient (h) of the model of chapter 1. This leads to higher wage and price inflation for a given target real wage.

Certain authors, notably Tavares (1978), Souza (1982) and Ramos (1981) have taken up the idea of financial cost-push inflation in the 1970s and 1980s and of the links between this and the foreign debt. It is argued that, in certain periods, high real interest rates exerted upward pressure on gross mark-ups in industry as the cost of borrowed working capital or of long-term debt increased.[51] This was exacerbated by the rise in average gearing ratios in Brazilian industrial firms.

Figure 2.4 points to a surge in real interest rates in 1977–8 and again, on a more dramatic scale, in 1980–2. The cost of consumer credit reached an

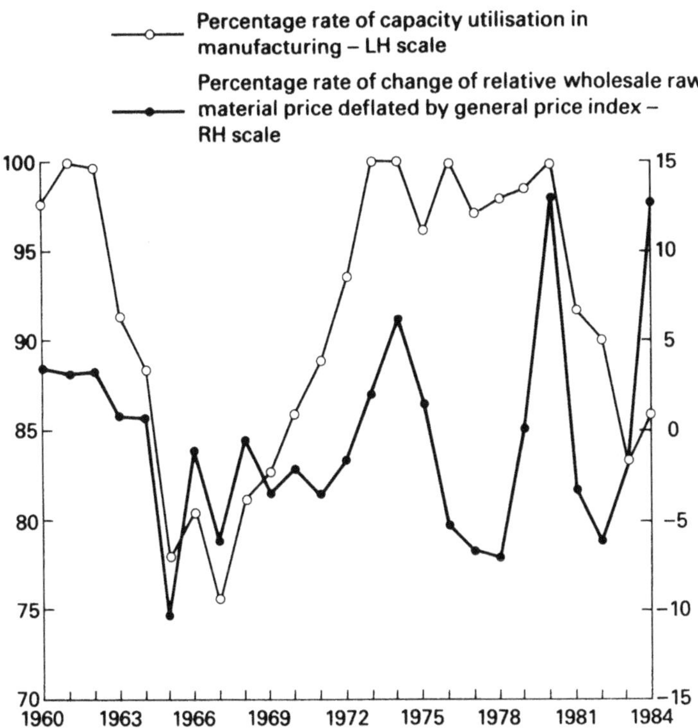

Figure 2.12 Raw material price changes and demand
Sources and definitions: See appendix 4 (A4.2)

unprecedented rate of over 60 per cent in real terms in the latter year. To explain high real interest rates, one recurrent line of argument is that domestic monetary policy was geared deliberately at maintaining high rates, conscious of the need to attract ever increasing inflows of foreign capital to finance large current account deficits associated with the rapid expansion of the debt service burden. A vicious circle developed as inflows exceeded current account financing requirements in many years and led to a build-up of reserves. The authorities sought to prevent these from enlarging the money base by open market sales of government securities. These attempts at sterilisation led to even higher interest rates and to increased capital flows.

A crucial linkage between the foreign debt and inflation derived from the conduct of exchange rate policy. During the 1980s in particular, enormous interest obligations and principal repayments owing on the foreign debt could only be met by generating increasing surpluses on the trade account of the balance of payments. This in turn required real devaluations of the exchange rate and also severely curtailed the flexibility to increase imports in the face of domestic supply shortages or unexpected increases in demand.

Of course, as noted by Souza (1982) and others, as the foreign indebtedness of Brazilian industrial companies expanded, real devaluations of the currency had an ever more profound expansionary impact upon the debt burden in cruzeiro terms. Therefore real devaluations may have added to financial cost inflation.

2.3.4 *Econometric analyses of inflation from a neo-structuralist perspective*

In the 1980s a small quantitative literature emerged as a counterpoint to the commodity market Phillips curve explanations for Brazil's inflation.

Initially econometric treatment was limited to estimation of reduced form models for the determinants of industrial wages and prices. Lara Resende and Lopes (1981) found strong evidence to support the view that official wage policy and external price shocks were the main determinants of industrial price inflation in the 1960s and 1970s. Demand pressures, operating through the labour market, were found to exert no influence upon inflation or, according to Lopes (1982), only a limited and secondary influence.

Modiano (1983a) adopted a different tack in the empirical analysis of Brazilian inflation by abandoning the estimation of reduced form models in favour of a simple simultaneous model of wage and price inflation. His model included three endogenous variables: inflation of average manufacturing earnings, industrial price inflation and overall wholesale price inflation. Earnings are determined by official wage adjustments coupled with free market factors that create a functional dependency between earnings inflation and the GDP output gap as well as between price inflation in the current and previous periods. Industrial prices are assumed to be determined by a fixed mark-up over unit labour costs and domestic raw material prices. The latter variable is exogenous and no role is posited for imported input prices. Overall inflation is a weighted average of industrial price and exogenous agricultural price inflations. While rudimentary, this specification has the value of allowing for supply shocks from agriculture, for raw material prices and for demand factors, albeit in a limited way.

Modiano estimated his model with a very short sample of 16 observations covering 1966–81. From the estimated coefficients of the structural model he computed the reduced form coefficients. Demand was found to be a significant determinant of earnings inflation but the total impact of the output gap variable on overall inflation was quite low; a 10 per cent fall in capacity utilisation leading to a 1.4 per cent fall in inflation. This contrasts with the 6–11 per cent fall in inflation that the commodity market Phillips curves, estimated over the same period, suggest would result from a similar change in capacity utilisation.

Modiano (1985) developed further the approach used in his earlier study. He expanded the wage and price model to include endogenous determination of agricultural prices and of the cruzeiro/dollar exchange rate. He replaced a composite domestic raw material price by oil and non-oil imported input prices. Dollar prices of tradable agricultural goods are assumed to be set exogenously in world markets, their cruzeiro price equalling the dollar price multiplied by the exchange rate. Non-tradable agricultural goods prices are modelled as a function of the GDP output gap and of the deviation from trend of an index of non-coffee food crop production. The two specifications are combined and a single equation is estimated for agricultural prices. While this specification captures the flavour of a competitive market for food it is not derived explicitly from such a model and exhibits some questionable features. In particular, not only is the GDP output gap an imperfect proxy for real household disposable income but it also embodies the same changes in agricultural output that enter the equation through the agricultural production variable.

Modiano (1985) went on to model the rate of exchange devaluation as a function of the inflation differential between Brazil and the U.S.A.[52] Earnings inflation is modelled as in Modiano (1983a) while two different specifications are experimented with for industrial price inflation. In one, the independent variables are the rates of change of earnings (not of unit labour costs) and of imported inputs. In the other, the mark-up is flexible and dependent upon the level or change in the output gap variable. In the preferred model, industrial price inflation apparently moves inversely with the rate of capacity utilisation. In other words, the mark-up rises (falls) continuously at low (high) levels of capacity utilisation. Modiano acknowledges this to be a surprising result and suggests some tentative explanations. In chapter 3 (3.6) we propose an alternative explanation and show why Modiano's result may be due to the omission of productivity growth from the model.

The main additional finding of Modiano (1985), relative to the results reported in Modiano (1983a), was that the endogenisation of agricultural prices makes inflation much more responsive to the rate of capacity utilisation, provided that the mark-up is fixed and does not move countercyclically. In this case a 10 per cent fall in capacity utilisation leads to a total 9 per cent fall in inflation. If the flexible mark-up model is accepted as valid,

Table 2.7. *Key macroeconomic indicators 1984–1988*

	Percentage rates of change						As percentage of GDP			
Year	Real GDP	Real agricultural output	Real industrial output	General price index	'Overnight' interest rates[a]	Average real salary in industry	Current account of balance of payments	Public sector 'operational' surplus (−deficit)[b]	Net taxation burden	U.S.$ billions Gross foreign debt
1984	5.1	3.0	6.4	220.6	231.0	2.9	0.0	−2.5	6.1	91.1
1985	8.3	9.8	9.0	225.5	250.2	24.4	−0.1	−4.3	2.5	95.9
1986	7.6	−8.2	11.7	142.3	76.7	25.2	−2.0	−3.6	5.2	101.8
1987	3.6	15.0	1.1	224.8	398.8	−5.0	0.3	−5.5	3.6	107.5
1988	−0.3	−0.4	−2.5	684.6	1061.3	5.3	1.3	−4.3	—	106.1

Notes: [a] Monthly averages annualised.
[b] Series from Banco Central do Brasil (includes state owned enterprises).

Sources and definitions: See appendix 4 (A4.2).

no statistically significant relationship can be discerned between capacity utilisation and inflation. The contrast between these findings points to the vital importance of properly specifying the major channels through which output and demand impinge upon prices and inflation.

Modiano's papers provide a very promising starting point for further work on the econometrics of Brazil's inflation and form an important building block for the present study. While the approach is potentially a fruitful one, the wage and price model needs more careful specification and estimation at the level of the individual equations and, more generally, the approach needs to be broadened to encompass additional variables. Chapters 3 to 6 are devoted to doing just this. Most importantly, perhaps, the assumptions of passive money and finance along with exogenous output determination require relaxation in order that the interrelationships between these variables and inflation can be examined. This is done in chapter 7.

2.4 Inflation and stabilisation post-1984

The analytical chapters of this study make use of data from the 1960s through to 1983–4 both to test certain hypotheses regarding price formation and to attempt to analyse the causes of, and the interrelationships inherent in, the inflationary process. Brazil's experience with inflation since 1984 has been a fascinating one due to the volatility of rates and the nature of the economic policy responses adopted. In briefly reviewing this experience, it is hoped to show that, despite important and frequent policy changes relative to the pre-1984 period, many of the major processes underlying the generation and propagation of inflation remain fundamentally the same. For this reason it is believed that the particular inflationary experience analysed in this study can continue to provide insights into Brazil's current inflation as well as, possibly, that of other countries with shared characteristics.

Brazil's macroeconomic policy and performance in the four and a half years since end 1984 have been enormously varied. Rates of price inflation have gyrated widely around a rising and historically unprecedented trend, punctuated by a series of failed but innovative attempts at achieving price stability. Up until mid-1987 price instability went hand in hand with rapid growth of output and employment and, throughout the period, Brazil generated trade surpluses that averaged in excess of 4.2 per cent of GDP. As a result, current account deficits were held to an average of only 0.5 per cent of GDP despite the enormous burden of foreign debt service. Certain key macroeconomic indicators are shown in table 2.7.

The economic recovery from the recession of the early 1980s, that began in 1984, gathered momentum in 1985 and 1986, and was evidenced by impressive rates of increase in industrial output of 9.0 per cent and 11.7 per cent in each year respectively. The principal engines of growth were net exports, particularly of manufactured goods, and consumer spending. The latter received enormous stimulus from rates of increase in real average industrial earnings of close to 25 per cent per year in 1985 and 1986.

The abandonment in early 1985 of attempts to reach agreement with the IMF on stabilisation measures marked the shift to a more heterodox, or eclectic, approach to achieving price stability. By virtue of the less restrictive monetary, fiscal and wage policies adopted from early 1985, aggregate demand and output growth received added stimulus. The cost was a substantial increase in the estimated 'operational' deficit of the public sector in 1985, expressed as a percentage of GDP, to 4.3 per cent.

The dramatic turnaround during 1984 in the current account of the balance of payments was reversed only to a limited extent in the following two years. Trade surpluses of U.S.$12.5 billion and U.S.$8.3 billion were achieved in 1985 and 1986 respectively. The current account position benefited from the effect upon imports of lower international petroleum prices and from falling interest rates in the major financial centres. While still rising during this period, 1984–6 saw a marked slowdown in the rate of growth of Brazil's foreign debt.

Average GPI inflation during 1985, at 225.5 per cent was close to the rate registered in the previous year. Intensive use of price controls held inflation in check through the first half of 1985. But, from August onwards, controls were eased and wage demands from industrial trade unions, which had intensified after the civilian government took office in March, combined to drive up the inflation threshold precipitously to approximately 15 per cent per month (535 per cent annualised) in January and February of 1986. Inflation rates quarter by quarter are shown in table 2.8.

Rapidly accelerating inflation led in February 1986 to the imposition of a wide-ranging and innovative stabilisation package that came to be called the Plano Cruzado (Cruzado Plan). The main elements comprised:

(a) the creation of a new currency, the cruzado, equal to 1000 cruzeiros,
(b) a general price freeze and a fixing of the exchange rate against the U.S. dollar,
(c) a wages and salary freeze at levels corresponding to average real values over the previous six months plus a bonus of 8 per cent (15 per cent in the case of the minimum wage),
(d) abolition of most forms of indexation – in the case of wages a 'trigger' mechanism was established so that these would be adjusted upwards by 20 per cent whenever accumulated inflation reached that threshold, and
(e) introduction of a scaling system for existing contracts with *ex ante*

Table 2.8. *General price index (average percentage rates of change by quarter)*

Quarter	Average monthly inflation	Annualised equivalent
1985 Q1	11.8	281.3
Q2	7.6	140.9
Q3	10.7	238.7
Q4	12.4	306.6
1986 Q1	10.6	235.0
Q2	0.1	11.4
Q3	1.0	13.0
Q4	3.8	57.0
1987 Q1	13.7	366.8
Q2	24.6	1300.3
Q3	7.3	132.9
Q4	13.9	376.7
1988 Q1	18.3	651.3
Q2	20.2	809.6
Q3	23.4	1246.8
Q4	28.2	1970.9
1989 Q1	17.5	692.5

Sources and definitions: See appendix 4 (A4.2).

indexation that was designed to eliminate built-in provisions for expected future inflation.

After a period of initial success aided by a high degree of public support, the Cruzado Plan foundered due to problems inherent in the price freeze and to the onset of a remarkable, consumption-led surge in aggregate demand and output.

The real wage boost occasioned by the Cruzado Plan, came on top of a major rise in the previous year and gave a sharp stimulus to consumer spending at a time when the economy had already been growing strongly for two years. There also occurred a process of remonetisation of the economy as demand for non-interest bearing assets surged. This led to average increases in $M1$ of 23.3 per cent in each of the six months following the Cruzado Plan's announcement. A by-product of remonetisation was to foster an illusion of increased wealth which in turn resulted in a marked fall in the savings ratio and further stimulus to demand.

The public sector too contributed to a major overheating of domestic demand. Despite a large rise in real tax receipts resulting from the temporary elimination of inflation, public sector spending expanded out of control and the overall deficit actually increased slightly over the course of 1986.

The value of wholesale trade rose by approximately 25 per cent in real terms in the three months to end May 1986. Industrial output surged and the IBGE/CEI survey based index of capacity utilisation in manufacturing reached the historically very high level of 86 per cent in the third quarter.

Policy-makers had tackled the problem of unsynchronised wage and salary adjustments prior to the Cruzado Plan by imposing the freeze at levels based upon the average value of incomes over the previous six months. Goods prices, on the other hand, were frozen at the nominal levels prevailing on 27 February without regard to the fact that periodic and unsynchronised adjustments prior to the freeze had left prices of many goods at unsustainably low relative levels. This led, in the months following the announcement of the package, to the emergence of shortages in the official market as goods were withheld from sale and to the rapid expansion of black markets. The demand boom greatly exacerbated this tendency.

Liberalisation of certain imports and hikes in interest rates in July 1986, designed to ease shortages and rein in consumer demand, were insufficient to prevent the re-emergence of inflation. GPI inflation, which had fallen to an annualised 12 per cent during the second and third quarters of the year, rose to 57 per cent in the last three months of 1986. The 20 per cent wage trigger acted to accelerate inflation as adjustments, based as they were on accumulated changes in past inflation, came to be made with ever increasing frequency.

A further series of measures introduced in late 1986 were aimed at reducing domestic demand and at restoring fiscal balance. The main weapon used was large increases in indirect taxation which had the side-effect of boosting cost inflation and igniting inflationary expectations. What was left of price restraint rapidly disintegrated.

By early 1987 the Cruzado Plan was in tatters. The combination of a fixed exchange rate and rising real labour and material costs had begun to make exports uncompetitive in the latter part of 1986. A sharp swing of the trade balance into a deficit position in late 1986/early 1987 precipitated the declaration of a moratorium on interest payments on the foreign debt in February, heightening the sense of economic crisis. Inflation continued to accelerate sharply, reaching an annualised 1,300 per cent in the second quarter.

Under Finance Minister Bresser-Perreira, a second attempt at stabilisation was made beginning in June 1987. The 'Bresser Plan' included a new 90 day wage and price freeze, the elimination of the 20 per cent wage trigger and its replacement by indexation based on inflation in the previous quarter, reduced spending by the public sector (notably on wheat and credit subsidies) and increased interest rates. A new cruzado was created equal to 1000 of the old units.

In its intent the plan was more orthodox than the Cruzado Plan had been in that it recognised the need to manage the growth of aggregate demand at the same time as breaking the wage-price spiral. In fact, attempts to impose fiscal restraint failed, the lack of spending cuts being exacerbated by declining real tax revenues. Accelerating inflation reduced the real value of tax collected and the sharp downturn in the industrial sector from mid-1987 caused indirect taxes levied on industrial output to fall. Real tax receipts declined by 14.8 per cent in 1987 and by a further 7.8 per cent in the following year. The extent of disequilibrium in public sector finances is illustrated by the fact that the net tax burden, as a percentage of GDP, collapsed to only 3.6 per cent; less than one third the comparable figure for 1980 and only one fifth that of 1972 (tables 2.1 and 2.7). The operational deficit of the public sector ended 1987 higher at 5.5 per cent of GDP.

The immediate impact of the Bresser Plan was to reduce inflation in the third quarter of 1987 to an annual 133 per cent, however, as price controls were lifted beginning in October, inflation again accelerated, driven in large part by expectations of a further price freeze. As shown in table 2.8, inflation began an inexorable rise that continued throughout 1988 and culminated in a monthly rate of 36.6 per cent (4,221 per cent annualised) in January 1989.

While the Bresser Plan singularly failed to meet its price stability objectives it did play a part in bringing the consumer boom to an abrupt halt. The rate of growth of industrial production began to slow during the second quarter of 1987, the slowdown gathering momentum as the year progressed. The re-introduction of lagged indexation precipitated a marked decline in real industrial wages from mid-year, culminating in a 5 per cent fall for 1987 as a whole.

A policy of induced high real interest rates – the bench mark 'overnight' rate averaged 17 per cent in real terms in the third quarter – was also intended to foster deflation. However, in addition to having an immediate inflationary influence through their impact on financial costs in industry, high real interest rates may even have had a perverse effect on private consumption by virtue of their effect upon private sector income and wealth. Given that a significant proportion of private wealth was held in the form of government debt or government linked savings instruments and that the private sector was a net creditor of the public sector, higher rates may have stimulated rather than dampened consumption.

The collapse of domestic demand in 1987–8 was tempered by impressive renewed growth in the foreign sector. Brazil's trade surplus widened to U.S.$11.2 billion in 1987 and U.S.$19.1 billion in 1988; the catalyst being a compound annual growth in manufactured and semi-manufactured exports over two years of more than 24 per cent. A resumption of interest payments on the foreign debt in the last quarter of 1987 was possible while generating a small current account surplus in the same year and a surplus in 1988 of U.S.$2.6 billion or approximately 1.3 per cent of GDP, unprecedented since the mid-1960s.

Due largely to a sharp recovery in the agricultural sector – where output rose by 15 per cent – as well as to growth in net exports, GDP registered a 3.6 per cent increase in 1987 despite slow or zero growth in much of the economy.

The recession in the industrial sector intensified from early 1988 with a decline in production over the year of 2.5 per cent. However, even more than in the previous year, GDP was sustained by the foreign sector and preliminary estimates suggest that it fell 0.3 per cent over the year. Recession in the domestic economy was accompanied by rapidly accelerating inflation, particularly in the last half of the year. On the side of costs, the real wage decline of 1987 continued into the early months of 1988 but was then reversed as widespread industrial unrest led to higher wage settlements. For 1988 as a whole real increases averaged over 5 per cent. Interest rates also remained high in real terms, especially during the second half.

At least as important in the 1988 inflation as rising costs was the impact of expectations. Indications of uncontrolled monetary expansion during the year heightened fears of hyperinflation and destabilised expectations. In the final quarter high-powered money grew by the annual equivalent of 4,770 per cent versus an inflation rate of 1971 per cent as the public sector deficit was financed by money creation. *M*1 rose at a rate of 3,536 per cent in the same period. Particularly in industry, a very important element in the acceleration of inflation appears to have been 'anticipatory' pricing, driven by rising expectations of a new freeze. Not wanting to be disadvantaged by being frozen at an unsustainably low level, industrialists fuelled a wage-price spiral by marking up prices with increasing frequency, to account not simply for increased costs but also for expected inflation.

As noted earlier, comprehensive and long-standing indexation, prior to 1986, had generally performed a stabilising function in the sense of ensuring a degree of relative price stability in times of high inflation and acting as an anchor for expectations. The unprecedented volatility in rates post-1986 owes much to the uncertainty created by the absence of such a mechanism.[53]

In January 1989 the so-called Summer Plan was introduced to deal with mounting instability in the price system. A new price freeze was combined with an end to indexation and an announced intention to reduce drastically the fiscal deficit in order to bring monetary and fiscal policy back under control. Within a matter of months it had become apparent that the political will to carry through the deficit reduction plans did not exist and at the time of writing little remains of the package except for an already disintegrating price freeze.

Brazil's recent experience with inflation and stabilisation highlights forcefully the importance for an analysis of the inflationary process of integrating a proper appreciation of aggregate and sectoral demand influences within a 'heterodox' framework.

At or near the peak in economic activity which was reached in 1985–6 industrial wages and prices appear to have been directly influenced by excess demand in labour and product markets. Nonetheless, the more powerful and direct influence of excess demand was upon the flexible price sectors of the economy, particularly agriculture. Price pressures originating in these sectors were quickly propagated throughout the economy via wages and other costs.

The experience of 1987–8 highlights the asymmetries inherent in the relationship between demand and inflation at high absolute rates of inflation. Whereas higher margins and increased real wage demands undoubtedly pushed up the inflation threshold in the expansionary phase of 1985–6, a significant subsequent fall in domestic demand had no discernible impact upon aggregate inflation which was, instead, propelled relentlessly upwards by rising costs and expectations of a further freeze.

The public sector played an important part in fuelling and sustaining inflation. Besides the direct stimulus of government spending, the effect upon asset creation of enormous public sector deficits was all important. An understanding of the complex interactions between the public sector deficit, its means of financing and the determinants of private sector income and wealth are crucial to an effective analysis of Brazil's inflation.

2.5 Conclusion

The foregoing review of the evidence and literature relating to Brazil's inflationary experience points to a complex and multi-faceted process. Cost-push factors, supply bottle-necks, demand pressures and changes in output combined – in different degrees at various points in time – to drive the rate of inflation up or down. In general terms these factors acted in a favourable, anti-inflationary way in the 1967–73 period, before turning noticeably unfavourable from about the time of the first oil shock onwards.

Three sets of issues, in particular, emerge from the review which are the subject of further investigation in subsequent chapters:

(a) indexation and inertial inflation,
(b) endogenous money and finance and the interrelationship with inflation, and
(c) the impact of demand on wage and price determination.

The indexation of wages, salaries and the exchange rate along with mark-up pricing in industry combined to ensure that shocks were propagated throughout the system. Largely due to lagged, fixed period indexation of wages and salaries, a tendency was created for inflation to remain at a new threshold until affected by a further shock; in other words, the inertial element was reinforced. Relative to a system in which wages and salaries are adjusted at ever shorter intervals in a vain attempt to maintain real living standards, the indexation rules prevailing prior to 1986 performed a stabilising role in the sense that they kept in check the forces that might otherwise have led to hyperinflation.

The expansion in the rate of growth of liquidity, required for the economy to sustain a higher rate of inflation, occurred in a largely endogenous fashion. However, money and finance were not always simply accommodating but also appear to have had an independent impact upon inflation at particular points in time, through the medium of demand.

There is still considerable uncertainty as to the impact of the level, or of changes in the level, of demand upon prices and inflation. The mechanisms through which demand pressures affect the price system and the strength of these effects are enquired into in chapters 3, 4 and 5. What is clear, however, is that attempts to couch an explanation for short-run inflation solely or predominantly in terms of the behaviour of aggregate demand have proved unsatisfactory. Costs have been crucial sources of basic inflationary pressure.

The review carried out in this chapter points to the need to organise the main factors in the inflation – both causal and propagating as well as demand and cost – into one coherent and explicit framework. Only in this way will it be possible to examine how they interacted and to obtain an indication, at the very least, of the relative importance of different processes and phenomena. Most existing studies focus either upon the side of costs or upon that of aggregate demand and money. The theoretical constructs implicit or explicit in these analyses are not sufficiently general to take account of 'other' factors. This has led, for instance, to little explicit treatment being given, in predominantly cost-push or neo-structuralist studies, to the mechanisms through which financial variables affect inflation.

The review of the existing literature points to the importance, when undertaking a study of inflation, of having a clear underlying theoretical framework. Some studies betray the absence of such a framework by placing contradictory or theoretically unsubstantiated interpretations on the data.

A theoretical framework, of the type sketched in chapter 1 (1.3), that allows explicitly for different mechanisms of price and output determination in industry and agriculture as well as being able to capture particular institutional characteristics of price determination, offers a promising basis for an enquiry into the nature of the inflation. It is much less limiting, for instance, than either a monetarist or a naive Keynesian one-good IS/LM type model without wealth effects.

PART II
THE DETERMINANTS OF WAGES AND PRICES

3 The manufacturing price index

3.1 Introduction

Theories of price determination are closely related to microeconomic theories of the firm. Among the latter, a key distinction is drawn between theories in which firms are essentially price-takers and those in which firms are better viewed as price-makers.[1]

Price-taking theories assume that firms are atomistic units that exercise no independent influence over price. A change in demand leads to a rapid adjustment in price with the consequence that prices, relative to costs, rise with an increase in demand and fall with a decrease. The relevance of these theories for explaining the behaviour of the firm in the industrial sector of a modern capitalist economy has long been called into question. Particularly in empirical investigations of industrial pricing, a more common starting point is to hypothesise some form of price-making behaviour.[2] This is the approach that we adopt here.[3]

3.2 Cost-plus pricing

Interest in price-making theories of the firm grew out of the pioneering survey of business pricing behaviour carried out by Hall and Hitch (1939).[4] Based on their survey results, Hall and Hitch concluded that price was not arrived at on the basis of equality between marginal revenue and marginal cost, as the existing body of marginalist theories suggested, but rather on the basis of what they called the 'full-cost principle'.[5] This implied that:

> prime (or 'direct') cost per unit is taken as the base, a percentage addition is made to cover overheads (or 'oncost', or 'indirect' cost), and a further conventional addition (frequently 10 per cent) is made for profit. (Hall and Hitch, 1939, p. 19)

Contrary to the predictions of conventional theories, prices were found to adjust in a more consistent and thorough fashion to changes in costs than to changes in demand. The survey results showed that, to varying degrees, oligopoly was present in virtually all sectors of industry and that the behaviour of firms could not therefore be properly explained by any of the models of the firm current at the time. In general, it was found that firms did not pursue short-run profit maximisation; in fact, they took no explicit account of marginal costs and revenues at all. Therefore they acted neither as independent monopolies as suggested by the Robinson-Chamberlin model of monopolistic competition nor as perfectly competitive nor monopolistic entities. Rather, they operated under conditions of oligopolistic interdependence.

The findings of Hall and Hitch, reinforced by subsequent business pricing surveys, gave rise to a vast literature on the question of industrial pricing.[6] On the theoretical front their work had left a major question unanswered, namely the determinants of the equilibrium price and output under oligopoly. Hall and Hitch and also Sweezy (1939) adopted the construct of the kinked demand curve to explain the phenomenon of 'sticky' or administered prices but they were unable to explain the more fundamental question of how these prices were arrived at initially. In other words, the level of the mark-up had still to be explained. This issue is not of direct relevance to the present study where causes of variation in the mark-up over time are the primary concern. However, since it is not possible to divorce completely the question of what determines the equilibrium mark-up from the issue of its variability over time, the former question is treated very briefly below.

Some have sought to reconcile the behaviour observed by Hall and Hitch with marginalist theories of the firm but this has been shown to require a series of stringent and unrealistic assumptions.[7] Following the line of enquiry first proposed by Hall and Hitch, the dominant tendency in the subsequent literature has been to seek an explanation for the cost-plus pricing principle within the context of oligopoly. Kalecki worked out an early formalisation of the cost-plus principle and also developed a theory of 'semi-monopolistic price formation' in which the mark-up is a positive function of the 'degree of monopoly' (Kalecki, 1943). The latter, he argued, depended upon the level of concentration in an industry, the development of sales promotion, overhead costs and the influence of trade unions. Implicit in the Kaleckian theory of semi-monopolistic pricing is the idea of collusion between firms. However, no explicit account is taken of the influence upon the mark-up of either the threat of new entry or the reactions of rival firms.

Building on the work of Kalecki, cost-plus pricing models were subsequently derived explicitly from within the framework of oligopoly. These models differ somewhat in their specification of the equilibrium mark-up and in their predictions regarding the time path of the mark-up.

Differences depend upon the exact strand of oligopoly theory from which they derive. For instance, models rooted in the Cournot-Nash solution to oligopoly link the mark-up positively to the concentration ratio in the industry and negatively to the price elasticity of demand for the industry's output.[8] In Sylos-Labini's limit pricing model, on the other hand, the principal determinant of the mark-up is the long-run target rate of profit (Sylos-Labini, 1969). The equilibrium price and therefore, given direct costs, the mark-up as well, is determined by leading firms in the industry and will settle between an upper barrier that implies a profit margin sufficient to induce new firms to enter the industry and a lower barrier required for the least efficient firms to cover costs and earn a minimum rate of profit. It is to the advantage of the leading firms to ensure the survival of existing smaller, less efficient firms. The need to prevent entry and to maintain group discipline limits the freedom of leading firms to alter the equilibrium price, independently of a change in conditions that affect firms throughout the industry.

Other pricing models have been advanced that also give a prominent role to the target rate of return. Notable in this context is the model due to Eckstein (1964) and refined further in Eckstein and Fromm (1968) and Eckstein and Wyss (1972). In this model the mark-up is set so as to yield a target return on capital at standard or normal output. The target is determined by the market structure and by long-run economic conditions in the industry.

3.3 Variations in price over time

Much of the literature – particularly the applied literature – on industrial pricing since Hall and Hitch has been less concerned with the determination of the equilibrium mark-up than with the variation of prices over time and particularly with the response of prices to changes in costs and demand. These issues are of direct relevance to the present study and are therefore discussed in some detail below.

Two themes have dominated the literature on econometric tests of the cost-plus model. The first is the precise definition of costs, encompassing the distinctions between direct and indirect costs as well as between normal and actual costs. The second is the behaviour of the cost-plus margin in the short run, and in particular over the trade cycle, raising the question of whether demand exerts any direct influence over price and, if so, in what direction. A related issue is the role in pricing of changes in overhead costs.

3.3.1 *The definition of costs – direct versus indirect costs*

The way in which costs are defined reflects underlying assumptions about the pricing policies of firms and has a direct bearing upon the interpretation of empirical results.

A number of analysts have favoured a strict definition of direct costs including only manual labour, raw materials and energy.[9] This leaves depreciation allowances (fixed capital costs), interest payments, costs of administrative services, direct taxes and salaries of managerial and technical staff as the main components of indirect costs. Salary expenses are classed as overheads on the basis that they are highly heterogeneous between firms. Another approach, which has also been widely applied, differs in that it includes administrative and technical salaries as part of direct costs along with manual labour costs.[10]

The distinction between direct and indirect costs is fundamental to the cost-plus principle. Starting with Hall and Hitch, firms have been shown to adjust prices more rapidly and systematically to changes in some costs as opposed to others. The most basic explanation for this behaviour is that direct costs are the firm's major costs, are directly associated with production and tend for these reasons to be more easily monitored. Overhead costs are more heterogeneous and, as a result, more difficult to monitor as well as being much more rigid with respect to changes in the scale of production. Moreover, according to Sylos-Labini, the distinction between direct and overhead costs is fundamental since the latter will vary greatly from firm to firm depending upon such factors as the capital intensity of production and age of machines (Sylos-Labini, 1979, p. 156). He argues that, because of the need to maintain price discipline among firms in an oligopolistic industry, there will be a tendency for price changes not to occur unless some of the 'general conditions' of the market vary. The latter are conditions that are clearly perceived by, and affect, all firms in a similar fashion. Since direct cost changes are frequent and have a similar impact upon all firms in the industry, these are among the most important 'general conditions'. Faced with a disturbance to equilibrium price, caused by say a change in labour or raw material costs, leading firms will quickly act to restore equilibrium by using the mark-up over direct unit costs, calculated at some normal or equilibrium level of output as a rule of thumb. On the other hand, a change in overhead costs, such as depreciation allowances, is more likely to be firm specific and will not in general occasion a systematic price response.

Certain statements of the cost-plus principle are open to interpretation as implying a much broader definition of direct cost than either of the two mentioned above. Sometimes a distinction is drawn between, on the one hand, 'true' full cost models in which firms respond to a disturbance in the equilibrium price taking account not only of direct costs but also of overheads and/or pure profit margins and, on the other, the more usual cost-plus models.[11]

3.3.2 *The definition of costs – actual versus normal costs*

In the literature on industrial pricing, the concept of normal or standard unit labour costs has been widely employed in place of actual unit labour costs. The rationale is that difficulties in accurately measuring actual costs often lead firms to base pricing decisions on unit costs calculated at some level of output that they expect to prevail on average. Actual unit costs tend to suffer reversible fluctuations of a cyclical nature, sometimes in ways that are hard to predict. The main cause of these fluctuations is variations in labour productivity, since employment tends to fall less than proportionally when output declines and to increase less than proportionally when output rises. It is also the case that the wage bill per worker varies cyclically, and possibly seasonally as well, due to short-term extensions or reductions of the standard working day, thereby introducing a second source of short-run, reversible change in unit labour costs.

In econometric price equations, a common procedure for approximating normal unit labour costs has been to correct for cyclical and seasonal variations in labour productivity by assuming that normal labour costs per unit of production can be proxied by dividing the wage rate by the level of trend productivity or by a moving average of the same.[12] This approach to normalisation is incomplete in that it makes no allowance for reversible changes in the basic wage and/or hours worked. A more thorough normalisation procedure was adopted by Godley and Nordhaus (1972) and Coutts, Godley and Nordhaus (1978). They attempted to remove all reversible cyclical elements from hours worked, earnings, employment and output. This they did by estimating standard hours worked and standard earnings as well as trend productivity.

Some economists maintain that actual unit labour costs, rather than normal costs, are the true decision variable of firms in the pricing process.[13] They assume that firms are able to track actual unit costs reasonably well, which might be the case if, for instance, productivity does not vary greatly or unpredictably over the cycle. Firms then take these short-run cost variations into account in pricing their output. It may also be the case that, as accounting and production control methods become more sophisticated, industrialists can more easily and rapidly monitor actual unit costs and are therefore less likely to rely on approximations. Sylos-Labini (1979) argues that the choice of time units used in an econometric study will to some extent influence *a priori* judgements as to the plausibility of the actual, relative to normal, cost hypotheses. Where annual averages are used for cost, price and output variables, the averaging process itself serves to eliminate seasonal fluctuations in labour productivity and earnings and, consequently, can be viewed as a particular, albeit incomplete, form of normalisation. He suggests that where annual data are used, actual average unit costs may often represent a sufficient normalisation (Sylos-Labini, 1979, p. 155). It is not clear, however, that the normal cost principle has anything to do with seasonal fluctuations in output. Rather, it is concerned with cyclical changes. In the final analysis the appropriate definition of unit labour costs becomes an empirical question.

The near universal assumption is made in cost-plus models that the productivity of raw materials, that is the volume of input per unit of output, is constant over time, ensuring a one for one correspondence between the prices of raw materials and the final good. One would not expect to find great variability in the short run as raw material inputs and output tend to vary together, unlike labour inputs which have an important overhead component. The possibility of a long-run trend change in raw material productivity cannot be ruled out.[14] However, if raw material productivity does exhibit trend variation, this is often difficult to measure and is probably of limited relevance in an essentially short-run analysis of price.

3.3.3 *The behaviour of the mark-up over the trade cycle*

Models of cost-plus pricing under oligopoly provide explanations for the observed tendency for price to be more responsive to changes in direct costs than to changes in overhead costs or demand. Nonetheless, they do leave open the possibility that under certain conditions both overheads and demand may influence price, leading to some short-run, probably cyclical, variation in the mark-up. No immutable prediction as to the magnitude or direction of change in the mark-up can be derived from theory. This is especially true when trying to predict movements in the aggregate industrial mark-up as opposed to the mark-up in a specific, and therefore more homogeneous, industrial sector. Notwithstanding the inability to make firm *a priori* predictions, theoretical considerations and accumulated empirical results point to a series of factors that will likely influence the final outcome. These include: the level of industrial concentration, the extent of cyclical change in the same, the configuration of the demand curve facing firms in the industry (particularly as it relates to price elasticity at different output levels), the degree of excess capacity and the exposure of the industry to competition from abroad. These points will be elaborated upon in the discussion that follows.

3.3.4 *Responsiveness of price to changes in product market demand*

That industrial prices may be influenced indirectly over the trade cycle through the effects of demand upon prices of factors of production – labour and raw materials – is not in dispute. Long-run changes in demand may also affect industrial prices by altering profits, investment and thereby unit costs. The more contentious issue, and one that has long been at the centre of the debate about industrial price formation, is whether demand exerts any cyclical influence upon prices, independently of costs. This is equivalent to asking how, if at all, the cost/price margin or mark-up varies in response to alterations in product demand. Most, but by no means all, views concerning the role of demand that are encountered in the cost-plus pricing literature fall into one of three categories:[15]

(a) competitive forces will ensure that prices fall relative to either normal or actual direct costs during a recession and vice versa in a period of expansion, in other words, the mark-up moves pro-cyclically.[16]
(b) prices rise relative to direct costs (normal or actual) in recession and vice versa in a period of expansion, leading to counter-cyclical movement in the mark-up,[17] and
(c) prices do not change relative to normal unit costs either in recession or in periods of prosperity – a constant mark-up over normal unit costs.[18]

The accumulated evidence suggests that pro-cyclical pricing is most likely to result in less concentrated sectors of industry, often consumer goods industries where barriers to entry are fewer due to such factors as shorter gestation periods of investment. In these industries, product demand will tend to become somewhat more elastic during a recession thereby encouraging firms, provided that they are able to perceive these changes, to lower prices relative to costs in order to increase sales and vice versa in periods of boom.[19] Demand is also more likely to have some moderate influence on prices in closed economies where competition from imports does not impose a significant constraint on price changes of home produced goods. Finally, rising demand will have a greater tendency to induce an increase in the mark-up when capacity utilisation is at very high levels, making supply inelastic.

Mild counter-cyclical movement in the mark-up is a possibility that is fully consistent with most theories of oligopoly. It becomes more likely the higher the concentration ratio and the greater the tendency for concentration to increase in a recession and decrease in a period of boom. Counter-cyclical pricing is also facilitated if the price elasticity of demand decreases in periods of recession. Arguably this is most likely to be the case in industries engaged in the production of consumer durables and producer goods. Purchases of this class of goods tend to be postponed in a recession and therefore lower prices will not appreciably increase sales. In fact, leading firms may actually increase prices relative to costs slightly in order to protect profit margins, especially those of less efficient firms in the industry that might otherwise be tempted to break the group's discipline. In periods of boom, an analogous but opposite situation can arise; prices may be allowed to fall relative to costs in order to forestall new entry that might otherwise be encouraged were profit margins allowed to rise unchecked.

The third main view on the role of demand, that of mark-up constancy over normal unit costs, has received qualified support in the literature. If, however, labour productivity rises in periods of boom sufficiently to reduce actual unit labour costs below the normal level and vice versa in periods of recession, the constancy of the mark-up over normal unit costs is consistent with pro-cyclical variation in the mark-up over actual unit costs. It becomes very difficult, if not impossible, in such cases to distinguish by econometric means the true decision variable of the firm. This fact has led to a debate about the true role of demand in normal cost models that has become known as the identification problem.[20]

The diversity of demand variables used in applied studies and differences in the way that they enter econometric models, has contributed to the difficulty involved in comparing empirical results on the role of demand and identifying a consensus.[21] In price models rooted in oligopoly theories, demand variables are best thought of as proxies for the degree of competition, whereas in price-taking or competitive models they represent excess demand. A *change* in price is associated in the former case with a *change* in demand and in the latter with the *level* of demand. Often in the cost-plus literature, a price change is modelled as a function of *changes* in costs and the *level* of demand without explicit recognition of the hybrid nature of the implied model or of the implausible implications.[22] Such a specification implies that a once and for all decrease in demand will precipitate a continuous rise or fall in the mark-up. Where there occurs a fall in the mark-up, the model might be rationalised as deriving from a hybrid mark-up/pure competition model.[23] If the demand level term bears a negative sign, the model exhibits the most improbable characteristic that a once and for all drop in demand causes a continuous rise in the mark-up.

3.3.5 *Overhead or indirect costs*

The cost-plus principle starts from the premise that firms adjust price in a predictable manner to any change in direct unit costs of production, usually measured at some standard volume of output. Normally changes in overhead costs are assumed to be absorbed by firms, in the sense that they do not respond to changes in these by varying prices but rather allow the pure profit element of the mark-up to rise or fall. This will generally hold in the short run as long as the amount of variation is not great and is not perceived by leading firms to affect the whole industry in a more or less systematic way.[24] Some theorists, notably Kalecki (1943) and Sylos-Labini (1969) also allow for the possibility of limited short-run variability as well.

Pricing policies may be rather different in cases where certain important overhead costs are subject to frequent and pronounced changes relative to costs in general. If this phenomenon is somewhat generalised across a given industry, firms may take these relative price changes into account in determining price. This is not a possibility usually considered in the literature on industrial pricing in developed economies because such dramatic and frequent changes in overhead costs are rare. In many rapidly industrialising economies, on the other hand, such occurrences are more commonplace and therefore short-run changes in overhead costs may in fact play a role in the pricing decisions of the firm.

There has emerged in recent years a body of literature dealing with the role of particular overhead costs in industrial pricing in the middle-income developing economies.[25] The discussion has centred around the role of working capital, the need for which arises since producers must generally advance the cost of variable inputs into production, collecting back the sum advanced out of the value of sales realised at the end of the production period. If the cost of inputs is financed through borrowing and firms follow replacement cost pricing, the relevant cost of working capital is the real interest rate.[26]

The existence of a lag between the time direct production costs are advanced and recouped can have important consequences in economies where capital markets are underdeveloped. The absence of long-term capital markets means that firms tend to finance investment in fixed capital out of retained earnings while borrowing in short-term markets to cover working capital costs. Segmentation of capital markets, often related to the earmarking of a portion of available credit for lending at subsidised rates, tends to bring about high and volatile real interest rates in the free segment of the market. Because subsidised credit to firms from commercial banks or official institutions is often rationed, or simply unavailable to certain productive sectors, to a greater or lesser extent working capital will have to be funded at free market rates.

In an institutional setting, such as that described above, interest payments, which along with depreciation allowances are the most important components of overhead costs, cannot be ignored by firms in setting prices. Interest charges are not, however, viewed by firms as a direct production cost. They are relatively small compared with labour and raw material costs, not directly linked to production and will tend to vary noticeably from firm to firm. For these reasons, variations in interest charges are not directly and systematically reflected in price changes but rather they will tend to exert pressure upon the cost/price margin.

3.3.6 *Conclusion*

With the exception of the models that emphasise working capital costs, the body of literature on industrial pricing reviewed above refers, in the main, to the developed industrialised economies. Conditions prevailing in developing economies are substantially different and this may affect the applicability of pricing models and *a priori* expectations as to likely outcomes. Especially in middle-income LDCs, oligopoly is rife and foreign competition is generally severely limited. At the same time, demand grows more quickly, is subject to greater volatility and changes more dramatically in structure over time than in the developed nations. In many cases price inflation is also much higher and more volatile, creating added uncertainty about relative prices. Much of the discussion in the developed country literature is predicated upon changes in the level of costs and demand being circumscribed within 'conventional' bounds and upon the idea that firms can monitor changes in price, costs and output with a degree of accuracy. If conditions are substantially different in LDCs, so too may be price setting practices. In the empirical analysis to follow, we endeavour to address these concerns and to test a variety of hypotheses in order to minimise the risk of imposing a conventional but unsuitable model upon the data.

3.4 The price of manufactured goods in Brazil

3.4.1 *The general model*

The preceding discussion has highlighted the existence of differences in approach to formalising and testing the cost-plus principle; these differences can in many cases be thought of as competing hypotheses. In what follows, we test a subset of these using annual data for the Brazilian manufacturing industry covering the period 1960–83. It is impossible in a general study such as this one to test against the data all major variants of the cost-plus model. Consequently, we take as given at the outset certain facts. The most important of these are:

(a) that direct costs consist of total earnings of all employees plus the cost of domestic and imported raw materials,
(b) that firms do not take fluctuations in the productivity of raw materials into account in calculating prices,
(c) that foreign competition does not exert a significant influence upon manufacturing prices in Brazil, and[27]

(d) that price controls did not have a marked impact upon the behaviour of manufacturing prices over the sample period.[28]

The determination of Brazilian manufacturing prices, and industrial prices in general, has been the subject of a number of econometric studies.[29] As we develop and test the model used in this study, we compare and contrast some of the more important models and results reported in the literature with our own work.

A key distinction among cost-plus models concerns the level of output at which firms evaluate unit labour costs. We consider two hypotheses; the first is that, on average over the year, earnings per worker divided by output per worker adequately approximates the true decision variable of the firm, yielding the following expression for unit labour costs (ULC)

$$ULC_t^A = (W^I/pr)_t \qquad (3.1)$$

where (W^I) is average annual earnings per worker in manufacturing and (pr) is average output per worker. This we refer to as actual unit labour costs (ULC^A).

The second hypothesis is that firms calculate ULC on the basis of the long-run trend level of output and employment

$$ULC_t^N = (W^I/pr^T)_t \qquad (3.2)$$

where (pr^T) is the level of labour productivity given by fitting a linear trend to actual productivity over the period 1960–83. This we call normal unit labour costs (ULC^N). It was not possible to follow the procedure used by Coutts, Godley and Nordhaus (1978) to achieve a more thorough normalisation as no data are available on hours worked or the basic wage (as distinct from total earnings).[30]

For the mark-up, we specify the following general model

$$M = j(\underset{?}{D}, \underset{+}{r}) \qquad (3.3)$$

where the symbols under the RHS variables indicate the direction in which a positive change in the relevant variable may be expected, *a priori*, to affect (M). This states that the mark-up over direct costs (M) is a function of the level of demand pressure (D) and the real rate of interest (r), where to avoid negative values, the latter variable was defined as; $r + (1+R)/(1+\dot{P}^G)$ with (R) the average annual nominal rate of interest and ($\dot{P}^G$) the general rate of inflation.[31] The partial derivative of (M) with respect to (D) is indeterminate *a priori*, hence the question mark. A positive sign would indicate a pro-cyclical movement in the mark-up, a negative sign a counter-cyclical tendency and a partial derivative of zero, no independent role for demand. The inclusion of the real interest rate is to test for possible feedback from the cost of borrowed working capital to price. A positive sign on the partial derivative is expected.

We organise the various hypotheses about unit labour costs and the mark-up by setting up two general maintained hypotheses corresponding to the actual and normal unit labour cost cases. These can be written as the composite functions

$$P^{WI} = j_1(g_1(D, r), ULC^A, P^{WR}, P^{IMR}] \qquad (3.4)$$
$$\qquad ? \; + \quad + \quad + \quad +$$

$$P^{WI} = j_2[g_2(D, r), ULC^N, P^{WR}, P^{IMR}] \qquad (3.5)$$
$$\qquad ? \; + \quad + \quad + \quad +$$

where P^{WI} is the wholesale price index of manufactured goods,
P^{WR} is the wholesale price of domestically produced raw materials,
P^{IMR} is the cruzeiro price of imported raw materials,
ULC^A is actual unit labour costs,
ULC^N is normal unit labour costs, and
other variables are as defined above.

If, as hypothesised, firms mark up prices over unit labour costs along with domestic and imported raw material prices and if, in addition, all costs are passed through completely, the partial derivatives on the three direct cost terms (ULC, P^{WR}, P^{IMR}) should sum to unity.[32]

3.4.2 *Dynamic structure*

Adjustment in prices may lag behind changes in costs. These lags can be interpreted in economic terms using the notion of current versus historic cost. If prices are marked up over the current or replacement cost of inputs, lagged cost terms are less likely to prove significant in an econometric price equation than if firms value stocks on an historic cost basis. The evidence suggests that Brazilian industrial firms follow replacement cost valuation (Calabi, 1982, p. 150). Lags in adjustment of prices to changes in demand may result if, for instance, firms delay their reaction to a given change in conditions until they are able to make a judgement about its permanency, or lack thereof. Where annual data are used, lagged variables are less likely to be significant than in studies using quarterly data since much of the adjustment may have taken place within the year.[33] One would assume this to be all the more true in a high inflation economy where agents learn quickly to distinguish and to act upon changes in economic circumstances. Having argued that lags are unlikely to be important, it would nevertheless constitute bad empirical practice to impose undue prior restrictions on the model. Ideally, a general dynamic specification should be adopted for the two price models, including at least one lagged value for each of the explanatory and dependent variables. With only 23 observations, lack of degrees of freedom prevented us from doing this here in a meaningful way so instead we included a lagged dependent variable in the general models and tested for misspecification of the dynamics in the preferred versions of the models through the addition of other lagged variables, separately and together.[34]

3.4.3 *Functional form*

Cost-plus models are most often estimated in log levels, log first differences or percentage rates of change.[35] Linear models in levels are seldom employed, in part because, when using highly trended data, problems of multicollinearity and heteroscedasticity are often acute. Preliminary tests using our data set showed this to be the case here as well, there being a very strong common trend in Brazilian price data. Moreover, a simple linear levels model does not ensure proportionality between changes in costs and the mark-up on the one hand and prices on the other.[36] For these reasons we adopt a log-linear form for the models, experimenting with both levels and first-difference specifications.

Adding an error term and lagged dependent variable to equation (3.4) and, assuming that the error enters in a multiplicative fashion, the first pricing model can be written in specific functional form as

$$P_t^{WI} = \sigma_0 ULC_t^{A\sigma 1} P_t^{WR\sigma 2} P_t^{IMR\sigma 3} P_{t-1}^{WI\ \sigma 4} D_t^{\sigma 5} r_t^{\sigma 6} e^u \tag{3.6}$$

$$\sigma_1 + \sigma_2 + \sigma_3 + \sigma_4 = 1 \quad \sigma_5 = ? \quad \sigma_6 > 0$$

Taking natural logs yields the model to be estimated

$$\begin{aligned} \ln P_t^{WI} = \ln \sigma_0 + \sigma_1 \ln ULC_t^A + \sigma_2 \ln P_t^{WR} + \sigma_3 \ln P_t^{IMR} \\ + \sigma_4 \ln P_{t-1}^{WI} + \sigma_5 \ln D_t + \sigma_6 \ln r_t + u_t \end{aligned} \tag{3.7}$$

Price models are often estimated in rates of change, usually on the grounds that models estimated using price level data may imply spurious correlation when there is a strong common trend in the data. As the possibility of spurious correlation cannot be rejected in the present instance, we also estimated log first-difference versions of the pricing models. In the case of the actual unit labour cost model, the maintained hypothesis was

$$\begin{aligned} \Delta \ln P_t^{WI} = \ln \alpha_0 + \alpha_1 \Delta \ln ULC_t^A + \alpha_2 \Delta \ln P_t^{WR} \\ + \alpha_3 \Delta \ln P_t^{IMR} + \alpha_4 \Delta \ln P_{t-1}^{WI} + \alpha_5 \Delta \ln D_t \\ + \alpha_6 \Delta \ln r_t + u_t \end{aligned} \tag{3.8}$$

$$\alpha_1 + \alpha_2 + \alpha_3 + \alpha_4 = 1 \quad \alpha_5 = ? \quad \alpha_6 > 0$$

An identical set of procedures was used to derive the maintained hypotheses, assuming normal cost pricing, from equation (3.5)

$$\ln P_t^{WI} = \ln \psi_0 + \psi_1 \ln ULC_t^N + \psi_2 \ln P_t^{WR} + \psi_3 \ln P_t^{IMR} + \psi_4 \ln P_{t-1}^{WI} + \psi_5 \ln D_t + \psi_6 \ln r_t + u_t \quad (3.9)$$

$$\psi_1 + \psi_2 + \psi_3 + \psi_4 = 1 \quad \psi_5 = ? \quad \psi_6 > 0$$

and,

$$\Delta \ln P_t^{WI} = \ln \zeta_0 + \zeta_1 \Delta \ln ULC_t^N + \zeta_2 \Delta \ln P_t^{WR} + \zeta_3 \Delta \ln P_t^{IMR} + \zeta_4 \Delta \ln P_{t-1}^{WI} + \zeta_5 \Delta \ln D_t + \zeta_6 \Delta \ln r_t + u_t \quad (3.10)$$

$$\zeta_1 + \zeta_2 + \zeta_3 + \zeta_4 = 1 \quad \zeta_5 = ? \quad \zeta_6 > 0$$

We also tested the level of demand (D) in equation (3.10) in place of the change in the same variable. As noted in the literature review above, the former specification is often encountered in applied work despite the difficulties involved in relating it to the underlying theory.[37]

3.5 The data

A full description of the data including sources and techniques used to construct certain series, is presented in appendix 4. Here we discuss briefly various characteristics and shortcomings of the data used in the subsequent estimations that have a direct bearing upon the quality and interpretation of the empirical results.

3.5.1 *Manufacturing price index* (P^{WI})

This series is contaminated in that it refers not only to prices of finished goods sold outside the manufacturing sector but also to prices of semi-finished goods that are used as inputs within the sector. Conceptually it is preferable to use an index in which these latter prices are netted out in order to eliminate double counting that may bias the estimates of the coefficient values. If cost indices refer to purchases outside the sector, while the price index includes prices of intermediate and final sales, changes in the relative prices of intermediate and final goods will cause prices to change independently of variations in direct costs or the mark-up. However no index of final manufactured goods prices is available and it is beyond the scope of the present study to attempt to construct one.[38]

A second problem with Brazilian manufacturing price data is that a published series dates back only to 1970. A much longer series is available that includes unprocessed mining and mineral product prices as well as those of manufactured goods. This series is widely used in econometric applications even though a bias is introduced by doing so since mining products are inputs into manufacturing and their prices are also included in the wholesale raw material price index. Rather than use the biased index for the entire sample period, we spliced together this series for the years prior to 1970 with the manufacturing price index for the subsequent period.

Being wholesale prices constructed as a modified Laspeyres index, the manufacturing price series corresponds more closely to list as opposed to transactions prices. It has been argued that list prices may not correspond exactly to the prices at which trade is actually transacted and that, by using the former in an analysis of price determination, we may not capture the true parameters of the pricing process (Coutts, Godley and Nordhaus, 1978). The analysis here is carried out on the premise that the results are not materially affected by the use of list rather than transactions prices.

3.5.2 *Domestic wholesale raw material price index* (P^{WR})

Before 1970 the only aggregate raw material price index published included prices of semi-processed raw materials that are in fact value added of manufacturing industry and are therefore also captured by the dependent variable (P^{WI}). We spliced together the overall raw material index for the pre-1970 period with the conceptually preferable crude raw material index that became available in published form only in 1970.

3.5.3 *Earnings and employment in manufacturing*

Data are available from industrial surveys to allow construction of a continuous series for these aggregates dating back to 1963. There are some differences in coverage that may affect the consistency of the data, particularly in the pre-1966 period, but, as Modiano (1983a) noted, gross inconsistencies can be avoided by not combining census and survey data, which were collected on quite different bases.

Average earnings data refer to compensation received by all employees, from unskilled workers to managers, whose jobs are directly linked to production. Earnings include not only the basic wage or salary but also additional payments for overtime, year-end bonuses, etc., that make up gross remuneration. No data series are available that refer only to non-managerial wages in manufacturing. In order to allow a few extra degrees of freedom for estimation of the price equation, proxy data are used for the years prior to 1963, as explained in appendix 4.

3.5.4 *The interest rate*

The choice of proxies for the average borrowing costs of firms is severely circumscribed by data availability. As pointed out in chapter 2, the only complete interest rate series that go back to 1960 relate to the rate charged by finance companies for consumer credit and the yield on bills of exchange (exchange acceptances) issued by these same institutions.[39] While the latter is not a rate charged to borrowers at all, it is generally acknowledged that this series probably more accurately reflects changes in, although not the absolute level of, the true cost of borrowing than do consumer lending rates. Posted lending rates were subject to explicit government controls through much of the sample period and do not reflect hidden costs of borrowing due to the wide use by financial institutions of such devices as commissions and compulsory deposits to raise the effective cost of finance. Bills of exchange, on the other hand, escaped controls to a greater degree as yield was measured in terms of capital gains rather than interest payments.

3.5.5 *Product market demand*

Three proxies for product market demand (*D*) were experimented with. These variables, discussed and compared in appendix 3, are:

(a) one minus the GDP output gap (*GDPCU*), constructed using a single trend line through peaks to approximate potential output in the economy as a whole,

(b) capacity utilisation in manufacturing (*CU*2), constructed using trend through peaks (assumed to occur in 1961, 1973, 1976, 1980 and 1986) to approximate potential output in the sector, and

(c) capacity utilisation in manufacturing (*CU*3), constructed using a five year moving average of actual output to approximate potential output.

For reasons set out in appendix 3, (*CU*2) followed by (*CU*3) is the preferred demand proxy.

3.6 Estimation results[40]

3.6.1 *Actual unit labour cost model – levels equations*

OLS estimation results for the maintained hypothesis, equation (3.7), using (*CU*2) as a measure of demand, are presented in table 3.1 as equation (3.7a). In an initial estimate the restriction of homogeneity in degree one of the direct cost terms and lagged dependent variables with respect to prices $(\sigma_1+\sigma_2+\sigma_3+\sigma_4=1)$ was tested for and could not be rejected. In (3.7a) the restriction is imposed; (Z7) being the *F* test for the restriction. All direct cost terms plus the real interest rate bear the expected signs and, with the exception of (P^{IMR}), are significant at the 5 per cent level. The lagged dependent variables (P^{WI}_{t-1}) and ($CU2_t$) are not however significant and an F test of the hypothesis that both coefficients equalled zero was not rejected by the data.

Test results using the other two proxies for demand are not reported as these were inferior to those obtained using ($CU2$). In none of the cases was current demand found to be a significant regressor. To allow for possible misspecification of the dynamics in the maintained hypothesis, equation (3.7) was re-estimated with one period lagged values of each of the demand proxies, with and without current demand and the lagged dependent variable constrained to zero. Changes in demand were also experimented with. None of the demand terms proved significant. A series of regressions was also run that included lagged direct cost terms but this revealed no evidence of an omitted variables problem. Lagged cost terms were included with and without the interest rate constrained to zero in case its significance was due to the omission of lagged direct costs.

Application of successive F tests led to the choice of equation (3.7b) in table 3.1 as the preferred parsimonious model using the OLS estimator. Homogeneity of the direct cost coefficients was once again easily accepted (Z7) and therefore imposed. All direct cost coefficients and the real interest rate are significant, although the t ratio on (P^{IMR}_t) is still rather low. This probably results from a high degree of multicollinearity between it and the domestic raw material price term. Other researchers have also noted this problem, pointing out that a number of raw materials that are imported are also produced domestically and that the prices of these substitutes tend to move together. This is particularly true of petroleum products.[41]

There is no evidence of first- or second-order autocorrelation in equation (3.7b). The log-likelihood test statistics for serial independence (Z1) and (Z2) being well below the critical value for χ^2 (1) of 3.84. The equation was re-estimated with the shorter sample period 1968–83. The results are reported as equation (3.7c) in table 3.1. Parameter stability in the preferred OLS specification is attested to by a value for the Chow test F statistic of 1.3(7,11). This is largely borne out by visual comparison of the estimated coefficients in equations (3.7b) and (3.7c). The coefficient on the interest rate term is however noticeably lower in the shorter sample estimate. Also, in the shorter sample, the interest rate and imported raw material prices lose significance. The interest rate variable may become a less adequate proxy for interest charges in the latter part of the period as innovation led to the development of new and varied financial instruments. As regards (P^{IMR}), this term probably loses significance since, after the first oil shock, the domestic raw material price index came to be very heavily influenced by

Table 3.1. *Estimated price formation equations: log level equations – dependent variable* ($\ln P^{WI}$)

	(3.7a) OLS (1961–83)	(3.7b) OLS (1961–83)	(3.7c) OLS (1968–83)	(3.7d) OLS (1961–83)	(3.7e) OLS (1961–83)	(3.7f) IV (1961–83)	(3.7g) IV (1968–83)	(3.9a) OLS (1961–83)	(3.9b) IV (1961–83)
Variables[a,b]									
Constant	0.272	−0.039	−0.023	−0.039	0.792	−0.039	−0.031	1.626	1.070
	(2.72)	(−4.49)	(−1.38)	(−1.47)	(1.60)	(−3.57)	(−1.81)	(3.63)	(2.37)
$\ln ULC^A$	0.422	0.429	0.426	0.425	0.506	0.283	0.330	—	—
	(5.75)	(6.28)	(5.58)	(5.76)	(5.72)	(4.36)	(5.10)		
$\ln ULC^N$	—	—	—	—	—	—	—	0.484	0.356
								(5.48)	(4.43)
$\ln P_t^{WR}$	0.531	0.524	0.545	0.524	0.433	0.634	0.606	0.450	0.560
	(6.85)	(9.77)	(9.86)	(6.63)	(6.13)	(12.05)	(12.13)	(6.05)	(8.28)
$\ln P_t^{IMR}$	0.046	0.051	0.029	0.051	0.061	0.083	0.064	0.066	0.084
	(1.04)	(2.14)	(0.79)	(1.28)	(1.64)	(3.12)	(1.87)	(2.50)	(2.96)
$\ln P_{t-1}^{WI}$	0.001	—	—	—	—	—	—	—	—
	(0.14)								
$\ln CU2_t$	0.001	—	—	—	—	—	—	−0.371	−0.247
	(0.01)							(−3.71)	(−2.45)
$\ln CU2_{t-1}$	—	—	—	—	−0.188	—	—	—	—
					(−1.70)				
$\ln r_t$	0.272	0.282	0.197	0.283	—	0.322	0.377	0.192	0.248
	(2.72)	(4.68)	(0.96)	(3.00)		(4.39)	(1.85)	(2.60)	(3.13)
TL	—	—	—	−0.00002	—	—	—	—	—
				(−0.01)					

Statistics[c]									
$\bar{R}^2$	0.99	0.99	0.99	0.99	0.99	0.99	0.99	0.99	0.99
SEE	0.029	0.027	0.026	0.028	0.037	0.034	0.027	0.030	0.034
DW	2.04	2.04	1.88	2.04	0.87	1.98	1.57	1.80	2.09
Z1	0.20	0.24	0.40	0.26	8.08	0.08	2.30	0.01	0.01
Z2	0.60	0.80	0.43	0.88	1.34	0.09	1.12	7.20	1.00
Z7	0.72 (1,16)	0.01 (1,18)	0.14 (1,11)	0.03 (1,17)	3.80 (1,18)	0.44 (1,18)	2.3 (1,11)	0.80 (1,17)	2.50 (1,17)

Notes: [a] Figures in brackets under the coefficient estimates are t ratios.

[b] Variables are defined as:

P^{WI} – index (1970 = 100) of average wholesale prices of manufactured goods,
ULC^{A} – index (1970 = 100) of actual average unit labour costs in manufacturing,
ULC^{N} – index (1970 = 100) of normal unit labour costs in manufacturing,
P^{WR} – index (1970 = 100) of average wholesale prices of domestically produced raw materials,
P^{IMR} – index (1970 = 100) of average cruzeiro prices of imported raw materials,
$CU2$ – rate of capacity utilisation in manufacturing,
r – index of average real yield on bills of exchange $(1+R)/(1+\dot{P}^{G})$, and
TL – a linear time trend.

[c] $\bar{R}^2$ is the multiple correlation coefficient, SEE the standard error of the regression, DW the Durbin–Watson test statistic, Z1 and Z2 the χ^2 statistics, each with one degree of freedom, for the log likelihood ratio test for first- and second-order serial correlation in the error term and, Z7 is the F test statistic for the null hypothesis of homogeneity in degree one of price with respect to direct costs.

foreign prices, aggravating the problem of multicollinearity referred to above. The stability of the error variance, or the homoscedasticity assumption, could not be rejected by the application of the Goldfeld-Quandt test. This yielded an F ratio of 1.19(8,7). Similar results regarding parameter and variance stability were obtained when the sample was divided at other points in time.

The evidence of stability of the direct cost coefficients suggested that multicollinearity between (ULC^{A}) and (P^{WR}) was not an insurmountable problem despite the high simple correlation, equal to 0.92 in equation (3.7b). We re-estimated equation (3.7b) with the addition of a linear time trend to test for a strong common trend remaining in the data. A significant coefficient on the trend variable would imply that the cost terms were explaining deviations around the trend and that the mark-up experienced a secular rise or fall. If the inclusion of the trend disrupted the parameters of the cost terms, we might conclude that there existed a problem of spurious correlation. In that case, the levels model might be judged to be inadequate. This expanded regression is reported as equation (3.7d) in table 3.1. In the results we find no evidence to suggest spurious correlation or the presence of a strong trend that is unexplained by the cost terms.

Both the yield on bills of exchange and the consumer credit rate were experimented with. The former was found to perform better in the model and showed itself to be an important explanatory variable. When the interest rate coefficient was constrained to zero in the general model and tests carried out for omitted variables, equation (3.7e) resulted. In this equation there is clear evidence of misspecification due to pronounced first-order autocorrelation. The goodness of fit is inferior to that of equation (3.7b) and the homogeneity restriction on the direct cost terms (Z7) is rejected by the data.[42] ($CU2$), lagged one period, is of borderline significance and bears a negative sign, suggesting counter-cyclical movements in the mark-up. However, the significance of the demand variable disappeared once autocorrelation was corrected for by using a Cochrane-Orcutt second-order procedure.

Given the evidence of misspecification and the relatively low simple correlation between ($CU2$) and the real interest rate it seems unlikely that the latter is acting simply as a better proxy for demand than ($CU2$). Instead the data point tentatively to an acceptance of the hypothesis of an explanatory role for the real interest rate in price determination (see section 3.7 below). The estimated elasticity of 0.28 in equation (3.7b) suggests that a 10 per cent rise in the real interest rate leads to a 2.8 per cent increase in the nominal manufacturing price level. If the statistical results are reliable, this effect cannot be dismissed as insignificant given that real interest rates were high and subject to an extremely large degree of variability.[43] The important implication is that the pursuit of tight money policies has a perverse impact on inflation in the short run. Considering the problems inherent in the interest rate data themselves and in their use as a proxy for average borrowing costs of firms, acceptance of the interest rate-push hypothesis must however be treated as tentative pending further testing.[44]

In an indexed economy there is bound to be a high degree of simultaneity in the determination of wages and prices. Potentially, such simultaneity, may lead to biased and inconsistent parameter estimates when OLS is applied. If the dependent and independent variables are jointly determined, the exogeneity assumption of OLS is violated as the residual term is not orthogonal, or independent, of the deterministic variables of the model. In order to test for simultaneous equation bias brought on by the joint determination of earnings and manufacturing prices, equation (3.7b) was re-estimated using an instrumental variable estimator.[45] This estimate appears as equation (3.7f) in table 3.1. The coefficients of ULC and raw material prices change quite dramatically compared with the OLS estimate of equation (3.7b). The elasticity of labour costs falls to 0.28 while that of domestic and foreign raw material prices rises to a combined 0.72.[46] A Wu-Hausman test for simultaneous equation bias was also performed on equation (3.7b). The t test statistic value obtained of 1.45(17) does not allow rejection of the null hypothesis of orthogonality despite the obvious change that occurs in the parameter values. Given the uncertain power of the Wu-Hausman test and the fact that the IV estimates are more in keeping with *a priori* expectations regarding cost shares – as discussed below – the IV estimate is preferred over OLS.

A test of the economic consistency of an estimated price model is to compare estimates of the direct cost coefficients with extraneous data on the composition of costs in manufacturing. The estimated values of the unit labour cost and raw material price terms should be approximately equal to the average share of labour and raw materials in total 'direct' inputs into manufacturing production.[47] An indication of these shares for Brazil can be obtained from industrial census data on the wage bill, raw material costs and total sales in manufacturing.[48] For 1970, this source shows labour costs equal to approximately 16 per cent of total direct costs of production and raw materials 84 per cent (IBGE, 1975). Our econometric estimates of the labour share are noticeably higher than the outside estimate while those of the raw materials share are lower. Still, the IV estimates are considerably closer than the OLS estimates obtained here or reported in other Brazilian pricing studies.[49] It has been suggested that the overstatement of the labour share results from the use of a contaminated manufacturing price index which includes prices of intermediate as well as final goods (Considera, 1981, pp. 670–1). Since the cost of intermediate inputs into production are not included among the explanatory terms, the labour cost variable is capturing not only the direct but also the indirect impact of these costs as they affect intermediate goods prices. Our results suggest that, in addition to the problem of contaminated data, some of the very high estimates obtained in other studies may be upward biased due to the use of inappropriate single equation estimators.

3.6.2 *Normal unit labour cost model – levels equations*

By following a similar procedure to the one employed in the previous section, we arrived at the best obtainable estimate of the normal unit labour model using OLS. This regression is presented as equation (3.9a) in table 3.1. The coefficient on ULC is somewhat higher, and that on (P^{WR}) lower, than in the corresponding OLS estimates of the actual unit labour cost hypothesis. The t ratio on the labour cost term is also lower. In contrast with the earlier results, the coefficient of demand is significant and again negative. There is however clear evidence of misspecification due to the presence of second-order autocorrelation (Z2).

Re-estimating using an IV estimator yielded equation (3.9b). As with the actual ULC models, the elasticity of labour costs falls while that of domestic raw material prices rises. The parameter values obtained for (ULC^{N}) are slightly higher and for domestic raw material prices slightly lower than in the actual ULC tests. There is no longer evidence of autocorrelated errors and the model generally fits the data well. Nonetheless, the combination of mark-up pricing over normal unit labour costs with a negative sign on the demand level term implies a rather unbelievable pricing hypothesis.[50] The implication is that firms not only pass on to prices cost savings due to productivity improvements in a boom period, as in the case of a fixed mark-up over actual labour costs, but they also go beyond this and reduce prices further, and continuously, as long as demand remains buoyant. A similar process occurs in reverse during a recession.

Economic theory and business logic do not accord easily with the results obtained. It is important to note that these are consistent with the hypothesis that the true decision variable of the firm is actual, and not normal unit labour costs and that the mark-up is unresponsive to demand. This is because actual unit labour costs will tend to fall relative to normal costs in an expansion and to rise in a recession, due to the pro-cyclical pattern of variation in productivity. The significance of the demand variable in equation (3.9a) may not therefore be symptomatic of an independent and counter-cyclical role for demand but rather of misspecific-ation due to the omission of a relevant variable, namely productivity; the effect of which is partially captured by the demand term. Rising productivity has the effect, *ceteris paribus*, of reducing actual unit labour costs; hence the negative coefficient on the ($CU2$) term. Serial correlation in the error term (of the OLS but not the IV estimate) is a reflection of the omitted variable problem.

Given the slightly better statistical properties of the actual unit labour cost model and its closer correspondence with accepted views on pricing, it seems preferable to conclude that firms mark-up price over actual unit labour costs and not over normal unit labour costs, as approximated using trend productivity.

3.6.3 *Actual unit labour cost – rate of change equation*

In the rate of change specification we report results from testing the actual ULC model only. No new or additional insights were obtained from experiments with the normal ULC model in rates of change form.

Estimation results for the maintained hypothesis, equation (3.8), are shown as (3.8a) in table 3.2. The restriction of homogeneity of price in degree one with respect to the direct cost terms and the lagged dependent variable was initially tested for and, being accepted, was subsequently imposed. The relevant F test statistic is (Z7). A more parsimonious version was arrived at through a test down procedure in which lagged price, the change in demand and the interest rate were all constrained to zero. This equation, however, exhibited evidence of misspecification due to serial correlation in the error term. In testing for the source of the misspecification the following variables were added to the equation individually and together: (a) lagged values of each explanatory variable, and (b) the proportional error correction mechanisms $[\ln(P^{WI}/ULC^{A})_{t-1}]$ and $[\ln(P^{WI}/P^{WR})_{t-1}]$.[51] The inclusion of these variables did not improve the specification. A one period lagged value of the log change in the interest rate was however found to be a significant explanatory variable. Re-estimating with the latter yielded equation (3.8b). While an improvement over the earlier specifications, this version suffers from parameter instability as can be seen by comparison with the short sample estimate of equation (3.8c).[52] It is not clear why in the levels specification the current real interest rate should be significant while in the changes model only its lagged value is significant. We would expect the same relationship to hold in first differences. It may be that the restrictions imposed by differencing, especially as regards the timing of changes, obscures the relationship.

No significant explanatory role could be found for any of the three demand proxies in their rate of change form. However, using a specification commonly adopted in the Brazilian literature, the lagged interest rate was constrained to zero and the level of demand was added to the set of

Table 3.2 *Estimated manufacturing price relationships: rates of change equations – dependent variable* ($\Delta \ln P^{WI}$)

	(3.8a) OLS (1962–83)	(3.8b) OLS (1962–83)	(3.8c) OLS (1968–83)	(3.8d) OLS (1962–83)	(3.8e) OLS (1962–83)	(3.8f) IV (1962–83)
Variables[a,b]						
Constant	0.627	−0.003	−0.001	0.773	−0.172	−0.040
	(0.128)	(−0.45)	(−0.13)	(1.91)	(2.14)	(−0.08)
$\Delta \ln ULC^{A}$	0.574	0.595	0.502	0.630	0.621	0.356
	(6.17)	(8.04)	(9.44)	(9.05)	(9.05)	(4.87)
$\Delta \ln P_t^{WR}$	0.318	0.314	0.464	0.235	0.256	0.666
	(2.29)	(3.37)	(6.63)	(2.63)	(2.87)	(7.34)
$\Delta \ln P_t^{IMR}$	0.100	0.091	0.034	0.135	0.123	−0.023
	(1.75)	(1.99)	(0.911)	(3.04)	(2.78)	(−0.33)
$\Delta \ln P_{t-1}^{WI}$	0.123	—	—	—	—	—
	(0.971)					
$\Delta \ln CU2_t$	−0.062	—	—	—	—	—
	(−0.43)					
$\ln CU2_t$	—	—	—	−0.226	−0.172	0.010
				(−3.21)	(−2.14)	(0.80)
$\Delta \ln r_t$	−0.086	—	—	—	—	—
	(−0.43)					
$\Delta \ln r_{t-1}$	—	0.259	0.050	—	0.141	0.346
		(2.55)	(5.14)		(1.31)	(2.06)

Statistics[c]						
$\bar{R}^2$	0.98	0.98	0.99	0.98	0.98	0.96
SEE	0.035	0.030	0.020	0.028	0.027	0.043
DW	2.14	2.21	1.87	2.50	2.51	2.71
Z1	3.20	1.96	1.29	1.28	2.78	3.69
Z2	0.56	0.16	0.47	2.25	1.00	0.87
Z7	1.89 (1,15)	1.89 (1,15)	0.09 (1,11)	0.29 (1,17)	0.73 (1,16)	0.04 (1,16)

Notes: [a] Figures in brackets under the coefficient estimates are t ratios.

[b] Variables are defined as:

P^{WI} – index (1970 = 100) of average wholesale prices of manufactured goods,

ULC^{A} – index (1970 = 100) of actual average unit labour costs in manufacturing,

P^{WR} – index (1970 = 100) of average wholesale prices of domestically produced raw materials,

P^{IMR} – index (1970 = 100) of average cruzeiro prices of imported raw materials,

$CU2$ – rate of capacity utilisation in manufacturing and

r – index of average real yield on bills of exchange $(1+R)/(1+\dot{P}^{G})$.

[c] $\bar{R}^2$ is the multiple correlation coefficient, SEE the standard error of the regression, DW the Durbin–Watson test statistic, Z1 and Z2 the χ^2 statistics for the log likelihood ratio test for first- and second-order serial correlation in the error term and, Z7 is the F statistic for the null hypothesis of homogeneity in degree one of price with respect to direct costs.

explanatory variables. OLS estimation results for this model are presented as equation (3.8d). The level of demand is significant, with a negative sign that implies counter-cyclical pricing. In the context of the underlying oligopoly pricing theory the implication is that a fall in the level of demand occasions a continuous rise in the mark-up. It is hard to see how else this result can be interpreted, certainly recourse cannot easily be made to the concept of excess demand effects in a competitive market. When re-estimated with the addition of the lagged interest rate, as in equation (3.8e), demand became less significant and the goodness of fit, as measured by the SEE improved slightly. Results from this version of the model, estimated using IV, are reported under equation (3.8f). The demand variable ($CU2$) changes sign and loses significance while the interest rate term becomes increasingly significant. Also of note is that relative to equation (3.8e), there occurs a substantial change in the estimates of the cost parameters. The labour cost coefficient falls and the domestic raw material price coefficient rises. Compared with the estimates obtained from the IV version of the levels equations, the elasticity of ULC is higher and that of raw material prices lower. Imported raw material prices lose significance and have a very low coefficient value.

3.6.4 *Preferred specification*

The IV estimate of the actual unit labour cost model in the log levels form is the one preferred and used in the overall macromodel of chapter 7. Since no clear statistical preference could be found for a first-difference specification, the levels model, which conforms best to the underlying theory, was adopted instead. Equation (3.7f) of table 3.1 is set-out again below with additional diagnostic statistics

$$\begin{aligned} \ln P_t^{\mathrm{WI}} = &-0.04 + 0.28 \ln ULC_t^{\mathrm{A}} + 0.63 \ln P_t^{\mathrm{WR}} \\ &(-3.57)\quad (4.36) \qquad\qquad (12.05) \\ &+0.08 \ln P_t^{\mathrm{IMR}} + 0.32 \ln r_t \\ &(3.12) \qquad\qquad (4.39) \end{aligned} \tag{3.7f}$$

IV $n=23$ $\bar{R}^2=0.99$ SEE$=0.034$ DW$=1.98$ LL$=47.34$

Z1$=0.08(1)$ Z2$=0.09(1)$ Z3$=2.00(7,11)$ Z4$=1.52(8,7)$

Z7$=0.44(1,18)$

The statistics (Z3) and (Z4) are the F ratios for, respectively the Chow test for parameter stability and the Goldfeld-Quandt test for stability of the model variance. These tests do not allow us to reject model stability. Other statistics are as defined in table 3.1.

This equation performs a key role in the complete macromodel. It shows that, in the manufacturing sector, prices respond to changes in costs and not to demand. Through the mark-up mechanism, changes in wages, domestic and foreign raw material prices, the exchange rate and the real interest rate are all transmitted rapidly throughout the wage and price system.

3.7 Conclusion

The analysis of this chapter suggests that the mark-up pricing hypothesis is capable of explaining the determination of manufacturing prices in Brazil. Prices appear to be set by marking up over actual unit labour costs and raw material prices. The use of normal unit labour costs receives some support from the data but only when demand is included in the equation with a negative coefficient. Of course it must be noted that we experimented extensively with only one, fairly crude, normalisation. Intuitively the concept of a normal level of output is of limited significance in a rapidly industrialising economy subject to large and precipitous variations in output. The measurement and tracking of actual costs may, therefore, be of more consequence to industrialists in this context than in a more stable economic setting.

The finding in favour of an actual unit labour cost hypothesis lends support to the view, expressed in chapter 2, that cyclical changes in labour productivity played a role in reducing inflationary pressure in the years of the 'miracle'.

No credible evidence could be found for an independent role for demand in the determination of aggregate manufacturing prices. The signs obtained for the demand coefficients point to a counter-cyclical role, if any at all. Other researchers have also been unable to demonstrate convincingly the existence of such a role in aggregate studies, although there is some evidence that demand does influence prices in either a counter or pro-cyclical manner at the level of disaggregated industrial sectors.[53] Given the great diversity of Brazilian manufacturing, it is not surprising that on aggregate no clear tendency is evident.

What the results reported here do show clearly is that the hypothesis of a fixed mark-up over direct costs is untenable. To help illustrate this point, the mark-up over direct costs implied by the preferred model is plotted along with the rate of capacity utilisation (*CU2*) in figure 3.1 and, along with two measures of the real interest rate in figure 3.2.[54] The econometric results reported in this chapter show that the real interest rate explains short-run changes in the mark-up better than the level of demand, as proxied here. The closer correlation of the interest rate series, rather than

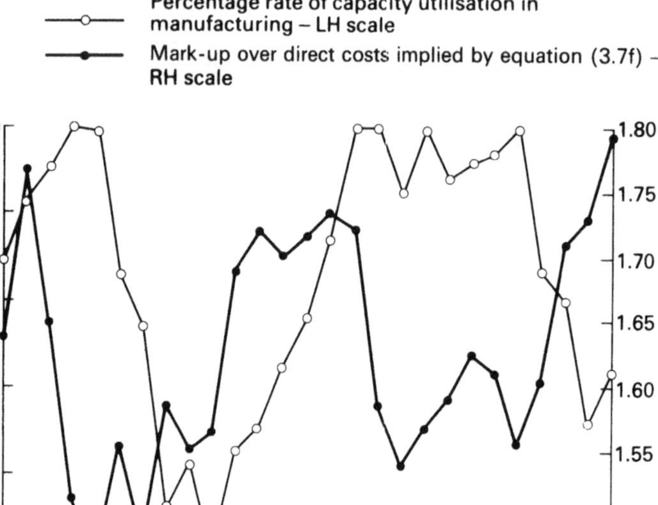

Figure 3.1 Capacity utilisation in manufacturing and implied mark-up of manufacturing prices over direct costs

(*CU*2), with the implied mark-up is evident from figures 3.1 and 3.2. The indications are that changes in an important component of overhead costs, the financial costs of borrowed working capital – which may have had a cyclical component – affected price, while product market demand did not. Although it cannot be claimed that the present study has offered conclusive evidence that the true parameters of the pricing process were as outlined, the results do cast serious doubt upon the findings of other studies that claimed to find some support, even if acknowledged to be slim, for countercyclical pricing. As argued above, these results appear to emanate from misspecified models.

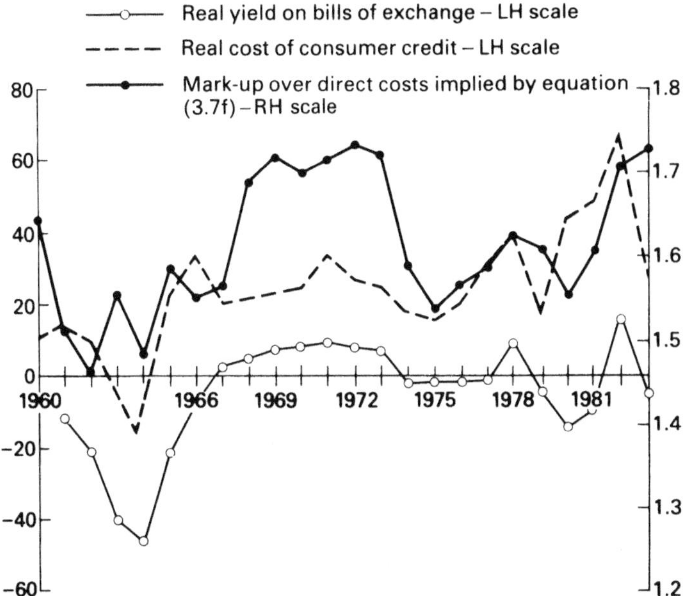

Figure 3.2 Real interest rates and implied mark-up of manufacturing prices over direct costs

4 Average earnings in manufacturing industry

4.1 Models of wage inflation

Two basic models dominated the econometric literature on wage inflation in the 1970s and early 1980s: the expectations augmented Phillips curve and the real wage resistance or target real wage models.[1] The first can be thought of as a model which asserts the primacy of the market while allowing only a reduced role for institutional or non-market processes to impinge upon wage determination. The real wage resistance model, in contrast, gives a prominent role to a certain type of institutional arrangement, namely a strong trade union presence in markets. More recently, there appears to have occurred a degree of convergence in views on the determinants of wage inflation in the industrialised countries. An eclectic model, combining elements of both the real wage resistance and Phillips curve hypotheses is now widely used in applied work.

4.1.1 *The augmented Phillips curve*

The expectations augmented Phillips curve is usually expressed in linear form in the following way[2]

$$\dot{W}_t = \beta_0 + \beta_1 U_t + \beta_2 \dot{P}^E \tag{4.1}$$

$$\beta_0 > 0 \quad \beta_1 < 0 \quad 0 \leqslant \beta_2 \leqslant 1$$

where $\dot{W}$ is the rate of change of wages or earnings,
U is the unemployment rate – employed as a measure of the inverse of the excess demand for labour, and
$\dot{P}^E$ is expected price inflation.

The equation represents the hypothesis that the rate of change of nominal wages varies inversely with the unemployment rate. Given unemployment, nominal wage inflation is a function of expected inflation plus an exogenous time path (β_0), assumed to be related to growth in labour productivity.

Lipsey (1960) was the first to use econometrics to estimate the inverse relationship between the unemployment rate and wage inflation proposed by Phillips (1958). He estimated a linear equation similar to (4.1) but used actual current price inflation instead of an explicit expectations term and included, as Phillips had suggested, the change in the rate of unemployment as well as its level. Friedman (1968) and Phelps (1968) published critiques of the simple Phillips relationship that brought the role of expectations into the forefront of debate. Armed with some evidence of a breakdown in the inverse long-run relationship between unemployment and inflation during the mid-1960s, Friedman argued that the relationship was more apparent than real, and essentially due to an accidental result generated by an underlying economic mechanism with fundamentally different long-run properties. In fact, he argued, wages would tend to rise by the expected rate of inflation in the absence of excess demand. It was unrealistic to assume that workers suffered from significant money illusion, in the longer run at least.

In terms of equation (4.1), Friedman's hypothesis amounts essentially to imposing the restriction $\beta_2 = 1$.[3] With this restriction imposed, the Phillips relationship can be rationalised as a Walrasian price adjustment process where excess demand for labour leads to adjustments in the expected real wage.[4] Provided that expectations are accurate in the long run and, for simplicity of exposition, assuming a constant relationship between changes in wages and overall prices, it follows that over the longer term only one rate of unemployment will be possible. Since

$$\dot{W}_t - \dot{P}^E_t = \beta_0 + \beta_1 U \tag{4.2}$$

and $\dot{W}_t - \dot{P}^E_t = 0$ then

$$0 = \beta_0 + \beta_1 U \tag{4.3}$$

Equation (4.3) defines the 'natural rate' of unemployment. Although in this model a short-run trade-off may exist between ($\dot{W}$) and (U), once expectations have adjusted fully to actual inflation, wage inflation will accelerate as long as actual unemployment is below the natural rate and decelerate if above. Any attempt on the part of government to maintain unemployment at a rate below the natural rate will be incompatible with stable inflation and will lead instead to a continuous acceleration of inflation. For this reason, the natural rate hypothesis is also referred to as the accelerationist hypothesis. From this perspective, the only option open to policy-makers wishing to influence the long-run rate of inflation is to shift the vertical Phillips curve by changing the parameters (β_0) and (β_1).

A competing hypothesis is that a long-run trade-off between ($\dot{W}$) and (U) is possible, although the slope of the long-run Phillips curve will be steeper than that of the short-run curve. Once expectations have adjusted fully to actual inflation ($\dot{W}_t = \dot{P}_t^E$)

$$\dot{W}_t - \beta_2 \dot{P}_t^E = \beta_0 + \beta_1 U_t \quad (4.4)$$

$$\dot{W}_t = \beta_0/(1-\beta_2) + \beta_1/(1-\beta_2)U_t \quad (4.5)$$

The policy implications of the long-run trade-off (LRTO) hypothesis are very different from those associated with the accelerationist view. In principle, if a trade-off persists in the long run, any target rate of unemployment can be achieved provided one is prepared to accept the implied rate of inflation.

Assuming expectations can be correctly measured or proxied, failure to reject the restriction $\beta_2 = 1$ in an estimate of equation (4.1) can be taken as acceptance of the accelerationist hypothesis. The LRTO hypothesis will be preferred if $\beta_2 = 1$ is rejected along with the restriction $\beta_1 \geqslant 0$. Were the latter restriction not rejected as well, a positive or zero trade-off would be implied between ($\dot{W}$) and (U) in the short run. In practice it is not often this easy to distinguish between the two hypotheses. Since inflationary expectations are not usually measurable, a test of the competing hypotheses must be carried out conditional upon some auxiliary hypothesis about the formation of expectations. The rejection of the restrictions $\beta_2 = 1$, $\beta_1 \geqslant 0$ does not necessarily point to the existence of a long-run trade-off if the assumptions made about expectations do not fit the true data generating process.

There exists a very broad literature on the empirical application of the augmented Phillips relationship to a wide spectrum of countries. Debate has centred around the success of the model in explaining wage inflation, which amounts essentially to a test for the strength and significance of excess demand effects, the most appropriate assumptions regarding expectations and the presence or absence of a long-run trade-off between ($\dot{W}$) and (U).

Attempts to fit the augmented Phillips curve to U.K. data for the 1960s and 1970s met with mixed success; the results seemingly closely dependent upon the time period over which the model was fitted. Artis (1981) reviewed a number of important applied studies and reached the tentative conclusion that in the U.K. context the augmented Phillips relationship had not up to that point proven a particularly robust one.[5] Subsequently, however, Sumner and Ward (1983) and Grubb, Jackman and Layard (1982) estimated augmented Phillips curves using U.K. data from 1957–8 to 1980 and obtained some evidence of the sensitivity of wage inflation to excess demand for labour. However, the homogeneity of the sample periods used is in doubt.[6]

In the United States, the augmented Phillips curve has been widely employed with more consistent results than in the U.K. It has long been used in the wage and price sectors of important large-scale macroeconometric models.[7] The apparent greater and more consistent success of the model in explaining U.S. versus U.K. wage inflation may be due to institutional differences in labour markets. A bargaining theory of wage determination that explicitly takes into account institutional factors such as the impact of trade unions and incomes policies may well be better suited to a study of wage inflation in the relatively more unionised and regulated Western European economies than a model which ignores these factors while asserting instead the primacy of the market.

Early estimates of the augmented Phillips curve used first-order adaptive, and in some cases extrapolative, schemes to generate expectations.[8] Faced with the well-known limitations of simple adaptive expectations that centre around their mechanical nature and the fact that when inflation changes they represent a non-optimal forecasting rule, considerable interest has been generated in alternative expectations generating schemes. Turnovsky and Wachter (1972) estimated a Phillips curve for the U.S. assuming an error learning process. Most efforts have been directed towards experimenting with higher-order time series models and rational or semi-rational formation of expectations. One approach to making operational the rational expectations hypothesis is to assume that agents use a time series model, including lagged values of inflation and certain other key macroeconomic variables. Predicted values from such a model can then be used to proxy expectations (McCallum, 1975). This really amounts to pseudo-rational expectations, as not all available information is considered. Another way used to implement the hypothesis has been to draw on existing macroeconomic models, or subsectors thereof, to obtain inflation predictions.[9] This is a more efficient method than the single equation prediction but the results may not always prove significantly better than those obtained using simpler methods.[10]

A number of recent studies have employed higher-order autoregressive time series models of price inflation to generate predictions for the same variable (Britton, 1983, chapter 5, Artis *et al.*, 1984 and Ormerod, 1982). Yet another approach has been to use observed data on expectations from surveys. Adopting this procedure, an attempt has been made, in the context of wage determination, to distinguish between expectations of workers and employers. These may diverge due to the fact that the relevant price index for workers relates to consumer prices as opposed to product prices, which are of greater relevance to employers (Parkin *et al.*, 1976, Sumner, 1978 and Sumner and Ward, 1983).

Recent empirical studies lend support to the accelerationist hypothesis, pointing to little or no long-run trade-off between wage inflation and unemployment.[11] Tests carried out in the early 1970s, on the other hand, especially in the U.S., tended to come down in favour of some long-run trade-off.[12] This may be explained by the idea that a trade-off in the long run is more likely to exist in periods of mild inflation whereas, beyond some threshold rate, agents become more conscious of the implications of inflation and are consequently less prone to money illusion.

Instances of the application of the Phillips curve to the study of inflation in developing countries are quite numerous.[13] Generally the estimation results are of poor statistical quality and, at times, hard to rationalise on grounds of economic consistency. Tests of the model are complicated by the virtually complete absence of unemployment data for developing countries, necessitating use of proxies that relate to demand conditions in product markets, and by poor wage data that often lead to the substitution of wage inflation by price inflation.[14] Where data problems can be overcome and a significant inverse relationship between changes in basic unskilled wages and the level of demand is identified, the explanation for this result may often have more to do with the conduct of official wage policies than with the free interplay of market forces. Another recurrent problem in applications of the augmented Phillips curve to LDCs concerns the choice and interpretation of the expectations variable as well as the sensitivity of the overall results to this choice. Until very recently, first-order adaptive expectations were almost universally assumed, despite the fact that this choice is even more inappropriate for a developing economy than for an industrialised economy if, as is often the case, inflation is higher and more volatile in the former. Where adaptive expectations are assumed, the coefficient on the expectations term is often well below unity implying an impossible degree of money illusion given the high rates of prevailing inflation.[15] Furthermore, a problem arises with any scheme that relies on current or lagged values of inflation as a proxy for expectations in a setting where wage indexation is pervasive. It becomes very difficult to disentangle the impact of a wage policy that establishes an administrative link between wages and inflation from expectations that are independently formed and acted upon by employers and employees.

In applying the Phillips curve analysis to LDCs, researchers are adopting the hypothesis, implicitly more often than explicitly, that wages are essentially market determined even where there is clear evidence of government intervention in labour markets in the form of trade union repression and/or mandatory wage indexation.[16] Employees and employers are assumed able to evade any floor or ceiling that might be thought to exist due to wage fixing policies. For instance, employers will resort to job turnover to reduce the cost of mandatory wage increases by hiring new workers at lower absolute levels of pay and employees and employers together will bargain at the level of the firm for increases over and above mandatory adjustments. Implicitly it is being assumed that there is no obstacle, such as a pool of excess labour, to real wages being bid up in periods of high demand. Furthermore, this approach assumes that workers are able to form expectations of future inflation and incorporate these wholly or partially into contracts negotiated. In other cases, in a small concession to the institutional environment, it is argued that price expectations may affect wages in a roundabout way, for instance, through pressure being brought to bear on government to raise official wage adjustments (Bomberger and Makinen, 1976).

The propensity to seek explanations for wage inflation in LDCs through the indiscriminate application of the Phillips curve paradigm is symptomatic of the tendency to apply, to developing countries, models formulated against the background of the socio-economic conditions prevailing in the industrialised world. This is all too often done without due regard to the particular economic and institutional conditions prevailing in LDCs.

4.1.2 *The real wage resistance model*

The basic premise of the model is that increases in nominal wages are due to discrepancies between real wage aspirations and actual real wage achievements. The model was first proposed and tested by Sargan (1964) and developed further by him in Sargan (1971) and (1980a). The concept of a net of tax definition of the real wage was introduced into the model by Jackson, Turner and Wilkinson (1975) and Coutts, Tarling and Wilkinson (1976).[17]

Ignoring complications due to taxes, which amounts to assuming that the ratio of gross to net pay remains constant over time, and all but the most rudimentary disequilibrium dynamics, the model can be written in linear form as

$$\dot{W}_t = \mu_0 + \mu_t U_t + \mu_2 \dot{P}_t^{E} + \mu_3 (W/P)_{t-1} + \mu_4 TL \tag{4.6}$$

$$\mu_1 < 0 \quad 0 < \mu_2 \leqslant 1 \quad \mu_3 < 0 \quad \mu_4 > 0$$

where (TL) is a linear time trend, (P) a measure of the overall price level and other variables are as defined previously.

The model differs from the expectations augmented Phillips curve in that the level of the real wage, lagged one period, is an argument in the wage equation. The negative sign expected on the real wage coefficient can be rationalised in economic terms on the basis that, when the actual real wage falls below its equilibrium or target path, there will be upward pressure on money wages in subsequent periods. Alternatively, the lagged real wage can be interpreted as a proportional control term or error correction mechanism that ensures long-run convergence on to the path implied by the model for the target real wage level (see chapter 3 (3.6.3)). Money wages change to ensure long-run adherence to the equilibrium path for the target real wage.

A priori, the coefficient on the expectations variable (μ_2) is expected to be close to or equal to unity as workers are assumed able to protect the real value of their wages even in the short term. But, even if $\mu_2 < 0$, long-run homogeneity of wages with respect to prices is inherent in the model due to the presence of the error correction mechanism.

Slightly different theoretical justifications for an equation such as (4.6) are encountered in the literature. One that is widely used, and is close to the original rationale offered by Sargan (1964), proceeds in the following manner. The target real wage is defined as

$$(W/P)_t^* = \xi_0 + \xi_1 TL + \xi_2 U_t \qquad (4.7)$$

$$\xi_1 > 0 \quad \xi_2 < 0$$

Generally the long-term growth of the real wage target is assumed exogenous and proxied, as done here, by a linear time trend. This is widely viewed as an unsatisfactory characteristic of the model.[18] Not only is no light shed on the underlying determinants of the long-term growth of real wages, but also an exogenous target can imply inconsistency between equilibrium in the labour market and elsewhere.[19] This would occur if, for instance, an external shock to the economy reduced productivity growth to below the implied trend growth in real wages. Attempts have been made to avoid possible inconsistencies by endogenising the long-run target – usually by equating it with some measure of the level or rate of growth of productivity.[20] In general, however, it has been found that a linear time trend performs best.

Having defined the target real wage, it is then necessary to postulate some form of adjustment mechanism to ensure long-run consistency between target and actual levels of the real wage. A very common procedure is to assume partial adjustment of the nominal wage to any discrepancy between the actual and target real wages

$$\dot{W}_t = \lambda[(W/P)_t^* - (W/P)_{t-1}] + \phi \dot{P}_t^E \qquad (4.8)$$

$$0 < \lambda < 1 \quad 0 < \phi \leqslant 1$$

where the coefficient (λ) measures the speed of adjustment. Nominal wage changes also depend upon expectations. Some formulations of the real wage resistance model make (λ) a variable that depends upon the state of the labour market and the severity of incomes policies (see for instance Artis, 1981). In this case, the target real wage becomes a function only of the time trend.[21]

Substituting equations (4.7) into (4.8) and re-arranging gives the expression for wage inflation that corresponds to the real wage hypothesis, equation (4.6). The following relationships hold between the parameters of equation (4.6) on the one hand and equations (4.7) and (4.8) on the other: $\mu_0 = \lambda\xi_0$, $\mu_1 = \lambda\xi_2$, $\mu_2 = \phi$, $\mu_3 = \lambda$, $\mu_4 = \lambda\xi_1$.

Certain modellers view equation (4.6) as a bargaining equation representing the demands of trade unions for wage increases which are then implicitly met by employers (Sargan, 1964, Britton, 1983). A more involved interpretation views the equation as a reduced form solution to a wage bargaining model for a unionised economy. A rigorous derivation of an equation essentially the same as (4.6) is provided by Nickell (1984), rooted in just such a model. Demands for money wage increases by the union side are modified by variables representing the ability or willingness of employers to accept these demands.

The wage equations derived from the augmented Phillips curve and real wage resistance models share many characteristics and both approaches have, to a considerable degree, become merged in recent practice. Attempts have been made to link formally the two models by arguing, from a neo-classical stance, that, since the real wage level is a major determinant of the excess demand for labour, its inclusion among the explanatory terms of the wage equation can be viewed as a proxy for the state of the labour market, along with the unemployment rate (McCallum, 1975, Holden and Peel, 1979).[22] Sargan (1964) preferred the view that the real wage term enters the equation due to the bargaining aims of unions but acknowledged that it could also be interpreted as adjusting the measured unemployment rate to give a better measure of the excess demand for labour.

Although first proposed in the early 1960s the real wage resistance model only came into vogue in the 1970s and is still much more widely applied to analyses of wage behaviour in the U.K. and Western Europe than elsewhere.[23] Estimated equations closely resemble equation (4.6) with the addition of more complicated disequilibrium dynamics, an error term and sometimes tax variables.[24]

Instances of the application of the real wage resistance model to developing economies are still very limited, partly due to the fact that the institutional arrangements generally thought to be implied by the model, i.e. the existence of trade unions with substantial bargaining power, are usually not to be found in developing countries.[25]

4.2 Wages and wage policy in Brazil – the institutional setting

Before formulating a model of earnings in Brazilian manufacturing, it is imperative to consider the institutional arrangements that governed the operation of labour markets over the sample period. Prior to 1965, collective wage negotiations between trade unions and firms within given regional groupings were permitted and conducted regularly under the supervision of government bodies and the Labour Courts. The right to strike, while circumscribed, was guaranteed by law. A system of regional minimum wages was in place. Minimum wages were adjusted at irregular intervals and may have exerted some influence over private sector settlements but automatic escalator clauses were never used in wage contracts.

After the military *coup d'état* of 1964, most important unions were subject to police intervention. The right to strike was withdrawn and collective wage negotiations ceased to be vehicles for free bargaining between employers and employees, becoming instead a means to implement official wage readjustments.

To replace the old system of wage settlements, in July 1965 the authorities imposed compulsory wage readjustments of fixed periodicity for all registered workers.[26] The measures had their greatest impact upon the formal sector of the labour market that operates in manufacturing and parts of the service and agricultural sectors. Since urban workers without regular jobs, the self-employed urban poor, domestic servants and a large proportion of rural workers were not classified as 'registered workers', their wages were not directly affected by these statutory readjustments.

By law, firms were not permitted to give workers less than the compulsory readjustment, although the law was mute on absolute wage levels. Firms could only evade compulsory indexation through labour turnover. While the wage laws had a binding effect upon all collective agreements at the industry level, firms were free to negotiate individual agreements with their workers that provided for increases over and above the compulsory adjustments.[27]

The wage law of 1965 established a system of annual readjustments for all registered workers but on staggered and non-uniformly distributed dates that varied between industry and regional groups.[28]

Under the original formula nominal wages were adjusted so that, given the expected rate of inflation, the average real wage at the time of adjustment would be equal to the average of the previous 24 months plus a productivity gain decreed by the authorities.[29] An important implication of this formula was that real wages fell, *ceteris paribus*, whenever expected inflation was underestimated as it deliberately was in 1965, 1966 and 1967.

The adjustment formula was altered in 1968 in order to compensate more fully – but still less than 100 per cent – for past underestimation of inflation. Full compensation for past underestimation was introduced in 1974, when nominal wages also came to be adjusted on the basis of average real wages over the past 12 instead of 24 month period. Basically the wage adjustment formula prevailing from 1968 through 1979 was a simple lagged indexation scheme of the form

$$\log W_t = \log W_{t-1} + \log P^{CG+}_{t-1} - \log P^{CG+}_{t-2} + \log z_t \tag{4.9}$$

where W is the average nominal wage,
P^{CG+} is end of period cost of living, and
z_t is the exogenously determined productivity gain.

Abstracting from productivity increases, this rule ensured that average real wages remained unchanged as long as inflation was constant but fell (rose) with an acceleration (deceleration) of inflation.[30]

The rapid acceleration of inflation in 1979, coinciding as it did with a period of political 'opening-up', appears to have convinced policy-makers of the necessity of stemming real wage erosion and setting in motion a process aimed at improving income distribution.

From late 1979, wage contracts came to be adjusted at six monthly rather than annual intervals, leading to a once and for all increase in average real wages.[31] Productivity increases were henceforth freely negotiated between employees and employers and the degree of indexation came to be a function of the wage level.[32]

From 1966 through to 1984, mandatory wage increases, taking account of cost of living adjustments and productivity awards, were on balance very close to changes in the cost of living index, thereby guaranteeing formal sector workers an approximately constant real wage. As there is little evidence to suggest that employers were able to evade systematically their obligation to award this minimum increase through labour turnover, official adjustments can be thought of as having provided an effective floor rate for formal sector wage adjustments.

The existence of a regime of institutional wage fixing in which all wages and salaries are approximately protected against inflation, calls into question the applicability of conventional models of wage inflation that give a prominent role to price expectations, independently formed and acted upon by workers and employers.

4.3 Wages and earnings in Brazilian manufacturing

This section focuses on the determination of average earnings of all employees whose jobs are linked to production in Brazilian manufacturing industry. Earnings in manufacturing, deflated by the cost of living index, rose by a compound annual rate of 2.9 per cent between 1963 and 1984, this contrasts with -1.6 per cent for the real minimum wage.[33] Only fragmentary data are available on earnings by class of employee in manufacturing, making it difficult to ascertain with certainty the time paths of the various series that make up the average of earnings for all manufacturing employees. On balance, the evidence suggests that changes in the earnings of unskilled workers were quite closely linked to official adjustments and, as a consequence, rose only slightly in real terms over most of the sample period.[34] In the late 1970s and early 1980s, some upward drift in real earnings of these workers may have occurred independently of wage policy as labour militancy re-emerged. On the other hand, it is also clear that after 1964 a broadening of earnings' differentials occurred as real wages and salaries of skilled workers and managers rose dramatically over the sample period.[35] These growing disparities are fundamental to an explanation of the upward trend in real earnings of all manufacturing employees.

Disparities arose not only within given industries but also across industries. Average earnings appear in general to have risen faster in industries that experienced relatively higher growth in output and productivity. Given that the composition of manufacturing shifted increasingly away from more traditional low productivity sectors – paying lower wages – to more capital intensive activities paying higher wages, the overall average of earnings in manufacturing was skewed upwards over time.[36] The causes of widening differentials in wages and earnings in Brazil, especially between different classes of employees, have been the subject of a considerable debate, not least because of the importance of this issue for an understanding of the causes of the post-1964 deterioration in income distribution.[37] Very briefly, much of the most promising work done to date has sought explanations in dualistic models of the formal labour market.[38] Wages of unskilled formal sector workers are determined by official wage policy, absolute levels being tied to the minimum wage. The pressures of rural urban migration, widespread urban underemployment and the lack of worker militancy ensured that increases in unskilled wages deviated insignificantly from officially decreed adjustments. In contrast, a more conventional market operated for skilled and managerial labour. With these classes of labour in short supply and, given the investment that employers make in training, skilled workers were in a position to reap some benefit from rising productivity in the form of secular increases in real wages. This class of wages is likely also to exhibit some cyclical variation linked to prevailing levels of excess demand for skilled labour services.

The primary relevance to the present study of these widening disparities resides in the fact that the averaging of earnings across skill levels and industries masks enormous differentials between the constituent series.[39] Whereas average earnings series are often employed in wage inflation studies of industrialised countries on the assumption that labour is to a large extent homogeneous, this same procedure raises important difficulties in the Brazilian context, and more generally in LDCs as a whole, since it is likely that different behavioural models will be required to explain skilled as opposed to unskilled wages and possibly also to explain wages in higher technology, capital intensive subsectors versus those in traditional labour intensive activities.

4.3.1 *A testable model of earnings inflation in Brazilian industry*

The first step in the derivation of such a model is to adopt the hypothesis that the average percentage mandatory wage adjustment ($\dot{W}^{A}$) can be approximately represented by the following function

$$\dot{W}^{A}_{t}=\tau_0+\tau_1\dot{P}^{CG}_{t}+\tau_2\dot{P}^{CG}_{t-1}+\tau_3\dot{P}^{CG}_{t-2}+\tau_4 DU7984+u_t \qquad (4.10)$$

$$\tau_1+\tau_2+\tau_3=1 \quad \tau_4>0$$

The cost of living adjustment depends upon the rate of change of the average cost of living index ($\dot{P}^{CG}$) in the current and two past periods.[40] A dummy variable ($DU7984$) with value of unity in each year from 1979 to 1984 and zero elsewhere is included to account for the introduction of semi-annual nominal wage adjustments in 1979 that *ceteris paribus* put upward pressure on the rate of change of wages. The constant term is included in the model to account for mandatory productivity adjustments awarded up until 1979.

Given that official adjustments ($\dot{W}^{A}$) appear to have constituted an effective minimum, or floor rate of increase in all manufacturing wages, changes in average earnings in manufacturing ($\dot{W}^{I}$) can be viewed as equal to the sum of a function of official adjustments plus a vector of additional variables that explain real earnings growth. A general specification that nests a variety of more parsimonius models can be expressed algebraically as

$$\dot{W}^{I}_{t}=\dot{W}^{A}_{t}+\rho_0+\rho_1 D_t+\rho_2 pr_t+\rho_3(W^{I}/P^{CG})_{t-1}+e_t \qquad (4.11)$$

$$\rho_1>0 \quad \rho_2>0 \quad \rho_3<0$$

where (D) is now a labour market demand pressure term and (pr) an index of manufacturing productivity. Given the lack of uniformity in disaggregate earnings behaviour, no *a priori* judgement is possible as to whether average real earnings contain a significant cyclical component or not. It is of course true that earnings as opposed to the basic wage are to some degree inherently cyclical due to their dependence upon hours worked. But the probable behaviour of the basic wage is less clear. Real wages of skilled workers and managers may have exhibited some pro-cyclical tendency while the same is less likely, although not impossible, for unskilled wages especially if official adjustments were the outcome of a policy reaction function in which productivity and cyclical variables had a role. This is not inconceivable given that the authorities retained important degrees of freedom in wage setting decisions.[41] Productivity is included to test for a link between this variable and the trend growth in real earnings. The real lagged earnings term can be rationalised either as a proxy for excess demand in the labour market, reinforcing the effect of the direct demand pressure term (D), or as a real wage catch up term. Subsumed within the constant are the impact of growing skill differentials and changes in manufacturing industry structure.[42]

Substituting the expression for official adjustments (equation (4.10)) into equation (4.11) yields the maintained hypothesis

$$\dot{W}_t^{\mathrm{I}} = \theta_0 + \theta_1 \dot{P}_t^{CG} + \theta_2 \dot{P}_{t-1}^{CG} + \theta_3 \dot{P}_{t-2}^{CG} + \theta_4 D_t + \theta_5 pr_t + \theta_6 (W^{\mathrm{I}}/P^{CG})_{t-1} + \theta_7 DU7984 + v_t \qquad (4.12)$$

$$\theta_0 > 0 \quad \theta_1 + \theta_2 + \theta_3 = 1 \quad \theta_4 > 0 \quad \theta_5 > 0 \quad \theta_6 < 0 \quad \theta_7 > 0$$

$$v_t = e_{1t} + e_{2t}$$

where the following relationships hold between the parameters of equations (4.10), (4.11) and (4.12), $\theta_0 = \rho_0 + \tau_0$, $\theta_1 = \tau_1$, $\theta_2 = \tau_2$, $\theta_3 = \tau_3$, $\theta_4 = \rho_1$, $\theta_5 = \rho_2$, $\theta_6 = \rho_3$, $\theta_7 = \tau_4$.

A particularly short sample consisting of only 19 observations prevented the adoption of a more general dynamic specification although, as reported further below, misspecified dynamics were subsequently tested for.

4.3.2 *The measurement of demand pressure*

Data relating directly to the state of demand in labour markets in Brazil is scarce and, where available, often unreliable. Unemployment figures, which are commonly used as approximate measures of the excess supply of labour in industrialised countries, are available in Brazil only from 1980 onwards. Even these data are of questionable reliability given the difficulties of defining the active labour force and in distinguishing between 'genuine' employment and underemployment in an LDC. In Brazil, as in many other LDCs, excess demand for labour is commonly proxied by a measure of product market demand, such as capacity utilisation in a particular sector of the economy or the GDP 'gap'. Appeal is made to 'Okun's Law' to link these variables to the rate of unemployment (see

appendix 3). Following this approach, we experiment here with the same measures of product market demand that were used in chapter 3, namely:
(a) capacity utilisation in the economy as a whole (*GDPCU*);
(b) capacity utilisation in the manufacturing sector (using trend through peaks to proxy potential output) (*CU*2); and
(c) capacity utilisation in the manufacturing sector (using a five year moving average of actual output to proxy potential output) (*CU*3).

4.3.3 *Model estimates*

The model developed above is specifically intended to explain manufacturing earnings in the period subsequent to the abolition of trade unions and the introduction of mandatory wage adjustments. The first full year in which the new policies were in effect, 1966, was chosen as the starting point for the sample period used, with 1984 as the end point. This gave only 19 data points for estimation, imposing constraints on the analysis. However, this approach must be preferred over the use of a longer, non-homogeneous sample period.[43]

Initial estimates of the maintained hypothesis revealed the presence of an outlying observation in 1983. This was a year in which the wage adjustment formula underwent four changes, as policy-makers sought to cut real wages as part of the government's stabilisation programme. Consequently the model over-predicts wage inflation in that year.[44] A dummy variable (*DU*83) was added to the model with value of unity in 1983 and zero elsewhere to neutralise this observation.

Results from an OLS estimate of the maintained hypothesis, using (*CU*2) to proxy demand (*D*) and with the inclusion of the dummy variable for 1983 (*DU*83), are summarised in table 4.1, equation (4.12a). The restriction $\theta_1+\theta_2+\theta_3=1$ in equation (4.12a) was initially tested for and, being accepted by the data, was subsequently imposed; the value of the *F* statistic on the restriction (Z3) being 2.45.[45] If productivity was a determinant of the rise in trend earnings its impact is probably subsumed within the constant, as no role could be found for productivity, irrespective of the proxy used for demand. The level of demand is significant. Tests using the alternative demand proxies yielded less significant coefficients and the estimates obtained exhibited instability over time. Lagged values of all the demand proxies were also experimented with but none was found to increase the explanatory power of the model. Lagged productivity as well as the rate of change of productivity were also found to be insignificant.

A test down procedure was applied to equation (4.12a) which yielded the more parsimonious specification of equation (4.12b). Homogeneity in

Table 4.1. *Estimated manufacturing earnings relationships – dependent variable, the rate of change of average earnings* ($\dot{W}^1$)

	(4.12a) OLS (1966–84)	(4.12b) OLS (1966–84)	(4.12c) CO (1) (1966–84)	(4.12d) OLS (1966–78)	(4.12e) OLS (1966–84)	(4.12f) OLS (1966–78)	(4.12g) IV (1966–84)	(4.13a) OLS (1966–84)
Variables[a,b]								
Constant	−0.188	−0.166	−0.152	−0.282	0.071	0.072	0.076	−0.147
	(−2.30)	(−2.14)	(−2.60)	(−2.54)	(7.66)	(7.75)	(9.08)	(−1.53)
$\dot{P}^{CG}_t$	0.655	0.649	0.670	0.544	0.676	0.656	0.701	0.756
	(10.42)	(11.78)	(13.49)	(5.83)	(9.84)	(5.47)	(7.55)	(12.55)
$\dot{P}^{CG}_{t-1}$	0.608	0.503	0.463	0.556	0.506	0.588	0.509	0.244
	(4.61)	(5.18)	(5.39)	(4.09)	(4.12)	(2.98)	(3.17)	(4.05)
$\dot{P}^{CG}_{t-2}$	−0.263	−0.152	−0.133	−0.100	−0.182	−0.244	−0.178	—
	(−2.38)	(−2.69)	(−2.72)	(−1.20)	(−2.60)	(−2.49)	(−2.44)	
$CU2$	0.452	0.259	0.242	0.383	—	—	—	—
	(2.42)	(3.06)	(3.81)	(3.20)				
$GDPCU$	—	—	—	—	—	—	—	0.233
								(2.22)
pr	−0.183	—	—	—	—	—	—	—
	(−0.81)							
$(W^1/P^{CG})_{t-1}$	0.048	—	—	—	—	—	—	—
	(0.34)							
$DU7984$	0.075	0.0653	0.058	—	0.044	—	0.029	0.082
	(2.23)	(2.80)	(4.19)	—	(1.90)		(1.17)	(3.37)
$DU83$	−0.143	−0.185	−0.207	—	−0.209	—	−0.178	−0.250
	(−2.41)	(−4.87)	(−6.14)	—	(−4.45)	—	(−3.29)	(−5.94)

Statistics[c]								
$\bar{R}^2$	0.99	0.99	0.99	0.96	0.99	0.92	0.98	0.99
SEE	0.026	0.026	0.024	0.023	0.032	0.031	0.050	0.034
DW	2.71	2.52	—	2.19	1.92	1.96	1.87	2.70
Z1	5.00	3.00	—	0.26	0.02	0.04	0.39	3.38
Z2	4.80	0.12	—	3.48	0.22	0.28	1.23	0.31
Z3	2.45 (1,10)	0.22 (1,12)	—	0.45 (1,8)	1.80 (1,13)	0.003 (1,9)	0.90 (1,12)	4.22 (1,13)

Notes: [a] Figures in brackets under the coefficient estimates are *t* ratios.

[b] Variables are defined as:

$\dot{P}^{CG}$ – the percentage rate of change of the average annual Rio de Janeiro cost of living index,

*CU*2 – capacity utilisation in manufacturing constructed using the trend through peaks method to measure potential output,

GDPCU – the real GDP gap constructed using trend through peaks,

*DU*7984 – a dummy variable with value one for the years 1979–84 and zero elsewhere, and

*DU*83 – a dummy variable with value one in 1983 and zero elsewhere.

[c] $\bar{R}^2$ is the multiple correlation coefficient, SEE the standard error of the regression, DW the Durbin–Watson test statistic, Z1 and Z2 the χ^2 statistics (each with one degree of freedom) for the log likelihood ratio tests for first- and second-order serial correlation in the error term and Z3 is the *F* ratio test statistic for the null hypothesis of homogeneity in degree one of wages with respect to the cost of living.

degree one of the price inflation terms with respect to wage inflation was once again tested for and imposed. The lack of a significant role for the lagged real earnings term can be interpreted as lending support to the view that, under the prevailing institutional setting, workers were not in a position to fight to maintain a target real wage. While it is true that the homogeneity restriction fulfils the role of ensuring long-run proportionality between rates of price and wage inflation, the lack of an error correction mechanism means that homogeneity in levels is not ensured. A rise or fall in the real wage that occurs due to a deceleration or acceleration of price inflation will be maintained since it will not set in motion a process aimed at restoring a 'target' real wage. The values and sign pattern of the price inflation variables ($\dot{P}^{CG}$) point to less than complete adjustment of changes in earnings to a change in the price level in the initial period (t) followed by overshooting in ($t-1$) which is then corrected in ($t-2$). The negative coefficient on the second lagged inflation term can be interpreted as resulting from the form of the indexation rule followed (see note 40 to this chapter).

Both equations (4.12a) and (4.12b) exhibit clear indications of first-order autocorrelation that could not be removed by re-specifying the dynamic structure. Re-estimating, using a Cochrane–Orcutt procedure, gave the results shown as (4.12c).

In equation (4.12c) demand is significant and its coefficient bears the positive sign expected *a priori*. The value of this parameter suggests that a 1 per cent rise in manufacturing output, relative to its potential level, would result directly in a rise in earnings inflation relative to current and lagged cost of living inflation of approximately one quarter per cent. The problem with the model is that it exhibits severe parameter instability. This is apparent from a visual comparison of the coefficient values in (4.12c) and (4.12d), where the latter is an estimate of the model using data covering 1966–78.[46] Errors in this shorter sample exhibit second-order serial correlation.

The stability problem, combined with a certain scepticism as to the usefulness of ($CU2$) as a labour market demand proxy, led to the suspicion that the misspecification of the model might be due to the presence of the demand term. The significance of this variable might result from spurious correlation due, for instance, to its capturing the influence of productivity growth upon real earnings.

OLS estimation results for a more parsimonious specification in which the demand proxy was constrained to zero as presented in table 4.1 as equation (4.12e). While constraining the model caused a slight reduction in the SEE and in the t ratios on the inflation variables, no longer was there evidence of autocorrelation or parameter instability. The summary estimation results for this model are reproduced below with additional diagnostic statistics

$$\dot{W}^{\mathrm{I}}_t = \underset{(7.66)}{0.071} + \underset{(9.84)}{0.676}\, \dot{P}^{\mathrm{CG}}_t + \underset{(4.12)}{0.506}\, \dot{P}^{\mathrm{CG}}_{t-1} - \underset{(-2.60)}{0.182}\, \dot{P}^{\mathrm{CG}}_{t-2}$$

$$+ \underset{(1.90)}{0.044}\, DU7984 - \underset{(-4.45)}{0.209}\, DU83 \qquad (4.12e)$$

OLS $n=19$ $\bar{R}^2=0.99$ SEE $=0.032$ DW $=1.92$

LL $=41.11$ Z1 $=0.02(1)$ Z2 $=0.22(1)$ Z3 $=1.80(1,13)$

Z4 $=0.74(6,9)$ Z5 $=1.18(6,5)$ Z6 $=0.92(13)$

The diagnostic statistics are as defined in table 4.1 with the addition of LL for the log of the likelihood function and (Z4) through (Z6) which are statistics for, respectively, the Chow F ratio test for parameter stability, the Goldfeld–Quandt F ratio test for stability of the variance and, the Wu–Hausman t ratio test for orthogonality of the residuals. Estimation results for the short sample estimate are reported as equation (4.12f). Parameter values change only slightly and the Chow test statistic value of 0.74(6,9) allows easy acceptance of stability. When the demand proxy is excluded, the constant takes on significance and a more plausible positive value of 0.07. Given constant inflation, the intercept captures the rate of growth of real average earnings. There is no evidence to suggest instability of the variance or a distribution of the residuals that is not normal.

As with the manufacturing price equation, here too it was essential to consider the possibility of simultaneous equation bias arising from the joint determination of earnings and prices. The coefficient on the current consumer price inflation term would tend to be upward biased if the error term in equation (4.12e) was not orthogonal with respect to the regressors. To choose an instrument for current price inflation we experimented with a number of specifications that included a wide range of the model's predetermined variables as well as lagged values of consumer price inflation. The predicted values from the equation with the highest SEE were used as the instrument.[47] Re-estimating equation (4.12e) using instrumental variables gave equation (4.12g) of table 4.1. Compared with the OLS estimate (equation (4.12e)), the coefficient of current inflation is slightly higher and that of twice lagged inflation, slightly lower. The differences do not suggest a problem of serious simultaneous equation bias. This conclusion is borne out by the Wu–Hausman t ratio statistic for the null hypothesis of residual orthogonaltiy in the OLS model (Z6).

4.3.4 *Comparison with other studies*

There are very few econometric time series studies on the wage equation in Brazil.[48] In the most notable of such studies, Modiano (1983a, 1985) uses the following model

$$\dot{W}_t^{\mathrm{I}} = \omega_0 + \omega_1 \dot{P}_t^{\mathrm{WG}} + \omega_2 \dot{P}_{t-1}^{\mathrm{WG}} + \omega_3 (1 - GDPCU)_t \tag{4.13}$$

where ($\dot{P}^{\mathrm{WG}}$) is the rate of wholesale price inflation used in place of cost of living inflation. Homogeneity in degree one of price inflation with respect to wage inflation is imposed on the relation so that ($\omega_1 + \omega_2 = 1$). The lag structure and homogeneity restriction are imposed *a priori*, the rationale being that this was how the wage adjustment rule worked. A demand pressure variable is added to explain cyclical real earnings variations.

A model similar to Modiano's but using cost of living inflation and including the two shift dummies was estimated for a slightly longer sample period, and is presented in table 4.1 as equation (4.13a). The model exhibits first-order serial correlation. The homogeneity restriction is imposed but only just accepted at the 5 per cent level; (Z3) being the relevant *F* test. The goodness of fit as measured by the SEE is lower than in the preferred models and when estimated over the full and shorter samples – using both OLS and Cochrane/Orcutt first- and second-order procedures – there was evidence of parameter instability.[49] This was apparently related to the inclusion of a demand pressure term, as in the specifications estimated above. Moreover, as discussed in appendix 3, GDP gap variables constructed using a single trend through peaks line to proxy potential output exhibit dubious properties. This model suggests a role for demand but, given the problems of misspecification and of the nature of the demand proxy used, the results are open to question.[50] As regards the dynamics of wage and price adjustment, our results suggest that this model is misspecified and that a model with a second lagged price inflation term fits the data better.

4.4 Conclusion

The results reported in this chapter provide some evidence of a pro-cyclical role for the level of demand in the determination of the rate of change of average manufacturing earnings. However, the unreliability of the econometric results means that these findings must be treated with care. A model excluding demand is statistically much more robust and, on balance, is preferred for use in the macromodel developed further on. The choice of this specification is important in that it negates the existence of what is usually thought of as a key channel through which prices and inflation respond to aggregate demand, even in an economy with a large mark-up pricing sector.

The analysis of the institutional set-up of the Brazilian labour market pointed to reasons why average earnings were unlikely to exhibit cyclical behaviour, even if a sub-class of earnings, namely those of skilled workers and managers did respond to demand conditions. The evidence supports an essentially institutional view of wage setting in Brazil, where official policy determines nominal earnings adjustments. Real average earnings rose in a secular fashion which the current model was ill-equipped to explain.

Equation (4.12e) fulfils an important function in the macromodel as it establishes a channel through which increases in consumer food and manufactured goods prices feed back into further price changes. The model also has the important property of ensuring that workers absorb a large share of any real income loss that is sustained due to an adverse supply shock to the system. Accelerating inflation forces real earnings down. Of course, decelerating inflation increases the real wage, thereby dampening the speed at which an anti-inflationary shock leads to lower overall inflation.

5 The price of food and food supply

5.1 Introduction

Whereas the appropriate characterisation of the functioning of markets for industrial goods and services is the subject of considerable debate, there exists a good deal of consensus among economists regarding the fundamental determinants of prices and output in agricultural markets.[1] A high degree of product homogeneity and large numbers of independent producers are among the typical characteristics of agricultural markets that make the model of pure competition, in which equilibrium price is determined by the intersection of the demand and supply schedules, a relevant starting point for price analysis in agriculture.

The relative lack of controversy regarding the fundamentals of agricultural market behaviour has meant that the literature on the subject is primarily applied and mostly concerned with the many non-trivial issues that arise in specifying and estimating a testable model of market behaviour, rather than with the characterisation of the basic structure.[2] This body of literature is mainly North American, the importance and diversity of agricultural production in the U.S.A. and Canada having spawned an enormous body of applied research in agricultural economics. Econometric models of agricultural price and output in developing economies, particularly in Latin America, are less plentiful despite the undisputed importance of the agricultural sector in aggregate output, employment, foreign trade and price determination in most LDCs. The tendency, prevalent until quite recently, to play down the contribution and importance of agricultural activities while concentrating on industrial development, coupled with particularly serious (and not unrelated) problems of data availability, reliability and coverage, probably help explain this lacuna.[3]

In the American literature, there is a tendency towards increasing degrees of complexity in models of agricultural price and output determination.

Specific commodity markets or even parts thereof are now much more often the focus of analysis rather than markets for composite goods such as food. The increasing micro emphasis has led to detailed consideration of the role of complements and substitutes, thereby increasing the number of explanatory variables that enter demand functions. Often demand and supply are disaggregated into several component parts in order to build more information into the model. Yet another source of increasing complexity is the more frequent use of very short time units in econometric price studies, leading to more involved dynamics and the need to model changes in stocks and speculative demand. The result has been a tendency towards larger and more highly simultaneous systems. The model developed below is very simple in comparison, although its fundamental structure is not dissimilar. The high degree of aggregation used in this study, coupled with a paucity of data pertaining to the agricultural sector in Brazil, limits the degree of sophistication possible in the present study.

5.2 Agricultural markets in Brazil: the role of government and problems of data availability

Brazil's agricultural production can be thought of as being made up of two rather broad categories of goods: first those produced primarily for domestic consumption, which are neither exported in significant quantities nor freely importable and consist in large part of basic foodstuffs and, secondly, food or raw materials destined principally for export markets. Prices of basic foodstuffs are determined in the domestic market while, to a considerable degree, prices of export goods are governed by international prices. In Brazil, the weights applied to export agricultural commodity prices in the general price index (domestic supply measure) are relatively low. For these reasons, we seek here to explain only the price of basic foodstuffs, taking export goods prices as given. Two price indices relating to food products in Brazil are available for a sample period long enough to be suitable for use in an annual econometric analysis. These are the wholesale price index of food products consumed domestically (P^{WF}) and the Rio de Janeiro consumer food price index (P^{CF}).[4] The model developed here sets out to explain these two prices as well as the closely linked process of supply determination.

Scant data on production of foodstuffs in Brazil posed a serious challenge in the context of the present study. As noted in chapter 2, no aggregate data series are available for Brazil's output of foodstuffs. There we presented a simple index of selected food crop production. This index, while adequate as an indicator of trends, is not suitable for use in the econometric exercises. It excludes many crops and all animal by-products that are represented in the aggregate price indices, and is also inadequate because of the fixed weights used. The share of many important crops in total output changed so markedly over the sample period as to render unrepresentative a fixed weight index, particularly when the price indices used are themselves based on three year moving average value weights. As discussed in chapter 2, aggregate agricultural production indices are inadequate in the present context because of the preponderance of food products for export and non-food raw materials for domestic consumption. Instead, we proxy food production by an imprecise indicator of non-coffee agricultural output that is consumed domestically. This series was constructed by subtracting from agricultural value added, agricultural exports and domestic coffee production – all measured at constant 1970 prices. The use of this proxy involves some double counting arising from the fact that a portion of current coffee production is included among agricultural exports. However, the extensive use of coffee stockpiles means that current production and current exports cannot be equated.[5] The proxy adopted for food suffers further slight contamination due to the inclusion of non-food agricultural goods that are not exported.

The simple examination of food prices and output data carried out in chapter 2, lent *prima facie* support to the hypothesis that the competitive model provides a useful characterisation of market behaviour. Nonetheless, the prevailing institutional setting had an important impact upon the functioning of the market that requires explicit consideration.

Over the period of analysis, Brazilian governments intervened in agricultural markets in an attempt to influence output, investment and prices.[6] The main mechanisms used were price controls, producer and consumer subsidies and direct marketing. Government involvement appears to have been quite effective at influencing consumer prices. Several key food prices including those of wheat, maize, milk and beef were subject to strict retail control over most of the sample period. Retail prices were insulated to a considerable extent from changes in producer or wholesale prices through the use of consumer subsidies. Prices at the producer and wholesale levels, on the other hand, seem to have been to a larger extent market determined; what controls there were being less effective. These considerations underlie the structure of the model developed below.

5.3 A simple disequilibrium model of the Brazilian food market

In the literature on agricultural pricing two principal types of market models are encountered: those which assume continuous market clearing and those which start from the premise that, even in competitive markets, inertia may prevent prices from changing rapidly enough to maintain continuous equilibrium between demand and supply. These disequilibrium models have been most often adopted in studies based on quarterly, monthly or even daily data.[7] In these cases it can be argued that over the time unit chosen markets do not clear even if, over a longer time horizon, competition does ensure that equilibrium prevails. There are reasons to suspect that in a developing country disequilibria in agricultural markets are more pronounced and longer lasting than in the more efficient agricultural markets of developed countries. Production in the former, particularly of basic food crops, is more likely to be subject to volatility, given the unsophisticated technology used and the uneven supply of inputs. Alternative sources of supply such as stockpiles and imports are less readily available to restore equilibrium quickly in the event of a poor harvest. Information is less rapidly disseminated, causing greater lags in the response of prices to changing supply and demand conditions. Price signals may be obscured by government controls, high inflation (which makes it difficult to discern relative price shifts) and underdevelopment of spot and futures markets. Here we adopted as a working hypothesis the assumption that continuous market clearing did not obtain.[8]

With the demand and production functions in implicit functional form, the proposed model is given by the following set of equations

$$df = f_1(\underset{-}{P^{CF}/P^{CG}}, \underset{+}{y^{DC}}, \underset{+}{N}) \tag{5.1}$$

$$sf_t = q_t^{AF} + im_t^{W} \tag{5.2}$$

$$q^{AF} = f_2(\underset{+}{P^{WF}/P^{CG}}, \underset{+}{le^{PA}}, \underset{+}{TL}) \tag{5.3}$$

$$P^{CF} = P^{WF}(1-\tau) \tag{5.4}$$

$$\Delta(P^{WF}/P^{CG}) = \delta(df - sf) \tag{5.5}$$

where df is the quantity of food demanded,
P^{CF} is the retail or consumer price of food,
P^{CG} is the consumer price index,
y^{DC} is real private sector disposable income,
N is population,
sf is the total quantity of food supplied,
q^{AF} is the quantity of food produced domestically,
im^{W} is the quantity of imported wheat,
P^{WF} is the wholesale price of food,
TL is a linear time trend,
le^{PA} is the real value of outstanding loans from the monetary authorities to the agricultural sector, and
τ is the rate of food consumption subsidy.

Equation (5.1) is the demand schedule for food; the quantity demanded is a negative function of relative retail prices and a positive function of private real disposable income[9] – used as a proxy for personal sector income – and of population.[10] Total supply (equation (5.2)) equals domestic production (q^{AF}) plus wheat imports, where the latter are used as a proxy for total food imports.[11] Food imports are taken to be pre-determined in the model. This is a simplifying assumption but given that imports were subject to government control and response lags existed, it may not be an unreasonable one. We abstract from 'on-farm' consumption, for which no data are available, to equate supply directly with the marketable surplus; the latter being the relevant variable in price determination. No role is allowed in the model for changes in stocks. Evidence for the U.S.A. shows that in the short term – less than one year – stocks can vary a great deal relative to demand with a concomitant influence upon prices. However, from year to year, with storage facilities limited, changes in stocks tend to be small (See Heien, 1977, p. 127). In Brazil, with very limited stockpiling facilities for basic foodstuffs, changes in stocks are likely to be even less important in price determination although, given the lack of data on stocks, there is no way to test this assertion. Domestic production is given in equation (5.3) as a positive function of relative wholesale price, where the latter is used as a proxy for producer prices (see note 4 above), real subsidised credit outstanding to agriculture from the monetary authorities and a linear time trend to capture technological improvements leading to rising yields.[12]

Equation (5.4) is a definition that sets retail prices equal to wholesale prices multiplied by one minus the rate of consumer food subsidy. For a given wholesale price, a rise in the subsidy rate implies a decrease in consumer price. This specification is rather different from that customarily used to explain price spreads. In order to explain the specification it is useful to consider the issue of causation between prices at different marketing levels. There are two conflicting notions in the literature on the relationships between demands at the farm or wholesale and retail levels (see Waugh, 1964b, p. 19). One view, that which is adopted here in a modified form, is that prices are made at the farm level and that retail prices consist of farm prices plus charges associated with processing, transport and marketing. There is wide acceptance of the validity of this notion in the short run in particular. Shortages or surpluses in supply are noticed at the farm level first, leading farm prices to be adjusted while retail prices charged on existing stocks remain unchanged. The second view, and that which is most widely adhered to, is that, in the longer run at least, consumer demand controls farm demand and, therefore, prices are determined at the retail level. As Heien (1977) shows, short-run farm to consumer price causation is compatible with the hypothesis that, in the long run, consumer prices and demand are controlling. In disequilibrium models, because the fundamental concern is with short-run price changes, the convention is to adopt the hypothesis of farm to retail price causation. In the present context there is an additional reason for adopting this specification. As stated above, it would appear that farm and wholesale prices were market determined to a larger degree than consumer prices which were largely administered; changes being made in reaction to alterations in prices at other marketing levels as well as to policy changes.

A series of difficulties arose in trying to model the price spread. Ideally we would wish to model retail prices as a stochastic function of wholesale prices, marketing and processing costs and, because of the particular institutional setting, also as a function of the rate of subsidy. In chapter 2, the divergent paths of wholesale and consumer food prices in the 1970s were remarked upon. This divergence was attributed primarily to the administered nature of consumer prices coupled with the widespread use of subsidies.[13] It is unclear what role was fulfilled by marketing and processing costs and it is impossible to test for their role due to a lack of relevant data. It is also difficult to test properly the hypothesis of the role of subsidies because of the absence of independent data from which to construct a continuous series on the rate of subsidisation. It was necessary instead to adopt the simplifying hypothesis that the spread between relative prices at the wholesale and retail levels was a function only of the subsidy rate, where the latter was proxied by the residually defined expression

$$\tau = 1 - P^{CF}/P^{WF}$$

The final equation (5.5) can be interpreted as a Walrasian adjustment mechanism in which the change in relative prices is a function of excess demand. The speed of adjustment of prices is given by (δ).

5.4 Recursive versus simultaneous systems

A recursive system consists of a set of equations, each containing a single endogenous variable other than those which have been treated as dependent in prior equations. As a consequence, the model can be solved within each time period in a specified order without a problem of simultaneity occurring.[14] In the model used here, the determination of demand and supply will be a recursive process if current supply is found to depend solely upon lagged, as opposed to current relative prices. Where current price is an explanatory variable in both the demand and supply functions, simultaneity is present.[15]

Particularly during the 1950s and early 1960s, much of the literature on agricultural pricing was concerned with the relative merits and drawbacks of working with recursive versus simultaneous models (Tomek and Robinson, 1977). The use of a recursive system has certain practical advantages in that the parameters are identifiable and in general OLS estimators will be consistent. Also a prediction of prices can be derived directly from the demand equation without first having to specify a complete model, including the process of supply determination. The accumulated evidence suggests that single equation models, in which supply is treated as exogenous, often provide satisfactory predictions of prices whereas in other applications, such as predicting demand for a commodity in a particular use, a simultaneous system may perform better (Tomek and Robinson, 1977, pp. 334–5). The appropriateness of a recursive as opposed to simultaneous model to characterise the functioning of a particular market will depend upon the nature of the commodity and, to a more limited extent, be governed by the time units used in the analysis. For a crop or livestock product with a long production cycle, the response lags will be longer than for commodities with a short cycle, suggesting that a recursive system may be adequate. On the other hand, in the case of the commodity with a short cycle, a simultaneous system may be more appropriate. It is also true that the shorter the time units used in the analysis, the greater the likelihood that a recursive system will be appropriate, as there are limited possibilities for variables to interact. The consensus, based on a large body of applied price studies which cover a variety of agricultural commodities and use time units up to and including one year, is that the linkage between demand and supply is generally recursive (Heien, 1977, p. 126 and Tomek and Robinson, 1981, p. 317). However, in the final analysis, the issue is one that must be addressed in each specific case.

5.5 The domestic output of food

Because of the interdependence of prices and output, whether the system is simultaneous or not, it is of vital importance for the consistency and completeness of the overall macromodel developed in chapter 8 that output of food be treated as endogenous. The nature of the link between demand, supply and prices in the food market is crucial in the determination of inflation, as was shown in chapter 1. The supply function is appropriately estimated here rather than later, as this allows us to form a judgement as to whether demand and supply should be treated as simultaneous or recursive. This in turn has a direct bearing upon the way in which prices are estimated.

If we assume initially a linear form for the production equation, with an additive disturbance and generalise the model to allow for short-run dynamics, equation (5.3) can be re-written[16]

$$q_t^{AF} = \gamma_0 + \gamma_1 (P^{WF}/P^{CG})_t + \gamma_2 (P^{WF}/P^{CG})_{t-1} + \gamma_3 (le_t^{PA}) + \gamma_4 le_{t-1}^{PA} + \gamma_5 q_{t-1}^{AF} + \gamma_6 TL + u_{1t} \quad (5.6)$$

Simultaneity of demand and supply is implied if the linear restriction ($\gamma_1 = 0$) is rejected by the data. If not rejected, this indicates that the system is more appropriately viewed as recursive. Both current and lagged real credit to agriculture may influence current output depending upon the average length of commodity cycles and the stage in the cycle at which most credit is conceded. *A priori*, however, one would expect lagged credit to be a more significant explanatory variable.

An outlying observation for food production in 1965 was identified in initial estimates. As a result, in subsequent estimations, a dummy variable was introduced with a value of one in 1965 and zero elsewhere.

Equation (5.6) was estimated using both OLS and IV estimators. In the latter case an instrumental variable was used for current relative prices.[17] An OLS estimate of the general model is reported as (5.6a) in table 5.1 and an IV estimate of a more parsimonious specification is shown as (5.6b).[18] Irrespective of the estimator used, support could not be found for the hypothesis of simultaneity between prices and output. The inability to reject the restriction ($\gamma_1 = 0$) and the significance of (γ_2), lend support to the hypothesis of a recursive link instead. As anticipated, lagged real credit performed better than its own current value or than both variables taken together. No explanatory role could be found for the lagged dependent variable.

The application of successive F tests yielded equation (5.6c) as the preferred parsimonius specification. Estimation results are reproduced below with additional diagnostic statistics

$$q_t^{AF} = \underset{(-24.38)}{-1298.0} + \underset{(6.73)}{0.042}\,(P^{WF}/P^{CG})_{t-1} + \underset{(8.01)}{0.219}\,le_{t-1}^{PA} + \underset{(24.34)}{0.665}\,TL + \underset{(2.40)}{1.21}\,DU65 + u_{1t} \quad (5.6c)$$

OLS $n = 25$ $\bar{R}^2 = 0.99$ SEE $= 0.478$ DW $= 1.92$

LL $= -14.23$ Z1 $= 0.002(1)$ Z2 $= 3.20(1)$ Z3 $= 0.82(7,14)$

Z5 $= 1.32(9,8)$

The diagnostic statistics do not point to serious misspecification. The Chow test (Z3) that compares parameter stability in the full sample with a shorter sample estimate (equation (5.6d)) suggests that the model is robust, although the parameters can be seen to change slightly. The Goldfeld–Quandt F statistic (Z5) does not allow us to reject the null hypothesis of homoscedasticity.

Table 5.1. *Estimated food production relationships: dependent variable – real food production* (q^{AF})

	5.6a OLS (1960–84)	5.6b IV (1961–84)	5.6c OLS (1960–84)	5.6d OLS (1967–84)
Variables[a,b]				
Constant	−1476.5	−1348.4	−1298.0	−1395.0
	(−6.58)	(−24.79)	(−24.38)	(−7.89)
$(P^{WF}/P^{CG})_t$	0.0008	−0.04	—	—
	(0.064)	(−1.77)		
$(P^{WF}/P^{CG})_{t-1}$	0.046	0.092	0.042	0.035
	(3.04)	(3.13)	(6.73)	(2.49)
le_t^{PA}	−0.0014	—	—	—
	(−0.18)			
le_{t-1}^{PA}	0.246	0.204	0.219	0.198
	(2.64)	(7.71)	(8.01)	(4.37)
q_{t-1}^{AF}	−0.135	—	—	—
	(−0.83)			
TL	0.756	0.69	0.665	0.714
	(6.57)	(24.82)	(24.34)	(7.89)
*DU*65	1.35	1.49	1.21	—
	(2.27)	(3.08)	(2.40)	
Statistics[c]				
$\bar{R}^2$	0.99	0.99	0.99	0.99
SEE	0.507	0.44	0.478	0.48
DW	1.86	2.25	1.92	2.23
Z1	0.47	0.32	0.002	0.46
Z2	3.34	2.90	3.20	3.13

Notes: [a] Figures in brackets under the coefficient estimates are *t* ratios.

[b] Variables are defined as:

q^{AF} – food production in billions of 1970 cruzeiros,

P^{WF} – index (1970 = 100) of the wholesale price of food,

P^{CG} – index (1970 = 100) of consumer prices,

le^{PA} – average loans outstanding from the monetary authorities to the agricultural sector in billions of 1970 cruzeiros,

TL – a linear time trend, and

*DU*65 – dummy variable with value of unity in 1965 and zero in other years.

[c] $\bar{R}^2$ is the multiple correlation coefficient, SEE the standard error of the regression, DW the Durbin–Watson statistic and Z1 and Z2 the χ^2 statistics, each with one degree of freedom, for the log likelihood ratio test for first- and second-order serial correlation in the error term.

The average elasticities of production with respect to lagged price and credit implied by the model are 0.26 and 0.10 respectively.[19] Both values are very low and, given the simplicity of the model, must be treated with caution. Price inelasticity fits with the traditional structuralist view on food supply response. As regards the apparent inefficiency of credit, it is important to note that credits destined for use in agriculture were often diverted to other uses due to the high subsidies implicit in the terms of lending. The average rate of output growth over the sample period implied by the time trend (adjusted by the constant) is a rather high 6.9 per cent. This almost certainly overstates true trend growth in food output and reflects inaccuracies in the production proxy data used.

In the applied agricultural market literature, both linear and log-linear specifications are adopted for supply functions.[20] There is no clear presumption in favour of one or the other and therefore the correct procedure is to test both specifications for data compatibility. A log-linear version of the supply function was estimated although no significant relationship could be identified between current and/or lagged relative price and production when using this specification. The fit of this model was clearly inferior to that of the linear version.[21]

5.6 The determination of wholesale food prices

Before solving the model for price and estimating the parameters of the resulting expression, it is useful to consider the reaction of the model to a rise in real income. This causes the demand for food to expand and, with supply predetermined in the current period, excess demand develops. Relative wholesale prices start to rise and, for a given rate of subsidy, retail prices also increase. This will have the effect of dampening demand. Whether this effect will be sufficient to restore equilibrium depends upon the price elasticity relative to the income elasticity of demand and the speed of wholesale price adjustment in the face of excess demand (equation (5.5)). On plausible assumptions as to the size of the relevant coefficients, disequilibrium is unlikely to be eliminated in one period. If not, in the subsequent period the higher wholesale price will stimulate greater production. Although not modelled here, food imports may also increase. Excess demand will be further reduced.

In order to obtain an expression for price from the structural model we must first specify a functional form for the demand equation. Since the explanatory variables enter the retail-wholesale spread equation (5.4) in multiplicative form, there is an *a priori* reason to adopt a constant elasticity specification for demand. In a linear specification, the identity of equation (5.4) cannot be maintained. As with supply functions, both linear and constant elasticity specifications are found in the literature. The main disadvantage of a constant elasticity model being that, in defiance of Engel's Law, it implies an unchanging income elasticity of demand for food over time. For this reason, the coefficients are best interpreted as average elasticities.

In adopting a constant elasticity specification for the demand function it is also necessary to posit proportional adjustment of prices to excess demand. On these assumptions the demand function, price spread equation and adjustment equation can be rewritten

$$\ln df_t = \ln\phi_0 - \phi_1 \ln(P^{CF}/P^{CG})_t + \phi_2 \ln y_t^{DC} + \phi_3 \ln N_t \tag{5.7}$$

$$P_t^{CF} = P_t^{WF} \cdot m_t \tag{5.8}$$

$$\Delta\ln(P^{WF}/P^{CG})_t = \delta(\ln df_t - \ln sf_t) \tag{5.9}$$

where $[m=(1-\tau)=P^{CF}/P^{WF}]$ and other symbols are as defined above. We derive a reduced form by substituting equation (5.8) into (5.7). The resulting expression is then substituted into equation (5.9). Because supply is directly observed and predetermined it enters the adjustment equation directly. Collecting terms and rearranging gives

$$\begin{aligned}\ln(P^{WF}/P^{CG})_t = {} & \delta\phi_0/(1+\delta\phi_1) + \delta\phi_2/(1+\delta\phi_1)\ln y_t^{DC} \\ & - \delta/(1+\delta\phi_1)\ln sf_t - \delta\phi_1/(1+\delta\phi_1)\ln m_t \\ & + \delta\phi_3(1+\delta\phi_1)\ln N_t + 1/(1+\delta\phi_1)\ln(P^{WF}/P^{CG})_{t-1} \\ & + u \end{aligned} \tag{5.10}$$

This specification was generalised to allow for additional adjustment lags by including income and supply in period $(t-1)$ among the explanatory terms. Initial estimates of the general model revealed outlying observations for 1982 and 1983. These years saw pronounced swings in the relative wholesale price of food, related in large measure to changes in official price and subsidy policies. In 1983 relative price rose by 23 per cent as the partial elimination of wheat subsidies led to a 264 per cent increase in the nominal wheat price. As the model could not be expected to capture the impact of this phenomenon, two dummy variables, with values of unity in 1982 and 1983 respectively and zero in other years (*DU*82 and *DU*83), were included in subsequent estimations.

The generalised version of equation (5.10) was estimated by OLS. Summary results are presented in table 5.2 as (5.10a). A test of the hypothesis that demand is homogeneous in degree one with respect to population ($\phi_3=1$ in equation (5.7)) amounted to testing the linear restriction that the coefficients on the supply and population terms (sf) and

(N) summed to zero. The relevant F test statistic was 1.3(1,15), not allowing us to reject the null hypothesis of homogeneity. In subsequent regressions, this restriction was imposed.

The general dynamic model suffers from multicollinearity that affects the t statistics. Lagged income and supply are both insignificant and a 'test' down' yielded the preferred specification, which excludes these variables. This is equation (5.10b) in table 5.2 – reproduced below along with additional diagnostic statistics

$$\ln (P^{WF}/P^{CG})_t = \underset{(-1.35)}{-0.241} + \underset{(2.67)}{0.166} \ln y_t^{DC} \underset{(-3.29)}{-0.372} \ln sf_t$$

$$\underset{(-1.20)}{-0.226} \ln m_t + \underset{(3.29)}{0.372} \ln N_t + \underset{(9.12)}{0.937} \ln (P^{WF}/P^{CG})_{t-1}$$

$$\underset{(-2.67)}{-0.125} \quad DU82 + \underset{(2.12)}{0.117} \quad DU83 \qquad (5.10b)$$

OLS $n=23$ $\bar{R}^2=0.95$ SEE$=0.035$ DW$=2.00$

LL$=48.4$ Z1$=0.36(1)$ Z2$=0.06(1)$ Z3$=1.54(4,16)$

Z4$=2.09(2,14)$ Z5$=2.92(6,3)$ Z6$=1.41(1,15)$

All coefficients bear the expected signs and are significant at the 5 per cent level except the constant and (m), the subsidy factor. To maintain consistency in the overall macromodel, this latter variable was not constrained to zero. Z6 is the F test for the restriction of homogeneity in degree one of demand with respect to income. In (5.10c) the model was re-estimated over the shorter sample period 1961–79. The value of the coefficients changed little and the Chow test (Z3) does not allow rejection of parameter stability. However, it was found that the results regarding parameter stability were somewhat sensitive to the choice of sub-sample period. The Goldfeld–Quandt F test (Z5) is well below the critical 5 per cent level of 6.09, not allowing us to reject the hypothesis of homoscedasticity.

In order to examine the possibility of simultaneous equation bias due to bi-directional causality between relative food prices on the one hand, and real disposable income and the unit subsidy factor (m) on the other, the model was re-estimated using instruments for (y^{DC}) and (m).[22] This result is presented as equation (5.10d). The parameters of the IV estimate do not differ greatly from those obtained using OLS. The hypothesis of residual orthogonality is further supported by the F statistic for the Wu–Hausman test (Z4). We conclude that simultaneous equation bias is not a sufficiently serious problem to invalidate the use of an OLS estimation.

From the estimated coefficients of equation (5.10b) it is possible to solve

Table 5.2. *Estimated food price equations – dependent variable, relative wholesale price of food* ($\ln(P^{WF}/P^{CG})$)

	5.10a OLS (1961–83)	5.10b OLS (1961–83)	5.10c OLS (1961–79)	5.10d IV (1961–83)
Variables[a,b]				
Constant	0.072	−0.241	−0.187	−0.194
	(0.213)	(−1.35)	(−0.85)	(−0.68)
$\ln y_t^{DC}$	0.185	0.166	0.149	0.159
	(2.11)	(2.67)	(2.28)	(1.98)
$\ln y_{t-1}^{DC}$	0.0004	—	—	—
	(1.06)			
$\ln sf_t$	−0.196	−0.372	−0.356	−0.361
	(−1.22)	(−3.29)	(−3.46)	(−2.77)
$\ln sf_{t-1}$	0.043	—	—	—
	(0.389)			
$\ln m_t$	−0.665	−0.226	−0.236	−0.306
	(−1.89)	(−1.20)	(−0.95)	(−1.14)
$\ln N_t$	−0.679	0.372	0.356	0.364
	(−1.07)	(3.29)	(3.46)	(3.33)
$\ln(P^{WF}/P^{CG})_{t-1}$	0.678	0.937	0.984	0.91
	(3.05)	(9.12)	(5.36)	(9.86)
*DU*82	−0.042	−0.125	—	−0.138
	(−0.63)	(−2.67)		(−1.95)
*DU*83	0.169	0.117	—	0.123
	(2.66)	(2.12)		(3.05)
Statistics[c]				
$\bar{R}^2$	0.96	0.95	0.82	0.94
SEE	0.035	0.035	0.358	0.043
DW	1.98	2.00	1.81	2.09
Z1	0.94	0.36	0.32	0.97
Z2	0.27	0.06	2.60	0.18

Notes: [a] Figures in brackets under the coefficient estimates are t ratios.
[b] Variables are defined as:

P^{WF} – index (1970 = 100) of the wholesale price of food,
P^{CG} – index (1970 = 100) of consumer prices,
y^{DC} – disposable income of the private sector in billions of 1970 cruzeiros,
N – index (1970 = 1) of average annual population,
sf – food supply in billions of 1970 cruzeiros,
m – one minus an index (1970 = 0) of the food consumption subsidy rate,
$DU82$ – a dummy variable with value of unity in 1982 and zero in other years, and
$DU83$ – a dummy variable with value of unity in 1983 and zero in other years.

[c] $\bar{R}^2$ is the multiple correlation coefficient, SEE the standard error of the regression, DW the Durbin–Watson test statistic and Z1 and Z2 the χ^2 statistics, each with one degree of freedom, for the log likelihood ratio test for first- and second-order serial correlation in the error term.

for the parameters of the structural model. Doing this we obtain estimates for the proportional speed of price adjustment (δ) of 0.4 and for price and income elasticities of demand for food of -0.61 and 0.45 respectively. As we would anticipate, demand for food is found to be both price and income inelastic. The adjustment speed appears rather low.

An indirect indication of the appropriateness of a disequilibrium, as opposed to an equilibrium model, is provided by the significance and high value of the lagged price variable in equation (5.10b). A price dependent, derived demand function from a model that assumes continuous market clearing includes the same variables as the latter equation, excluding lagged price. The structural coefficients of that model, and therefore the interpretation of the estimated parameters, are of course different. Nonetheless, when equation (5.10b) was re-estimated with the lagged dependent variable constrained to zero, there was clear evidence of misspecification due to serial correlation in the errors and the fit of the equation also deteriorated markedly.

In order to illustrate the significance of the parameter values for adjustment in the face of disequilibrium, it is useful to consider a simple arithmetic example. Imagine a 10 per cent rise in real income. Ignoring secondary effects upon prices due to a wage-price spiral, this leads in the first period to a 4.5 per cent rise in demand for food and a 1.8 per cent rise in both wholesale and retail relative prices. This in turn reduces demand by 1.1 per cent. In fact, because the overall consumer price level will move up slightly, the actual change in relative prices and the fall in demand will be marginally less. In the second period, we can expect a rise in food production of just under 0.5 per cent (average price elasticity of supply of 0.26) and a further round of relative price increases.[23] The simple example given here shows that, even ignoring wage-price spiral effects, the estimated parameters of the model imply a slow adjustment of prices to disequilibria. This is attested to in a more comprehensive way by the simulation exercises of chapters 8 and 9.

5.7 Conclusion

In this chapter we set out to examine the nature of the market for food in Brazil. To date no work of a similar nature has appeared in the literature. In setting out the analytical model, care was taken to incorporate, to the extent possible, salient features of the institutional setting peculiar to Brazil. However, given the aggregate nature of the analysis, many simplifying assumptions were made. In the empirical part of the chapter, the quality of the analysis undertaken was constrained by inadequacies in the data that led to the use of some rather problematic proxy variables, especially in the cases of production and subsidies. Nonetheless, despite these problems, the results do help to clarify the process of price and output determination in a key segment of the agricultural market. They point to the applicability of a modified competitive market model to explain food prices and output and also highlight how the combination of slow price adjustment with price inelastic demand and supply for food means that any disequilibrium is not easily or quickly reversed.

6 Other price relationships

6.1 The cruzeiro/U.S. dollar exchange rate

In August 1968, the Brazilian authorities introduced a system of small and frequent currency devaluations, a system often referred to as a 'crawling peg'. The main objective was to reduce the speculative capital flows and consequent extreme fluctuations in the foreign component of high-powered money that the previous system of large and infrequent parity changes had encouraged. The principle behind the new system was to maintain approximate short-run purchasing power parity (PPP) between the cruzeiro and the currencies of Brazil's major trading partners.[1] The benchmark used to guide decisions regarding the frequency and magnitude of 'mini-devaluations' was the cruzeiro/U.S. dollar parity, adjusted for the inflation differentials between the two countries. Nevertheless, parity changes were in no way automatic or fully predictable. The size and frequency of devaluations remained a discretionary decision arrived at after taking into account a series of factors besides movements in the adjusted, or real, cruzeiro/U.S. dollar rate. The most important of these additional factors appear to have been fluctuations in the U.S. dollar relative to other major currencies, inflation differentials between major OECD countries, changes in Brazil's external terms of trade and balance of payments performance.

The average annual real cruzeiro/U.S. dollar exchange rate (e) can be defined as

$$e_t = (P^{WUS*}/P^{WG})_t \cdot E_t \tag{6.1}$$

where P^{WUS*} is the U.S. wholesale price index (1970 = 100),
P^{WG} is the Brazilian wholesale price index – internal supply (1970 = 100), and
E is the average nominal cruzeiro/U.S. dollar exchange rate.

A rise in (e) denotes a real devaluation of the cruzeiro.[2] Although the crawling peg was not introduced officially until mid 1968, from 1967 onwards, policy-makers had begun to adjust the exchange rate so as to maintain, on average, a reasonably constant real rate (see chapter 2, figure 2.10).

Through 1978, deviations from strict purchasing power parity between the cruzeiro and the U.S. dollar were contained within a fairly narrow range. Starting in 1979, however, this changed as the authorities varied the operation of the crawling peg and made occasional use of large once and for all parity changes that came to be known, as 'maxi-devaluations'. The first maxi-devaluation occurred in December 1979 in an attempt to improve the balance of payments situation in the face of a growing disequilibrium aggravated by the second oil shock. In a reversal of previous policy, in 1980 the authorities announced a depreciation target for the exchange rate of 40 per cent, aimed at combating accelerating inflation by attempting to influence inflationary expectations. In the event, actual devaluation over 1980 was 54 per cent but still well below domestic inflation of 109 per cent. This led to a major appreciation of the real exchange rate which was only partially reversed in 1981 and 1982. A second maxi-devaluation occurred in February 1983, followed by a further gradual real devaluation in 1984. The trend depreciation in the real cruzeiro/U.S. dollar exchange rate that occurred from late 1978 through to 1984 coincided with the appreciation of the U.S. dollar against other major currencies.[3]

6.1.1 *A model of the exchange rate*

Very little detailed empirical work has been done on the determinants of the cruzeiro/U.S. dollar exchange rate. Customarily, in econometric models it is treated as an exogenous policy variable in the period preceding the introduction of the crawling peg and its rate of change is linked to domestic and foreign inflation in the post-1966 period. In the latter case, the percentage rate of change of the exchange rate has been explained as a function of the rates of change of domestic and U.S. wholesale price inflation.[4] The usual approaches to modelling free floating exchange rates in the industrialised world are of little relevance in the Brazilian context, given the absence of a free market in foreign exchange and the dominance of the institutionalised crawling peg system. For the purposes of this study a simple model is adequate which captures the link between exchange rate changes and the inflation differentials while accounting for maxi-devaluations by the use of dummy variables.[5]

To test the hypothesis that changes in the exchange rate were a function primarily of an attempt to maintain purchasing power parity *vis-à-vis* the

U.S. dollar, we proceeded as follows. Re-arranging equation (6.1) and taking logs gives a definition for the nominal exchange rate (E)

$$\ln E_t = \ln P_t^{WG} - \ln P_t^{WUS*} + \ln e_t \tag{6.2}$$

or, taking first differences,

$$\Delta \ln E_t = \Delta \ln P_t^{WG} - \Delta \ln P_t^{WUS*} + \Delta \ln e_t \tag{6.3}$$

If PPP holds, (e) is a constant. With (E_t) redefined as an index with base 1970 = 1, PPP implies a constant value of one for (e_t). To derive a testable model from equation (6.3), we specify the stochastic relationship[6]

$$\Delta \ln E_t = \eta_0 + \eta_1 \Delta \ln P_t^{WG} + \eta_2 \Delta \ln P_t^{WUS*} + \eta_3 DU81 + \eta_4 DU83 + \eta_5 \Delta \ln E_{t-1} + \eta_6 \Delta \ln P_{t-1}^{WG} + \eta_7 \Delta \ln P_{t-1}^{WUS*} + u_t \tag{6.4}$$

$$\eta_1 + \eta_6 > 0 \qquad \eta_2 + \eta_7 < 0$$

where ($DU81$) and ($DU83$) are dummy variables with value of unity in 1981 and 1983 respectively and zero in other years, used to account for the large variations that occurred in those years in the rate of change of the real exchange parity as a result of the maxi-devaluations. Lagged values of the dependent and independent variables are included to allow for the possibility of adjustment lags between changes in inflation rates and in the rate of devaluation that might help to explain deviations from PPP. If, after allowing for the impact of the maxi-devaluations, strict PPP holds then

$$\eta_0 = \eta_6 = \eta_7 = 0 \qquad \eta_1 = 1 \qquad \eta_2 = -1.$$

6.1.2 *Model estimates*

A summary of the OLS estimation results for the maintained hypothesis of equation (6.4) are presented in table 6.1 as equation (6.4a). All the lagged variables as well as the constant are insignificant and a test down procedure yielded the more parsimonius specification of equation (6.4b). A joint F test (Z3) did not allow rejection of the restrictions $\eta_1 = 1$ and $\eta_2 = -1$, the statistic having the value 1.34 (2,14). This indicates that we cannot reject the proposition that the domestic and U.S. wholesale inflation rates were fully taken into account in deciding upon the rate of exchange devaluation. In other ways the estimation results for equation (6.4b) are acceptable. There is no evidence of serial correlation in the error terms that might point to an omitted variables problem. Re-estimating with a shorter sample period, 1967–79, excluding the years in which the most pronounced alterations occurred in the real exchange rate, gave equation (6.4c) of table 6.1. There is no visual evidence of significant parameter instability and the Chow test did

Table 6.1. *Estimated exchange rate equations – dependent variable, rate of change of the average nominal cruzeiro/U.S. dollar exchange rate* ($\Delta \ln E$)

	(6.4a) OLS (1967–84)	(6.4b) OLS (1967–84)	(6.4c) OLS (1967–79)	(6.4d) IV (1967–84)	(6.4e) OLS (1967–84)
Variables[a,b]					
Constant	−0.014	—	—	—	—
	(−0.47)				
$\Delta \ln P_t^{WG}$	1.039	0.994	1.048	0.988	1.0
	(6.18)	(41.85)	(8.46)	(15.0)	
$\Delta \ln P_t^{WUS*}$	−0.594	−0.741	−0.710	−0.57	−1.0
	(−1.77)	(−5.46)	(−3.10)	(−1.57)	
*DU*81	−0.116	−0.118	—	−0.236	−0.100
	(−2.24)	(−3.24)		(−2.31)	(−2.71)
*DU*83	0.198	0.209	—	0.342	0.206
	(3.12)	(5.18)		(3.22)	(5.58)
$\Delta \ln E_{t-1}$	−0.031	—	—	—	—
	(−0.16)				
$\Delta \ln P_{t-1}^{WG}$	0.004	—	—	—	—
	(0.02)				
$\Delta \ln P_{t-1}^{WUS*}$	−0.126	—	—	—	—
	(−0.34)				
Statistics[c]					
$\bar{R}^2$	0.98	0.99	0.85	0.93	0.99
SEE	0.038	0.034	0.037	0.092	0.037
DW	1.80	1.68	1.83	1.84	1.54
Z1	0.02	0.12	0.06	0.84	0.44
Z2	1.34	0.36	0.92	0.40	2.00
Z3	—	1.34 (2,14)	1.26 (2,11)	—	2.58 (2,14)

Notes: [a] Figures in brackets under coefficient estimates are *t* ratios.
[b] Variables are defined as follows:

P^{WG} – index (1970 = 100) of wholesale prices – internal supply,
P^{WUS*} – index (1970 = 100) of U.S. wholesale prices,
*DU*81 – a dummy variable with value of unity in 1981 and zero elsewhere, and
*DU*83 – a dummy variable with value of unity in 1983 and zero elsewhere.

[c] $\bar{R}^2$ is the multiple correlation coefficient, SEE the standard error of the regression, DW the Durbin–Watson test statistic, Z1 and Z2 the χ^2 statistics (each with one degree of freedom) for the log likelihood ratio tests for first- and second-order serial correlation in the error term and, Z3 is the *F* ratio statistic for the null hypothesis that the coefficients of the current domestic and U.S. inflation rates are jointly equal to 1 and −1 respectively.

not allow rejection of the null hypothesis. The relevant F ratio was equal to 0.64(5,10).

The exchange rate is a determinant of industrial prices and therefore also of overall wholesale prices (P^{WG}). For this reason (E_t) and (P_t^{WG}) are jointly determined and we cannot discount the possibility of simultaneous equation bias in an OLS estimate of equation (6.4b). Consequently, this equation was re-estimated using an instrumental variables estimator. Results are presented as equation (6.4d) in table 6.1. As an instrument for (P_t^{WG}) we used the predictor from an equation explaining this variable by its own lagged values and other pre-determined variables from the overall macromodel.[7] The value of the estimated coefficient on the domestic inflation term is virtually unchanged in the IV as compared with the OLS estimate. The coefficient on foreign inflation is lower but insignificant in the IV case. A Wu-Hausman test using equation (6.4b) yielded a t test statistic of $-0.44(13)$ that did not allow us to reject the null hypothesis of orthogonality of the residuals. As simultaneous equation bias does not appear to be serious we continue to make use of the OLS estimates. The Goldfeld-Quandt test for the stability of the equation variance gave an F ratio of 1.3(5,7), not allowing rejection of the null hypothesis.

The restriction of complete adjustment for changes in domestic and foreign inflation is imposed in equation (6.4e). The F test for the restriction appears in table 6.1 as (Z3). The standard error of the regression is only marginally higher than in equation (6.4b) but still rather large relative to an outside yardstick at over 7 per cent of the mean value of the dependent variable. Nonetheless, given the simplicity of the model, this is judged to be acceptable. In other respects the results are quite adequate. It is equation (6.4e) that is used in the macromodel of chapter 7.

6.1.3 *Conclusion*

The model estimated is a very simple one that emphasises the institutional arrangements governing exchange rate adjustments. It points to the importance of the *de facto* indexation of the exchange rate, based on the adherence to a PPP rule *vis-à-vis* the U.S. currency. This policy played an important role in the process of overall price formation and inflation by ensuring that changes in dollar import prices were, in general, rapidly and fully reflected in their cruzeiro counterparts. Ideally, one would wish to find an economic explanation for the few major changes in the real exchange rate that did occur over the period. For reasons presented earlier, this could not be done here.

6.2 Aggregate price indices

In order to link together the various price series that appear in the model, either as endogenous or exogenous variables, certain composite price indices are required. There is a role in the model for three such indices: the consumer price index (also referred to as the cost of living index), the wholesale price index (domestic supply) and the general price index (domestic supply). The latter brings together consumer and wholesale prices.

6.2.1 *The consumer price index*

The Rio de Janeiro consumer price index is used in this model as a proxy for a national index, as no such series existed prior to 1980. The index is calculated using a modified Laspeyres formula in which three year moving average weights are employed. Seven different component indices make up the composite index (see definition in appendix 4(A4.2)). One of these, consumer food prices, accounted on average over the sample period for between 40 per cent and 50 per cent of total weighting. It is outside the scope of this study to attempt to model each of the six remaining non-food component indices. To do so in a meaningful way would involve a detailed study of various service sector markets and of government pricing policies. However, to have included these six indices in the model as exogenous variables would have been uninformative and would have made nonsense of counter-factual simulations by ignoring all links between these and other consumer and wholesale prices. These considerations precluded the use in the model of a purely definitional equation for the consumer price index. Instead, we chose to approximate the actual index by a stochastic relationship based on the hypothesis that the non-food components of the composite index can be adequately proxied by current and lagged values of wholesale manufactured prices and consumer food prices. As just over half the weighting in the actual index applies to food or manufactured articles, this assumes that the prices of services and housing follow manufacturing prices or, less probably, food prices, either with or without a lag.

Given the very strong common trend in Brazilian price data, problems of multicollinearity and heteroscedasticity preclude acceptable estimates being carried out using a linear model in levels. A log-linear model is not compatible with the actual index because of the implied constant elasticity specification. Consequently we opted for a percentage rate of change specification. Allowing for a fairly general dynamic structure, the maintained hypothesis was

$$\dot{P}_t^{CG} = \omega_0 + \omega_1 \dot{P}_t^{CF} + \omega_2 \dot{P}_t^{WI} + \omega_3 \dot{P}_{t-1}^{CF} + \omega_4 \dot{P}_{t-1}^{WI} + \omega_5 \dot{P}_{t-1}^{CG} + u_t \tag{6.5}$$

where P^{CG} is the composite Rio de Janeiro consumer price index, P^{CF} is the Rio de Janeiro consumer food price index, and P^{WI} is the wholesale manufacturing price index.

A percentage rate of change is denoted by a dot over the variable.

6.2.2 *Model estimates*

OLS estimation results for the maintained hypothesis are reported in table 6.2, equation (6.5a). The full available sample period, 1960–84, is used for estimation. The maintained hypothesis was re-estimated applying successive F tests in order to eliminate redundant variables. Results for a more parsimonious specification appear as (6.5b) of table 6.2. All lagged terms, save lagged manufacturing price, have their coefficients constrained to zero along with the constant. A significant value for the constant would imply that the consumer price series varied independently of what are hypothesised to be its component parts. The restriction $(\omega_1 + \omega_2 + \omega_4 = 1)$, or homogeneity in degree one of the RHS terms with respect to consumer price inflation, was initially tested for and, since accepted by the data, subsequently imposed. The F test for this restriction, (Z3) in equation 6.5b), does not allow rejection of the null hypothesis. The finding of homogeneity suggests that the composite index is exhausted by current consumer food price and by current and lagged wholesale manufacturing price. However, there is evidence of first-order autocorrelation that may be an indication of an omitted variable problem. However, as this hypothesis could not be tested, we re-estimated using a first-order Cochrane-Orcutt estimator. These results are presented as equation (6.5c).

The coefficient on the food price variable in (6.5c) is very close in value (0.40) to the actual average weight of food in the consumer price index. The manufacturing price terms appear, therefore, adequately to proxy the prices of manufactured consumer goods, housing and various services. The goodness of fit of (6.5c), as measured by the SEE is reasonable, at about 4 per cent of the mean value of the dependent variable. In other respects the model appears adequate. Results from re-estimates over the shorter sample period 1967–84 are presented as equation (6.5d). On visual inspection, the coefficients can be seen not to change substantially. A Chow test yielded an F ratio of 1.3(7,14); not permitting rejection of the null hypothesis of stability.

Table 6.2. *Estimated consumer price relationships – dependent variable, the percentage rate of change of the consumer price index* ($\dot{P}^{CG}$)

	(6.5a) OLS (1960–84)	(6.5b) OLS (1960–84)	(6.5c) CO (1) (1960–84)	(6.5d) CO (1) (1967–84)
Variables[a,b]				
Constant	0.007	—	—	—
	(0.71)			
$\dot{P}^{CF}_{t}$	0.411	0.390	0.400	0.437
	(6.73)	(7.75)	(10.83)	(9.17)
$\dot{P}^{WI}_{t}$	0.318	0.331	0.338	0.282
	(4.46)	(6.20)	(8.81)	(5.40)
$\dot{P}^{CF}_{t-1}$	−0.021	—	—	—
	(−0.23)			
$\dot{P}^{WI}_{t-1}$	0.149	0.279	0.262	0.281
	(1.54)	(13.16)	(11.89)	(12.01)
$\dot{P}^{CG}_{t-1}$	0.136	—	—	—
	(1.05)			
Statistics[c]				
$\bar{R}^2$	0.99	0.99	0.99	0.99
SEE	0.026	0.026	0.023	0.021
DW	1.32	1.39	1.81	1.67
Z1	3.56	4.33	—	—
Z2	0.22	0.14	—	—
Z3	—	0.003 (1,22)	—	—

Notes: [a] Figures in brackets under the coefficient estimates are t ratios.

[b] Variables are defined as follows:

P^{CF} – index (1970 = 100) of Rio de Janeiro consumer food prices, and

P^{WI} – index (1970 = 100) of wholesale manufacturing prices.

[c] $\bar{R}^2$ is the multiple correlation coefficient, SEE the standard error of the regression, DW the Durbin–Watson test statistic, Z1 and Z2 the χ^2 statistics (each with one degree of freedom) for the log likelihood ratio tests for first- and second-order serial correlation in the error term, Z3 is the F ratio test statistic for the null hypothesis of homogeneity in degree one of consumer price inflation with respect to the RHS variables.

6.2.3 *The wholesale price index*

This is a modified Laspeyres index covering prices of a wide range of goods sold in the domestic market. Prices of export goods are excluded. Two component indices are wholesale food prices (P^{WF}) and raw material prices (P^{WR}), both endogenous to the model. The remaining component prices refer to manufactured goods. Together, these can be closely approximated by the wholesale manufacturing price index (P^{WI}), which is also endogenous to the model.[8] The weighting in the overall wholesale price index changed over time as weights were based on moving averages. On average however, over the period 1960–84, the index can be represented by the following formula

$$P_t^{WG} = 0.33P_t^{WF} + 0.15P_t^{WR} + 0.52P_t^{WI} \tag{6.6}$$

6.2.4 *The general price index – domestic supply*

This is a fixed weight index constructed from the Rio de Janeiro consumer price index (P^{CG}), the wholesale price index (domestic supply) (P^{WG}) and the Rio de Janeiro construction cost index (P^{H}). The index is defined by

$$P_t^{G} = 0.3P_t^{CG} + 0.6P_t^{WG} + 0.1P_t^{H} \tag{6.7}$$

PART III

THE INFLATIONARY PROCESS

7 A macroeconomic model for Brazil

7.1 Introduction

In the preceding chapters we investigated the determinants of certain important prices in the Brazilian economy. The focus was upon price formation in specific markets or sectors of the economy. Output, with the exception of food, was treated as exogenous along with demand and all financial variables. We know however that real aggregates and prices are not independent of one another. Not only do changes in demand feed back into prices but also alterations in price levels and inflation may set in motion processes that lead to changes in stocks of financial assets, interest rates and demand, thereby occasioning further price changes. In order to analyse these feedbacks and, more generally, to examine the process of continuous inflation, as distinct from price formation, it is necessary to relax the assumptions of exogenous output and finance, bringing together the individual price equations within the framework of a more general macromodel.

The macromodel proposed here is a relatively simple one designed for the study of a particular set of issues, namely inflationary pressures and propagation mechanisms. As such, certain aggregates and processes are modelled in more detail than is customary in small macroeconometric systems while, in other cases, variables normally endogenised are here treated as exogenous. Three main simplifications made relate to: (1) the financial sector, (2) current and real national accounts aggregates, (3) factor markets. While principal monetary flows between the private, governmental and overseas sectors are modelled explicitly, we do not examine the monetary and financial markets in which the amounts and prices of financial assets are determined. The banking system and credit multiplier are abstracted from, the only monetary asset being high-powered money. Examination of previous work on Brazil, suggests that interest rates are not easily modelled in a meaningful way, nor do they play an important role in the determination of private expenditure. Therefore we treat them as exogenously determined and include no asset demand functions in the model. Another important simplification is the lack of current value national accounts aggregates. Rather than complicate the system through the introduction of implicit national accounts deflators alongside the many consumer and wholesale price indices used, in the few cases where aggregates must be expressed in nominal terms, we simply reflate the constant value national accounts series using fixed weight price indices from the wage and price sector of the model. In one essential case, the discrepancy between the fixed base index and the current base implicit deflator is accounted for through the use of an exogenous adjustment factor. The model is also incomplete in that it does not include an explicit modelling of factor markets.

None of the simplifications made radically impair the model's usefulness in studying the issues at hand. There exist other models of the Brazilian economy that examine in some depth issues and processes given scant treatment here, particularly foreign trade, federal government fiscal affairs and the financial system.[1]

It was beyond the scope of the study to undertake from scratch the specification and estimation of a real sector model of the Brazilian economy, even in a simple form. Given constraints on time and space, we drew instead on existing Brazilian econometric modelling work in choosing specifications for the stochastic demand equations and to a more limited extent in defining the overall structure of the model. It proved impossible, however, simply to borrow equations from other sources and incorporate these directly into the model. Poor data documentation in many of the original studies made it difficult to identify the precise data sets used to estimate the models. In some cases unpublished and otherwise not readily available series were used. Moreover, sample data employed in the estimations did not extend sufficiently far into the present to cover the final years of the period used in the present simulation exercises; namely 1966–83. Neither were forecasts from the original models sufficiently accurate to enable us to use the original model estimates. Therefore, we chose from the literature model specifications for most of the required variables but re-estimated these using data from as close to the original sources as possible and extended the sample period up to 1983. In some cases the re-estimates yielded results quite close to those reported in the original studies. In others, however, results were sufficiently different that it proved necessary to change somewhat the original specifications. Summary estimation results and sources for the original models are given in the notes, at relevant points during the exposition of the complete model below.

The method used to obtain the stochastic equations for the real sector left something to be desired in that it fell half way between a true attempt at modelling properly the relevant relationships and outright borrowing of existing models. Some of the resultant models, as well as some of the original ones, clearly exhibit statistical deficiencies or dubious economic properties. However, it was felt that the method did provide an acceptable solution given the prevailing constraints.

To create a small but workable model capable of elucidating the nature of the inflationary process, it was determined that six stochastic relationships, in addition to those price, inflation and food production equations estimated previously, were required along with numerous new definitional statements. For five of these six, the equations used were based closely on the existing literature and explained:

(a) private investment in fixed capital,
(b) goods exports,
(c) goods imports excluding wheat and petroleum,
(d) petroleum product imports, and
(e) non-food value added.

In the case of the sixth stochastic equation – the consumption function – a review of the Brazilian literature showed the existing econometric estimates to be inadequate on several counts. We are not aware of any specialised econometric analyses of the Brazilian consumption function and, where estimates have been made, the results are often suspect. In some cases unacceptably short samples having been used for estimation and models are often clearly misspecified. Deficiencies in the original specification searches that led to the omission or misspecification of key variables appear to be the cause. Specifically, attempts to identify wealth effects have at best been limited to rudimentary tests for an explanatory role for real money balances. Serious data deficiencies impair any attempt to estimate consumption functions in the Brazilian context but it was felt that, given the pivotal role of the consumption function in linking holdings of private financial assets with aggregate demand and inflation, the existing work could be improved upon. We therefore specified and estimated a consumption function, summary estimation results and further details of which are reported when presenting this equation in section 7.2.2 below.

7.2 The model

A complete model of the Brazilian economy is set out below. Numerous identities, a series of aggregate demand equations and an equation to explain non-food value added are combined with the price equations and food supply relation developed in previous chapters. Where an equation has been discussed previously, the rationale for it is not restated here.

Instead, the reader is referred back to the relevant chapter. All variables are defined and sources given in appendix 4. Salient characteristics of the model are discussed further in section 7.3 which also includes a comparison with other models of Brazil's economy. Section 7.4 is devoted to a short conclusion.

7.2.1 *National income and output*

Identity for real GDP (expenditure measure) at market price

GDP comprises private expenditure on consumption (c), gross investment in fixed capital (i^{F}) and stock building (i^{S}), expenditure by general government on goods, services and fixed capital investment (g) as well as exports (x) minus imports (im), all valued in constant 1970 cruzeiros. Stock building, along with government consumption and investment expenditure are treated as exogenous

$$y_t = c_t + i_t^{\mathrm{F}} + i_t^{\mathrm{S}} + g_t + x_t - im_t \tag{7.1}$$

Identity for GDP (production measure) at market price and factor cost

A second measure of GDP is required in order to maintain consistency given the supply constraint in agriculture. If GDP is built up only from the expenditure side, the real income loss from an exogenously given reduction in food output cannot be accounted for properly. Since the Brazilian national accounts include no income measure of GDP, we follow the procedure used in other models of Brazil's economy in building up GDP from the perspective of production. GDP at factor cost ($\hat{y}^{\mathrm{FC}}$) is defined as the sum of the value added of the food (q^{AF}) and non-food (q^{NF}) sectors. To convert this measure of GDP back into market prices ($\hat{y}$) we must add the factor cost adjustment ($t_t^{\mathrm{I}} - su_t$). This is explained below

$$\hat{y}_t^{\mathrm{FC}} = q_t^{\mathrm{AF}} + q_t^{\mathrm{NF}} \tag{7.2}$$

$$\hat{y}_t = q_t^{\mathrm{AF}} + q_t^{\mathrm{NF}} + t_t^{\mathrm{I}} - su_t \tag{7.3}$$

Factor cost adjustment

Market price measures of national accounts aggregates are equal to factor cost measurements plus indirect taxes net of subsidies. In the constant price accounts, indirect tax and subsidies are valued at constant base year rates. To obtain these real series, we adopt the assumption that both variables can be represented as functions of GDP. From the current price national accounts data for the base year, 1970, we derive the effective rates of indirect taxation and subsidisation and use these combined with the real GDP (expenditure) series at market prices to generate the required data

$$t_t^I = 0.167 y_t \tag{7.4}$$

$$su_t = 0.008 y_t \tag{7.5}$$

Real national income (expenditure measure) at market price

This is a measure of real national purchasing power. For a country susceptible to pronounced changes in its terms of trade, real GNP alone is an inadequate proxy for real national income. Real national income equals real GNP – itself equal to real GDP (y) plus real net factor income from abroad (nre) – adjusted for the terms of trade effect (tg). The latter variable is endogenous to the model and explained below. Real net factor income from abroad is held exogenous and the terms of trade effect is explained further below

$$nin_t = y_t + nre_t + tg_t \tag{7.6}$$

Statistical discrepancy between two measures of GDP

Due to accounting errors in the measurement of variables as well as to some inevitable misspecification of the linkages between supply and demand and of the dynamic adjustment mechanisms that operate to equate these, some means is required to bring GDP, measured on the production side, in line with GDP as measured by final expenditures. Rather than force the accounting identity we define a statistical discrepancy. This is equal to real GDP (expenditure measure) minus real GDP (production measure), both at market price

$$sd_t = y_t - \hat{y}_t \tag{7.7}$$

7.2.2 *Private sector income, domestic financial wealth and domestic expenditure*

Real private disposable income

This is defined as real national income at factor cost – equal to GDP (production measure) at factor cost ($\hat{y}^{FC}$) plus net factor income from abroad (nre), adjusted for the terms of trade effect (tg) – plus the real value of interest payments on the government debt in private hands ($0.07 \cdot B_{t-1}/P_t^{CG}$) and the real value of non-interest transfers (tr^{NI}), minus direct taxes (t^D). Non-interest transfers are treated as exogenous while interest payments and taxes are explained further below. Capital gains or losses on financial assets, which are of decisive importance in a high inflation economy, do not enter this equation as it seems hardly sensible in a high inflation economy to view these as components of the income stream. Rather, net capital gains are explicitly modelled in the consumption function as additions to, or subtractions from, real wealth

$$y_t^D = \hat{y}_t^{FC} + nre_t + tg_t + 0.07 \cdot B_{t-1}/P_t^{CG} + tr_t^{NI} - t_t^D \tag{7.8}$$

Private disposable income deflated by the consumer price index

In the relative wholesale food price equation, the income variable used is nominal disposable income of the private sector deflated by the consumer price index – a fixed base index. Real private disposable income as defined above was obtained by deflating the nominal aggregate by the implicit national accounts deflator for GDP – a current base, or Paasche index. Since neither nominal disposable income nor the national accounts deflator for GDP are identified as endogenous variables in the model, the two different measures of real disposable income are linked here simply by using the ratio of the implicit deflator to the consumer price index. This ratio (RES) is treated as exogenous

$$y_t^{DC} = y_t^D \cdot RES_t \tag{7.9}$$

Real consumption

The model proposed is based on the relation first estimated by Ando and Modigliani (1963) and now widely used in the literature on industrialised economies. Real consumption depends upon:

(a) real disposable income of the private sector (y^D), used as a proxy for personal sector disposable income for which no data are available,[2]
(b) the stock of privately held financial assets (as a proxy for personal sector wealth) at the start of the period (WE_{t-1}), adjusted for inflation loss on money fixed assets ($\dot{P}_t^{CG} \cdot H_{t-1}$) and for capital gains (indexation of principal) on government bonds $[(\dot{P}_t^G - 0.7) \cdot B_{t-1}]$ – all deflated by the current consumer price ($\dot{P}_t^{CG}$) (see explanation below),
(c) lagged consumption, and
(d) a dummy variable ($DU75$) with value one in 1975 and zero elsewhere used to account for the sharp disruption in patterns of savings and consumption that occurred in the wake of the first oil shock.

Because population growth in developing countries tends to be rapid, it is necessary to take account explicitly of the upward shift in consumption over time due to population expansion. The easiest means to do this is to impose the restriction of homogeneity in degree one of consumption with respect to population by deflating both sides of the relation. Therefore, the model used here is estimated in *per capita* terms. Population (N) is exogenous. Following Pesaran and Evans (1984), the opening stock of financial assets is deflated by the current rather than the lagged price to avoid misspecification when prices change and, especially, overprediction of consumption when prices rise rapidly. High-powered money is used in the expression for inflation loss as a proxy for personal sector monetary assets. The inclusion of a lagged dependent variable can be interpreted as capturing habit persistence in consumption patterns but may also reflect the influence of wealth, which is only imperfectly captured by the variable (WE).[3] The impact upon consumption of capital gains and losses is restricted equal to the impact of the opening stock of assets themselves. Other less restrictive specifications were experimented with but were rejected by the data[4]

$$\begin{aligned}(c/N)_t = & -3.92 + 0.43\,(y^{D}/N)_t \\ & + 0.18\{[WE_{t-1} + (\dot{P}_t^{G} - 0.7)\cdot B_{t-1} \\ & - (\dot{P}_t^{CG}\cdot H_{t-1})]/N\cdot \dot{P}_t^{CG}\} \\ & + 0.47\,(c/N)_{t-1} - 12.03DU75 \end{aligned} \qquad (7.10)$$

$$c_t = (c/N)_t \cdot N_t \qquad (7.11)$$

Real gross private investment in fixed capital

The determinants of investment is an area in which little econometric work has been done in the Brazilian context. It was not possible to fill this lacuna here despite the fact that a number of models based on the simple and flexible accelerator principles were experimented with without great success. A serious problem in this context is the lack of adequate estimates of the private sector capital stock. In the end we were obliged to use a rudimentary specification which is questionable on theoretical grounds due to the absence of both a conventional stock adjustment mechanism and of long-run homogeneity of degree one of investment with respect to income. Private investment depends upon real GDP (expenditure) (y) and the average real value of loans outstanding from the monetary authorities to the private sector during the current period (le^{PT}). The monetary authorities, including the Bank of Brazil, are a major supplier of the rationed credit that is available for investment purposes[5]

$$i_t^{F} = \exp\,(-0.53 + 0.66 \ln y_t + 0.29 \ln le_t^{PT}) \qquad (7.12)$$

The inclusion of a credit availability term among the explanatory variables and the absence of an interest rate variable conform to a common practice in Brazilian and other developing country models of investment. With no linkage between interest rates and investment, an important channel connecting the financial and real sectors of the economy in conventional models is here closed off. This reflects the reality of the Brazilian economy in which very little longer-term finance is available at any level of interest rates. The availability of credit, rather than its cost, is more likely to be a binding constraint on investment. The introduction into the model of the credit variable creates a new and potentially very important channel through which real and financial variables may interact.[6]

Nominal domestic financial wealth of the private sector

This equals the stock of high-powered money (H) along with federal, state and municipal securities (B) held in private portfolios. The latter two variables are both explained elsewhere in the model. No composite data are available on private or personal sector wealth and (WE) is only an imperfect proxy for total private financial wealth, particularly as it excludes foreign financial assets for which no data exist

$$WE_t = H_t + B_t \tag{7.13}$$

7.2.3 *General government*

Expenditure on goods, services and investment

These expenditures are treated as exogenous in real terms

$$g_t = c_t^{\mathrm{G}} + i_t^{\mathrm{G}} \tag{7.14}$$

Direct and indirect taxes

A number of simple estimated tax functions were experimented with which linked direct and indirect taxes to a variety of current and lagged measures of national income and expenditure. However, these functions, which assumed constant average tax rates, caused the model to perform very poorly in dynamic simulations. Consequently we opted instead to use definitional equations for both direct and indirect taxes in which rates were determined residually from actual data on tax and income or expenditure. These effective rates vary over time. Indirect tax equals the product of the indirect tax rate (δ^{I}) and GDP (expenditure) (y) reflated by the general price index (P^{G}). Direct tax equals the direct tax rate (δ^{D}) multiplied by GNP (expenditure) ($y + nre$), reflated by the general price index.

An important consequence of the approach adopted is that government tax revenues are completely protected against changes in the price level. This is a reasonable approximation to reality given that indexation of tax brackets prevailed

$$T_t^{\mathrm{I}} = \delta^{\mathrm{I}}(y \cdot P^{\mathrm{G}})_t \tag{7.15}$$

$$T_t^{\mathrm{D}} = \delta^{\mathrm{D}}[(y + nre) \cdot P^{\mathrm{G}}]_t \tag{7.16}$$

Food subsidies

Subsidies to consumption were widely employed in Brazil during the 1970s as an anti-inflation device, in conjunction with price controls. They were most widely applied to foodstuffs and petroleum products. The financing of these subsidies through the government budget influenced the determination of asset flows within the economy and therefore also potentially affected demand and inflation. In this model, food subsidies play an important role in linking consumer prices to market determined wholesale food prices. By contrast, subsidies to petroleum products have been abstracted from. The modelling of the financing of food subsidies is greatly complicated by the fact that no data are readily available on the breakdown of subsidies, as measured in the national accounts, into their component parts. The cost of food subsidies comprises many diverse elements including losses on regulatory stocks and on resale of food imports on government account as well as price support.

In the absence of actual data, we create an approximate food subsidy series by making the simplifying assumption that the evolution of food subsidies over time can be represented by the product of:

(a) an exponential time trend $[e^{(r \cdot t - t0)}]$ where (e) is now the base of natural logarithms and (t_0) represents the 1970 base year,

(b) the current rate of subsidisation, defined as the base year rate of subsidy (scaled to 1970=0) and equal to $(1-m_t)$,[7] and

(c) the wholesale value of current food supply $(sf \cdot P^{WF})$.

No data could be found on food subsidies in the base year 1970 therefore it was necessary to make an estimate based solely upon data for total subsidies combined with information on agricultural prices and subsidy policies in that year. On this basis food subsidies were estimated at CR$ 400 million or 3.0 per cent of the estimated value of total food supply.[8] Subsidies were estimated at CR$ 126 billion in 1980. Using the estimates for 1970 and 1980 combined with data on the price and quantity of output, it was possible to calculate the implied trend rate of growth of real subsidies (r) to be 0.13.

The food subsidy series constructed can only be thought of as a highly approximate representation of the probable time path of actual subsidies. Its validity rests upon the acceptance of two main hypotheses. First, that actual food subsidies were of the order of magnitude assumed and, secondly, that they were generated by a process such as that suggested here. Assuming acceptance of these hypotheses, by capturing the links between price differentials in retail and wholesale markets and total subsidies, the method employed serves the aim of helping to understand the major repercussions of changes in subsidy policy

$$SU_t^F = 1.03 - m_t \cdot (sf \cdot P^{WF})_t \cdot [e^{0.13 \cdot (t - t0)}] \qquad (7.17)$$

Interest and indexation on government securities

These comprise fixed interest payments and indexation of principal on government bonds as well as discounts on treasury bills. Only payments made to security holders outside the monetary authorities or government are of relevance. For simplicity, bills are treated here in the same way as bonds, i.e. as if they bore monetary correction and interest rather than being sold at a deep discount to face value.[9] The actual rate of indexation on the most important subset of total government securities, federal treasury bonds bearing monetary correction (ORTNs), averaged 93 per cent of general price inflation over the period 1965–83.[10] These bonds also bore a coupon of 6 per cent or 8 per cent depending on maturity.

We generate an approximate series for interest and indexation payments received by the private sector where, for all securities, average indexation equal to general price inflation less 7 per cent is assumed along with a coupon of 7 per cent. In other words, total real yield is assumed to equal zero; a reasonable approximation to reality. Were we to assume 100 per cent indexation of principal plus interest, the behaviour of the model would not be altered substantially

$$DS_t = \dot{P}_t^{G} \cdot B_{t-1} \tag{7.18}$$

Total value of government securities in private portfolios

The total end of period value of government securities in private hands (B_t) equals the stock of federal, state and municipal bonds and bills at $(t-1)$, (B_{t-1}), indexation paid on this stock in (t) $[(\dot{P}_t^{G} - 0.7) \cdot B_{t-1}]$, and the net increase during (t) of new debt held by the private sector $(nrb_t \cdot P_t^{G})$. The real value of the latter variable is found residually by inverting equation (7.19). The net increase in new debt held by the private sector is treated as exogenous in real terms so as to ensure that, when the system is shocked and the price level rises or falls relative to the base run, the ratio of bonds to high-powered money in private wealth does not change dramatically in real terms. In reality the ratio of bonds to high-powered money rose over time

$$B_t = [1 + (\dot{P}_t^{G} - 0.7)] \cdot B_{t-1} + (nrb \cdot P^{G})_t \tag{7.19}$$

Average loans outstanding to the overall private sector

A crude average of the total real stock of loans outstanding from the monetary authorities to the private sector during period (t) may be obtained using end period stocks in (t) and $(t-1)$

$$le_t^{PT} = (le_t^{PT*} + le_{t-1}^{PT*})/2 \tag{7.20}$$

Average loans outstanding to the agricultural sector
This variable is derived in the same way as the previous one

$$le_t^{PA} = (le_t^{PA*} + le_{t-1}^{PA*})/2 \qquad (7.21)$$

Total loans outstanding to the private sector – end of period
Real end of period loans outstanding from the monetary authorities to the overall private sector comprise loans to agriculture (le^{PA*}) as well as loans to manufacturing and other non-agricultural activities (le^{PNA*}). The latter two variables are both treated as exogenous policy variables. It was assumed that the volume of lending was invariant with respect to inflation and the price level. In fact, as we discussed in chapter 2 (2.3.2), over part of the sample period there was a tendency for real loans outstanding to rise with inflation because, with fixed nominal interest rate payments on loans, the real value of the loan servicing stream fell as inflation rose [11]

$$le_t^{PT*} = le_t^{PA*} + le_t^{PNA*} \qquad (7.22)$$

Budget constraint of the combined general government and monetary authorities – current cruzeiros
Because the Central Bank of Brazil and the Bank of Brazil – together referred to as the monetary authorities – both perform fiscal as well as monetary functions, it is necessary to consolidate their operations with those of the federal treasury as well as state and municipal governments to derive a meaningful expression for the deficit of general government (see chapter 2 (2.3.2)). This can only be done very approximately as no official consolidated data are available and the complexities of the relationships between the federal treasury, the monetary authorities and other governmental and semi-governmental bodies make it impossible to effect a consolidation with complete accuracy (Horta, 1981). However, for the purposes at hand, it suffices to ensure basic consistency between stocks and flows without identifying or precisely quantifying each and every source and application of funds.

The budget constraint is of crucial importance in the model because changes in the price level and inflation affect financial flows through the budget thereby allowing us to examine the secondary consequences for inflation of government expenditure policy: particularly as it relates to debt service and food subsidies. As written here, the budget constraint treats changes in high-powered money as the endogenous financing variable. As noted above, new issues of government bonds are treated as exogenous in real terms. Therefore, given a shock to the system with no change in bond indexation rules, the value of real bonds are substantially independent of the price level. Were indexation of principal equal to 100 per cent of inflation, this independence would be complete. As the model stands, any addition to, or reduction in, the financing requirement of the government deficit brought on by a shock to the system, is met by changes in high-powered money. Other financing assumptions could, of course, be adopted.

The budget constraint states that the change in the stock of high-powered money depends upon the sum of:

(a) changes in the value of the end of period stock of loans outstanding from the monetary authorities to the private sector $[\Delta(le^{PT*} \cdot P^{G})_t]$,
(b) interest and indexation on government securities in private hands (DS),
(c) government expenditure on food subsidies (SU^{F}),
(d) government expenditures on goods, services and fixed investment ($g \cdot P^{G}$),
(e) government expenditures on non-food subsidies ($su^{NF} \cdot P^{G}$),
(f) government expenditure on non-interest transfers ($tr^{NI} \cdot P^{G}$), and
(g) the change in net foreign assets of the monetary authorities expressed in domestic currency terms (ΔFR_t)

minus the following,

(h) total tax receipts ($T^{I} + T^{D}$),
(i) the change in the value of total government securities in private hands (ΔB_t), and
(j) other net receipts ($nro \cdot P^{G}$).

Other net receipts are calculated as a residual item in equation (7.23). Since it includes receipts and expenditures that tend to rise in line with the price level, it is treated as exogenous in real terms. If it were fixed in nominal terms, the model would throw up anomalous results when, as a result of a shock, the price level departed from base run values

$$\begin{aligned} \Delta H_t = {} & \Delta(le^{PT*} \cdot P^{G})_t + DS_t + SU^{F}_t \\ & + [(g + su^{NF} + tr^{NI}) \cdot P^{G}]_t + \Delta FR_t \\ & - [(T^{I} + T^{D}) + \Delta B + (nro \cdot P^{G})]_t \end{aligned} \tag{7.23}$$

Stock of high-powered money

$$H_t = \Delta H_t + H_{t-1} \tag{7.24}$$

7.2.4 *Foreign sector*

Total real exports of goods and services

These are equal to the volume of exports of goods (x^G) and services (x^S). Service exports were quantitatively unimportant and are therefore treated as exogenous. In a common simplifying assumption, the export price in dollars is also held exogenous on the assumption – probably not strictly correct – that Brazil had no influence over prices in export markets

$$x_t = x_t^G + x_t^S \tag{7.25}$$

Real goods exports

Goods exports depend upon real U.S. GNP (y^{US}) – used as a proxy for foreign demand – relative price and a shift dummy variable with value one in 1981–3 and zero elsewhere. Relative price is defined as the ratio of the effective cruzeiro export price – an index of real subsidies to exports (z^E) multiplied by the dollar export price (P^{EX*}) and the nominal cruzeiro/dollar exchange rate (E) – to the Brazilian general price index (P^G)[12]

$$x_t^G = \exp\{-9.56 + 1.60 \ln y_t^{US} + 0.54 \ln [(z^E \cdot P^{EX*} \cdot E)/P^G]_t\} \\ + 0.42\, DU8183 \tag{7.26}$$

Total real imports

These comprise imports of petroleum products (im^P), wheat (im^W), other goods (im^{NWP}) and services (im^S), expressed in constant cruzeiros. Imports of wheat are held exogenous following a common practice in the Brazilian literature that reflects the institutional setting. Over the sample period foreign trade in wheat was a government monopoly. Rather than try and model a policy reaction function to explain these imports, we treat them as an exogenous policy variable. Service imports are treated as exogenous for the sake of simplicity. The disaggregation of non-wheat imports into petroleum products and other commodities also follows a procedure used in the literature that reflects the very different income and price elasticities that apply to petroleum versus the bulk of other imports.

$$im_t = im_t^P + im_t^W + im_t^{NWP} + im_t^S \tag{7.27}$$

Real goods imports excluding wheat and petroleum

These are explained by a model developed in Abreu and Horta (1982).[13] Imports depend upon real GDP (y), relative price, demand pressure and a dummy variable with value one in 1974 and zero in all other years. The inclusion in the equation of a demand pressure variable,

($GDPCU$), is aimed at capturing certain costs of obtaining domestically produced import substitutes that are not measured directly in the price. As capacity utilisation increases, so too do bottle-necks and delays in domestic supply, causing consumers to turn increasingly to foreign suppliers. The dummy variable is included to capture the impact of extraordinary stockbuilding brought on by the oil shock. Relative price is given by the ratio of the effective cruzeiro price of imports – an index of real tariffs (z^{I}) multiplied by the dollar price of non-petroleum imports (P^{IMNP*}) and by the nominal cruzeiro/dollar exchange rate (E) – to the Brazilian wholesale price index (P^{WG})

$$im_t^{NWP} = \exp\{-3.83 + 1.20 \ln y_t - 0.71 \ln[(z^{I} \cdot P^{IMNP*} \cdot E)/P^{WG}]_t + 2.05 \ln GDPCU_t\} + 0.20\, DU74 \qquad (7.28)$$

Real petroleum imports

Petroleum and allied imports are a function of real GDP (y), relative price and their own value lagged. Relative price equals the product of the dollar price of imported petroleum (P^{IMP*}) and the nominal cruzeiro/dollar exchange rate (E) divided by the wholesale price index (P^{WG})[14]

$$im_t^{P} = \exp\{-5.47 + 1.09 \ln y_t - 0.192 \ln[(P^{IMP*} \cdot E)/P^{WG}]_t + 0.287 \ln im_{t-1}^{P}\} \qquad (7.29)$$

Terms of trade effect

There are many ways to quantify this. The most frequently used method, which is also that employed in Brazil's national accounts, is as the excess of the volume of imports that can be purchased from the proceeds of actual exports over the volume of these exports. This can be simplified to read

$$tg_t = x_t \cdot (P_t^{EX*}/P_t^{IM*} - 1.0) \qquad (7.30)$$

Net foreign assets of the monetary authorities (official foreign reserves) – in cruzeiro terms

The change in total foreign reserves equals the sum of the current and capital accounts of the balance of payments, expressed in nominal cruzeiro terms. The current account balance equals the trade balance plus net factor income from abroad on current account – where the latter is equal to real net factor income reflated by the cruzeiro import price ($nre \cdot P^{IM*} \cdot E$). Subtracting the current balance from changes in foreign reserves yields a residually defined value that we call net capital inflows (nk). In fact, in addition to changes in the net foreign indebtedness of the government and private sectors as well as in the long-term position of the monetary authorities and the government, net capital inflows as here defined also include changes in the foreign assets of commercial banks. This variable is treated as exogenous in real terms; its nominal value being linked to the U.S. wholesale price index expressed in cruzeiros $(nk \cdot P^{WUS*} \cdot E)$

$$FR_t = FR_{t-1} + E_t[(x \cdot P^{EX*}) - (im \cdot P^{IM*}) + (nre \cdot P^{IM*}) + (nk \cdot P^{WUS*})]_t \quad (7.31)$$

7.2.5 *Production and supply*

Food production

Production of food depends upon the real value of average loans outstanding from the monetary authorities to the agricultural sector in the previous period (le^{PA}_{t-1}), the previous period's wholesale food price relative to the cost of living index $[(P^{WF}/P^{CG})_{t-1}]$, a linear time trend (TL) and a dummy variable with value one in 1965 and zero in other years (see chapter 5 (5.5))

$$q^{AF}_t = -1298.0 + 0.219\, le^{PA}_{t-1} + 0.042\,(P^{WF}/P^{CG})_{t-1} + 0.665TL + 1.21DU65 \quad (7.32)$$

Total food supply

This equals domestic food production plus wheat imports

$$sf_t = q^{AF}_t + im^{W}_t \quad (7.33)$$

Non-food production

This consists of the real value added by industry and the service sector as well as non-food agriculture.[15] Our modelling of this variable is based on a technique extensively discussed in Behrman and Klein (1970) and applied by them and others in macroeconometric models for Brazil.[16] The variable is explained by a 'value added function' that, while including elements of final demand as explanatory terms, is interpreted by Behrman and Klein as deriving from the transformation of an input-output type of production process and therefore combining demand and supply elements.[17] Non-food output is related to total consumption, investment and export demands[18]

$$q^{NF}_t = -2.58 + 0.70(c + c^{G})_t + 0.68(i^{F} + i^{G})_t + 1.09x_t \quad (7.34)$$

7.2.6 *Prices and inflation rates*

The relative wholesale price of food

This depends positively upon real private disposable income – deflated by the consumer price index – (y^{DC}), population (N), and lagged relative price. It is negatively related to the real supply of food (sf) and the food subsidy factor (m). Two dummy variables are also included in the model (see chapter 5 (5.6))

$$(P^{WF}/P^{CG})_t = \exp[-0.241 + 0.166 \ln y_t^{DC} - 0.372 \ln sf_t - 0.226 \ln m_t + 0.372 \ln N_t + 0.937 \ln (P^{WF}/P^{CG})_{t-1}] - 0.125\,DU82 + 0.117\,DU83 \quad (7.35)$$

$$P_t^{WF} = P_t^{CG} \cdot (P^{WF}/P^{CG})_t \quad (7.36)$$

$$\dot{P}_t^{WF} = P_t^{WF}/P_{t-1}^{WF} - 1.0 \quad (7.37)$$

Consumer food price

Consumer food price equals wholesale food price multiplied by (m_t), where $(1-m)$ equals the rate of consumer food subsidy (see chapter 5 (5.3))

$$P^{CF} = P_t^{WF} \cdot m_t \quad (7.38)$$

$$\dot{P}_t^{CF} = P_t^{CF}/P_{t-1}^{CF} - 1.0 \quad (7.39)$$

The wholesale price of manufactured goods

This variable is a function of unit labour costs – the index of manufactured earnings divided by an exogenous index of output per worker in manufacturing (W^1/pr) – domestic raw materials prices (P^{WR}), imported raw materials prices in cruzeiros ($P^{IMR*} \cdot E$) and an index of the real rate of interest (r). The latter is defined as $[(1+R)/(1+\dot{P}^G)]$, where (R) is the nominal yield on bills of exchange. Imported raw materials prices in dollars (P^{IMR*}) and the real interest rate are treated as exogenous (see chapter 3 (3.6.4))

$$P_t^{WI} = \exp[-0.039 + 0.283 \ln (W^1/pr)_t + 0.634 \ln P_t^{WR} + 0.083 \ln (P^{IMR*} \cdot E)_t + 0.322 \ln r_t] \quad (7.40)$$

$$\dot{P}_t^{WI} = P_t^{WI}/P_{t-1}^{WI} - 1.0 \quad (7.41)$$

Average earnings in manufacturing

These are a function of current and two period lagged consumer price inflation ($\dot{P}^{CG}$) as well as two dummy variables (see chapter 4 (4.3.3))

$$\dot{W}_t^{\mathrm{I}} = 0.071 + 0.676\dot{P}_t^{\mathrm{CG}} + 0.506\dot{P}_{t-1}^{\mathrm{CG}} - 0.182\dot{P}_{t-2}^{\mathrm{CG}} + 0.044\,DU7984 - 0.029\,DU83 \quad (7.42)$$

$$W_t^{\mathrm{I}} = W_{t-1}^{\mathrm{I}} \cdot (\dot{W}_t^{\mathrm{I}} + 1.0) \quad (7.43)$$

The rate of consumer price inflation

This variable depends upon consumer food price inflation ($\dot{P}^{\mathrm{CF}}$) as well as both current and lagged wholesale manufacturing price inflation ($\dot{P}^{\mathrm{WI}}$) (see chapter 6 (6.2.2)).

$$\dot{P}_t^{\mathrm{CG}} = 0.40\dot{P}_t^{\mathrm{CF}} + 0.338\dot{P}_t^{\mathrm{WI}} + 0.262\dot{P}_{t-1}^{\mathrm{WI}} \quad (7.44)$$

$$P_t^{\mathrm{CG}} = P_{t-1}^{\mathrm{CG}} \cdot (\dot{P}_t^{\mathrm{CG}} + 1.0) \quad (7.45)$$

The cruzeiro/U.S. dollar exchange rate

Domestic and U.S. wholesale price inflation are the determinants of the rate of change of this variable along with two dummy variables. U.S. price inflation is exogenous (see chapter 6 (6.1.2))

$$E_t = \exp(\ln E_{t-1} + 1.0\Delta \ln P_t^{\mathrm{WG}} - 1.0\Delta \ln P_t^{\mathrm{WUS*}}) - 0.10DU81 + 0.206DU83$$

$$\dot{E}_t = E_t/E_{t-1} - 1.0 \quad (7.47)$$

The wholesale price index – domestic supply

This is made up of prices of goods sold in the domestic market. Export prices are excluded. The three component indices are food prices (P^{WF}), raw material prices (P^{WR}) and manufacturing prices (P^{WI}) (see chapter 6 (6.2.3))

$$P_t^{\mathrm{WG}} = 0.33P_t^{\mathrm{WF}} + 0.15P_t^{\mathrm{WR}} + 0.52P_t^{\mathrm{WI}} \quad (7.48)$$

$$\dot{P}_t^{\mathrm{WG}} = P_t^{\mathrm{WG}}/P_{t-1}^{\mathrm{WG}} - 1.0 \quad (7.49)$$

The general price index

The three component indices of this aggregate are wholesale prices (P^{WG}), consumer prices (P^{CG}) and construction costs (P^{H}). The relative construction cost ($p^{\mathrm{H}} = P^{\mathrm{H}}/P^{\mathrm{CG}}$) is treated as exogenous, allowing us to define the general price index as (see chapter 6 (6.2.4)).

$$P_t^{\mathrm{G}} = 0.6P_t^{\mathrm{WG}} + 0.4P_t^{\mathrm{CG}} + 0.1p_t^{\mathrm{H}} \quad (7.50)$$

$$\dot{P}_t^{\mathrm{G}} = P_t^{\mathrm{G}}/P_{t-1}^{\mathrm{G}} - 1.0 \quad (7.51)$$

The wholesale raw material price index

Ideally a stochastic model should be advanced to explain this variable. A useful initial hypothesis might be that relative raw material prices are determined by domestic supply and demand coupled with some influence of foreign raw material prices (see chapter 2 (2.3.3) and figure 2.12). The latter influence appears to have been especially important during the 1970s when foreign prices of commodities, which were both domestically produced and imported, experienced dramatic increases. Petroleum was of course the most important good in this category. Some rudimentary econometrics were performed on raw material prices but with little success. Data deficiencies make a test of the market model hypothesis very difficult to set up. Given these factors and the time constraint, we chose simply to define the variable as a weighted average of imported raw material prices, in cruzeiro terms ($P^{IMR*} \cdot E$) and a residually defined 'domestic' price component ($p^{WR+} \cdot P^{WG}$) where (p^{WR+}) is the exogenously given relative price. The weighting is based upon an estimate of the influence of foreign prices upon the domestic price index

$$P_t^{WR} = 0.15(P^{IMR*} \cdot E)_t + 0.85(p^{WR+} \cdot P^{WG})_t \tag{7.52}$$

7.3 Salient features of the model

The complete model is made up of 52 equations, 12 behavioural and 40 definitional. In addition to the 52 endogenous variables, there are 56 predetermined variables, 40 exogenous and 16 lagged endogenous. We now describe intuitively some of its important features.

7.3.1 *Indexation of prices, government expenditure and financial assets*

As discussed in the introduction, an important aim of this study is to examine the relationships between inflationary pressures of a structuralist or cost-push variety and the propagating mechanisms that can cause these to set off a continuous inflation. In specifying the individual pricing equations, account was taken of formal and informal price and wage indexation. When the equations of the wage and price sector are combined, the close interrelationship between prices is clear. With mark-up pricing and indexation of wages and the exchange rate, an incipient relative price change is not easily absorbed but rather tends to set off a continuous series of additional price changes, leading to a higher rate of inflation.

In this chapter financial factors have been built in – private financial wealth is a determinant of consumption expenditure and official lending influences investment expenditure. Through the food market, rising expenditure creates inflationary pressures. Therefore, a causal link is established between finance and inflation.

Through the budget constraint and the trade balance, causality also runs from changes in the price level to changes in high-powered money. This acts to validate, to some degree, inflations that originate in the 'real' sector. A price shock tends to set in motion a process of validating increases in the stock of financial assets that prevents a large contraction in private expenditure and output. Public sector consumption and investment expenditure are determined exogenously in real terms. Given an overall deficit, a rise in the price level calls forth an increase in the nominal stock of financial assets in order that government may finance the increase in its nominal outlays. The nominal value of food subsidies and of interest payments on the public debt rises with the value of food output and the face value of government securities, respectively. All these factors combine to mitigate the contractionary impact of a rise in the price level via the real balance effect by increasing net nominal asset accumulation of the private sector and so maintaining, to some degree, private sector expenditure. What is more, a large and rising proportion of private financial wealth (indexed bonds) is largely insulated in real terms from higher prices, thereby attenuating the importance of the real balance effect.

7.3.2 *Output, demand and price determination*

An important feature of the model and one crucial to the structuralist approach, is the disaggregation of domestic production into food and non-food items with the adoption of different hypotheses concerning output and pricing decisions in each sector. Food output is supply constrained, with relative price acting slowly to clear the market. By contrast, the price of manufactured goods and, implicitly, that of other non-food items as well, is determined by a mark-up over direct costs and is insensitive to demand and supply. Output adjusts to clear this market in response to alterations in demand. The model is designed essentially for short-run analysis and as such non-agricultural supply is assumed to be elastic. There is no link between net investment flows and productive capacity in either industry or agriculture. Food output grows along a trend line which represents in part the effects of new investment.

In the model demand pressures cause inflation through the food market. In contrast to many conventional Keynesian models, there is no Phillips curve linking demand to inflation through the labour market, nor does demand directly affect the industrial mark-up. Labour productivity in the model is treated as exogenous. However it was shown in chapter 2 that changes in industrial output relative to capacity were positively linked to productivity. Changes in productivity in turn alter unit labour costs in manufacturing. This establishes an inverse causal link between output and inflation – rising output putting downward pressure on inflation. Although, it would have been useful to endogenise productivity so as to allow this process to operate in the simulation exercises, after initial testing it proved difficult to model the employment/output link in a sensible way. As the model stands, neither earnings nor productivity are influenced by deviations in output or demand from their base run solution levels. Therefore, unit labour costs are insulated from these changes. Variations in absolute as well as in certain key relative prices cause demand and output to change in the model in the following ways:

(a) a rise in the overall price level causes existing money balances to fall, with a negative impact upon expenditure and inflation,
(b) changes in the real exchange rate or in dollar prices of imports or exports influence demand for these variables and, therefore, through the multiplier lead to changes in demand for food and inflation,
(c) changes in the external terms of trade imply a direct change in real national income, and
(d) a rise in relative wholesale food price leads to a rise in food output.

7.3.3 *Comparison with other models*

There exist a number of macromodels of the Brazilian economy. These are differentiated by their theoretical underpinnings, levels of aggregation and purposes for which they were designed. It is not intended here to describe or even to make reference to all the models documented in the literature. Rather, we mention briefly the most important structural models and point out how the present one is similar or dissimilar to these.

The earliest attempts at modelling the Brazilian economy are reviewed by Souza and Monteiro (1974) and by Jul (1977). As might be expected, these models were generally very unsophisticated by today's standards and are not referred to further here. The most important models have been developed since the first oil shock. Sahota (1975) developed a large model with a particularly detailed specification of the fiscal system. He used the model for a number of control experiments. Jul (1977) constructed a detailed model with 230 variables, 53 of them behavioural. It incorporates the structuralist feature that output is disaggregated into four main sectors with secondary and tertiary sector output demand determined and coffee and non-coffee agricultural production supply constrained. However, the system falls short of conforming fully to the structuralist paradigm in that there is no sectoral differentiation in price setting mechanisms. All prices are a function of one overall index which is itself a function of costs and real money supply growth.

Taylor *et al.* (1980) built two versions of a growth model designed to examine issues related to income distribution. The approach includes many structuralist features.

A small model with a typical Keynesian structure and only one composite good, was developed by Assis (1981). It has a detailed specification of the financial sector as it is designed to analyse the determination of stocks and flows of financial assets. However, an explicit link between stocks of assets and expenditure is not established. In Assis (1983) the same author proposed another model with more emphasis on aggregate demand and output determination. It conforms to the structuralist paradigm in that pricing and output decisions are arrived at differently in agricultural and non-agricultural sectors.

Modiano (1983b) sketches the make-up of a macromodel with some structuralist features. The model itself is not presented formally. Aggregate demand is determined by a single reduced form equation in which growth in real income is a function of real money growth and the share of government expenditure in total income. Agricultural output is supply determined, with price a function of demand and supply. Non-agricultural output is implicitly demand determined. The industrial wage and price sector is specified so as to take account explicitly of mark-up pricing and indexation of wages and the exchange rate.

Contador (1984) sets out a model designed specifically to account for the effects of supply and price shocks upon the system. Reduced form equations are proposed for output, income and money supply growth. It is assumed that rational expectations hold in a weak form and that unexpected shocks cause only short-run deviations in real output from its long-run path and only temporary changes in the rate of inflation.

The present model distinguishes itself from existing models in a variety of respects. Of these, one of the most notable resides in the fact that the process of price level and inflation determination is modelled in detail following a systematic research strategy that is well documented. In particular, much more attention has been paid to food price determination at the wholesale and retail levels than has been customary in the Brazilian literature. Institutional features of the food market, particularly food subsidies, are combined with market forces. In modelling prices and inflation rates, an important difference between the present study and others carried out previously is that an explicit research methodology has been set out and followed. We have endeavoured to consider alternative hypotheses and variants of the same hypotheses in a systematic manner and to present sufficient detail regarding the method used, the findings achieved and the statistical properties of the estimates made for the reader to be able to form judgements of his own as to the quality and relevance of the results.

A second distinguishing feature of the present model is the treatment of the process of financial asset accumulation. Private sector wealth is defined and changes in it are linked to changes in the financial assets of the public and overseas sectors. The government budget constraint is modelled in a consistent, if still very rudimentary, fashion in a way that does not ignore levels of government below the federal treasury. Asset flows are linked to the determination of private expenditure through the consumption function and the implications for both the public and private sectors of interest payments and indexation on government debt are modelled explicitly. While these features are, to a large extent, standard in macromodels of industrialised countries, the same has not been true in the Brazilian context. The effect of doing this has enabled us to capture, in a way not done before, the bidirectional causal links between prices and output that were discussed above.

7.4 Conclusion

In this chapter the detailed specification of key prices and rates of inflation developed in part II of the study was combined with a simple model of endogenous demand and output to form a small macroeconomic system. Extensive use was made of the existing modelling literature for Brazil, updating and in many cases modifying previously obtained results. The overall structure and emphasis does however differ in significant ways from that of existing models.

The model developed offers a representation of the structure of the Brazilian economy. The possibility cannot be ruled out that the actual structure might be better represented by an alternative model. A number of factors point to the need to treat with caution the results obtained. A short sample was used in estimation of the parameters of the model and, since the short sample properties of many of the diagnostic tests applied are not well understood, we can have only limited confidence in the apparent statistical properties of the results obtained. Not all estimation results were equally robust. The poor quality of much of the data used in estimation is another factor that must bear upon the reliability of the results. Notwithstanding these qualifications, care was taken to obtain the best results consistent with the constraints imposed by data availability and the limited degrees of freedom.

The model would benefit from extension and improvement in a number of areas. Its usefulness as a tool for understanding inflation would be enhanced were the financial sector to be developed further, allowing for the endogenisation of the interest rate in order to permit a more complete examination of the phenomenon of interest rate-push inflation. Asset demand functions would allow us to capture substitution between monetary and non-monetary assets as inflation rose. Likewise, a proper modelling of domestic raw material prices is required as these clearly play a most important role in overall price formation. In addition, it would be desirable to supplement endogenous food subsidies with both endogenous petroleum and implicit credit subsidies in order to enquire more fully into the interaction between short-term anti-inflationary measures and longer-term stimulus to demand and inflation through private wealth expansion. As regards aggregate demand and output determination, investment in fixed capital requires a more adequate modelling along with non-food output. The model would be further enriched were it possible to endogenise the income and expenditure streams of important social groups, such as industrial workers, industrialists and farmers. This would permit an explicit consideration of the complex interactions between inflation, anti-inflationary policies and income distribution.

8 Model validation and evaluation

8.1 Introduction

In this section the model is put through a number of exercises and tests designed to assess its adequacy as a simplified representation of the Brazilian macroeconomy. The model is found to be adequate in this respect and is therefore employed for policy analysis purposes in the next chapter. The exercises performed were carried out using the Cambridge Model Processing System (MPS), a programme that uses a generalised Newton–Raphson iterative procedure to obtain solution values for each endogenous variable given a set of starting values (Cambridge Economic Policy Group, 1983).

Customarily, to test the validity of a simultaneous equation model – in other words to assess whether or not it reaches an acceptable standard of performance:

(a) procedures are applied to the individual equations of the system in order to test for misspecification,
(b) other measures are adopted to test the ability of the model as a whole to track historical data, whether within or outside the sample period used in parameter estimation, and
(c) exercises are performed with the model to investigate whether or not it responds to stimuli – which usually take the form of substantial changes in exogenous variables or policy parameters – in a manner consistent with economic theory and empirical observation.

Step (a) above has already been carried out for each of the stochastic equations, in considerable depth for the price, food output and earnings equations and in a cursory fashion for the demand and output relationships that were adapted from other studies. As regards whole system validation of the variety referred to under item (b), no data points were available for out-of-sample tracking tests at the time this part of the study was completed. Instead, an historical, or *ex post* simulation was performed, yielding a control or base solution that was in turn compared with the actual historical record; in other words the model's historical tracking capacity was scrutinised. This exercise is reported in section 8.2. In section 8.3, the model's response to stimuli is examined through dynamic multiplier analysis.

8.2 Historical tracking

In order to generate the base run, historical values were supplied for all endogenous variables as initial conditions only. Also supplied were historical series for all exogenous variables, covering the entire simulation period. The simulation performed was therefore dynamic, since solution values were used for endogenous variables at each stage beyond the initial year, as well as deterministic, since all residuals were set equal to zero. In the control run, as in all subsequent 'shocked' runs, a solution was obtained for each variable over the period 1966 to 1983. This was the longest time period that could be employed given variations in the sample sizes used to estimate the various stochastic equations.[1]

While historical tracking can be of use for evaluating a simultaneous model, one should not attach undue importance to this technique. This is particularly true when the model in question is designed, as it is here, for descriptive purposes and hypothesis testing rather than for forecasting. In the former case overall tracking errors are arguably less crucial than the statistical robustness of the individual equations and their theoretical derivations. Moreover, the validity of historical simulation as an evaluation technique has come in for criticism. The most basic complaint is that good tracking performance of a series of individual equations under dynamic simulation may have more to do with offsetting errors than with a genuine capacity to replicate history. On a more sophisticated level, Hendry and Richard (1982) argued that the goodness of fit of a dynamic historical simulation is an invalid technique for model selection and one that reveals less about the model's correspondence to reality than it does about the model's structure. This is the case as the accuracy of the simulation is related primarily to the degree to which the model attributes variance in the data to outside, or exogenous, factors. Thus, there exists a negative relationship between the number of endogenous variables and tracking performance. A poor track does not imply necessarily that a complex model is inferior to another simpler one. Hendry and Richard (1982) also show that it is an inherent property of a closed, stationary and linear model that the simulation track converges on the unconditional data means as the sample size increases. Consequently, the inability of the model to replicate the variability in the data series does not necessarily indicate that the model is inadequate.

To assess the model's tracking performance, for each of twelve key endogenous variables – eleven of these stochastically determined plus the GDP identity – the base solution and historical values are plotted together against time. Direct inspection of the plots can yield valuable information about the quality of the tracking. An especially important criterion is how well the model simulates the turning points, or rapid changes in the data. Also computed were three summary measures of tracking performance based upon simulation errors. These are: the root mean square error (*RMSE*), root mean square percentage error (*RMSPE*) and Theil's inequality coefficient (U).

For a given variable, the root mean square error summarises the deviations of the solution from the historical time paths over all observations. It is defined as

$$RMSE=\sqrt{1/n\Sigma(v_t^s-v_t)^2}$$

where (n) is the number of observations in the simulation period, (v_t) is the observed or historical value of a given endogenous variable at time (t) and, (v_t^s) is the corresponding base or control run solution value. The *RMSE* is expressed in the same units as the endogenous variable in question and can therefore be difficult to interpret. In many cases a unit free tracking statistic can be usefully applied. One such measure is the root mean square percentage error, given by

$$RMSPE=100\sqrt{1/n\Sigma[(v_t^s-v_t)/v_t]^2}$$

For both *RMSE* and *RMSPE*, perfect tracking is captured by a value of zero. Therefore, the model builder aims to achieve the lowest possible values for each.

While, in general, *RMSPE* is the preferred measure, if the observed values of the endogenous variable are low or if they switch back and forth between positive and negative values, then *RMSPE* is not recommended. In such cases, a moderate error can be associated with a large *RMSPE* simply because the observed value is very close to zero. For variables such as rates of change, *RMSE* will be the preferred measure.

Theil (1961) proposed a useful simulation statistic related to the *RMSE* which he termed the inequality coefficient

$$U=\frac{\sqrt{1/n\Sigma(v_t^s-v_t)^2}}{\sqrt{1/n\Sigma(\bar{v}_t^s)^2}+\sqrt{1/n\Sigma(\bar{v}_t)^2}}$$

where ($\bar{v}$) indicates the mean of (v). The numerator of (U) is simply the *RMSE*. The scaling of the denominator is such that the value of (U) always falls between zero and unity. If $U=0$, we have a perfect fit as $v^s=v$ for all (t). Conversely, if $U=1$, the predictive performance is as bad as it can be. The Theil coefficient is also decomposed into the bias, variance and covariance proportions, (U^m), (U^s) and (U^c) respectively.[2] The bias proportion (U^m) is an indicator of systematic error, measuring as it does the extent to which average values of the simulated and historical series deviate. We expect a good track to yield a low value for this proportion since systematic error is a troubling property. (U^s), the variance proportion, points to the model's success at replicating variability in the series of interest. A high value of (U^s) indicates that the simulated series fluctuates much less than its historical counterpart. The covariance proportion (U^c) represents that portion of the error that is neither systematic nor represents deviations from average variability. Ideally, one would like to find the following distribution of values; $U^c=1$, $U^m=0$, $U^s=0$.

8.2.1 *Tracking of output and demand variables*

Figures 8.1 through 8.7 contain tracking plots for the principal national accounts aggregates in the model as well as for food production. The model tracks the GDP identity well, as evidenced by the plot and attendant statistics. Of the constituent parts of GDP, the model succeeds in adequately tracking consumption and investment, with *RMSPE*s of just under 3 per cent and 4 per cent respectively. With low values for (U^m) and (U^s), there is no indication of serious systematic bias or uncaptured variance. Foreign trade aggregates – figures 8.4 to 8.6 – are much more volatile components of national income than consumption or investment and, partly as a consequence, the tracking achieved is much less impressive. *RMSPE*s vary from 9.4 per cent for exports to almost 12 per cent for non-wheat and petroleum product imports. For both categories of imports, relatively high values of (U^s) point to the difficulty the model has in matching the variability of the historical time paths. Instances of large underprediction of imports occur in 1973–6. Even a small deviation in the time path of national income has a powerful impact upon imports because of the high income elasticity of the latter. The model succeeds in capturing the major turning points in the historical time path of imports that occurred in 1974 and 1979–80. Lesser turning points, notably that which occurred in 1975–6, are however missed.

The model is able to replicate quite well the behaviour over time of domestic food production, figure 8.7. Simulation statistics have acceptable values and major turning points are correctly predicted.

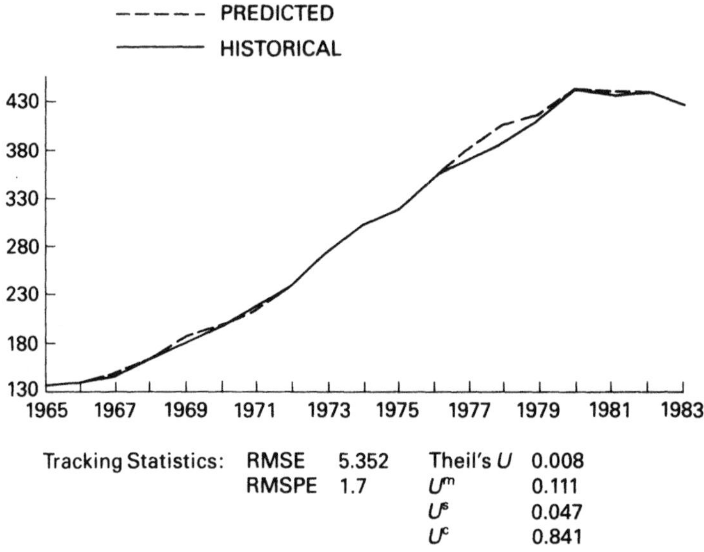

Figure 8.1 GDP – base solution and historical values (billions of 1970 cruzeiros)

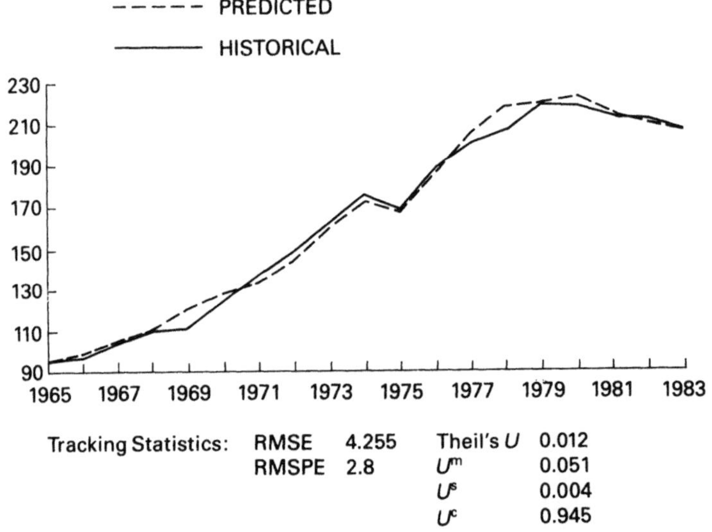

Figure 8.2 Private consumption per capita – base solution and historical values (billions of 1970 cruzeiros)

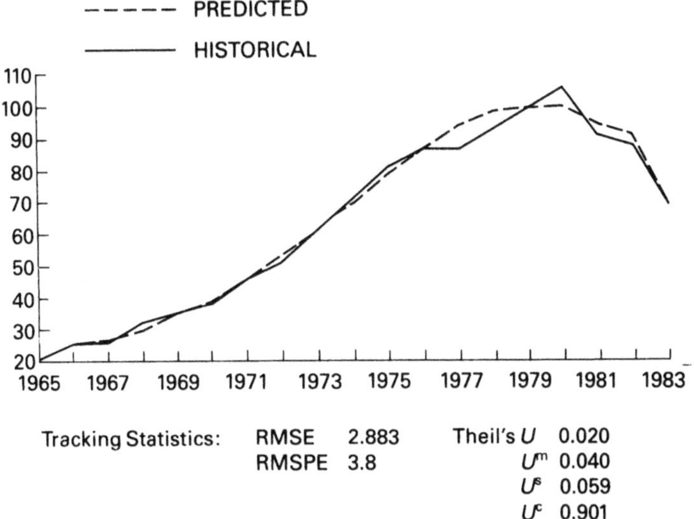

Figure 8.3 Private gross fixed investment – base solution and historical values (billions of 1970 cruzeiros)

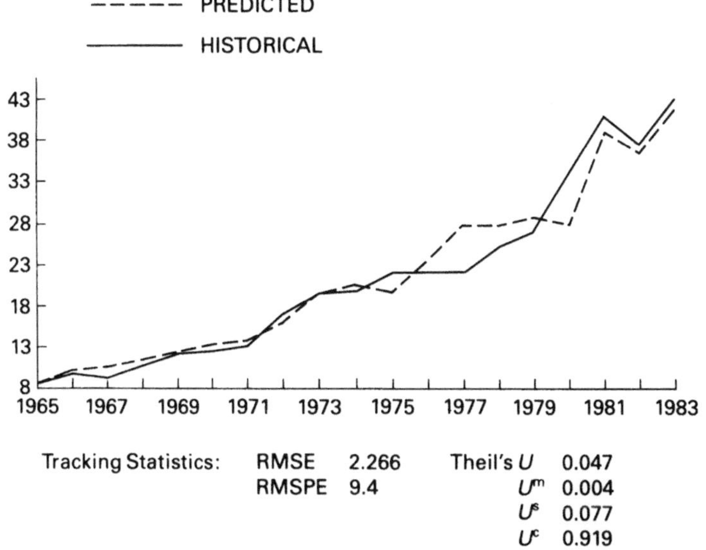

Figure 8.4 Goods exports – base solution and historical values (billions of 1970 cruzeiros)

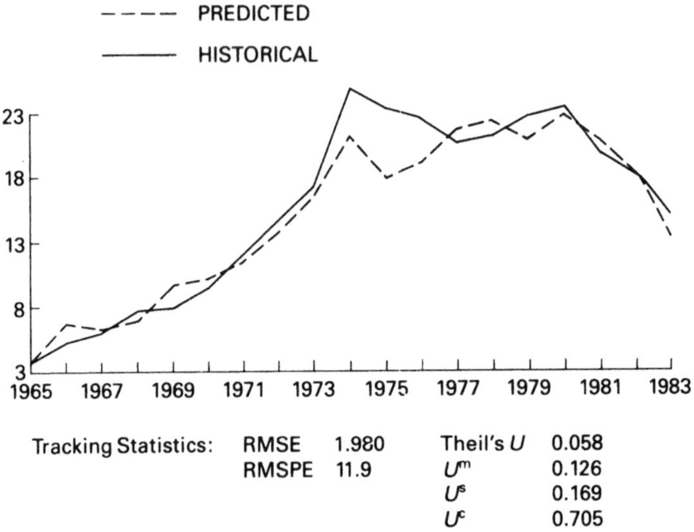

Figure 8.5 Imports of goods other than wheat and petroleum products – base solution and historical values (billions of 1970 cruzeiros)

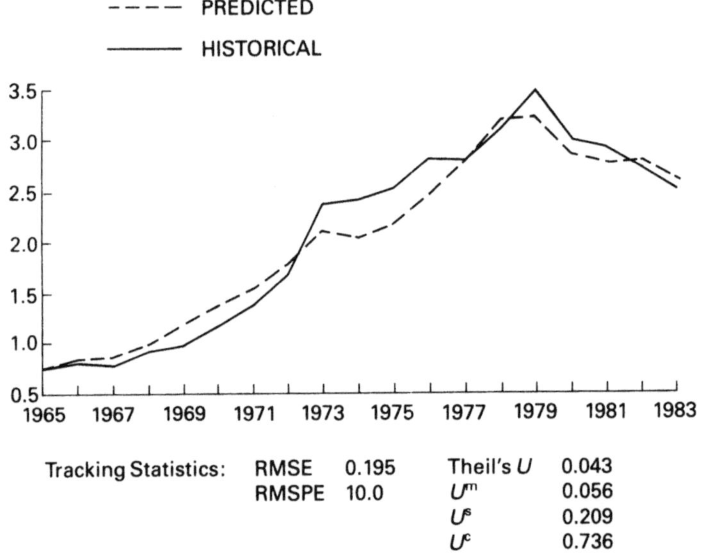

Figure 8.6 Imports of petroleum products – base solution and historical values (billions of 1970 cruzeiros)

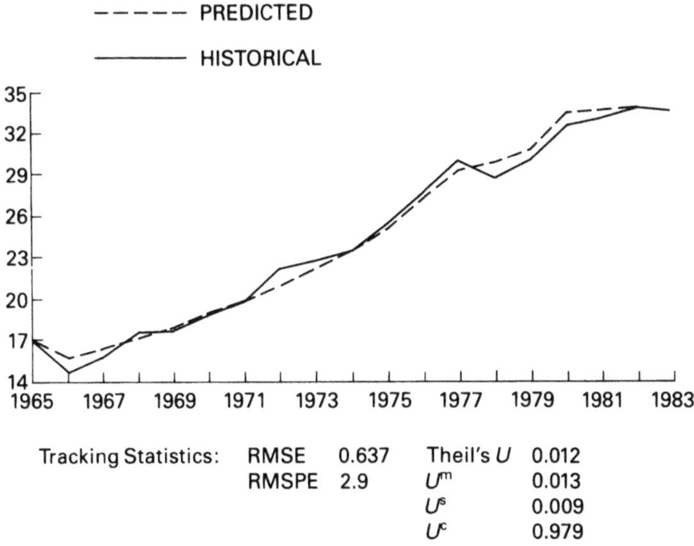

Figure 8.7 Domestic production of food – base solution and historical values (billions of 1970 cruzeiros)

8.2.2 *Tracking of inflation variables*

Base solution and historical values for the rates of change of consumer prices, manufacturing earnings and the nominal cruzeiro/U.S. dollar exchange rate are graphed in figures 8.8 through 8.10. Tracking performance is mediocre, with *RMSE*s of about 8.0 (eight percentage points) being achieved. There is considerable evidence, both visual and in the values of the (U^s) statistics, that the simulations fail to capture adequately the variability in the historical series. This is particularly true for earnings and consumer price inflation.

Deficiencies in tracking do not primarily reflect inadequate single equation models but rather the fact that, due to the high degree of interdependence between inflation rates and price levels in the model, even a small error in one equation is rapidly transmitted throughout the system. It is especially the case that any turning point errors in the relative food price equation have a marked impact upon the rate of change of prices. A prediction error in the food equation in 1970–1, combined with a series of single equation prediction errors in various inflation terms in 1973–4, is the root cause of the major overprediction of price changes in 1973–6.

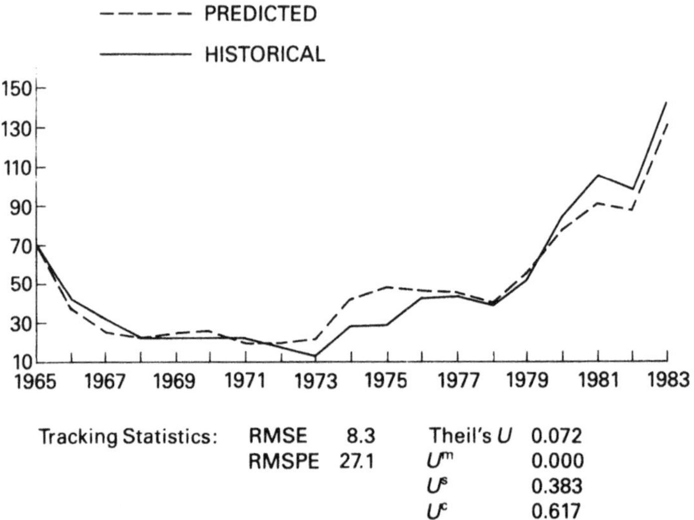

Figure 8.8 Consumer price inflation – base solution and historical values (percentage rate of change)

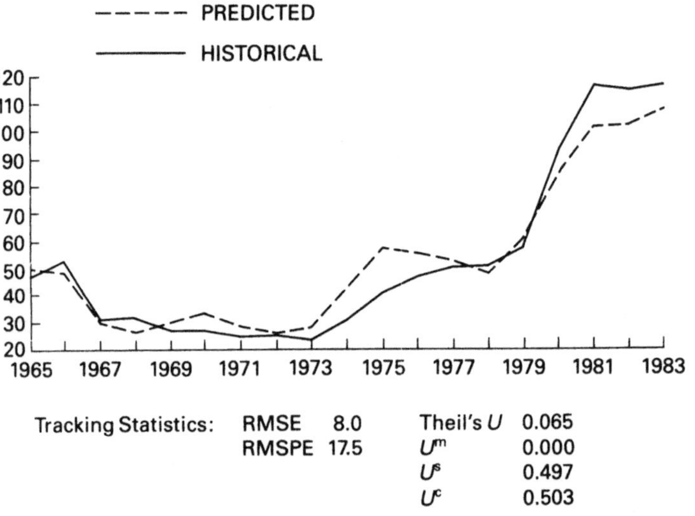

Figure 8.9 Earnings inflation in manufacturing – base solution and historical values (percentage rate of change)

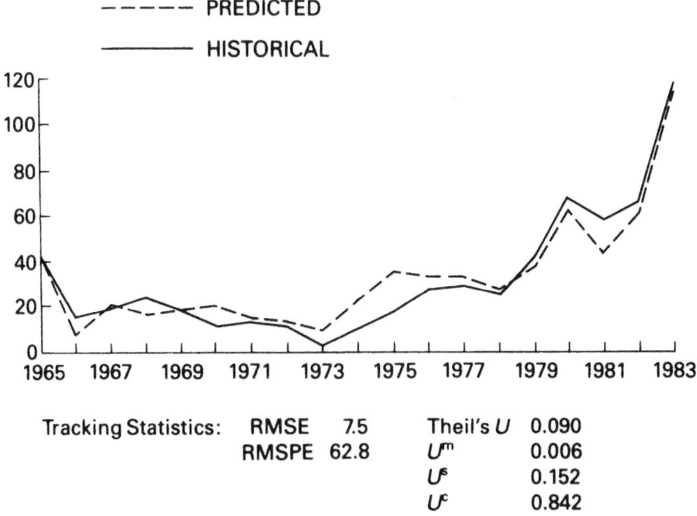

Figure 8.10 Rate of devaluation of the cruzeiro against the U.S. dollar measured in log first differences – base solution and historical values (percentage rate of change)

8.2.3 *Tracking of the manufacturing price index*

The relevant plots are figures 8.11 and 8.12. The first reveals that the price level is noticeably overpredicted by the model during much of the latter half of the simulation. The Theil statistic is not a good indicator of tracking performance in a case such as this where data are highly trended. Theil himself applied the statistic only to change variables. To allow for a more precise visual inspection of tracking performance, the first differences of the logs of base solution and historical values are plotted in figure 8.12. The model's noticeable overprediction in 1974–81 is quite clearly evident and is directly related to the high simulated values of the inflation terms obtained during 1973–6. With manufacturing price almost wholly determined by other current endogenous prices, any errors in the latter feed immediately into the former.

8.2.4 *Tracking of the relative wholesale price of food*

When the model was first simulated it was found that turning point errors in this equation – present even when historical values were used for all independent terms – had a powerful impact upon the tracking performance of other variables. Even a relatively small error in the predicted relative

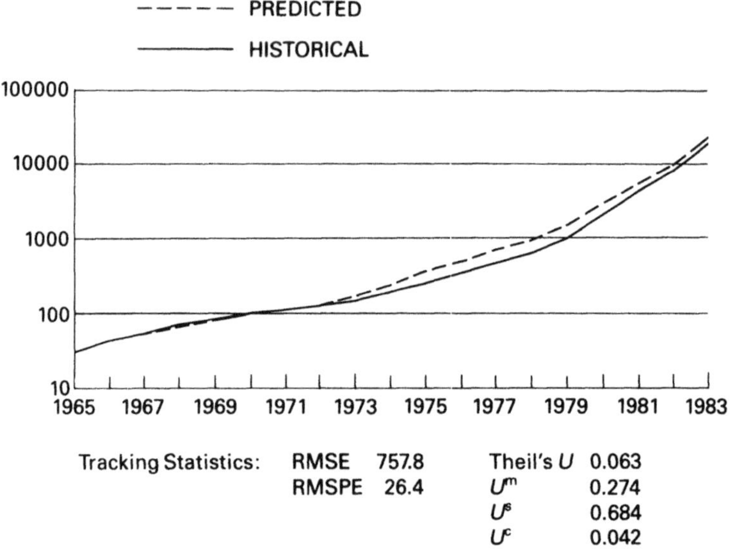

Figure 8.11 Index of wholesale prices of manufactured goods – base solution and historical values (log scale with base 1970 = 100)

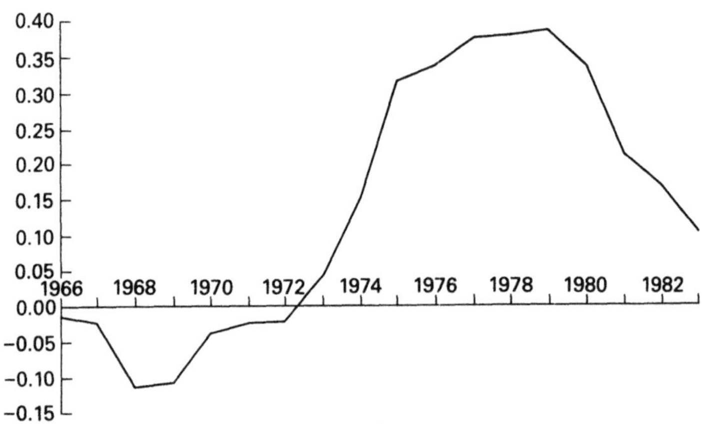

Figure 8.12 Index of wholesale prices of manufactured goods – tracking error (log difference of base and historical values)

food price level can imply a large alteration in the change in relative price which in turn translates into a big prediction error for inflation rates throughout the system. The dynamic structure of the food price equation helps to perpetuate the impact of any error through time. Single equation errors were found to be particularly pronounced in 1973–5 and 1980. When used in a full dynamic simulation, this version of the food equation caused all the model's inflation terms and price levels to experience noticeable and sustained deviations relative to base. To reduce this problem, two additional dummy variables were included in the food price equation – for simulation purposes only – with values of one in 1973–5 and 1980 respectively and zero in other years. Coefficient values for the dummy variables were imposed. The simulation discussed here was performed with this latter version of the model. The track of the adjusted model is shown in figures 8.13 and 8.14, both in levels and also in first differences to aid interpretation. Tracking is adequate given an *RMSPE* of 3.3 per cent and there is only limited evidence of systematic prediction error as indicated by the value of (U^m). While the result achieved owes much to the use of the dummy variables, it is not altogether surprising that a model without dummy variables performs badly, given the number of large turning points in the data, the institutional complexities of the food market and important data deficiencies.

8.3 Multiplier analysis

As discussed earlier, adequate historical tracking is not in itself sufficient to establish the validity of a model. It is also imperative to consider the dynamic behaviour of the model over time. One objective of this analysis is to check for evidence of structural instability in the model that is not representative of the economy that we are seeking to explain. The model may exhibit a tendency to yield stable, explosive oscillatory or explosive non-oscillatory solutions that empirical observation and/or theory do not predict. This can be the case even when each of the model's equations are not by themselves unstable. Instability may arise if these are combined and solved simultaneously. In the case of linear models, or non-linear models that are linearised around a particular simulation solution, stability can be analysed by examining the characteristic roots. This option is not available in the case of non-linear models. Instead, it is customary to enquire into stability in an imprecise way through the application of simulation experiments in which shocks are applied to exogenous variables or policy parameter values and a new solution obtained. This is then compared with the base run.[3] Where these experiments take the form of shocks to the time

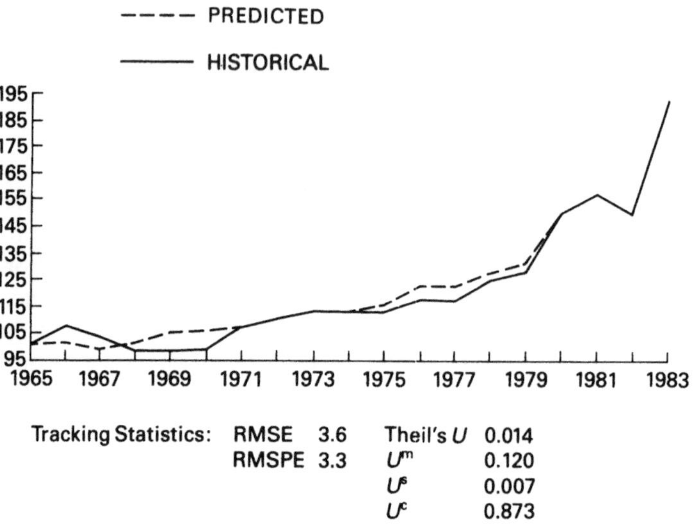

Figure 8.13 Index of relative wholesale prices of food – base solution and historical values (base 1970 = 100)

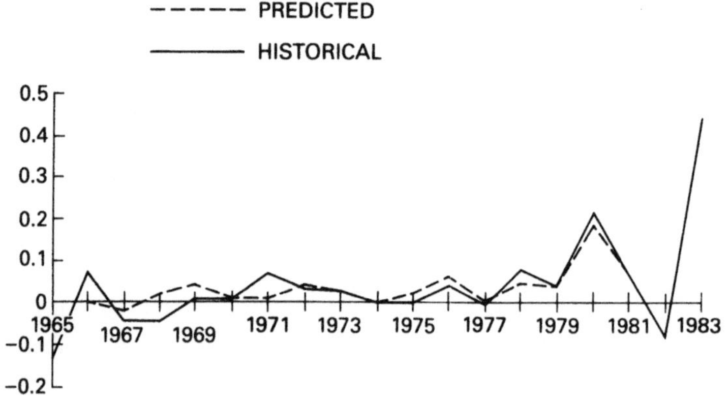

Figure 8.14 Absolute change in index of relative wholesale prices of food – base solution and historical values

path of exogenous variables the technique is often referred to as multiplier analysis.

Multiplier analysis is also useful, contingent upon consistency of the empirical results with underlying theory and outside empirical evidence, as a means to enquire into the way in which the economy may respond to policy induced or stochastic changes in particular variables over time. Thus multiplier analysis can be thought of as a form of counter-factual experimentation, often referred to as 'causal analysis', in which the aim is to illuminate the causes of past or present macroeconomic behaviour. Lucas (1976) mounted a powerful critique of the use of structural macromodels in causal analysis. He argued that the parameters of the economic system reflect optimal decision rules of economic agents that are in part based upon agents' expectations about the future time paths of the exogenous variables of the system. If these expectations were to change, we would expect the parameters of the system, and presumably the estimated parameters of any model of the system, also to change. Since an alteration in the historical time path of the exogenous variables can be expected to lead to adjustments in expectations, Lucas maintained that it was therefore invalid to enquire into the consequences of changes in these variables on the assumption of an unaltered economic structure.

The validity of the Lucas critique appears to have been widely accepted without however having precipitated, at least as yet, much change in empirical practice. Challen and Hagger (1983) suggest that causal analysis continues to be widely used due in part to our lack of knowledge about the quantitative significance of Lucas' point. Until such time as it can be established that the results obtained from causal analyses are truly misleading, it seems appropriate to make continued use of them while bearing in mind the possible impact of exogenous changes upon the model's structure.

Three validating shocks were applied to the Brazilian model under two hypotheses regarding the food supply process. In all cases, the shocks were applied in 1966 and continued through 1983. In other words, they were sustained rather than impact shocks. By shocking the system first with food production endogenised, as in the standard model, and then again with food production exogenised, it was possible to gauge the importance for the dynamic adjustment process of a supply response in the food market. The three shocks administered were:

(a) an import price shock taking the form of a sustained 10 per cent increase in each of the four exogenously given dollar import price indices in the model,
(b) an aggregate demand shock in which the real value of fixed investment by government was increased by a sustained 10 per cent, and

(c) a negative food production shock consisting of a sustained fall in *per capita* food output equal to 10 per cent of the simulated 1966 volume.[4]

In order to evaluate the impact of shocks to the system, solution values for a series of key endogenous variables from the shocked runs were compared with their corresponding base run values. Deviations between shocked and base solution values were graphed for each of these endogenous variables. The exact way in which deviations were measured varies slightly between variables, as explained below.[5]

The impact of a shock upon real GDP (expenditure measure) is represented graphically by the percentage deviation of shocked GDP from its own base solution values

$$\Delta y_t = [(y_t^{sh} - y_t)/y_t] \cdot 100$$

where the superscript (sh) signifies shocked solution values; variables without a superscript are base solution values. The impact of a shock upon foreign trade is measured by the change in the dollar value of the balance of trade in goods and services $(tb_t^{sh} - tb_t)$ as a percentage of base run GDP, also expressed in dollars $(y \cdot P^{WUS*})_t$

$$\Delta tb_t = [(tb_t^{sh} - tb_t)/(y \cdot P^{WUS*})_t] \cdot 100$$

where

$$tb_t = (P^{EX*} \cdot x - P^{IM*} \cdot im)_t$$

By expressing deviations in the trade balance relative to GDP, the magnitude of any change is more readily interpreted. The use of base run GDP as opposed to shocked values for the same variable allows us to isolate changes in the trade balance due to a shock from changes due to variations in national income. The measurement of the trade balance in dollars rather than cruzeiros is justified by the importance of isolating what happens to foreign reserves in dollars. A change in the real exchange rate will cause dollar reserves to behave differently from their cruzeiro equivalent.

The response to shocks of consumer price inflation is measured by the simple deviation of shocked run from base run values and is therefore expressed in numbers of percentage points

$$\Delta \dot{P}_t^{CG} = (\dot{P}_t^{CGsh} - \dot{P}_t^{CG})$$

Finally, the response of price levels to the shocks is expressed in percentage deviations:

$$\Delta P_t = [(P_t^{sh} - P_t)/P_t] \cdot 100$$

For each shock, the percentage deviation is calculated for the overall consumer and wholesale price indices, for the wholesale food price index

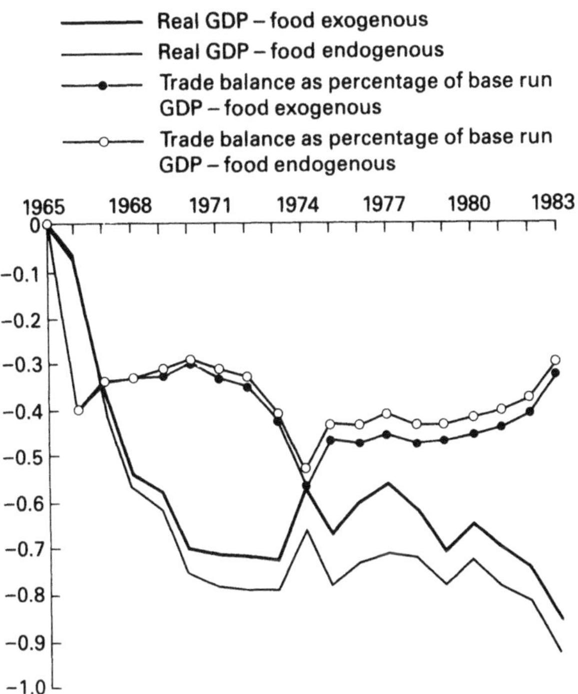

Figure 8.15 Responses of GDP and trade balance to import price shock – with and without endogenous food production (percentage differences relative to base run)

and, in one case, for the index of manufacturing earnings as well. For each shock, deviations of endogenous variables as defined above are also shown in tabular form.

8.3.1 *An import price shock with endogenous food*

Deviations in the time paths of the key endogenous variables relative to base run values are plotted in figures 8.15, 8.16 and 8.17 for the case of a 10 per cent dollar import price rise (terms of trade deterioration). Also plotted are the outcomes for the exogenous food case to be discussed below. The impact of the shock is shown numerically in table 8.1.

An immediate effect of the terms of trade worsening is to reduce real national income via a reduction in (tg), a terms of trade loss. This leads to decreased real demand for domestic output and to a fall in production. This is only partially offset by expenditure switching from higher priced imports to domestic output, with the result that GDP falls. This fall is limited in the

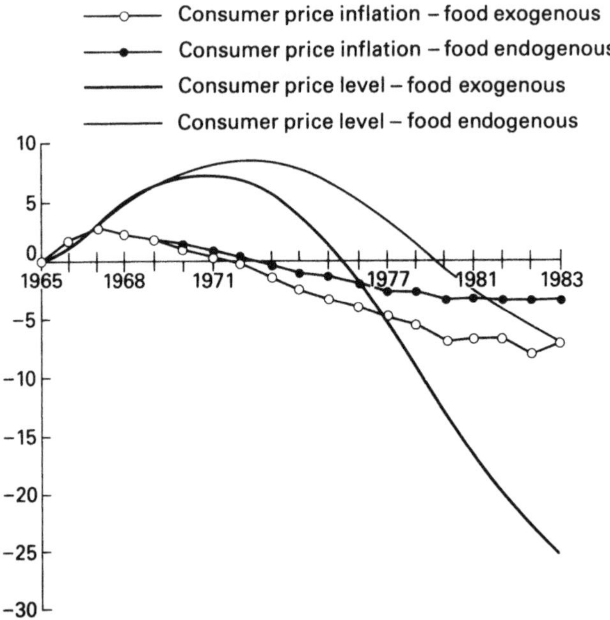

Figure 8.16 Responses of consumer price level and inflation to import price shock – with and without endogenous food production (percentage differences relative to base run)

first period but becomes more accentuated subsequently as the multiplier effect takes hold.

Despite a reduction in the volume of imports due to higher relative prices and reduced demand, price elasticities of import demand are low enough so that the value of imports rises with the rise in prices. As a consequence, the trade balance deteriorates after the shock by an average 0.4 per cent of base GDP in each period.

Inflation accelerates slightly in the first two periods – delayed adjustment being a function of lags in the wage and consumer price equations – as higher imported raw material costs feed into domestic raw material prices and directly into manufacturing costs. This price levels increase sets off a wage-price spiral as wages chase prices in a manner discussed more fully below. The 10 per cent rise in import prices leads in time to an 8.7 per cent increase in the consumer price index. Inflation at its peak in period 2 is 2.6 per cent above base. From period 3 onwards inflation starts to decelerate – led by falling food price inflation. This comes about as falling national income reduces demand for food and in turn leads to smaller increments in

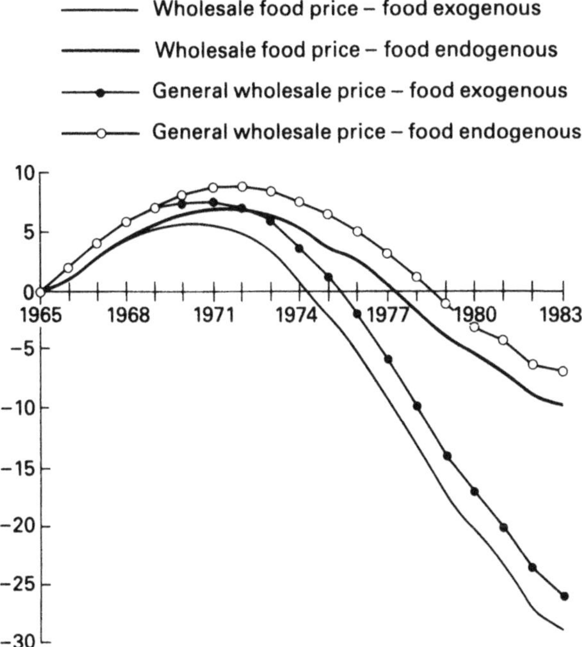

Figure 8.17 Responses of key wholesale price levels to import price shock – with and without endogenous food production (percentage differences relative to base run)

relative price than in the base solution. Lower levels of demand lead to lower rates of inflation. This tendency is however dampened over time as the lower relative price of food translates, with a lag, into reduced food production and therefore into reduced excess demand for food.

On top of the initial downward pressure on GDP that is triggered by the terms of trade loss, output, and consequently inflation as well, is further reduced by a reduction in real wealth that acts upon the level of consumption. While the real value of bonds falls only slightly given near perfect indexation, real money balances are reduced by the higher price level. Moreover, a reduction in foreign reserves in each period due to the increased trade deficit acts as a drain on money. This is only partially offset by a somewhat larger government deficit resulting from lower real tax revenue combined with expenditure and lending commitments that are to a substantial degree fixed in real terms.

Stagflation ensues for the first seven periods after the shock. Later, as the

Table 8.1. *Dynamic elasticities – import price shock with endogenous food*

Year/ period	Trade balance/ base GDP	Real GDP	Consumer price inflation	Consumer price level
1966/1	−0.40	−0.07	1.70	1.22
1967/2	−0.34	−0.38	2.60	3.28
1968/3	−0.33	−0.57	2.20	5.09
1969/4	−0.31	−0.62	1.90	6.63
1970/5	−0.29	−0.76	1.30	7.69
1971/6	−0.31	−0.78	0.80	8.39
1972/7	−0.33	−0.79	0.30	8.65
1973/8	−0.40	−0.80	−0.30	8.39
1974/9	−0.53	−0.66	−1.00	7.63
1975/10	−0.43	−0.78	−1.40	6.59
1976/11	−0.43	−0.73	−1.80	5.23
1977/12	−0.41	−0.71	−2.30	3.50
1978/13	−0.43	−0.72	−2.70	1.45
1979/14	−0.44	−0.78	−3.30	−0.76
1980/15	−0.42	−0.72	−3.10	−2.55
1981/16	−0.41	−0.79	−3.00	−4.13
1982/17	−0.38	−0.82	−3.40	−5.92
1983/18	−0.29	−0.92	−3.30	−7.31

price level falls below base, real wealth begins to grow again sufficiently for the economy to settle temporarily at a point where GDP is below base but growing at the base rate, inflation is lower and the trade balance is worse. Given time, the falling price level would tend to boost both GDP and inflation further, bringing them back towards the base line path. The prevailing outcome is only sustainable provided that the current account deficit can be financed.

8.3.2 *An import price shock with exogenous food*

The impact of this shock is documented in figures 8.15 through 8.17 as well as in table 8.2. When food production is exogenised – equivalent to an exogenous total supply since the other components of food supply are determined outside the model – the inflationary impact of the import shock is reduced. GDP does not deteriorate quite as much since a lower level of

Table 8.2. *Dynamic elasticities – import price shock with exogenous food*

Year/ period	Trade balance/ base GDP	Real GDP	Consumer price inflation	Consumer price level
1966/1	−0.40	−0.09	1.70	1.17
1967/2	−0.34	−0.37	2.80	3.25
1968/3	−0.33	−0.54	2.30	5.06
1969/4	−0.32	−0.58	1.70	6.36
1970/5	−0.30	−0.70	1.00	7.13
1971/6	−0.32	−0.71	0.30	7.38
1972/7	−0.35	−0.72	−0.40	7.03
1973/8	−0.42	−0.72	−1.40	5.81
1974/9	−0.57	−0.58	−2.60	3.86
1975/10	−0.46	−0.67	−3.40	1.36
1976/11	−0.48	−0.60	−4.00	−1.61
1977/12	−0.46	−0.56	−4.90	−5.26
1978/13	−0.48	−0.62	−5.50	−9.18
1979/14	−0.47	−0.71	−6.90	−13.31
1980/15	−0.46	−0.65	−6.70	−16.63
1981/16	−0.44	−0.70	−6.90	−19.65
1982/17	−0.41	−0.74	−7.90	−23.04
1983/18	−0.32	−0.85	−7.10	−25.45

prices – relative to the endogenous food case – preserves real balances, wealth and consumption to a greater extent than before. Import volume is higher and the trade balance worse than before.

Inflation behaves much as in the endogenous food case during the first three periods but subsequently decelerates much more rapidly. This result is due to the fact that food output does not fall with the drop in relative price as it does in the earlier experiment. There is no longer a built in mechanism to dampen or absorb part of the deflationary pressure of a fall in food prices.

In figure 8.16 a salient feature is the very long length of adjustment in the face of a shock. We observe long swings in price levels and inflation rates and no convergence back to the base-run solution path within the expanse of 18 periods. Some specific reasons for this sluggish adjustment are discussed below. It cannot be ruled out, however, that the inflationary process has a built in momentum, causing overshooting, which may lead to long-run unstable, oscillatory behaviour.

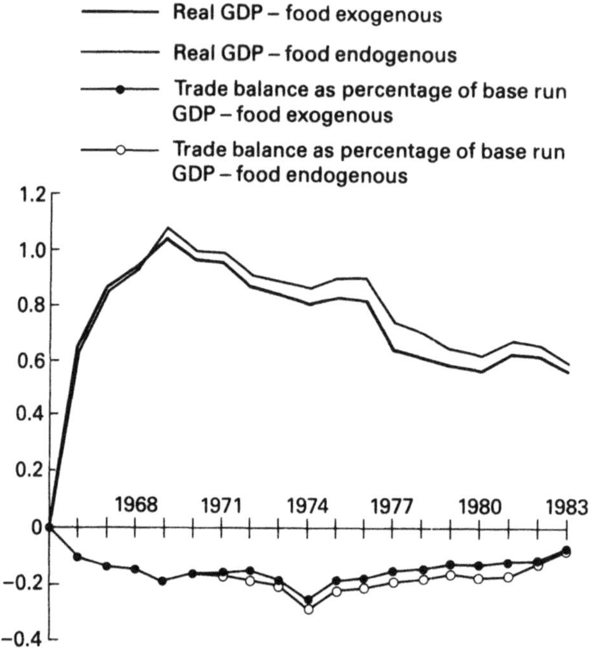

Figure 8.18 Responses of GDP and trade balance to government investment shock – with and without endogenous food production (percentage differences relative to base run)

8.3.3 *A government investment shock with endogenous food*

This shock, taking the form of a 10 per cent rise in real government investment, is reported in figures 8.18, 8.19, 8.20 and in table 8.3. The increase in exogenous demand directly boosts real GDP through its effect upon demand for non-food output. Through the multiplier, aggregate demand expands, driving real GDP up progressively to a level about 1 per cent above base by period 4. Higher GDP is substantially sustained over time, falling back only gradually towards the base path. Falling real wealth is responsible for this trend. Not only are real balances reduced by the higher price level but also the increased trade deficit means less high-powered money is created. Higher aggregate demand brings with it increased imports, leading to a deterioration in the trade balance that averages about 0.2 per cent of base GDP.

The impact upon inflation of demand expansion depends crucially upon the market for food. Higher aggregate demand creates excess demand for

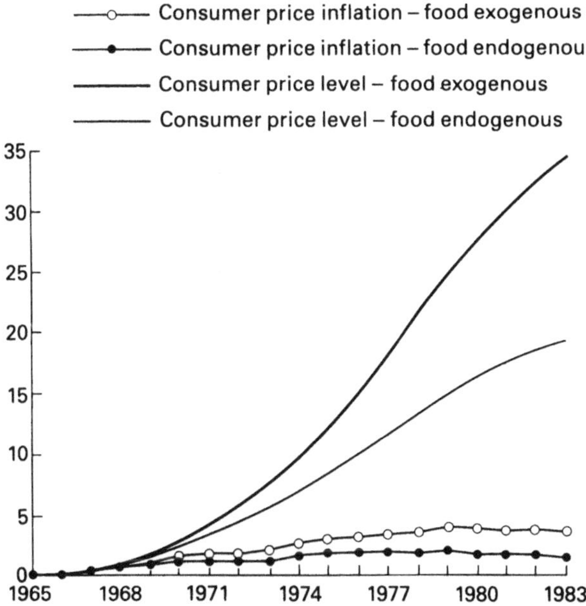

Figure 8.19 Responses of consumer price level and inflation to government investment shock – with and without endogenous food production (percentage differences relative to base run)

food, leading to larger relative food price increases. But, given indexation of earnings and mark-up pricing in manufacturing, nominal wages and prices chase nominal food prices up in an attempt to undo the increase in relative food prices. This simply leads to yet larger increases in nominal food prices and to accelerating inflation as the process repeats itself. As long as food price inflation exceeds consumer price inflation, the price of food relative to the cost of living (as well as to manufactured goods prices) rises, real wages fall and inflation accelerates. This is the fundamental dynamic process inherent in Latin American structuralist models of inflation, as discussed analytically in chapter 1.

Were there no real balance effect operating in the model, inflation would accelerate until all adjustment lags worked themselves out and nominal wages chased manufacturing prices, which in turn chased nominal food prices at a rate sufficiently high to ensure unchanging relative food prices. At this new relative price excess demand may still persist but, as shown in chapter 1, the wage-price spiral is halted as industrial prices rise at a rate equal to that of nominal food prices, thereby preventing any further rise in

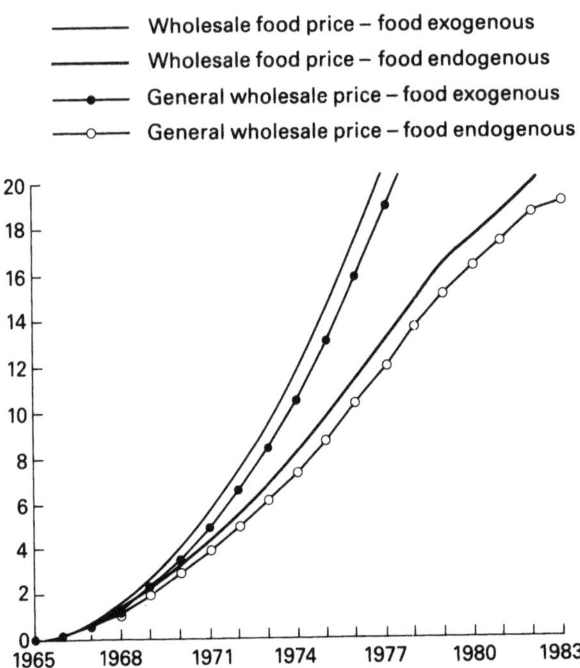

Figure 8.20 Responses of key wholesale price levels to government investment shock – with and without endogenous food production (percentage differences relative to base run)

the relative price of food that might help eliminate excess demand. Depending upon the strength of the wage-price spiral, equilibrium may, on the other hand, be re-established if the relative price is high enough to choke off demand and/or to bring about an increase in supply. In the present model the price elasticity of demand for food and the price elasticity of food supply are both low, necessitating a large relative price increase either to dampen food demand significantly or to bring forth sufficient new food production to help restore equilibrium in subsequent periods.

The speed of adjustment in the absence of real balance effects would be governed solely by lags in the model. These depend primarily upon the rate at which food prices adjust to excess demand – shown in chapter 5 to be slow – and, to a lesser extent, upon the coefficients of wage adjustment. After wage increases are passed on to manufacturing prices, there occurs another lag before this adjustment is fully reflected in the consumer price index because lagged as well as current (P^{I}) is a determinant of this index. As

Table 8.3. *Dynamic elasticities – government investment shock with endogenous food*

Year/ period	Trade balance/ base GDP	Real GDP	Consumer price inflation	Consumer price level
1966/1	−0.11	0.65	0.20	0.14
1967/2	−0.14	0.87	0.40	0.46
1968/3	−0.15	0.94	0.70	1.02
1969/4	−0.19	1.06	1.00	1.80
1970/5	−0.17	0.99	1.20	2.73
1971/6	−0.17	0.99	1.20	3.72
1972/7	−0.18	0.92	1.20	4.74
1973/8	−0.20	0.88	1.30	5.83
1974/9	−0.29	0.87	1.80	7.17
1975/10	−0.22	0.91	1.90	8.58
1976/11	−0.22	0.91	2.00	10.11
1977/12	−0.19	0.75	2.10	11.76
1978/13	−0.18	0.70	2.00	13.41
1979/14	−0.16	0.64	2.20	15.05
1980/15	−0.17	0.62	1.90	16.32
1981/16	−0.17	0.67	1.80	17.46
1982/17	−0.14	0.65	1.80	18.62
1983/18	−0.08	0.59	1.50	19.41

a consequence of adjustment lags in the model, inflation accelerates, albeit at a gentle pace, for twelve periods in response to the demand shock.

The impact of a real balance effect is that the adjustment process stabilises at a lower rate of inflation than would otherwise be possible, since higher inflation reduces real wealth and thus puts downward pressure on the demand for food. Equilibrium between demand and supply of food is obtained with a lower relative price than in the absence of a real balance effect. However, in the case of the government investment shock, because of the importance of indexed assets and because new high-powered money is created through the government deficit and trade balance, the real balance effect is not strong.

The government investment shock is a useful one for evaluating the strength of demand-pull factors upon inflation. If we rescale the results reported in table 8.3 to set shocked GDP equal to 1.0 per cent above base in each period, these indicate that a 1.0 per cent rise in GDP causes a 0.3 per cent rise in inflation in the first period and a further 0.5 per cent and 0.7 per cent rise in the second and third periods respectively.[6] Thereafter, the impact is greater still. This result suggests that demand has a reasonably powerful effect upon inflation. Reference was made in chapter 2 to the strength of demand effects implied by commodity market Phillips curve for Brazil. The results reported in table 2.3 show that these suggest a 1.03 per cent to 1.84 per cent rise in inflation during the current period consequent upon a 1 per cent increase in GDP. Modiano (1985), using a framework more akin to that employed here, finds an impact of 0.90 per cent over one period. Our results point to a much slower reaction lag between changes in demand and inflation than do these studies. Inflation in the first period is only one quarter to one fifth that implied by the above-mentioned studies. However, even the impact multiplier from the present model is somewhat greater than what Lopes (1982) reports to be the equivalent coefficient for the United States (see chapter 2 (2.3.1)).

It is noteworthy that the underlying causal mechanism linking demand and prices, namely food market disequilibrium, is completely different to that posited by the commodity market Phillips curve analyses.[7] As a consequence, the policy prescriptions for fighting inflation that derive from this model are very different to those that flow from the commodity market Phillips curve.

8.3.4 *A government investment shock with exogenous food*

The impact of the same demand shock upon the key variables, under the assumption of a fixed food supply, is also plotted in figures 8.18 through 8.20 and shown in table 8.4. With food output unresponsive to rising relative prices, inflation accelerates more rapidly than in the endogenous food case. An important food market equilibrating mechanism that was at work previously is now crippled. The restoration of balance between food supply and demand requires much more rapid inflation and higher relative prices. Since the higher price level (relative to the endogenous food case) reduces real wealth by a greater amount, real GDP is slightly lower in the latter part of the simulation. Accordingly, the trade balance deteriorates by marginally less than in the endogenous food case.

8.3.5 *A food production shock with endogenous food*

This shock, which takes the form of a fall in output equal to 10 per cent of period 1 production, is reported in figures 8.21 through 8.24 and in table 8.5. To a much greater extent than was the case with the earlier shocks, this one has a dramatic quantitative impact upon real and price variables in the

Table 8.4. *Dynamic elasticities – government investment shock with exogenous food*

Year/ period	Trade balance/ base GDP	Real GDP	Consumer price inflation	Consumer price level
1966/1	−0.11	0.64	0.20	0.14
1967/2	−0.14	0.88	0.50	0.51
1968/3	−0.15	0.93	0.80	1.12
1969/4	−0.19	1.04	1.20	2.00
1970/5	−0.16	0.96	1.60	3.19
1971/6	−0.17	0.96	1.70	4.52
1972/7	−0.17	0.87	1.90	6.12
1973/8	−0.18	0.84	2.10	7.94
1974/9	−0.26	0.81	2.80	10.08
1975/10	−0.20	0.83	3.00	12.42
1976/11	−0.19	0.82	3.20	15.05
1977/12	−0.16	0.64	3.50	18.10
1978/13	−0.15	0.61	3.60	21.31
1979/14	−0.13	0.59	4.10	24.58
1980/15	−0.15	0.57	3.80	27.28
1981/16	−0.15	0.62	3.60	29.69
1982/17	−0.12	0.62	4.00	32.46
1983/18	−0.07	0.56	3.50	34.50

system. An immediate effect is to reduce production and real income.[8] This effect is multiplied through the system as reduced real expenditure drives down non-food output as well. To the very limited extent that rising food prices choke off food demand, there occurs some substitution in consumption in favour of non-food items. This will dampen slightly the downward movement in non-food output. GDP reaches its nadir relative to base in period 4 at minus 1.8 per cent. The trade balance improves with the fall in domestic demand.

Lower supply immediately creates excess demand for food and starts to drive up relative food prices. Earnings, manufacturing prices and consumer prices all chase nominal food prices in an attempt to remove the relative price change. This is shown graphically in figure 8.24. However, lags in wage adjustment and in adjustment of consumer prices to industrial prices mean that nominal food prices rise more rapidly than either wages or overall prices. The price of food relative to overall consumer price increases

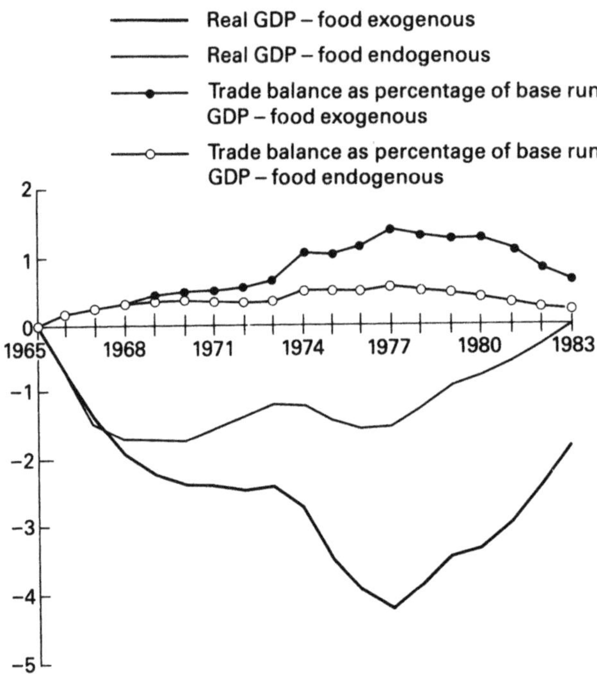

Figure 8.21 Responses of GDP and trade balance to food production shock – with and without endogenous food production (percentage differences relative to base run)

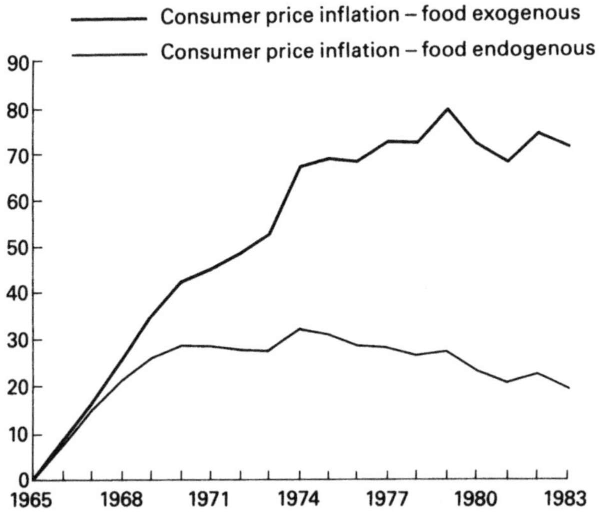

Figure 8.22 Responses of consumer price inflation to food production shock – with and without endogenous food production (percentage differences relative to base run)

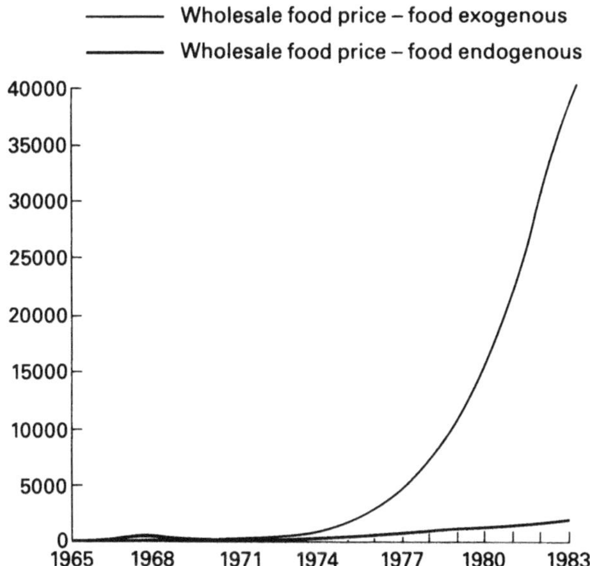

Figure 8.23 Responses of wholesale food price levels to food production shock – with and without endogenous food production (percentage differences relative to base run)

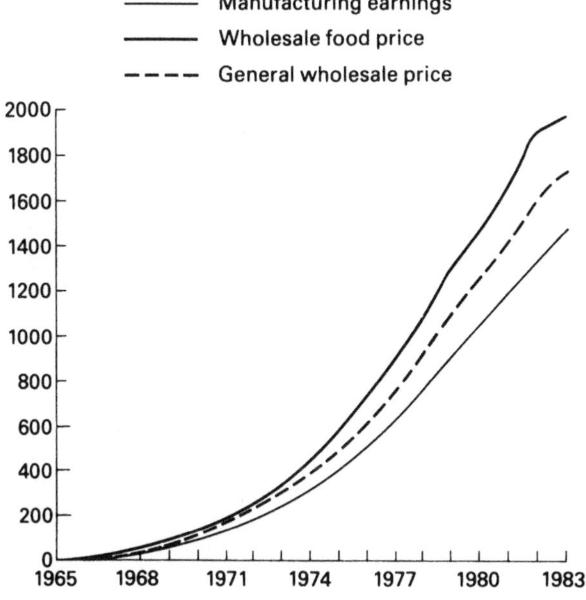

Figure 8.24 Responses of key price levels to food production shock – food production endogenous (percentage differences relative to base run)

Table 8.5. *Dynamic elasticities – food production shock with endogenous food*

Year/ period	Trade balance/ base GDP	Real GDP	Consumer price inflation	Consumer price level
1966/1	0.15	−0.89	8.50	6.10
1967/2	0.24	−1.47	15.90	19.29
1968/3	0.30	−1.72	21.60	39.86
1969/4	0.35	−1.76	26.20	68.15
1970/5	0.34	−1.73	28.90	105.33
1971/6	0.32	−1.57	28.40	152.25
1972/7	0.33	−1.39	27.90	209.51
1973/8	0.35	−1.17	28.10	279.42
1974/9	0.50	−1.22	32.80	366.58
1975/10	0.46	−1.47	31.70	469.00
1976/11	0.50	−1.56	28.80	584.89
1977/12	0.56	−1.52	28.40	723.73
1978/13	0.50	−1.25	26.50	884.24
1979/14	0.43	−0.92	27.90	1065.25
1980/15	0.40	−0.76	23.40	1223.97
1981/16	0.31	−0.55	21.20	1375.85
1982/17	0.22	−0.29	23.00	1562.36
1983/18	0.18	−0.04	19.90	1709.98

more or less continuously up until period 9. At this point in time relative food price is 21 per cent above base and the resulting price stimulus has caused food output to rise to a level only 3.5 per cent below base. Implicit demand for food is lower due to the substitution effect of higher price and of a slightly lower real income. Since, by period 9, food market equilibrium is re-established and relative price stops rising, inflation no longer accelerates. Nevertheless, a rise of nearly 33 percentage points in the rate of inflation was required in order to re-establish this equilibrium.

If price elasticities of demand and/or supply and income elasticity of demand were higher, a smaller increase in relative food price and lower inflation would have sufficed to restore equilibrium. If the price adjustment coefficient were higher we would have seen a more rapid surge in inflation but equilibrium in the food market would have been restored sooner. Since food demand is below base and, given lower national income, excess supply emerges, causing a very gradual deceleration of inflation from period 9 onwards (see figure 8.22).

Adjustment in the food market comes about at the cost of a fall in real earnings in manufacturing of 10 per cent (period 9 level relative to base run).

The behaviour of financial variables, combined with the recovery of food output, enables GDP to rise gradually back towards base level after bottoming out in period 4. With lower GDP, real tax revenues are reduced. With most components of government expenditure fixed in real terms, the deficit expands. This, combined with the expansionary impact upon foreign reserves of the trade balance improvement, ensures that in the longer run sufficient new high-powered money is created to offset the erosion of existing real balances via price increases. Real wealth falls initially by some 25 per cent but then moves back up over time to a point only 4 per cent below base at the end of the simulation period. This helps to explain why inflation tapers off only slightly after period 9. Other things being equal, a fall in GDP sets in motion stabilising forces that tend to push it back up by stimulating private expenditure.

8.3.6 *A food shock with exogenous food*

This outcome is also pictured in figures 8.21 through 8.24 and is reported in table 8.6. With no food supply response, a much higher relative price of food is necessary than in the previous experiment to restore equilibrium by forcing down demand. With the speed of price adjustment the same as in the endogenous food model, the restoration of equilibrium now takes much longer. Inflation accelerates for twelve to thirteen years before reaching a plateau at a rate of 70–80 percentage points above the base rate, compared with 25–30 points in the endogenous food case. To choke off the excess demand for food, in the face of rigid supply, a substantially greater fall in domestic demand, real income and output is required along with a much higher relative food price. The demand reduction comes about primarily due to the effects of a large cut in real wealth brought on by a much higher price level. Were there no real balance effects, an even higher relative price and more inflation would be required to restore equilibrium. GDP falls quite dramatically, reaching a trough in period 12 at over 4 per cent below base. However, output starts rising again towards base after period 12 as a flood of new high-powered money enters the system, via the greatly improved trade balance and increased government deficit. This has an expansionary effect upon demand. With food supply static and income rising slightly, there is no mechanism operative to bring inflation back down to a lower rate.

The experiment demonstrates dramatically the importance of the food market in the inflationary process. The inflationary dangers of institutional

Table 8.6. *Dynamic elasticities – food production shock with exogenous food*

Year/ period	Trade balance/ base GDP	Real GDP	Consumer price inflation	Consumer price level
1966/1	0.14	−0.80	8.00	5.52
1967/2	0.24	−1.48	17.10	18.77
1968/3	0.33	−1.95	25.70	41.95
1969/4	0.42	−2.21	34.90	78.22
1970/5	0.46	−2.39	42.60	133.20
1971/6	0.48	−2.43	45.70	214.42
1972/7	0.56	−2.46	48.70	337.71
1973/8	0.68	−2.41	53.40	527.90
1974/9	1.06	−2.74	67.70	829.59
1975/10	1.02	−3.49	69.70	1288.46
1976/11	1.17	−3.96	68.70	1987.27
1977/12	1.40	−4.23	72.90	3138.27
1978/13	1.32	−3.88	72.50	4907.48
1979/14	1.24	−3.43	80.80	7574.62
1980/15	1.27	−3.30	72.60	10 753.04
1981/16	1.11	−2.93	69.20	14 703.75
1982/17	0.84	−2.36	75.30	20 655.28
1983/18	0.64	−1.79	72.30	27 260.06

or policy impediments to a flexible supply response in the traditional agricultural sector are manifest, as is the stabilising potential of removing such impediments.

8.4 Conclusion

In this chapter, two procedures were applied to the model in order to test whether it attained an acceptable standard of performance. The historical tracking can be judged adequate, bearing in mind the high level of aggregation used in modelling, particularly as regards the real sector of the economy. As noted, tracking errors in the wage and price variables owe a lot to prediction errors in the relative food price equation.

As the model is not designed to forecast specific values, consistency in its dynamic response to outside stimuli is a more important criteria for model evaluation than are its tracking properties. In this area, the model performed reasonably well. However, a possibility of potentially unstable long-run oscillatory behaviour was identified. The very long swings in price levels and inflation rates appear to be related to the combination of gradual adjustment of prices and inflation to changes in activity with sluggish downward pressure on activity, prices and inflation through the weak real balance effect. It is also true that the inflation adjustment process has a built-in momentum which keeps it rising even after real balances and aggregate demand have fallen back. This leads to overshooting. Having said this, the responses of the model to shocks generally accord with prior expectations based on theory – i.e. as set out in chapter 1 – as well as with outside empirical observation.

The exercises performed in this chapter show that a once and for all change in relative prices can easily produce a continuous inflation in an economy with mark-up pricing and widespread official or implicit indexation of key prices such as wages and the exchange rate. A powerful inertial component of inflation was identified that depended upon the interaction of different prices as well as upon the endogenous response of the model's financial sector. These findings, which fit well with the predictions of Latin American structuralism, are derived from a model that is quite general and able to account for cost-push, 'structuralist' and demand-pull inflations. Rather than assume simply that finance is accommodating, the model allowed for an explicit consideration of certain important interactions between primary inflationary pressures, government policies, stocks and flows of financial assets and continuous inflation.

9 Policy experiments

9.1 Introduction

The validating exercises carried out in the last half of chapter 8 not only served to enquire into the technical properties of the model but also yielded results of interest in understanding some of the processes underlying Brazil's inflation. The aim of the present chapter is to enquire further into the nature of inflation and particularly to examine the interaction between inflationary pressures and possible policy responses, on the assumption that the model provides an adequate, if simple, representation of the Brazilian economy. We wish to continue the process begun in chapter 8 of linking the model results both to the theoretical framework of chapter 1 and to some of the important issues and hypotheses raised in chapter 2 concerning the specific inflationary experience under study. We are now returning to the central theme of the study – namely a structuralist vision of inflation augmented to account for financial influences – and the experience of Brazil.

A large variety of policy experiments, of varying degrees of complexity, could be performed with the model. However, time and space precluded the implementation and reporting of a great number of experiments. The exercises selected do, nevertheless, illustrate many of the major insights to be gained from the model. The five experiments reported here were designed to help illuminate better the direct and indirect effects of inflationary shocks and of actual policy measures that characterised the Brazilian experience. Naturally the experiments are crude and simplistic in comparison with actual phenomena and policy packages but this does not detract from their usefulness in highlighting major implications of any given event or course of action. No attempt has been made to replicate, either quantitatively or qualitatively, inflationary conditions and policy packages corresponding to an historically precise experience. In the absence of constraints on time and space, such a procedure might be attempted in order, for instance, to examine the combined impact of real devaluation, terms of trade deterioration and a change in wage indexation policy, as actually occurred in 1979. However, the implementation of such an experiment would be complex and it is not clear that the model is equipped to deal with such a degree of complexity. Our analysis is at a higher level of generality.

The experiments performed fall into two broad categories. The first, comprising two experiments, involves an analysis of the system's response to a foreign price shock under alternative regimes of earnings and exchange rate indexation. The second category, comprising three experiments, examines how policy-makers might respond to a food production shock by manipulating the time paths of selected variables. Policy reaction functions are proposed for the food subsidy rate and for food imports, both of which were held exogenous in previous runs. In one experiment it is additionally assumed that the policy-makers set a target for the trade balance and assign the direct tax rate as an instrument variable.

The outcomes of the policy experiments are reported in a manner analogous to that used in the multiplier analysis of chapter 8. For each alternative policy, a base solution is obtained under the new assumptions regarding institutional regimes or policy objectives. The models are then subject to counterfactual shocks and the shocked solution values are compared with the relevant base solutions. Deviations of key endogenous variables from their base values are calculated as in the earlier exercises, plotted and also presented in tabular form. To facilitate an appreciation of the impact of the shocks under the new regimes, also plotted are the post-shock outcomes for the same endogenous variables in the absence of a policy response.

9.2 An import price shock with an alternative indexation rule for earnings

The object of this exercise is to consider how differently the system reacts to the same 10 per cent dollar import price shock applied in chapter 8 (8.3.1) (where an endogenous food response was allowed for), assuming slower and incomplete adjustment of nominal earnings to changes in consumer price. The parameters of the earnings inflation equation (7.42) were changed to make it read

$$\dot{W}^{1}_{t} = 0.71 + 0.4\dot{P}^{CG}_{t} + 0.4\dot{P}^{CG}_{t-1} + \text{DUMMIES}$$

where the constant term, dummy variables and their coefficients are as in the standard model. A simple two period adjustment scheme is proposed that ensures only 80 per cent pass through of price increases to wages. This

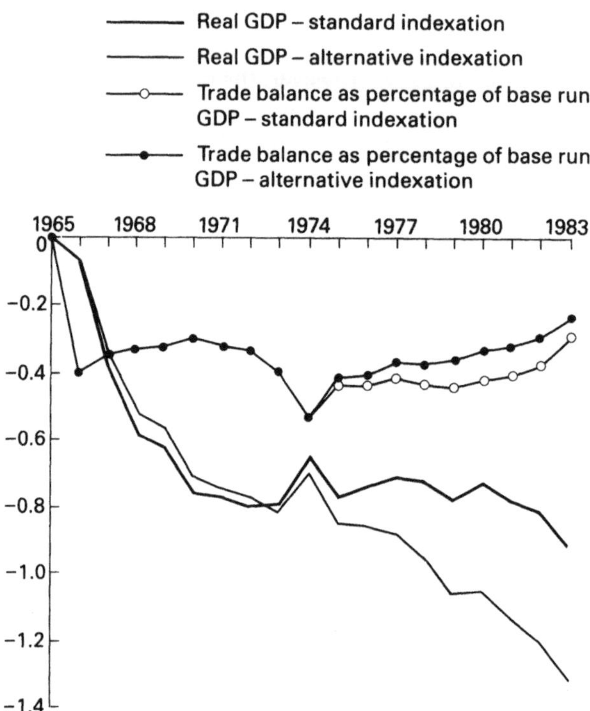

Figure 9.1 Responses of GDP and trade balance to import price shock – under two earnings indexation schemes (percentage differences relative to base run)

contrasts with the standard model in which 100 per cent pass through is assumed. Moreover, adjustment takes place more slowly with only 40 per cent occurring in period 1 as opposed to 68 per cent in the standard model. The changes made correspond to a reduction in the wage adjustment coefficient (h) in the model of chapter 1.

The manner in which the system responds to the price shock under the standard (100 per cent) and alternative (80 per cent) indexation schemes is portrayed graphically in figures 9.1, 9.2, 9.3 and in table 9.1. The latter shows the numerical impact of the shock relative to base under the alternative indexation scheme. Table 8.1 gives the numerical impact of the same shock under the standard indexation scheme. Inflation accelerates in both cases during the first two periods but the post-shock peak under the alternative is only 1.8 as opposed to 2.6 percentage points above base. The consumer price level, at its highest, is 4.0 per cent (periods 5 and 6) rather than 8.7 per cent above base (period 7). The inflationary impact of the

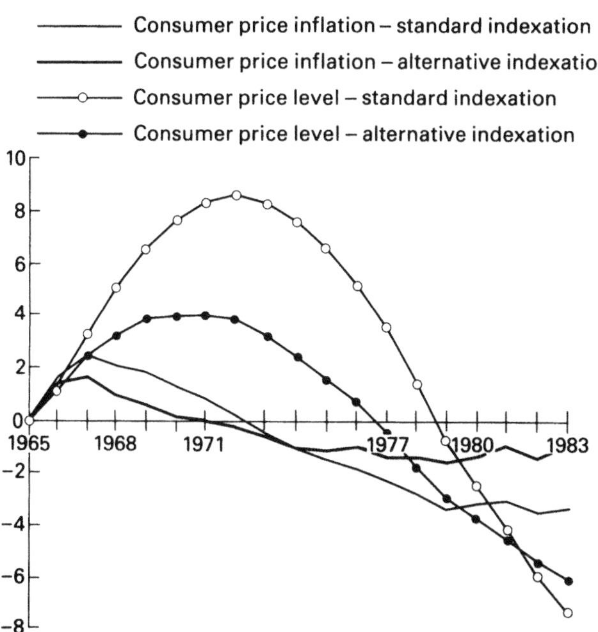

Figure 9.2 Responses of consumer price level and inflation to import price shock – under two earnings indexation schemes (percentage differences relative to base run)

shock is initially attenuated because wage and salary earners in manufacturing absorb more of the real income loss that results from the deterioration in the terms of trade than they do in the standard model. This is illustrated in figure 9.3, which shows the well-known result that the lower the adjustment coefficient, the more an acceleration in inflation reduces real earnings.[1] The corollary to this is that as inflation decelerates after period 2, real earnings rise more rapidly. This in turn dampens the pace at which overall inflation decelerates in that it implies higher rates of nominal earnings inflation relative to price inflation. Thus a greater stability of inflation rates and price levels is achieved at the cost of more variability in real earnings.[2]

Over the first nine to ten years there is little difference under the two indexation regimes in the impact of the shock upon GDP and the trade balance. The model does not capture the distributional impact of the shock upon income, output and the trade balance.[3] If, as we might assume, the propensity to consume out of wage income is higher than out of profits, the shock, by shifting income in favour of capitalists, would have the additional

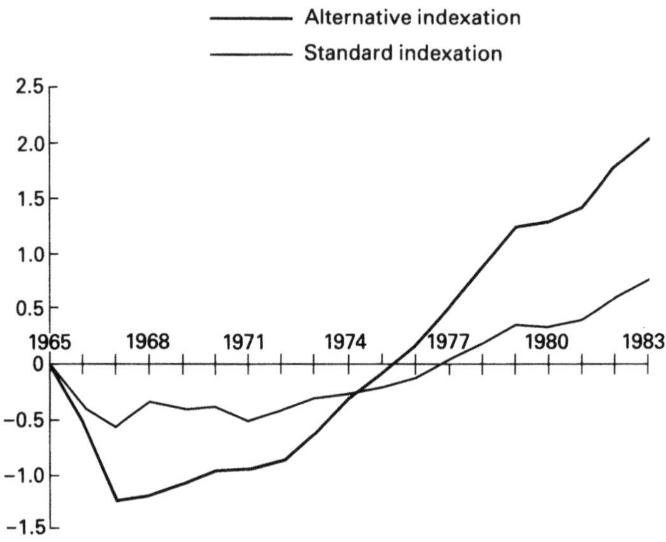

Figure 9.3 Responses of the level of real manufacturing earnings to import price shock – under two earnings indexation schemes (percentage differences relative to base run)

effect of further depressing domestic demand and output, taking more pressure off inflation and causing the trade balance to recover somewhat. Whether or not rising profits would boost investment sufficiently to compensate is another question.

The only way in which the exchange rate regime change does have a direct impact upon the real economy in the present model is through its effect upon the production costs of manufactured exports. A rise occurs in the relative price of exports as lower real earnings hold down manufacturing prices, giving added stimulus to exports. However, quantitatively, this effect is negligible because the interdependence of prices ensures that lower levels of the manufacturing price also contribute to a lower exchange rate, dampening the extent of the relative export price rise.

In the early years of the shock, real national income falls by very slightly less in the alternative, as opposed to standard, indexation case. This is due to the favourable impact of a smaller price rise upon real balances. A difference in the impact of the shock upon the trade balance under the two regimes is virtually imperceptible before the 10th period. The markedly faster drop in GDP that is registered under the alternative indexation scheme, beginning in period 10, can also be traced to the behaviour of real balances. In the standard model, the depressing influence upon real

Table 9.1. *Dynamic elasticities – import price shock with alternative (reduced) indexation of earnings (percentage differences relative to base run)*

Year/ period	Trade balance as a percentage of base run GDP	Real GDP	Consumer price inflation	Consumer price level
1966/1	−0.40	−0.07	1.50	1.08
1967/2	−0.35	−0.35	1.80	2.51
1968/3	−0.33	−0.52	1.00	3.34
1969/4	−0.32	−0.57	0.60	3.84
1970/5	−0.30	−0.71	0.20	4.02
1971/6	−0.32	−0.75	0.00	4.02
1972/7	−0.33	−0.78	−0.20	3.83
1973/8	−0.40	−0.81	−0.60	3.27
1974/9	−0.53	−0.69	−1.00	2.43
1975/10	−0.41	−0.85	−1.00	1.58
1976/11	−0.41	−0.85	−1.00	0.69
1977/12	−0.37	−0.88	−1.30	−0.47
1978/13	−0.38	−0.96	−1.30	−1.66
1979/14	−0.36	−1.08	−1.50	−2.89
1980/15	−0.33	−1.05	−1.10	−3.71
1981/16	−0.32	−1.14	−1.00	−4.42
1982/17	−0.30	−1.20	−1.30	−5.39
1983/18	−0.24	−1.33	−0.90	−6.02

balances of the leakage of foreign reserves through the enlarged trade deficit is to a great extent compensated for by the rapid fall in the price level after period 7. This leads only to a gentle fall in output below base. Because prices fall much more slowly under the alternative indexation regime, the leakage effect dominates, driving real balances and GDP down more rapidly. The trade balance improves accordingly.

The results of this exercise suggest that a reduction in the speed of adjustment and a partial de-indexation of earnings can be useful in checking the propagation of inflation after a relative price shock. Comparing the outcome of the import price shock under both indexation schemes shows that a rate of inflation that is 0.8 per cent lower on average in each of the seven years following the shock is achieved at the cost of a 0.5 per cent per year drop in average real earnings. There emerges a clear short-run trade-off between inflation and functional income distribution unless, of course, employment is stimulated significantly to compensate for the loss in the real earnings rate – an unlikely outcome. In the longer term, however, the downward rigidity of inflation is heightened by the alternative scheme and income is redistributed back to workers. These distributional consequences would likely have many implications, both economic and political, not captured by the present model. One of these, referred to briefly in chapter 2, is the reduction in the demand for food and, consequently, in the rate of inflation as well, that would likely result from a cut in real earnings in industry.

In the short to medium term, real aggregates are little affected by the change in earnings indexation. The long-term impact upon GDP of the shock under the alternative rule is of little practical interest as other policy measures would surely be introduced to counter continued deflation.

During the mid-1960s, changes in wage and salary indexation schemes were used in Brazil as a device to bring down inflation. The deterioration that occurred in the share of wages in national income during that period is certainly compatible with what the model suggests is an important consequence of such a policy. By contrast, in 1979 the authorities changed the wage setting rule to increase the speed at which price changes were passed on to wages. The model clearly predicts that such a change would have contributed to the steep rise in the inflationary threshold that took place in that year.[4]

9.3 An import price shock with an alternative indexation rule for the exchange rate

Another crucial instance of indexation in the Brazilian economy, albeit one of informal indexation, concerns the price of foreign currency. Here it is assumed that the one to one link between the domestic/foreign inflation differential and exchange devaluation is severed. The following rule is proposed to govern the rate of cruzeiro/U.S. dollar devaluation

$$\Delta \ln E_t = 0.8 \Delta \ln P_t^{WG} - 1.0 \Delta \ln P_t^{WUS*} + \text{DUMMIES}$$

where dummy variables enter the expression as in the standard model of equation (7.46).

No longer is the real exchange rate independent of domestic inflation. Instead, inflation now brings about a real currency appreciation because the coefficient of ($\Delta \ln P_t^{WG}$) is set equal to 0.8 rather than to 1.0 as in the standard model.

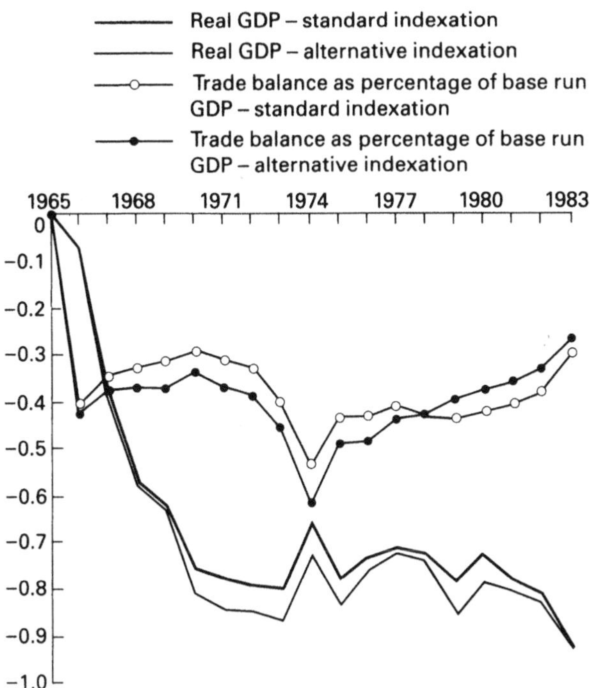

Figure 9.4 Responses of GDP and trade balance to import price shock – under two exchange rate indexation schemes (percentage differences relative to base run)

The results obtained when the model is subject to a 10 per cent import price shock with standard and alternative exchange rate indexation rules are shown in figures 9.4 and 9.5. Table 9.2 and table 8.1 contain the values for the alternative and standard cases respectively. Under the alternative regime, the inflationary impact of the price shock is reduced. Domestic prices are now somewhat shielded from the foreign price rise with the result that inflation peaks at 2.4 rather than 2.6 points above base in period 2. The consumer price index at its peak in period 6 is 6.6 per cent higher as opposed to 8.7 per cent higher in period 7 in the standard case.

The model allows for a change in the exchange rate regime to have a direct impact upon the real sector of the economy. Incomplete indexation leads to a real appreciation of the cruzeiro. By the end of the third period, the real exchange rate (deflated by the wholesale price index) is 16 per cent lower than in the shock experiment with standard 100 per cent indexation. This real appreciation in turn causes the relative cruzeiro prices of imports and exports to fall over time.

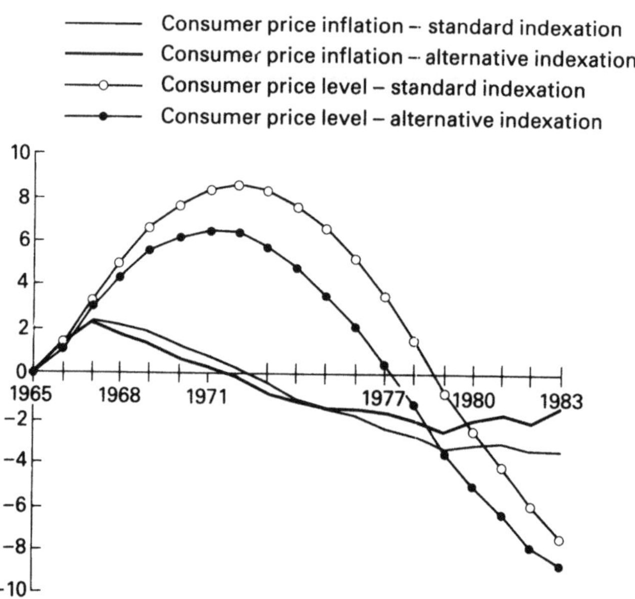

Figure 9.5 Responses of consumer price level and inflation to import price shock – under two exchange rate indexation schemes (percentage differences relative to base run)

Over the first twelve years of the simulation, imports are stimulated and exports depressed, with the result that the trade balance deteriorates by more than in the standard indexation case and pulls GDP down with it. Nevertheless, quantitatively the impact of the regime change is not great, with the cumulative deterioration over 12 years in the trade balance relative to average base level GDP equal to about 2 per cent. The weakness of this effect can be traced not only to the fact that exports and imports are price inelastic but also to the fact that upward pressure on the import price, emanating from the relative price change, is attenuated by lower domestic demand. This process is aided in as much as imports are much more income elastic than they are price elastic. The contractionary income effect upon the trade balance of the real appreciation of the currency largely dominates the expansionary price effect. It must be borne in mind that, given the simple specification of the foreign sector in the model, only a very approximate evaluation of the impact of real exchange rate changes upon trade flows is possible.

A portion of the real income loss associated with the terms of trade deterioration that results from the rise in dollar import prices is borne by

Table 9.2. *Dynamic elasticities – import price shock under alternative (reduced) exchange rate indexation (percentage differences relative to base run)*

Year/ period	Trade balance as a percentage of base run GDP	Real GDP	Consumer price inflation	Consumer price level
1966/1	−0.42	−0.10	1.50	1.09
1967/2	−0.37	−0.41	2.40	3.03
1968/3	−0.37	−0.57	1.80	4.57
1969/4	−0.37	−0.64	1.30	5.67
1970/5	−0.34	−0.81	0.70	6.28
1971/6	−0.37	−0.85	0.30	6.55
1972/7	−0.39	−0.85	−0.10	6.46
1973/8	−0.46	−0.87	−0.70	5.80
1974/9	−0.62	−0.73	−1.20	4.80
1975/10	−0.48	−0.83	−1.50	3.56
1976/11	−0.48	−0.75	−1.60	2.20
1977/12	−0.44	−0.72	−2.00	0.46
1978/13	−0.43	−0.75	−2.10	−1.44
1979/14	−0.39	−0.85	−2.50	−3.50
1980/15	−0.37	−0.78	−2.10	−5.00
1981/16	−0.35	−0.80	−2.00	−6.32
1982/17	−0.33	−0.83	−2.10	−7.77
1983/18	−0.27	−0.90	−1.40	−8.59

exporters whose incomes were previously fully insulated against inflation. In contrast, workers bear less of the brunt of adjustment than in the standard indexation case since the fall in real earnings is less pronounced due to a more limited acceleration of inflation.

After period 12, there occurs a reversal – relative to the standard indexation case – of the earlier improvement in the trade balance. In a process analogous to that observed for real earnings under the alternative indexation regime, the relative prices of imports and exports begin to rise more quickly compared with the standard case as inflation falls below the base line rate. However, the lagging behind of exchange rate changes that results from the partial de-indexation puts a break upon the fall in overall inflation.

This exercise suggests that there may be a role to be played by partial de-indexation of the exchange rate in an anti-inflationary policy package. The cost in terms of short-run balance of payments deterioration appears to be quite low. However, there are obvious limits to this course of action as was demonstrated by the Chilean experience with a fixed nominal exchange rate from mid-1979 to mid-1982 (see Parkin, 1983).

The authorities might decide to respond to a foreign price-shock not by bringing about a real appreciation of the currency, as in the experiment reported on above, but rather by stepped up devaluation aimed at staving off any deterioration in the trade balance. Although not examined explicitly here, our model suggests that a 'super indexation' of the exchange rate in the face of the shock would yield an outcome that is the mirror image of that obtained in the present experiment. The inflationary impact of the shock would be magnified with only limited favourable consequences for the trade balance and GDP. Instead, to be effective in combating the trade deficit, a policy of gradual real devaluation needs to be accompanied by expenditure reducing measures. Industrial price controls could be used to ensure a more pronounced change in the relative price of tradable goods and, therefore, a more powerful impact upon trade flows, by preventing a wage-price spiral that would otherwise be set off by the real devaluation.

Another possible course of action, and one that is similar to that followed in Brazil in 1979–80, would be to confront the terms of trade deterioration with a once and for all real devaluation while maintaining unchanged the exchange rate indexation parameters.[5] The model clearly predicts that such a policy would have a major inflationary impact without bringing about a significant improvement in the foreign sector. The incipient rise in the relative cruzeiro prices of imports would spark off strongly accelerating inflation as, first manufacturing prices, then wages chased the nominal exchange rate in an attempt to undo the relative price change. The policy would be inefficient since only by forcing demand down tremendously through the medium of an erosion of real balances could there occur a lasting improvement in the trade balance.

The role of devaluation in economic stabilisation in developing countries has long been a hotly debated issue. The experiment performed here lends support to the view, often associated with the structuralist school, that devaluation alone is not a particularly efficient stabilisation policy since the degree to which it causes expenditure switching is limited by the low price elasticity of imports and exports. On the other hand, it is clear that the inflationary consequences of devaluation cannot be overlooked.

9.4 A food shock with a food subsidy response

Here we take up again an issue considered repeatedly in earlier chapters, namely the macroeconomic impact of food subsidies. In chapter 1 we discussed the importance of assessing the direct price impact as well as the financial consequences of a subsidy policy. In chapters 2 and 5 the important role accorded to food subsidies in Brazil after 1974 was highlighted.

For the purposes of this experiment, the hypothesis adopted was that, faced with a negative food production shock, policy-makers manipulated the consumer food subsidy rate sufficiently to isolate the consumer food price from the impact of the shock. Instead of rising, along with the wholesale price of food, relative to the general level of prices, this policy ensured that consumer food prices remained unchanged relative to the overall consumer price index. In other words, subsidies were increased sufficiently to neutralise any incipient tendency for the relative consumer price of food to rise in the face of a fall in production. Controls on consumer food prices, combined with growing subsidisation, fulfilled this objective while allowing the wholesale price to respond to the altered supply conditions.

This policy rule was implemented by including a policy reaction function in the model of the form:

$$m_t^{\mathrm{sh}} = m_t^{\mathrm{b}} + [(P^{\mathrm{WF}}/P^{\mathrm{CG}})_t^{sh} - (P^{\mathrm{WF}}/P^{\mathrm{CG}})_t^{b}]$$

where (m_t^{b}) and $[(P^{\mathrm{WF}}/P^{\mathrm{CG}})_t^{b}]$ are the base run values for the unit subsidy factor (1 – the rate of subsidy) and the relative wholesale food price, both held exogenous in this experiment. The effect of this rule is to ensure that any upward pressure on the relative wholesale food price in the shocked run $[(P^{\mathrm{WF}}/P^{\mathrm{CG}})_t^{sh}]$ leads to an exactly offsetting fall in the unit subsidy factor (m^{sh}). This is equivalent to a rise in the rate of subsidy since $\tau = (1 - m)$. Given the configuration of the consumer food price equation, this ensures in turn that the change in the relative wholesale price of food is not passed on to the relative consumer price of food. Food production remains endogenous as in the standard model.

The dynamic behaviour of key variables in response to the same 10 per cent fall in *per capita* food production applied in chapter 8.3.5 is plotted in figures 9.6, 9.7 and 9.8, with and without the subsidy policy response. Numerical values for the endogenous subsidy case are reported in table 9.3 while the corresponding data, assuming no subsidy response, appear in table 8.5.

With the endogenous subsidy response, inflation reacts much more gradually and peaks at a lower rate in response to a sustained drop in food

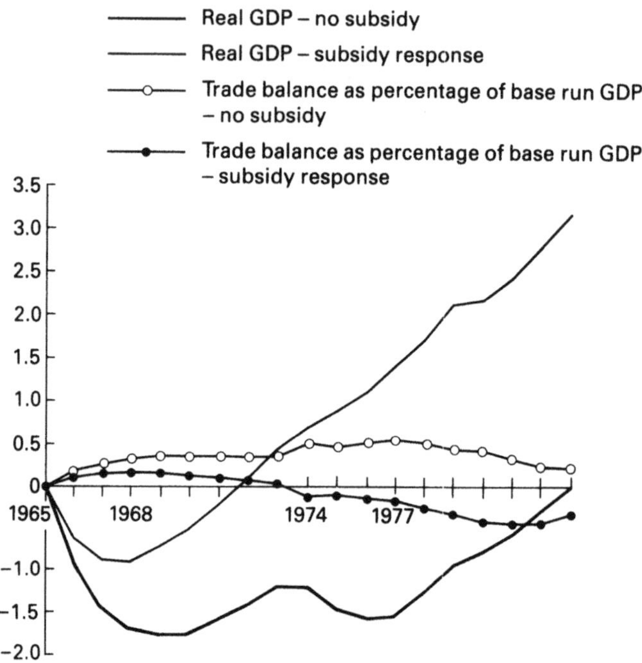

Figure 9.6 Responses of GDP and trade balance to food production shock – with and without subsidy response (percentage differences relative to base run)

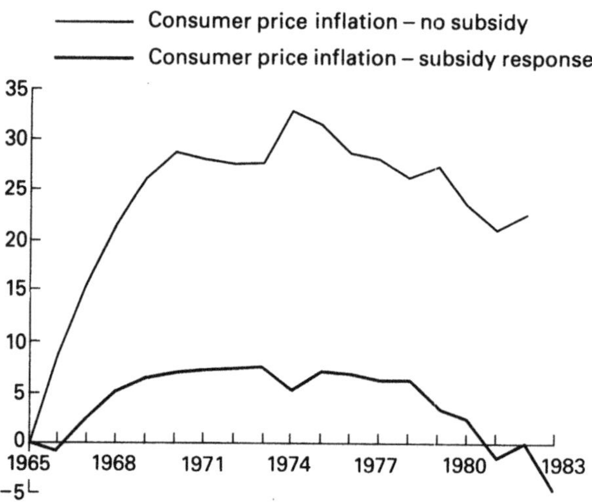

Figure 9.7 Responses of consumer price inflation to food production shock – with and without subsidy response (percentage differences relative to base run)

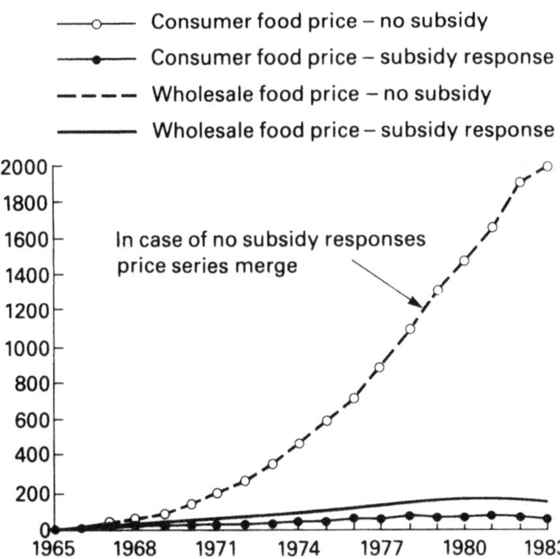

Figure 9.8 Responses of consumer and wholesale food price levels to food production shock – with and without subsidy response (percentage differences relative to base run)

production than in the case of a fixed rate of subsidy. There is virtually no impact felt upon consumer price inflation in the first period as the rise in the wholesale food price brought on by the shock affects the price system initially only by raising overall wholesale prices (P^{WG}). This in turn causes some exchange rate devaluation (but, of course, less than in the fixed subsidy case) and leads, therefore, to a small rise in manufacturing prices. It takes two periods for the latter to be fully reflected in the consumer price. Consumer prices are now therefore linked to demand and supply in the food market through an indirect and weak mechanism. No longer are overall consumer prices affected through the much more direct route of consumer food price increases, as the explicit link between wholesale and consumer food prices is now severed.

The divergent behaviour of wholesale and consumer food price series under the endogenous subsidy policy can be seen in figure 9.8 where a wedge develops as wholesale prices rise much more rapidly than do consumer prices. Consumer food prices increase in line with the overall consumer price index to maintain an unchanged relative food price at the retail level. Also plotted in figure 9.8 are consumer and wholesale food prices under the fixed subsidy case. The two series here merge visually into one as they follow virtually identical time paths. An unchanged rate of subsidy prevents the emergence of a significant wedge.

Table 9.3. *Dynamic elasticities – food production shock with subsidy response (percentage differences relative to base run)*

Year/ period	Trade balance as a percentage of base run GDP	Real GDP	Consumer price inflation	Consumer price level
1966/1	0.11	−0.63	−0.50	−0.34
1967/2	0.15	−0.89	2.60	1.65
1968/3	0.17	−0.89	5.30	6.15
1969/4	0.16	−0.70	6.50	11.95
1970/5	0.13	−0.48	7.00	18.48
1971/6	0.09	−0.20	7.30	25.60
1972/7	0.05	0.10	7.40	33.34
1973/8	0.00	0.44	7.30	41.17
1974/9	−0.12	0.71	5.40	46.42
1975/10	−0.12	0.91	7.20	53.69
1976/11	−0.14	1.11	6.80	61.18
1977/12	−0.19	1.42	6.40	68.68
1978/13	−0.26	1.70	6.20	76.39
1979/14	−0.35	2.12	3.60	80.66
1980/15	−0.45	2.20	2.40	83.17
1981/16	−0.48	2.41	−0.90	82.30
1982/17	−0.45	2.75	0.30	82.59
1983/18	−0.31	3.16	−4.60	78.81

The dramatic anti-inflationary impact of the subsidy policy is evident from figures 9.7 and 9.8. Whereas inflation accelerates to a peak of about 30 percentage points above the rate base with no increased subsidisation, this figure falls to only 7 percentage points when the subsidy is employed as a policy variable in the manner hypothesised.

As shown in figure 9.6, GDP falls marginally, relative to base, in the first four periods after the food production shock due to the real income loss and to a slight erosion of real balances. The trade balance improves with falling demand. Relative to the fixed subsidy case, however, the fall in GDP and the improvement in the trade balance are considerably less. GDP begins an inexorable rise relative both to the base run and to the fixed subsidy case. The trade balance deteriorates accordingly. This outcome results from burgeoning private financial wealth that is a consequence of a rapidly growing budget deficit required to finance ever increasing food subsidies. The effect of rising tax revenues on the government budget and a continuous fall in foreign reserve accumulation is insufficient to restore monetary equilibrium. The real wealth stimulus to aggregate demand and output leads to a level of GDP by the end of the simulation period that is some 3.2 per cent above base as opposed to the fixed subsidy case where GDP ends largely unchanged. The expansion of aggregate demand that occurs with an endogenous subsidy response puts additional upward pressure on wholesale demand for food, driving relative price at this marketing level up further, drawing out more subsidies and causing the multiplier effect to start all over again.

Within the present framework this demand expansion is not more inflationary because the linkage between demand and inflation through the food market is completely neutralised and the impact of rising demand on other sectors of the economy is, *ex hypothesis*, not directly inflationary. In fact, however, this policy would almost certainly result in rising inflation. A more complete model would allow for the possibility of inflationary pressures from such alternative sources as bottle-necks in the supply of essential imports (assuming that a foreign exchange constraint comes into play) or from skilled labour shortages as full capacity in manufacturing is reached. By the same token, the inexorable rise in the budget deficit and in the money supply would undoubtedly have a strong adverse impact on inflationary expectations. Even in the context of our own model, a more realistic policy of less than complete neutralisation of consumer food price increases would also allow some of the increase in demand to spill over into consumer prices. In this way a subsidy policy, conceived of as anti-inflationary, may in the longer run contribute to an aggregate demand inflation.

As regards the distribution of the burden of inflation, we arrive at the paradoxical outcome that farmers, consumers and industrialists are all better off as a result of the subsidy policy. The government, on the other hand, loses out by suffering a haemorrhaging of its deficit.

The outcome of this experiment is an extreme one and would almost certainly be completely unsustainable because of the sizes of both the trade balance and government deficits that are implied. While not captured in this simple model, we know that the financing of the trade deficit may be constrained by external factors while a continuous rapid expansion of the fiscal deficit would be likely to play havoc with the domestic financial system and, as noted above, might also fuel expectations of more rapid inflation especially if financed, as it is here, by the creation of new high-powered money. The outcome is also untenable as there is no mechanism in the model to bring the wholesale food price back down towards base, thereby reducing subsidies. Instead, rising demand and lagged supply response ensure that excess demand for food grows continuously, relative price rises, subsidies expand and demand is pushed ever higher.

The experiment performed does serve to illustrate, albeit in an extreme fashion, one of the mechanisms behind Brazil's inflation in the late 1970s and early 1980s. It also points to one of the ways in which inflation of a structuralist variety, i.e. due to food shortages, may lead to a rising government deficit as policy-makers seek to dampen an initial inflationary surge. This deficit not only acts to validate the initial inflation by ensuring a flow of financial assets into the private sector but also sets in motion an aggregate demand inflation. Subsidies of many kinds, especially food, petroleum and credit subsidies, were widely used in Brazil, especially from the mid-1970s onwards, in an effort to dampen the impact of price shocks and/or to maintain growth in the face of these same shocks. Consumer food subsidies alone were not of a sufficient magnitude to put great strain upon public finances, yet when combined with other agricultural subsidies, petroleum subsidies, export subsidies and implicit credit subsidies, the impact was very significant. One of the consequences of these policies was to enlarge greatly the fiscal deficit and probably to contribute to inflation by stimulating sectoral or aggregate demands.

9.5 A food shock with a food import policy response

Another way in which policy-makers responded to a shortfall in domestic food production was by allowing an expansion of imports in order to help restore equilibrium in the food market. In this model, food imports consist wholly of wheat imports over which the government has a trade monopoly; as in fact it did in Brazil during the period of analysis.

Faced once again with a 10 per cent drop in *per capita* food production, policy-makers are assumed now to react according to the following rule

$$im_t^{\mathrm{Wsh}} = im_t^{\mathrm{Wb}} + 0.5(q^{\mathrm{AFb}} - q^{\mathrm{AFsh}})_t$$

where (im^{Wb}) is the base level exogenous quantum of wheat imports and (q^{AFb}) is the base level domestic food output, held exogenous in this experiment, while (im^{Wsh}) and (q^{AFsh}) are the corresponding endogenous values under the food import policy regime. The reaction function ensures that a fall in food production is partially compensated for by a rise in imports, equal to exactly one half the original shortfall. The choice of 0.5 for the reaction coefficient is arbitrary, but probably better represents the possibilities open to policy-makers, given a balance of payments constraint, than would the imposition of a coefficient of unity. The impact of the food

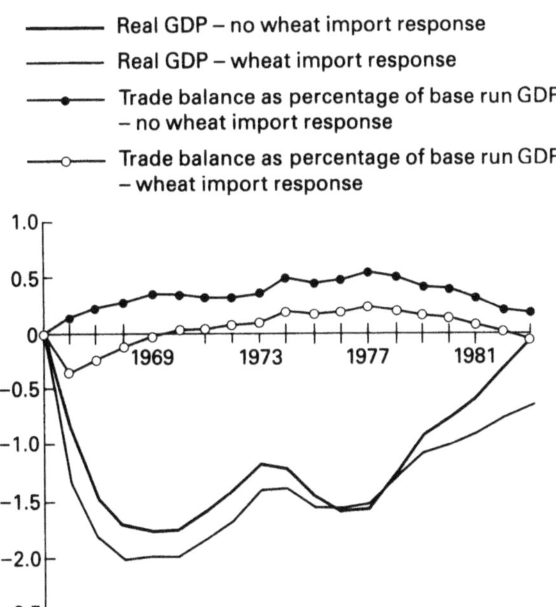

Figure 9.9 Responses of GDP and trade balance to food production shock – with and without wheat import response (percentage differences relative to base run)

shock under the proposed policy rule, as well as without it, is shown in figures 9.9 through 9.11. Numerical values are given in table 9.4 with the corresponding data for the case of no policy response appearing in table 8.5.

The flexibility in food imports has an important anti-inflationary influence as evidenced in figure 9.11. The extent of the excess demand that emerges in the food market after the shock is much less in this case than under the assumption of rigid wheat imports. The total food supply deficiency is only one half the amount of the contraction in production. As a consequence, a new equilibrium can be re-established at a relative price that is not as high as was required in the absence of additional imports. It follows therefore that the wage-price spiral set off by the shock is attenuated and that inflation and the price level peak at well below the levels previously recorded. Consumer price inflation peaks at just under 20 percentage points above the base run rate, as opposed to almost 33 points in the no policy response case.

The rise in the quantum of imports combines with the fall in food production and the real balance effect to drive real GDP down by 1.3 per cent in period 1 (figure 9.9). Through the operation of the multiplier,

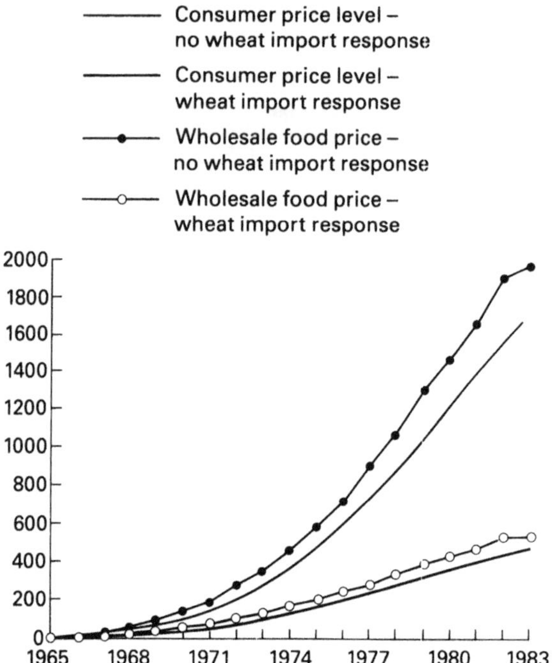

Figure 9.10 Responses of consumer prices and wholesale food price levels to food production shock – with and without wheat import response (percentage differences relative to base run)

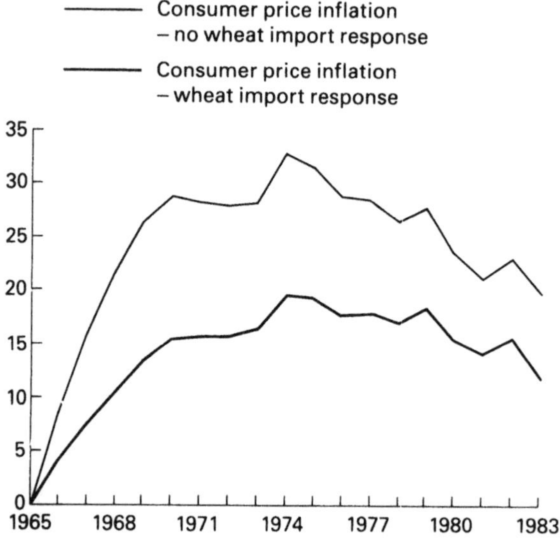

Figure 9.11 Responses of consumer price inflation to food production shock – with and without wheat import response (percentage differences relative to base run)

Table 9.4. *Dynamic elasticities – food production shock with wheat import response (percentage differences relative to base run)*

Year/ period	Trade balance as a percentage of base run GDP	Real GDP	Consumer price inflation	Consumer price level
1966/1	−0.36	−1.34	4.00	2.81
1967/2	−0.25	−1.80	7.60	8.73
1968/3	−0.13	−2.02	10.60	17.71
1969/4	−0.01	−1.97	13.40	29.60
1970/5	0.02	−1.96	15.40	44.52
1971/6	0.04	−1.82	15.60	62.26
1972/7	0.07	−1.64	15.70	83.04
1973/8	0.10	−1.40	16.40	107.54
1974/9	0.20	−1.37	19.60	136.45
1975/10	0.16	−1.56	19.30	168.66
1976/11	0.20	−1.57	17.90	203.51
1977/12	0.26	−1.50	18.00	243.92
1978/13	0.21	−1.27	17.00	287.58
1979/14	0.15	−1.05	18.20	334.14
1980/15	0.13	−0.96	15.40	372.65
1981/16	0.07	−0.87	14.10	408.20
1982/17	0.00	−0.73	15.40	450.59
1983/18	−0.05	−0.61	11.90	479.65

national income falls further in subsequent periods, averaging 1.9 per cent below base in periods 2 to 6. This is a somewhat greater fall in output than occurs in the absence of the import policy, the difference being due to the expansion of food imports. The latter brings about a marginal deterioration in the trade balance during the first three periods. Thereafter, the trade balance recovers but is still distinctly worse than in the unchanged imports case. After period 3, GDP begins to recover, but at a slower pace than occurred in the absence of flexible imports. This is due, as in the earlier case, to an expansion of real balances connected with the accumulation of foreign reserves.

The model suggests that food import flexibility combined with rapid import response is an effective policy to mitigate the otherwise serious inflationary consequences of a food shock. A large improvement is obtained in overall price levels and inflation at a relatively small cost in terms of additional forgone national income and output. Policy-makers may, however, face a trade balance financing constraint. This leads directly to consideration of a rather more sophisticated policy package to confront the food shock.

9.6 A food shock with a wheat import response and a target for the trade balance

In the last experiment the amount by which the trade balance deteriorates as a result of the wheat import policy is not great (0.75 per cent of base GDP in the first four years of the simulation), nonetheless we assume here that even this level of deterioration cannot be tolerated. Relative to the reduced level of GDP that prevails after the food shock, this deterioration is of course somewhat greater still.

We assume here that policy-makers set target values for the trade balance equal to the historical values for this variable. They assign the rate of direct taxation as an instrument. At the same time the policy rule governing imports of wheat is maintained as in section 9.5 above. The reaction of the system to the same 10 per cent food production shock under these assumptions is displayed in figures 9.12 through 9.14 along with the outcome assuming no policy response whatsoever. Tables 9.5 and 8.5 contain the relevant numerical data.

In order to forestall a deterioration of the trade balance resulting from the additional food imports required to mitigate the effects of the fall in food production, policy-makers increase the rate of direct taxation as an offsetting demand reducing measure. This depresses disposable income and drives real output down by 4 per cent in the first year of the shock (figure 9.12) which contrasts with a drop of less than 1 per cent in the absence of a policy response and of 1.3 per cent when food imports alone are allowed to respond. Output does however begin to recover rapidly as the tax rate is adjusted downwards again in subsequent periods and eventually, after period 4, is reduced to below the rates prevailing in the base run. From period 5 onwards, GDP is actually above the path upon which it would have been in the absence of any policy reaction, since now fiscal policy ensures that the economy grows at the limit imposed by the trade deficit target.

Under this set of policies, inflation accelerates at a markedly slower pace than in the case either of no policy response or of a food import response only (figures 9.13 and 9.14). The consumer price level is 69 per cent higher in period 7 as opposed to 210 per cent and 83 per cent higher in each of the latter cases respectively. The difference in the behaviour of inflation is a reflection primarily of the lower levels of demand that prevail in the present

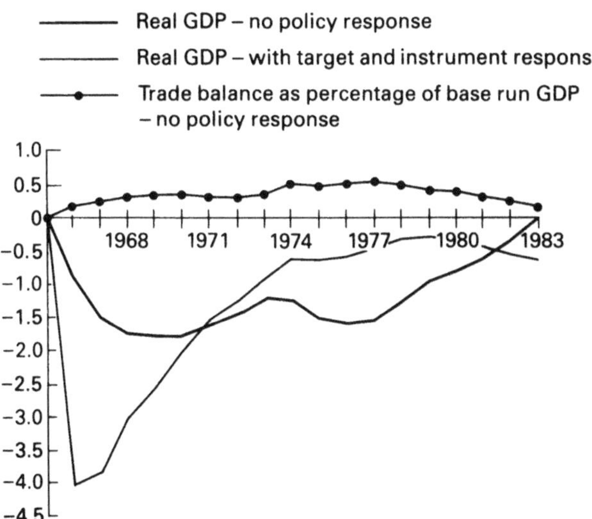

Figure 9.12 Responses of GDP and trade balance to food production shock – with and without wheat import response combined with trade balance target where tax rate used as instrument (percentage differences relative to base run)

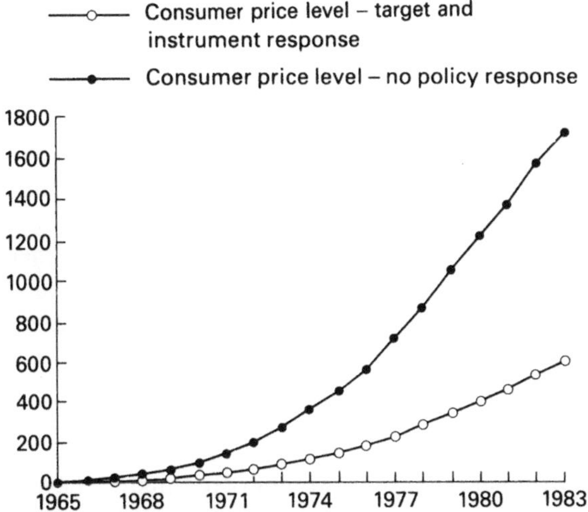

Figure 9.13 Responses of consumer price level to food production shock – with and without wheat import response combined with trade balance target where tax rate used as instrument (percentage differences relative to base run)

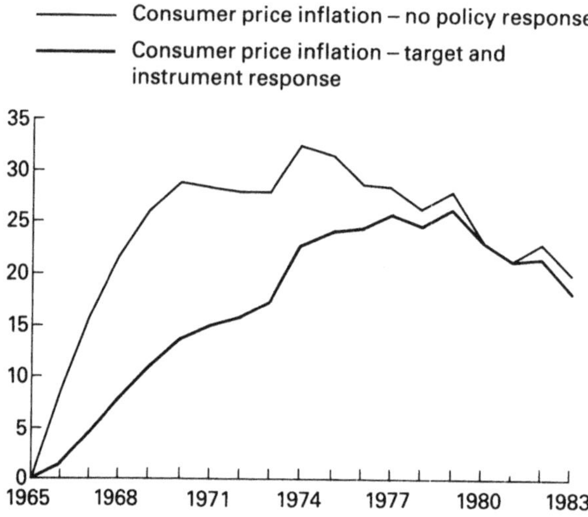

Figure 9.14 Response of consumer price inflation to food production shock – with and without wheat import response combined with trade balance target where tax rate used as instrument (percentage differences relative to base run)

experiment during the first four periods of the shock. Higher direct taxes reduce private disposable income and therefore also the demand for food and other commodities. With reduced excess demand for food, the pressure upon inflation is lessened. Nevertheless, inflation continues to accelerate over a longer period of time than in the other cases because of the continuously higher levels of demand that prevail in each period from 1970 to 1981.

The policy package investigated here constitutes a short, sharp response to lower food production. The tax rate manipulation can be thought of as representing an 'orthodox' fiscal deflationary answer to an inflationary shock. Although the short-term cost, measured in forgone output, is considerable, over the medium term, output levels are higher than in either the case of no policy response or of an import response alone. Adjustment in tax rates ensures that output growth proceeds as fast as is feasible given the trade balance constraint.

9.7 Conclusion

This chapter brought together the various strands of the analysis developed in previous chapters to bear upon the central theme of the study, namely the mechanics of structural and cost-push inflation and their interaction with financial influences. The overall macromodel – which in turn embeds the sectoral pricing models – was used to shed light upon the response of the

Table 9.5. *Dynamic elasticities – food production shock assuming wheat import response combined with trade balance target/direct tax rate as instrument (percentage differences relative to base run)*

Year/ period	Trade balance/ base GDP	Real GDP	Consumer price inflation	Consumer price level
1966/1	0.00	−4.06	1.40	1.01
1967/2	0.00	−3.83	4.60	4.59
1968/3	0.00	−2.97	8.10	11.19
1969/4	0.00	−2.54	11.20	21.04
1970/5	0.00	−1.97	13.80	33.81
1971/6	0.00	−1.51	15.00	49.49
1972/7	0.00	−1.24	16.00	68.78
1973/8	0.00	−0.89	17.50	92.15
1974/9	0.00	−0.62	22.90	120.00
1975/10	0.00	−0.64	24.20	150.73
1976/11	0.00	−0.54	24.40	186.78
1977/12	0.00	−0.40	25.70	234.49
1978/13	0.00	−0.32	24.70	291.12
1979/14	0.00	−0.27	26.60	352.50
1980/15	0.00	−0.34	23.40	409.64
1981/16	0.00	−0.48	21.30	467.97
1982/17	0.00	−0.55	21.40	536.64
1983/18	0.00	−0.67	18.20	589.33

economy to inflationary shocks of a type that have characterised Brazil's actual experience. Naturally, being a highly simplified representation of the macroeconomy, the model was not able to capture all the repercussions of the shocks that were suggested by outside observation or by theory. Nonetheless, the results obtained were generally consistent with what we know from other sources and sufficiently interesting to further the understanding of the problems at hand. The quantitative impact of the shocks upon the endogenous variables of the model can only serve as very approximate indications of the likely orders of magnitude. Notwithstanding this proviso, the quantitative results help to establish the importance and relevance of the many different, and often opposing, effects and tendencies that are engendered as a result of an inflationary shock. The chapter also examined some of the major costs and benefits of a range of policy responses on the part of the authorities. Here, too, the measures envisaged in the experiments, although highly stylised, bore a resemblance to those tried out at different times in Brazil.

10 Conclusion

At the outset of this study it was hypothesised that chronic inflation in Brazil could best be explained and analysed within a structuralist framework augmented to allow for stocks and flows of financial assets. In setting out to formulate and test this general hypothesis, we passed through a series of stages.

After reviewing the work of the Latin American structuralist school on the causes of inflation, we went on to construct a formal qualitative model encompassing the fundamentals of this approach as well as a rudimentary financial system. We proceeded to examine the dynamics of inflation given the economic structure hypothesised and to draw out a number of the basic conclusions on the causes and propagating mechanisms of inflation.

The next stage in the analysis involved switching from abstract theory to a review of Brazil's actual inflationary experience. Existing explanations for the inflationary record were reviewed and criticised. At the same time, simple analytical techniques were employed to examine important aspects of the inflationary process and to make an initial assessment of how these could best be understood. The weight of evidence pointed to the likely relevance for an analysis of this particular historical experience of a theoretical framework along the lines of that developed in the previous chapter.

In the third stage of our analysis we examined in much greater detail the pricing hypotheses underpinning the structuralist framework. The theoretical rationale for these sectoral pricing models was reviewed along with the literature on their empirical testing. The hypotheses were tested statistically using Brazilian data.

Having established that certain individual price series and inflation rates were explicable by processes compatible with a structuralist vision of overall inflation, the next stage in the analysis involved combining the estimated pricing equations with a set of other economic relationships to form a small statistical model of the Brazilian macroeconomy. The degree to which the model provided an adequate representation of the Brazilian economy was judged by using it to replicate the historical record and by subjecting it to dynamic shocks.

With a simulation model now in place, it became possible to take up once again the core hypothesis of the study, namely the adequacy of an 'asset augmented' structuralist explanation for inflation. Experiments with the model were designed to investigate the nature of inflation in a dynamic and quantitative context. We sought to derive indications of the relative importance of a number of underlying causes of inflation that had been analysed qualitatively using the theoretical model and/or considered when reviewing Brazil's inflationary experience. The model, being fully dynamic, enabled us to investigate the interaction between, on the one hand, basic inflationary pressures and propagating mechanisms such as indexation and, on the other hand, real and financial variables. The experiments performed with the simulation model were naturally highly stylised and intended to illustrate certain broad traits of the inflation rather than analyse in a detailed way the specific causes of inflation at any given point in the past.

We believe that the results of the study support the view that Brazilian inflation is explicable by an 'asset augmented' structuralist model. Although alternative explanations for Brazilian inflation, notably of a monetarist bent, are examined briefly and refuted in part I of the study, no attempt is made to compare and contrast our quantitative model with a monetarist counterpart and, therefore, we cannot be sure that other models may not offer equally convincing or better explanations for the inflation. However, having said this, we would argue forcefully that the balance of evidence deriving from theoretical considerations, previous empirical work on Brazil's inflation and our own analysis favours an augmented structuralist interpretation.

10.1 The nature of inflation

How can we now characterise succinctly the nature of Brazil's inflation? In what follows we bring together the principal findings of the study. No attempt is made to repeat the detailed results obtained nor to ascribe causes to the inflation at each specific point in time, instead we seek to define the nature of the inflation in fairly broad terms. This review can conveniently be grouped under the following headings:

(a) 'basic pressures' and 'propagating mechanisms',
(b) cost-push factors,
(c) structural inflation, the food supply and the external sector,
(d) demand pressures,

(e) financial assets and inflation,
(f) food subsidies and inflation,
(g) the income share conflict, wage and price indexation and inertia.

10.1.1 *'Basic pressures' and 'propagating mechanisms'*

Underlying the early structuralist vision of inflation was the distinction between basic pressures and propagating mechanisms. As noted earlier, the former are factors that cause the prevailing rate of inflation to move up (or down) significantly whereas propagating factors tend to perpetuate inflation at or close to any given level reached after the repercussions of a basic pressure have worked their way through the economic system. We have attempted to show that this distinction, while not absolutely clear cut, is fundamental to an understanding of Brazil's experience with inflation. The recognition of the distinction is important in formulating policies designed to arrest inflation. In contrast to the approach adopted here, most formulations of monetarist views on inflation reject, or at best, play down any dichotomy between basic pressures and propagating mechanisms – ultimately money is the culprit.

In Brazil, over the period of analysis, indexation of wages and prices at fixed intervals based on past inflation imparted a strongly self-perpetuating character to the inflation. Mark-up pricing in industry ensured that indexation of wages and the exchange rate fed directly into manufactured goods prices and thereby ensured a very high degree of simultaneity in the determination of prices and rates of inflation. Indexed financial assets and endogenous mechanisms for the creation of new financial assets helped to facilitate the liquidity growth that was required to sustain the rapidly increasing levels of nominal national income and expenditure caused by continuous inflation.

Basic pressures that were of importance in explaining Brazil's inflation ranged from cost-push pressures deriving from changes in dollar input prices or the real exchange rate to underlying structural bottlenecks in food production and expansionary aggregate demand. Factors such as these led to relative price shifts which, given the dynamics of price setting and inflation, sparked an acceleration in the prevailing rate of general price inflation. Once a new threshold was established for the rate of inflation, the propagating mechanisms would tend to ensure that inflation remained at or close to this rate.

10.1.2 *Cost-push factors*

One-off increases in key relative prices that fed into the cost of industrial goods were shown to have been the single most powerful cause of changes in the inflation threshold both in the early 1960s and again at repeated intervals in the years following the first oil crisis. Declining inflation during the years of the 'miracle' was also attributable in large measure to declining relative prices of certain important costs. In reviewing the data on Brazil's experience and again in the simulation exercises we drew attention to the importance at different points in time of rising dollar import prices of raw materials, real exchange devaluation, rising real wages and unit labour costs, as well as increases in real interest rates as catalysts for an acceleration of inflation.

Despite the relatively closed nature of Brazil's economy, which meant that the direct impact of a foreign price shock or real exchange depreciation was limited, the secondary effects of such a shock spread rapidly through the economy. It was found that a dollar import price rise led – in the absence of countervailing increase in subsidies or controls – to a rise in the overall price level equal to about 80 per cent of the dollar price increase. Alterations in the real exchange rate were also found to have similarly powerful repercussions for inflation. The model results support the widely held view, discussed in chapter 2, that the combination of the second oil shock – not substantially cushioned by subsidies – with the maxi-devaluation of 1979 had a powerful inflationary impact while also setting in motion recessionary forces. As regards the efficacy of the maxi-devaluation at ameliorating the foreign trade position, casual observation of the historical data combined with the model results leads one to question the extent to which expenditure switching occurred. Imports fell by 32 per cent in dollar terms in the four years comprising 1980–3 whereas exports expanded by only 9 per cent. The import contraction probably had more to do with the size of the recession of 1981–3 than with the devaluation directly.

Also in the case of wages the high degree of simultaneity in price determination meant that, assuming labour productivity remained unchanged, a rise in real wages in industry had an impact upon overall inflation of much greater magnitude than its relatively small direct influence upon industrial prices alone.

Yet another source of cost-push pressure in the industrial sector appears to have been financing costs. For reasons explained, it was difficult to measure accurately the importance of interest rate push. We did nonetheless identify, in a tenative fashion, a causal role for this factor – one which may help explain the often observed perverse short-term impact of tight money.

10.1.3 *Structural inflation, the food supply and the external sector*

Emphasised throughout the study was the fact that the dynamics of price determination in the market for domestic agricultural produce and the way in which this market interacts with the rest of the economy was crucial to an understanding of the inflationary process. We found evidence to support the view that the relative price of agricultural foodstuffs was determined by the excess demand for food.

Our analysis attested to the highly inflationary consequences of food supply disruptions as well as to the sensitivity of inflation to changes in the food supply process. Rescaling the food shock simulation results to allow a comparison with the GDP growth/inflation trade-off reported below, the model suggests that a 1 per cent fall in food production led to an approximately 0.85 per cent rise in inflation during the first period and to much higher inflation in subsequent periods – rising from 1.6 per cent in period 2 to a peak of 3.3 per cent in period 9.

The reaction of inflation to a food production shock is conditioned to a large extent by the price elasticities of demand and supply for food. When elasticity of supply was constrained to zero (exogenous food) the impact upon inflation was dramatic. Likewise when food imports were permitted to make up a portion of the shortfall in domestic production, the inflationary surge was much reduced.

Volatility in food production does not in itself constitute a structural bottle-neck capable of engendering a continuous 'basic' inflationary tendency. However, from an examination of the question of the trend rate of growth of food production and the adequacy of this in light of growth in demand, we concluded that there existed a more deep-seated problem of a potentially inflationary imbalance between demand and supply in Brazil during the 1970s and 1980s. We did not attempt to quantify the underlying pressure on inflation resulting from stagnant or declining *per capita* growth in domestic food production and the related trend rise in relative food prices. This phenomenon did without a doubt have inflationary consequences distinct from those of one-off shocks due, for instance, to poor harvests. These longer-term effects were obscured by the increasing use of food price controls and consumer subsidies.

Our results on food prices and inflation reinforce the relevance of a classic 'structuralist' prescription for increased price stability, namely the promotion of a more rapid trend growth in – and greater cyclical stability of – domestic food production, as well as increasing access to alternative sources of supply, be they domestic stockpiles or imports, so as to dampen fluctuations that do occur.

Latin American structuralists early on placed importance upon the foreign exchange constraint as a cause of inflation. They argued that such a constraint was often of a structural nature and created an inflationary bias. In the Brazilian context we have argued that the absence of a foreign exchange constraint during much of the 1960s and early 1970s allowed flexibility to meet demand for scarce consumer goods or intermediate inputs into production through importing. No pressing need existed for significant exchange devaluation and together these factors provided a potent anti-inflationary force.

On the other hand, a foreign exchange constraint emerged in a new guise in the late 1970s and, more forcefully still, in the 1980s. In this instance the root cause was not a chronic imbalance between the value of exports and imports but rather the need to generate increasing trade surpluses in order to meet interest payments and some principal repayments on the foreign debt. Further work is required to assess in detail the implications of this phenomenon for inflation. Clearly, as we noted, import contraction and diversion of domestically produced goods to export markets may have led to inflationary shortages in certain key goods at home and certainly reduced the flexibility that had previously existed to head off potentially inflationary supply short-falls through increased use of imports. The imperative of greater and more frequent use of exchange devaluation in order to ensure that the requisite trade surplus was generated, certainly influenced inflation.

10.1.4 *Demand pressures*

A recurring theme throughout this study has been the extent to which changes in the level or rate of growth of aggregate demand or of a particular sectoral demand influenced price determination and inflation. While the results of our analyses were far from conclusive, we did indentify the food market as an important conduit through which the level of demand influenced the overall rate of inflation.

The simulation model exhibits what, by an outside yardstick, appears to be a significant, although rather slow-acting sensitivity of inflation to changes in the level of aggregate demand. A 10 per cent rise in GDP due to an increase in public investment was found to boost inflation by 0.3 per cent after one period and by a further 0.5 per cent and 0.7 per cent after two and three periods respectively. The immediate impact is considerably less than suggested by commodity market Phillips curve estimates for Brazil. It takes two to three years for inflation to respond by as much as the Phillips curve results suggest it responds in one year.

In contrast to the process inherent in the Phillips curve, the main mechanism by which aggregate demand affects inflation in our model is through the food market. By way of the multiplier, higher domestic demand, whether or not attributable primarily to a surge in consumption, will spill over into increased demand for food. This in turn puts upward pressure on the relative food price and overall inflation.

No role was identified in the model for a direct effect of demand upon the mark-up in manufacturing. Nor could a reliable impact of demand upon real earnings be identified, although some evidence was found to suggest such a relationship. Problems with labour market demand proxies may have prevented identification of a causal link. If these could be overcome and a positive relationship identified between the real wage and the level of demand, the sensitivity of the model to demand inflation would be heightened. At the same time, however, the importance of pro-cyclical changes in productivity upon unit labour costs was noted in chapters 2 and 3. If it had been possible to endogenise productivity in the simulation model, a potentially quite powerful mechanism would have been introduced to link rising capacity utilisation inversely to inflation, thereby cancelling out, to some extent at least, any inflationary impact of rising capacity utilisation that operates through the labour market. Considering both real wage and productivity effects, the net impact upon unit labour costs and, therefore, upon inflation as well, remains uncertain.

While we have shown that the possibility of an aggregate demand inflation, fuelled say by an expansionary fiscal policy, cannot be ignored, the simulations pointed to the much greater inflationary potential of cost-push shocks. Examination of the relationship between inflation and output in the various experiments demonstrates the pitfalls of seeking an explanation for inflation solely in the behaviour of demand. No clear stable relationship is identifiable between these variables in isolation from costs. Undoubtedly, the contribution of demand factors to inflation must be viewed in conjunction with that of cost-push and structural elements. Theoretical constructs that unjustifiably restrict the scope of analysis are to be avoided.

10.1.5 *Financial assets and inflation*

In chapter 2, monetarist explanations for Brazil's inflation were subject to critical review. We argued that evidence on causality between various monetary aggregates and prices did not support the strict one way chain of cause and effect posited by monetarists. Moreover, money in a narrow sense was shown to have become increasingly irrelevant over the period of analysis as the spectrum of liquid or semi-liquid assets in private portfolios expanded dramatically after the mid 1960s. The commodity market Phillips curve analysis, which plays a pivotal role in most monetarist reasoning on inflation in Brazil, was shown to be rife with difficulties.

While firmly rejecting a monetarist explanation for Brazilian inflation, a central theme of this study has been the crucial importance of accounting explicitly for the role of money and other financial assets in the inflationary process.

The financial sector of the model, while rudimentary, served nonetheless to illustrate certain traits of relevance to an understanding of the inflationary process. One of these was the high degree of endogeneity of financial assets. Assuming, as we did, a completely passive stance on the part of policy -makers, basic inflationary pressures, whatever their origin, were found to propagate throughout the system and to lead to continuous inflation, ever increasing levels of nominal national income and expenditure and a corresponding expansion of nominal financial assets. The indexation of most assets that comprised private financial wealth, represented in the model by government securities, meant that the nominal value of these increased with inflation. In addition to a tendency for liquidity expansion to accommodate increases in national income, inflation did, under certain circumstances, actually lead to an expansion in real liquidity. This occurred through the balance of payments as well as through the public sector deficit, in the latter case because subsidies tended to expand in real terms in response to greater inflation. With a very small and diminishing proportion of non-indexed financial assets in private wealth portfolios, any potentially stabilising real balance effect was of limited significance in checking the progress of inflation.

Bond financing of the public sector deficit in our model is equally as inflationary as financing through the issuance of high-powered money. This results from the way in which we modelled the financial sector and specifically from the absence of endogenous interest rates which precludes any linkage between bond financing, rising interest rates and a reduction in the capital value of outstanding bonds in private portfolios. Where operative, such a mechanism may have a stabilising influence on inflation by mitigating the impact on real wealth expansion of a bond financed deficit. In the Brazilian context this effect appears to have been of limited and, over time, declining importance. Mechanisms were created whereby government securities became increasingly liquid and their effective maturities shorter and shorter. In other words, government securities came over time to be money substitutes in a wide range of transactions. Under the circumstances, rising interest rates had no appreciable wealth reducing impact.

Besides highlighting a considerable degree of endogeneity of financial assets, the simulations also showed that stocks of financial assets are linked in a causal sense to inflation through the impact of changes in private wealth upon consumption and the demand for food. The model therefore incorporates a specific channel through which an expansionary monetary and/or fiscal policy, or an endogenous non-policy related expansion of assets, can lead to inflation. The model in this respect encompasses explicitly certain elements of the inflationary process that are highlighted by monetarists.

10.1.6 *Food subsidies and inflation*

One focus, both of the qualitative modelling of chapter 1 and of the later simulation exercises, was the interaction between short-run anti-inflationary impacts of a food subsidy policy and longer-term consequences flowing from the financing of this policy through the issuance of government monetary debt. In a very un-monetarist way, an expansion of the fiscal deficit to finance increased subsidies was found to be anti-inflationary in the short run, despite the implications for private wealth, because it isolated a substantial part of the wage and price system from rising wholesale food prices. At the same time, however, the subsidy policy, by preventing a negative substitution effect upon food demand from operating and by stimulating aggregate demand, increased disequilibrium in the food market, thereby further driving up wholesale prices, subsidy payments and aggregate demand. The policy became rapidly unsustainable and itself contributed to an aggregate demand inflation.

Judging by the model's response, the inflationary experience of the post-1974 period might have been rather different if food subsidies had not been widely used along with price controls to drive a wedge between consumer and wholesale prices. Given the deteriorating supply conditions in the traditional agricultural sector, it seems inevitable that, had this not occurred, relative prices would have risen at all marketing levels but probably by less than the recorded rise in relative wholesale price. Significant additional upward pressure on inflation would have been the probable result as the model suggests that the additional supply response would not have been sufficient. The total value of food subsidies was not large enough for a cut-back to have significantly improved public finances and thereby altered appreciably the pattern of asset accumulation, private expenditure and aggregate demand.

10.1.7 *The income share conflict, wage and price indexation and inertia*

Albeit in a simplified form, the model captures many of the mechanisms that operated to help social groups protect their relative, although not absolute, shares in national income. The behaviour of manufacturing prices – being unresponsive to demand and set as a mark-up over direct costs with assumed 100 per cent pass-through of costs – acted to protect the relative income share of industrialists. Exporters were substantially protected by the informal indexation of the exchange rate. Workers, because of the lagged fixed period indexation scheme, were not as well protected. Real wages and salaries tended to rise and fall in an inverse pattern to inflation. This, while detrimental to workers' direct interests, clearly constituted one of few stabilising mechanisms without which supply or demand shocks would have had an even more pronounced impact upon overall inflation. Finally, changes in the public sector's relative share of national expenditure and income merit mention. By allowing taxes as a proportion of national income to fall during the 1970s, while expanding subsidies and transfers, the government was in effect compensating other groups or sectors for real income losses sustained and accepting a deterioration in its own income/expenditure balance.

The model simulations involving partial de-indexation of earnings and the exchange rate sought to examine the consequences for inflation of partially severing formal linkages between prices. Limited de-indexation forced the economy to absorb cost-push shocks with less inflation. The real income loss implicit, for instance, in a terms of trade deterioration or a shortfall in food output, was absorbed more readily than under the standard indexing rules.

The simulation results reinforce the view that backwards looking and fixed period indexation of key wages and prices contributed to a marked tendency for inflation to remain at a given rate until such time as a new shock caused it to rise or fall. Whereas, in the absence of formal indexation, particularly indexation of wages and salaries, unfavourable shocks at already high rates of inflation might have led to hyperinflation as periods between price adjustments were shortened and reference points for prices were lost, the system that prevailed pre-1986 imparted a degree of stabilising rigidity. Naturally this rigidity also meant that indexation slowed the process of inflationary deceleration in the presence of a favourable shock.

While the model results did point to a strong inertial tendency in the inflation they also brought out the fact that inertia was not the *cause* of inflation in a meaningful sense and that indexation was not the only propagating factor. Brazil's failed attempts at stabilisation post-1986 illustrate the dangers of a slavish adherence to a belief in inertial inflation to the exclusion of other factors. While a necessary condition for price stability is to break the inertial element in the inflation, by for instance imposing a temporary wage and price freeze, this is not a sufficient condition. Basic pressures must be addressed as well.

10.2 Unanswered questions and directions for further research

A great many issues connected with the nature of the Brazilian inflation remain unanswered or in need of further study. The adoption in this study of a modelling approach did in itself restrict the range of possibilities open to us in addressing the problem. Given the scope of the question at hand, some selectivity in treatment was inevitable and almost certainly desirable. On a more specific note, two main factors prevented a more detailed and comprehensive coverage of the inflationary experience within the confines imposed by an empirical modelling approach. The first relates to flaws and inadequacies in the structure of the model itself. Reworking parts of the existing structure and extending the model in new directions would greatly enhance its usefulness as a tool of analysis. Of particular interest would be to model afresh the supply side of industry and to expand the financial sector. While beset by data problems, the linkage via a production function of potential output to key inputs such as fixed capital, non-substitutable imported inputs and even working capital, would open up a new range of possibilities for hypothesis testing and for the setting up of interesting simulations. In a like manner, a more complete financial system, with credit, interest rates and asset demand functions might yield a similarly rewarding pay-off.

Constraints of time and space prevented use of the model, in its existing form, for a greater number of counter-factual and policy experiments. While there are very clear limitations in the capacity of the simple model used to illuminate specific causes of inflation and resulting implications for stabilisation policy, more insights could be drawn from additional experimentation with the model.

Brazil's lurch towards hyperinflation during 1989 brings into focus the pressing need for a fuller understanding of the causes and the effects of chronic inflation and also the need for appropriate policy responses. It is hoped that this study may serve as a basis for one avenue of further research.

Appendix 1 Derivation of analytical results for chapter 1

A1.1 *Comparative statistics for the model without asset effects*

In chapter 1 the following equations define the equilibrium values for relative prices, industrial output and inflation

$$\bar{\theta}=\frac{(1-\alpha)c\bar{g}}{[1-c-s(1-\alpha c)]\bar{Q}_{\mathrm{A}}} \tag{1.16A}$$

$$\bar{Q}_{\mathrm{I}}=\frac{[1-s-(1-\alpha)c]\bar{g}}{[1-c-s(1-\alpha)c]} \tag{1.17A}$$

$$\bar{\pi}=h\frac{(1-\alpha)c\bar{g}}{[1-c-s(1-\alpha c)]\bar{Q}_{\mathrm{A}}\theta^{*}}-1 \tag{1.18A}$$

Noting that (α) and (c) are positive fractions and making use of the stability condition we obtain the following results

$$\frac{\partial\bar{\theta}}{\partial g}=\frac{(1-\alpha)c}{[1-c-s(1-\alpha c)]Q_{\mathrm{A}}}>0$$

$$\frac{\partial\bar{Q}_{\mathrm{I}}}{\partial g}=\frac{[1-s-(1-\alpha)c]}{[1-c-s(1-\alpha c)]}>0$$

$$\frac{\partial\bar{\pi}}{\partial g}=\frac{h(1-\alpha)c}{[1-c-s(1-\alpha c)]\bar{Q}_{\mathrm{A}}\theta^{*}}>0$$

$$\frac{\partial\bar{\theta}}{\partial\bar{Q}_{\mathrm{A}}}=-\frac{\bar{\theta}}{\bar{Q}_{\mathrm{A}}}<0$$

$$\frac{\partial\bar{Q}_{\mathrm{I}}}{\partial\bar{Q}_{\mathrm{A}}}=0$$

$$\frac{\partial\bar{\pi}}{\partial\bar{Q}_{\mathrm{A}}}=-\frac{h(1-\alpha)cg}{[1-c-s(1-\alpha c)]\bar{Q}_{\mathrm{A}}^{2}\theta^{*}}<0$$

$$\frac{\partial\bar{\theta}}{\partial s}=\bar{\theta}\frac{(1-\alpha c)}{[1-c-s(1-\alpha c)]}>0$$

$$\frac{\partial\bar{Q}_{\mathrm{I}}}{\partial s}=\frac{\alpha c^2(1-\alpha)}{[1-c-s(1-\alpha c)]^2}>0$$

since

$$\pi=h\left(\frac{\theta}{\theta^*}-1\right)$$

$$\frac{\partial\pi}{\partial s}=h\partial\frac{(\theta/\theta^*)}{\partial s}$$

$$\frac{\partial\pi}{\partial s}=\frac{h}{\theta^{*2}}\left\{\theta^*\frac{\partial\bar{\theta}}{\partial s}-\bar{\theta}\frac{\partial\theta^*}{\partial s}\right\}$$

noting that

$$\frac{\partial\theta^*}{\partial s}=\frac{\theta^*}{(1-s)}$$

$$\frac{\partial\pi}{\partial s}=h\frac{\theta}{\theta^*}\frac{(1-\alpha)c}{(1-s)[1-c-s(1-\alpha c)]}>0$$

We may easily derive, from equations (1.5) and (1.11), the instantaneous effects of changes which occur before relative price (θ) has begun to respond. The results are

$$\frac{\partial\bar{Q}_{\mathrm{I}}}{\partial g}=\frac{1}{(1-\alpha c)}>0$$

$$\frac{\partial\pi}{\partial g}=0$$

$$\frac{\partial\bar{Q}_{\mathrm{I}}}{\partial\bar{Q}_{\mathrm{A}}}=\frac{\alpha c\theta}{(1-\alpha c)}$$

$$\frac{\partial\pi}{\partial\bar{Q}_{\mathrm{A}}}=0$$

$$\frac{\alpha\bar{Q}_{\mathrm{I}}}{\partial s}=0$$

$$\frac{\partial\pi}{\partial s}=-h\frac{\theta}{\theta^*(1-s)}<0,\ \text{because}\ \frac{\partial\theta^*}{\partial s}>0$$

Table A1.1. *Multipliers for the model with asset effects*

	Increase in		
Effects on	Q_A	g	s
θ	m_{11}	m_{12}	m_{13}
a	m_{21}	m_{22}	m_{23}
Q_I	$k_{11}m_{21}$	$k_{12}+k_{11}m_{22}$	$k_{14}+k_{11}m_{23}$
π	hm_{11}	hm_{12}	m_{44}

Note: $m_{44}=h[(1-\alpha)c(1-t)k_{11}t+(1-s)k_{21}k_{44}+k_{21}k_{30}]$.

A1.2 *Comparative statics for the model with asset effects*

Using equations (1.33) and (1.36) from chapter 1, we can derive (θ) and (a) in terms of the exogenous variables (Q_A), (g) and (s). The resulting (a) can be utilised in equation (1.32) to derive (Q_I) and similarly (θ) can be used to derive (π), following equations (1.11) and (1.12). Note also that all variables are measured as deviations around initial values

$$\hat{\theta}=m_{11}Q_A+m_{12}g+m_{13}s$$

$$\hat{a}=m_{21}Q_4+m_{22}g+m_{23}s$$

where

$$m_{11}=(k_{23}+k_{21}k_{43}/k_{11}t)/d$$

$$m_{12}=(k_{22}+k_{21}k_{42}/d_{11}t)/d$$

$$m_{13}=(k_{24}+k_{21}k_{44}/k_{11}t)/d$$

$$m_{21}=(k_{43}+k_{30}k_{23}/(k_{11}t\,d)$$

$$m_{22}=(k_{42}+k_{30}k_{22})/(k_{11}t\,d)$$

$$m_{23}=(k_{44}+k_{30}k_{24})/(k_{11}t\,d)$$

$$d=(1-k_{21}k_{30}k_{11}t)$$

$$\hat{Q}_I=k_{11}\hat{a}+k_{12}g+k_{14}s$$

$$\pi=h(\hat{\theta}-\theta^*)$$

The multipliers are collected and presented in table A1.1.

Appendix 2 Research methodology

A certain dissatisfaction with, and distrust of, econometrics has led in recent years to a new emphasis being placed upon research methodologies.[1] Too often, applied econometric research has failed to be clear and open about the processes used in:

(a) selection of a general model,

(b) simplification of the latter to arrive at a preferred specification, and

(c) 'quality control' of the preferred model.[2]

The selection of the general model involves drawing on economic theory and knowledge of the institutional setting. At this stage the model may be in implicit functional form and represent a steady state growth path, thereby by-passing the issue of disequilibrium dynamics. The next stage involves obtaining a more parsimonious representation of the data by making decisions as to which variables to include and which to exclude. At this stage, decisions are made as to functional form and dynamic structure. Finally, the preferred model must be adequately evaluated to ensure that it is: (1) consistent with theory; (2) both statistically and economically significant; (3) robust; and (4) able to encompass or reconcile previous research.[3] At all stages in the research, openness and a certain critical awareness are essential in order that weaknesses are unveiled rather than covered up.

Once a general model has been formulated, two broad strategies have been proposed for confronting the theory with the data in a systematic way. These are the encompassing principal (see Mizon, 1984 and Hendry, 1979) and the technique of variable addition (see Pagan and Hall, 1983).

The encompassing principle is to commence from as general a model as is feasible – i.e. one upon which undue *a priori* restrictions have not been placed in terms of variables included, functional form, and systematic and error dynamics – and 'test down' using 'specification' tests such as the F ratio, likelihood ratio, Lagrange multiplier or Wald test to arrive at a preferred parsimonious model. Ideally, at each stage in this procedure tests for misspecification should also be applied.

The method of variable addition reverses the above-mentioned procedure in that one begins with a parsimonious model and then subjects it to a barrage of tests for misspecification, including misspecification due to the omission of variables.

Irrespective of the exact strategy followed the intent is the same; to adopt a consistent approach to model specification that reduces the likelihood of arriving at final model forms that are misspecified. It is important to report sufficient information on the procedures used and tests performed to allow the reader to form a judgement as to the quality of the research undertaken.

In this study we have endeavoured to comply with these requirements. The specific strategy followed in the econometric investigation (of wage and price formation) draws on both the encompassing and variable addition techniques; being slightly closer to the former than the latter. Care is taken in formulating the general model based on theoretical and institutional factors. In many cases theory or convention dictates the functional form of the model. Where no clear *a priori* preference is identified, we estimate models in different functional forms and then compare these either on the basis of a formal test, such as the likelihood ratio test for linear versus log-linear forms, or using more *ad hoc* criteria.

To the limited extent possible we start the specification search from a more general rather than specific model. The main constraint here is the lack of sufficient degrees of freedom. The maximum sample size used in the estimation of the models is twenty-five; these being annual observations covering the years 1960–84. In some cases, samples of less than twenty observations are used. Lack of important data series for earlier periods precludes the use of longer, more adequate sample sizes. In this context the generality of the initial specification is limited to the incorporation of a relatively small set of current and lagged variables. A general specification is estimated using ordinary as well as first- and second-order autoregressive least squares. A log likelihood ratio test is applied to choose between these three estimates.[4] The general model is re-estimated applying successive F tests of the linear restriction that the estimated parameters of subsets of variables (initially broad then becoming narrower) are equal to zero. The coefficients of variables appearing in the general model are constrained to zero where the null hypothesis cannot be rejected.

In some cases it is impossible, given the degrees of freedom constraint, to include all the current or lagged variables of interest in the general specification. In these cases additional tests are made for misspecification due to omission of variables. This involves adding possible omitted variables, together and one by one, to the parsimonious model and evaluating their significance using t and F tests.

Once the parsimonious specification is identified, a series of diagnostic tests are performed to check for misspecification from sources other than serial correlation of the error term or variable omission. Specifically, we test for model instability and orthogonality of the residuals (absence of simultaneous equation bias).

Structural stability of the model involves both parameter stability over the sample period and stability of the variance (homoscedasticity). To test for the former we use a Chow F test (Chow, 1960), either by splitting the sample into two equal parts or, more often given the limited degrees of freedom, by comparing the full sample to a subsample chosen on the basis of where prior knowledge suggests structural breaks are likely to occur. To test for the stability of the variance we split the sample at mid-point and apply a Goldfeld–Quandt F ratio test (Goldfeld–Quandt, 1965).

The application of least squares to a single equation model assumes that the explanatory variables are truly exogenous, in other words that there is one way causation between the dependent and the explanatory variables. Where, however, the equation forms part of a larger system of simultaneous equations, the explanatory variables are very likely also to be determined by the dependent variable. In this case, the assumption that the error term is independent (or orthogonal) with respect to the explanatory variables is violated and least squares yield biased and inconsistent estimates. It is important to test for residual orthogonality to determine if a problem of simultaneous equation bias exists. This we do first by re-estimating the parsimonious model using an instrumental variables (IV) estimator. Because the number of predetermined variables in the complete macrosystem far exceeds the number of observations and also because of non-linearities in the variables of the model, it is not possible to obtain instruments by regressing all predetermined variables on the jointly determined variables, and using the predictors from these equations as instruments (as in two stage least squares). Instead we use an *ad hoc* approach to the selection of instruments, as is the norm in applied econometric studies. Initially a third-order autoregression (AR3) is run on the jointly determined variables. Depending on the goodness of fit of this model as measured by R^2 and standard error of the regression (SEE), we either use the predictors from this equation or experiment with other equations that include additional predetermined variables from the model. In this way we arrive at the preferred instrument generating equation.

The IV estimates are presented for visual comparison with OLS estimates. Where estimated parameter values differ substantially, this may point to a problem of simultaneous equation bias in the OLS regressions. More formally, a test for the statistical significance of the bias is carried out using the Wu–Hausman test.[5]

By carrying out the various procedures discussed above it is intended that weaknesses in the model be uncovered. Of course, the model selection strategy employed is far from comprehensive and without weaknesses of its own. As a result, deficiencies in the model may go undetected. Some possible problems may arise, for instance, from the use of OLS rather than IV as a vehicle for model selection and from the use of a hybrid encompassing and variable addition technique for the selection of certain models, leading to possible inconsistencies. It is also the case that the small sample properties of some of the diagnostic tests applied are not well known and their use is justified only by reference to asymptotic properties.

Where feasible, the preferred models are compared with existing models encountered in the literature and an attempt is made to reconcile the two by, for instance, showing how one can encompass the other.

Notes

1 See Leamer (1983), Hendry (1980) and McAleer, *et al.* (1985).

2 This is a categorisation used by McAleer, *et al.* (1985). Sargan (1964) is often quoted as an early example of good applied econometric research.

3 Again this categorisation is used by McAleer, *et al.* (1985).

4 The use of auto-regressive least squares in this way has attracted much criticism from advocates of the encompassing technique (see Hendry and Mizon, 1978). They maintain that, starting from a general dynamic model including lagged values of all independent as well as the dependent variables, one should test for a common factor in the data. Only if this is found are autoregressive least squares appropriate, i.e. there exists true error dynamics. Otherwise the equation exhibits systematic dynamics due to model misspecification that should be dealt with by estimating with free parameters on the lagged variables. Testing for common factors in the context of the present study was found to be unfeasible because a serious problem of multicollinearity arose when lagged values of all variables were added. Parameter values ceased to make economic sense. Rather than admit a problem of multicollinearity it was decided to risk the danger of imposing inadmissible common factors. However, by starting with fairly general dynamic models, the danger of assuming error autocorrelation when model misspecification was the true problem was less acute than it would have been had less general models been used and not thoroughly tested for misspecification.

5 Wu (1973) and Hausman (1978). Wu's *T*2 test is identical to Hausman's general specification test as Nakamura and Nakamura (1981) show. Wu's *T*2 statistic is generated by adding instruments for the jointly determined variables to the original set of regressors for the equation being tested and re-estimating. The statistic is easily computed as it is equivalent to the *F* ratio for the hypothesis that the parameters of the instruments are jointly equal to zero. Pagan (1984)

shows that using generated regressors as instruments, the t ratios (and F ratios) on the instruments will be downward biased. This means that if the F ratio exceeds the critical value and we reject the null hypothesis that the parameters of the instruments do not differ significantly from zero, there is a danger that we may conclude that simultaneous equation bias is a problem when it is in fact not. There will, however, be no danger of inappropriately accepting the null hypothesis.

Appendix 3 Measurement of demand pressure

The measurement of demand pressure in Brazilian product and labour markets is complicated by a scarcity of data. The only direct data available are a quarterly survey based index of capacity utilisation in manufacturing industry dating from mid-1968 and unemployment rates in selected major urban centres dating in most cases from 1980. To obtain a longer series, pre-dating 1968, it is necessary to infer an indicator of demand pressure from other available data.

Two methods have been employed in the Brazilian literature to infer rates of capacity utilisation, either in a particular sector or in the overall economy. The first and by far the most widely used approach has been to estimate potential output by 'trend through peaks'.[1] Actual output is plotted against time and 'major' peaks are selected where it is assumed that capacity was fully utilised. These peaks are then connected by constant exponential growth lines. The line connecting the last two major peaks is then extrapolated into the future, assuming an unchanging slope. The trend line through the peaks is taken to represent potential output. The percentage rate of capacity utilisation is calculated as

$$CU = q/q^{p} \cdot 100$$

where (q) is aggregate or sectoral output and (q^{p}) is the corresponding potential output. Excess capacity or the 'output gap' in percentage terms is simply

$$EC = 100 - CU$$

Many empirical studies of wage and price determination in Brazil over recent decades adopted the 'trend through peaks' method to derive measures of capacity utilisation on the assumption of only two peaks; generally 1961 and 1974 or 1976, whether for GDP, or for industrial or manufacturing output. In figure A3.1, we plot a capacity utilisation variable for manufacturing of this variety for 1960–86, in which it is

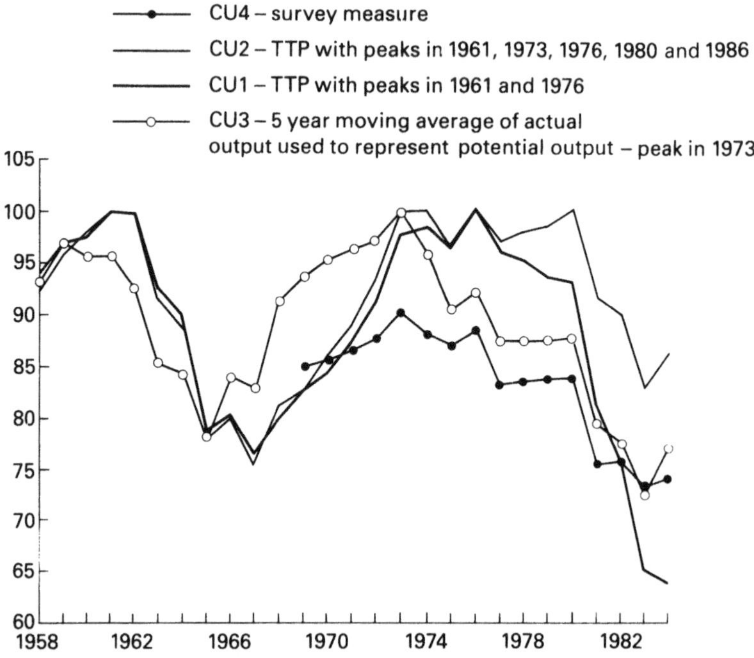

Figure A3.1 Measures of capacity utilisation in manufacturing industry

assumed that potential output grew at a compound annual rate of 8.1 per cent over the entire period and that peaks were reached in 1961 and 1976 ($CU1$). The values also appear in table A3.1.

Annual averages of capacity utilisation as measured by the survey data available from 1968 are also presented in the table and plotted as ($CU4$). The two measures coincide reasonably well as regards turning points over the years 1968–80.[2] However, in the post-1980 period, the relationship breaks down, with the data based measure ($CU1$) implying rapidly falling and improbably low rates of capacity utilisation. This reflects the fact that ($CU1$) implicitly assumes continued rapid growth of potential output, despite the dramatic fall in fixed investment that occurred in manufacturing in the 1980s.[3]

The assumption of a constant growth in potential output is clearly not adequate for constructing a measure of capacity utilisation that is to be used to proxy demand beyond 1980. We therefore relaxed the assumption of a constant growth in potential output and assumed instead that peaks occurred in 1961, 1973, 1976, 1980 and 1986. Three trend through peak lines were fitted with different slopes. As in the earlier example, growth of 8.1 per cent was assumed between 1961–76 while rates of 5.2 per cent and

Table A3.1. *Rates of capacity utilisation in manufacturing and in the overall economy*

Year	*CU*4	*CU*2	*CU*1	*CU*3	*GDPCU*
1958	—	92	93	93	97
1959	—	96	97	97	95
1960	—	98	98	96	97
1961	—	100	100	96	100
1962	—	100	100	93	98
1963	—	91	92	85	93
1964	—	88	90	84	89
1965	—	78	79	78	85
1966	—	81	80	84	82
1967	—	75	76	83	80
1968	—	81	80	91	83
1969	85	83	83	94	85
1970	86	86	84	95	86
1971	87	89	87	96	89
1972	88	93	91	97	92
1973	90	100	98	100	98
1974	88	100	98	96	100
1975	87	96	96	90	98
1976	89	100	100	92	100
1977	83	97	96	87	98
1978	84	98	95	88	96
1979	84	99	93	87	95
1980	84	100	93	88	95
1981	76	92	81	79	87
1982	76	90	76	78	82
1983	73	83	65	73	74
1984	74	86	64	77	72

1.9 per cent prevailed in 1976–80 and 1980–6 respectively. Capacity utilisation, calculated on this basis, is plotted in figure A3.1 as (*CU*2). The correlation with (*CU*4) is quite good and is maintained in the post-1980 period.

Another proxy for capacity utilisation in manufacturing was computed by generating a series for potential output in which the latter equalled the average of actual output in a given year as well as in the four previous years. 1973 was found to be the year in which the ratio of actual to potential output – as proxied by the five year moving average – was at its highest level. Setting capacity utilisation in that year equal to 100 per cent and rescaling the entire series gave a variable, (*CU*3), comparable with the others discussed above. This proxy is shown in figure A3.1 and table A3.1.

Another method employed in the Brazilian literature, and elsewhere, to estimate capacity utilisation has been to abstract from changes in the utilisation of factors other than fixed capital and to assume that deviations in output from potential are due solely to differences between the actual output/capital ratio and some peak or capacity value for the same ratio. Potential output becomes a function of the stock of fixed capital at the beginning of each time period. Malan and Bonelli (1977) and Baumann Neves (1978) both used this method to construct capacity utilisation indicators for the Brazilian manufacturing industry from 1954–5 to 1975.

This method is, in many ways, more theoretically defensible than the trend through peaks approach in that it does at least allow for the effect of changes in the capital stock over time. However, in the Brazilian context, an estimate of the capital stock must be built up from some base year estimate and from net investment flows, using the perpetual inventory method. With no data on depreciation, in both the studies reported above, gross investment flows are used as proxies for net flows. Contador (1977) compares Malan and Bonelli's capacity utilisation series with one constructed using the trend through peaks approach and finds little difference in the two.[4] However, our own attempt to update their series using post-1975 data on gross investment in manufacturing along with production data yielded implausible indications of capacity utilisation rates in the late 1970s and early 1980s. This was probably due to the compounding of errors in the capital stock series due to the failure to account for depreciation and, possibly as well, due to the failure to allow for trend variation in the capacity output/capital ratio.[5]

Given that changes in agricultural output, relative to trend or potential output, arguably have more to do with supply side conditions than with demand factors, it is questionable whether overall capacity utilisation in the economy (100 − GDP output gap) is a reasonable proxy for demand. On the assumption that industrial and service sector output is primarily demand driven, capacity utilisation in one or both of these sectors provides a more defensible proxy for demand pressures generally. For this reason our preferred measure of product market demand is the variable (*CU*2), derived above. Still, because GDP gap variables are widely employed in the existing Brazilian literature, we also test for demand effects using such a proxy. To be consistent with the other indicators used, we define a variable, (*GDPCU*), as 100 minus the percentage output gap, where the latter was constructed on the assumption that cyclical peaks were attained in 1961 and 1976. A compound annual rate of growth of potential GDP of 7.17 per cent was assumed. (*GDPCU*) is therefore the rate of 'capacity utilisation' in the overall economy.

In the absence of direct data on labour market demand, we follow the standard practice in the Brazilian literature of making appeal to Okun's Law to link capacity utilisation to the unemployment rate; the usual proxy for excess supply of labour. Okun (1962) found, using data for the U.S.A., a reasonably stable relationship between the rate of unemployment and output over the trade cycle, assuming potential output to be exogenous. His findings have been cited to justify the use of capacity utilisation measured by the 'trend through peaks' method as a proxy for one minus the unemployment rate. Turnovsky (1977, pp. 92–3), offers a theoretical derivation of this relationship taking as a starting point a short-run production function in which the capital stock is exogenous.

Notes

1 This method is associated with Klein and the Wharton Econometric Forecasting Associates as well as the President's Council of Economic Advisers. See Council of Economic Advisers (1970) and Klein and Summers (1966).

2 Christiano (1981) shows that survey based capacity utilisation indicators tend consistently to show lower rates of capacity utilisation and less amplitude of variation than do data based measures. He discussed some possible explanations for this phenomenon. Here we have not re-scaled (*CU*4) therefore turning points and slopes rather than absolute levels of capacity utilisation are relevant to the comparison.

3 The constant cruzeiro value of gross fixed investment in manufacturing industry fell by a cumulative 29 per cent between 1979 and 1981 and by a further 11 per cent between 1981 and 1984 (data from *Conjuntura Econômica*, annual surveys of investment in industry, various dates).

4 Christiano (1981) presents evidence for a series of industrial countries to show that trend through peak indicators show very similar patterns of change to those exhibited by more sophisticated measures based on methods like that used by Malan and Bonelli (1977) or even methods where potential output is given by a multi-factor production function.

5 Christiano (1981) shows that from the industrialised countries, output/capital ratios have tended to decline over time.

Appendix 4 Data: definitions and sources

In section A4.1 the symbols used in chapter 7 are defined and the sources of the data are shown in abbreviated form. Abbreviations are explained in section A4.3. Assorted data presented or referred to in chapters other than 7 are defined and their sources given in section A4.2. Where identical to, or functionally related to data defined in section A4.1, a cross reference is made. 1970 CR$b. refers to billions of constant 1970 cruzeiros.

A4.1 Data used in chapter 7

B	end of year stocks of federal treasury bonds (ORTNs) and bills (LTNs), outside monetary authorities, plus main state and municipal indexed securities; CR$b. BBCB (various dates).
c	private consumption of domestically produced goods deflated by implicit deflator for consumption; 1970 CR$b. From NA.
c^G	government consumption expenditure deflated by implicit deflator for consumption; 1970 CR$b. From NA.
DS	interest and indexation on government securities (B); CR$b. Constructed using $DS = \dot{P}^G \cdot B_{t-1}$.
$DU65$	dummy variable with value one in 1965 and zero in other years.
$DU74$	dummy variable with value one in 1974 and zero in other years.
$DU75$	dummy variable with value one in 1975 and zero in other years.
$DU7984$	dummy variable with value one in 1979 through 1984 and zero in other years.
$DU81$	dummy variable with value one in 1981 and zero in other years.
$DU8183$	dummy variable with value one in 1981 through 1983 and zero in other years.
$DU82$	dummy variable with value one in 1982 and zero in other years.
$DU83$	dummy variable with value one in 1983 and zero in other years.
E	index (1970 = 1) of nominal average annual cruzeiro/U.S. dollar exchange rate. Constructed from data in IFSY (1984) and IFS (Jan. 1986).

FR foreign assets of monetary authorities CR\$b. IFSY (1984) and IFS (Jan. 1986).

g real expenditure on goods, services and fixed capital investment by general government; 1970 CR\$b. Constructed using $g = c^G + i^G$.

$GDPCU$ overall capacity utilisation, where construction of $GDPCU$ is explained in appendix 3.

H end of year stocks of high-powered money; CR\$b. IFSY (1984) and IFS (Jan. 1986).

i^F private gross investment in fixed capital deflated by implicit deflator for investment; 1970 CR\$b. From NA.

i^G government gross fixed capital investment deflated by implicit deflator for investment; 1970 CR\$b. From NA.

i^S private stock building deflated by implicit deflator for GDP; 1970 CR\$b. From NA.

im total imports of goods and services deflated by implicit deflator for imports; 1970 CR\$b. From NA.

im^{NWP} imports of all goods except wheat and petroleum; 1970 CR\$b. Constructed, $im^{NWP} = im - im^S - im^P - im^W$.

im^P imports of petroleum; 1970 CR\$b. Constructed from quantum and dollar price indices for crude petroleum imports from CE, 'Comércio exterior' (various dates) rescaled to 1970 = CR\$1.17b, where this estimate of the 1970 value of petroleum imports was taken from foreign trade data in AE (1973).

im^S imports of services; 1970 CR\$b. Constructed, $im^S = im - im^G$, where latter is constant value of all goods imports computed from quantum and dollar price indices from CE, 'Comércio exterior' (various dates) rescaled to 1970 = CR\$11.5b.

im^W imports of wheat; 1970 CR\$b. Constructed from quantum and dollar price indices for wheat imports from CE, 'Comércio exterior' (various dates) rescaled to 1970 = CR\$0.48b.

le^{PA} average annual stocks of loans outstanding from the monetary authorities to the agricultural sector; 1970 CR\$b. Constructed using $le^{PA} = (le_t^{PA*} + le_{t-1}^{PA*})/2$.

le^{PA*} end of period loans from monetary authorities to the agricultural sector deflated by GPI; 1970 CR\$b. For 1960–71 from AE (various dates), for 1972–8 from IBRD (1981), and for 1979–84 from BBCB (various dates).

le^{PNA*} end of year stocks of loans from monetary authorities to the non-agricultural private sector; 1970 CR\$b. Constructed using $le^{PNA*} = le^{PT*} - le^{PA*}$.

le^{PT} average annual stocks of loans outstanding from the monetary authorities to the overall private sector deflated by GPI; 1970 CR$b. Constructed using $le^{PT} = (le_t^{PT*} + le_{t-1}^{PT*})/2$.

le^{PT*} end of year stocks of loans from the monetary authorities to overall private sector deflated by GPI; 1970 CR$b. From IFSY (1984) and IFS (Jan. 1986) – 'claims on private sector by monetary authorities'.

m index (1970 = 1) of unit food consumption subsidies. Constructed using $m = P^{CF}/P^{WF}$.

N index (1970 = 1) of estimated mid-year population. From data in IFSY (1984) and IFS (Jan. 1986).

nin national income; 1970 CR$b. Constructed using $nin = y + nre + tg$.

nrb net receipts from new government securities placed with the private sector; 1970 CR$b. Constructed using $nrb = \{B_t - [1 + (\dot{P}_t^G - 0.7)] \cdot B_{t-1}\}/P_t^G$.

nre net factor income from abroad deflated by P^{IM*}; 1970 CR$b. From NA.

nro other net receipts of general government deflated by GPI; 1970 CR$b. Calculated using equation (7.23).

nk net capital inflows deflated by P^{WUS*}; 1970 CR$b. Calculated using equation (7.32).

P^{CF} index (1970 = 100) of Rio de Janeiro consumer food price: for 1960–70 from CE (October 1971); for 1970–6 from CE (July 1979); for 1976–84 from CE (various dates).

P^{CG} index (1970 = 100) of Rio de Janeiro overall consumer price. Sources as for P^{CF}. See section A4.2 for component sub indices.

P^{EX*} index (1970 = 100) of dollar export prices from CE 'Comércio exterior' (various dates).

P^G index (1970 = 100) of the Brazilian general prices (domestic supply). Sources as for P^{CF}.

p^H index (1970 = 1) of Rio de Janeiro construction cost deflated by P^{CG}. Sources as for P^{CF}.

P^{IM*} index (1970 = 100) of overall dollar goods import prices. Source as for P^{EX*}.

P^{IMP*} index (1970 = 100) of dollar prices of imported petroleum. Source as for P^{EX*}.

P^{IMNP*} index (1970 = 100) of dollar prices of non-petroleum imports: for 1960–5 and 1983–4, proxied by P^{IM*}; for 1966–82 from Modiano (1985).

P^{IMR*} index (1970 = 100) of dollar imported raw material prices: for 1960–78 from CE 'Comercio exterior' (various dates), U.S.$

prices: – 'intermediate consumption goods – raw materials'; for 1979–84 from CE (various dates), 'U.S.$ prices – intermediate consumption goods'.

$P^{W\dot{F}}$ index (1970 = 100) of wholesale food prices. Sources as for P^{CF}.

P^{WG} index (1970 = 100) of overall wholesale prices (domestic supply). Sources as for P^{CF}.

P^{WI} index (1970 = 100) of wholesale manufacturing prices (general supply): for 1960–9 from CE (various dates), 'industrial product prices'; for 1970–84 from CE (various dates), 'industrial product prices – manufacturing industry'.

P^{WR} index (1970 = 100) of wholesale raw material prices (internal supply): for 1960–9 from CE (various dates), 'prices, production goods – non-food raw materials – total'; for 1970–84 from CE (various dates), 'non-food raw materials – unprocessed'.

p^{WR+} index (1970 = 1) of the relative price of the domestic component of wholesale raw material prices. Constructed from equation (7.52).

P^{WUS*} index (1970 = 100) of U.S. wholesale prices: from IFSY (1984) and IFS (Jan. 1986).

pr index (1970 = 1) of output per worker in manufacturing industry. Constructed using $pr = q^{M}/em$, where em is an index of employment in manufacturing industry. Sources; for 1958–62 from Musalem (1982), for 1963–84 as for W^{I}.

q^{AF} food production; 1970 CR\$b. Constructed by taking an index of real agricultural production from NA multiplied by 1970 value of agricultural output less real value of coffee production and real value of agricultural exports. Real value of coffee given by quantum produced (for 1960–79 from IBRD (1982) and for 1980–4 from CE (various dates)), multiplied by estimated 1970 value of coffee output of CR\$1.21b: from IBRD (1982). Real value of agricultural exports equals index of non-industrial exports from CE 'Comércio exterior' (various dates) multiplied by estimated 1970 value of agricultural exports of CR\$6.0b: from IBRD (1982).

q^{M} index of real output of manufacturing industry; NA.

q^{NF} non-food value added; 1970 CR\$b. Constructed using $q^{NF} = \hat{y} - q^{AF} - t^{I} - su$.

RES ratio of implicit GDP deflator to consumer price index. Constructed using equation (7.9).

r index of average annual real yield on bills of exchange. Constructed using $r = (1 + R)/(1 + \dot{P}^{G})$, where (R) is average yield over twelve months on bills of exchange of 180 days (for 1960–70) and 360 days (for 1971–83): data from Banco Central.

sd statistical discrepancy between GDP (expenditure measure) and GDP (production measure). Constructed using equation (7.7).

su real subsidies; 1970 CR\$b. Constructed using $su = 0.008y$.

SU^F consumer food subsidies; CR\$b. Constructed using equation (7.17).

su^{NF} non-food subsidies; 1970 CR\$b. Constructed using $su^{NF} = su - -(SU^F/P^G)$.

sf supply of food in constant value terms; 1970 CR\$b. Constructed using $sf = q^{AF} + im^W$.

T^D direct tax plus other non-tax current revenues of general government (other net receipts); CR\$b. NA.

t^D direct tax plus other non-tax current revenues of general government (other net receipts); 1970 CR\$b. Constructed using $t^D = T^D/P^G$.

T^I indirect tax revenues of general government; CR\$b. NA.

t^I indirect tax revenues of general government; 1970 CR\$b. Constructed using $t^I = 0.167y$.

tg index (1970 = 0) of terms of trade effect. Constructed using equation (7.30).

TL a linear time trend.

tr^{NI} non-interest transfers from government to the private sector; 1970 CR\$b. Constructed from data on total transfers to private sector (from NA) deflated by GDP deflator less interest expense on government debt $(0.07 \cdot B_{t-1}/P_t^{CG})$.

W^I index (1970 = 100) of average earnings in manufacturing industry. Observations for 1958–62 proxied by estimates of the average urban minimum wage taken from Jul (1977), 1963–9 constructed from data on total salary payments and employment from the following sources: for 1963 from *Indústria de transformação – dados gerais 1963/4*, IBGE; for 1964–5 from AE (1967); for 1966 from AE (1969); for 1967–8 from AE (1970) (original source *Produção Industrial*) and for 1969 from *Indústria de transformação – pesquisa trimestral*, IBGE. Data for 1970–84 on average earnings taken directly from: for 1970 from *Boletim Econômico – IPEA*; for 1971–84 from *Indicadores Conjunturais da Indústria* (various dates), IBGE.

WE domestic financial wealth of the private sector; CR\$b. Constructed using $WE = H + B$.

x exports of goods and services deflated by implicit deflator for exports; 1970 CR\$b: from NA.

x^G exports of goods; 1970 CR\$b. Quantum data from CE 'Comércio exterior' (various dates) multiplied by estimated 1970 value of goods exports of CR\$ 12.6b from AE (1973).

x^S exports of services; 1970 CR\$b. Constructed using $x^S = x - x^G$.

y GDP at market prices, expenditure measure; 1970 CR\$b: from NA.

$\hat{y}$ GDP at market prices, production measure; 1970 CR\$b: from NA.

y^D disposable income of the private sector deflated by implicit GDP deflator; 1970 CR\$b: from NA.

y^{DC} disposable income of the private sector deflated by the consumer price index P^{CG}; 1970 CR\$b. NA.

$\hat{y}^{FC}$ GDP at factor cost, production measure; 1970 CR\$b. NA.

y^{US} U.S. GNP; 1980 U.S.\$b; from IFSY (1984) and IFS (Jan. 1986).

z^E index (1970 = 1) of export subsidies: for 1960–78 from Musalem (1982) for 1979–84 assumed constant at 1978 value of one.

z^I index (1970 = 1) of real tariffs on non-petroleum imports: for 1960–5 assumed constant at 1966 level; for 1966–82 from Horta, reproduced in Modiano (1985) and for 1983–4 assumed constant at 1982 level.

A4.2 Data used in chapter 2 and elsewhere

In order of appearance in tables and figures.

Real GDP from NA2.

Real agricultural output – from NA2.

Real industrial output – from NA2.

GDP deflator – from NA2.

General price index – P^G.

Current account of balance of payments – from IFSY (1984), IFSY (1988) and CE (March 1989), converted into cruzeiros using (E).

Public sector 'operational' surplus (deficit) – estimates of the public sector surplus (as percentage of GDP) excluding monetary correction on the public debt. Series for 1970–83 from Centro de Contas Nacionais e Centro de Estudos Fiscais of the Fundação Getulio Vargas reproduced in Marques (1985) (excludes state owned enterprises). Series for 1981–8 from Banco Central do Brasil, *Indicadores Macroeconômicos do Setor Público* (September 1989).

Net taxation burden – equal to the sum of direct and indirect taxation less current transfers and subsidies, all expressed as a percentage of GDP. NA2.

Gross foreign debt – total registered foreign debt in U.S.\$b: from BBCB (various dates) and CE (various dates).

Aggregate inflation – $\dot{P}^G$.

Wholesale food price inflation – $\dot{P}^{WF}$.

Wholesale raw material price inflation – $\dot{P}^{WR}$.

Wholesale manufactured goods price inflation – $\dot{P}^{WI}$.

Consumer food price inflation – $\dot{P}^{CF}$.
Consumer miscellaneous price inflation – rate of change of index of 6 non-food items comprising the Rio de Janeiro cost of living index. Constructed residually from series for P^{CG} and P^{CF} assuming that the latter had constant 0.40 weighting in former. Weighting used corresponds to actual 1982 weighting. See below under *Consumer Price Index* for constituents.
Construction cost inflation – rate of change of $(p^{H} \cdot P^{CG})$.
High-powered money – H.
Wholesale price inflation – $\dot{P}^{WG}$.
$M1$ – narrow money, end of year levels from IFSY (1984) and IFS (Jan. 1986).
$M3$ – $M1$ plus time and savings deposits from IFSY (1984) and IFS (Jan. 1986).
Foreign assets of the monetary authorities – FR.
Urban minimum wage – average annual for urban South Eastern Brazil. Calculated as average of 12 monthly wages plus the 13th wage: from BBCB (various dates).
Official wage adjustments – Ministry of Labour figures on average annual officially decreed wage and salary adjustments.
Average manufacturing earnings – W^{I}.
Cost of living – P^{CG}.
Unit labour cost in manufacturing – Constructed using $ULC = (W^{I}/pr)$.
Food crop production – fixed weight quantum index of 8 major food crops. Weights taken from percentage shares in total value of output in 1973 (from IBRD (1982)). Crops with respective weights are: wheat (7.0), rice (20.5), maize (24.0), manioc (16.2), potatoes (5.1), peanuts (2.6), beans (20.1) and bananas (4.5). Production data from AE (various dates).
Overnight interest rate – from CE (May 1989), average of monthly rates annualised.
Average real salary in industry – from FIESP, reproduced in CE (May 1989), December to December changes.
Capacity utilisation in manufacturing – variable $CU2$ (see below).
Real yield on bills of exchange – r.
Real cost of consumer credit – 1 plus average interest rates charged by finance houses 'financeiras' for 360 day credit towards purchase of consumer durables, inflation divided by 1 plus general price inflation: data from Banco Central do Brasil.
Manufacturing price index – P^{WI}.
De-trended productivity in manufacturing – absolute deviations from a trend line through (pr).
Wholesale food price – P^{WF}.

External terms of trade – P^{EX*}/P^{IM*}.
Cruzeiro price of imported raw materials deflated by general price index (assuming no subsidies) – $P^{IMR*} \cdot E/P^{G}$.
Dollar price of imported raw materials deflated by U.S. wholesale price index – P^{IMR*}/P^{WUS*}.
Real cruzeiro/U.S. dollar exchange rate – $E \cdot P^{WUS*}/P^{WG}$.
Actual domestic price of fuel oil – index of actual cruzeiro price of fuel oil: for 1966–82 from Modiano (1985) (original data from *Anuário Estatístico do Conselho Nacional do Petróleo*, various dates) and for 1983–4 from CE (various dates).
Notional domestic price of imported petroleum (assuming no subsidies) – $P^{IMP*} \cdot E$.
Relative wholesale raw material price – P^{WR}/P^{G}.
CU1, CU2, CU3 and CU4 – measures of capacity utilisation in manufacturing industry constructed in the way described in appendix 3 using q^{M}.
Consumer Price Index – subindices with actual 1982 weights are: food (0.40), domestic articles (0.093), accommodation (0.118), clothing (0.021), health (0.053), private services (0.199), public services (0.116).

A4.3 Key to data sources

BBCB – *Boletim do Banco Central.*
UNNA – *United Nations National Accounts Yearbook.*
NA — National Accounts data nominal series: for 1960–4 from CE (Oct. 1969); for 1965–9 from CE (Feb. 1981) and for 1970–83 in CE (Mar. 1985). The first two series were rebased and spliced with 1970–83 data. Implicit deflators from: for 1960–9 from UNNA (1976); for 1970–82 from *Contas Nacionais do Brasil: Metodologia e Tabelas Estatísticas*, IBE/Centro de Contas Nacionais and for 1983 from CE (Mar. 1985).
NA2 – Revised National Accounts data for 1970–88 from IBGE, Diretoria de Pesquisas, Departamento de Contas Nacionais, *Contas Consolidadas para a Nação* (1989).
CE – *Conjuntura Econômica.*
IFSY – *International Financial Statistics (Yearbook).*
IFS – *International Financial Statistics (Monthly).*
AE – *Anuário Estatístico do Brasil.*
IBRD – *International Bank for Reconstruction and Development (see Bibliography for citations)*
IBGE – *Instituto Brasileiro de Geografia e Estatística*
FIESP – *Federação das Industrias do Estado de São Paulo*

Notes

1 *A theoretical framework for the study of inflation rooted in the Latin American structuralist approach*

1 There exists an extensive literature devoted to this polemic, see for instance, articles contained in Baer and Kerstenetzky (1964). Many of the major points of disagreement between monetarists and structuralists are addressed in the course of developing the theoretical model of section 1.3 of this chapter and also in the later empirical chapters of this study.

2 The ideas put forward by this school did not, of course, emerge in isolation and, as Seers (1962) shows, they owe a debt to the work of many non-Latin American economists. In tracing the intellectual developments of the tradition, Seers does not make mention of the work of Kalecki, whose contributions to economics have a strong structuralist flavour (see Kalecki, 1943, 1955). Other non-Latin American bodies of literature that can be termed structuralist have grown up either independently or due to cross-fertilisation with the Latin American school. Certain authors have, for instance, considered similarities and differences between Latin American structuralism and the 'Scandinavian Approach' to inflation as well as to Schultze's 'Structural Imbalance' inflation theory (see Wachter, 1976 and Canavese, 1980). In the short review that follows we use structuralism to refer to the Latin American structuralist tradition.

3 On the other hand, structuralists pointed out (Olivera, 1964) that output growth can contribute to price stability in as much as relative price changes may be effected more readily under those conditions than in a stagnant or declining economic environment. Social groups are more likely to accept a fall in relative, as opposed to absolute, income shares.

4 Olivera (1967a) showed this formally.

5 Of course, neither of these two bottle-necks are essential prerequisites for structural inflation nor are they necessarily the only possible bottle-necks that may arise.

6 See particularly Seers (1962) and Pinto (1968).

7 Although the model of section 1.3 is not couched explicitly in terms of income shares, this conflict is at the root of the inflationary mechanisms discussed. Olivera (1967a) provided a formalisation of the dynamics of the income share struggle in the context of a structuralist model.

8 Important contributions to this literature are to be found in: Taylor (1979, 1981, 1983), Chichilnisky and Taylor (1980) and Cardoso (1979, 1981).
9 See Rowthorn (1980) for an insightful exposition of a 'conflict' model.
10 The idea of inertial inflation is particularly associated with the work of Francisco Lopes, Andre Lara Resende and Persio Arida. See Arida (1982), Lopes (1982), Arida and Lara Resende (1985). A compendium of papers on the subject appears in Lopes (1986).
11 If wages are set not by administrative fiat but as the outcome of bargaining by workers and capitalists, the model will only hold as long as inflation is below what Rowthorn (1980) termed the 'expectations threshold'. Beyond this rate of inflation, workers will begin to fight for nominal wage adjustments based upon expected future inflation and not just upon past erosion of the real wage as in the present model. With institutionalised indexation and curbs on the possibility of settlements deviating from the mandatory path, the model may well be relevant, even at high rates of inflation, despite the fact that actual real wages will always be below a notional concept of a target real wage. See chapter 4(4.2) for a discussion of the Brazilian institutional setting.
12 Point (A) is not a long-run equilibrium point as, leaving aside for the moment financial questions, in time there may be pressure to increase the speed of adjustment in both the food and labour markets. Rising (λ) in equation (1.13) and particularly (h) in equation (1.11) will cause accelerating and eventually explosive inflation.
13 See for instance, Ott and Ott (1965), Christ (1967), Blinder and Solow (1973), Branson (1976) and Cripps and Godley (1976).
14 Were we to build in here demand effects in the labour and product markets as well, assets would also be linked to inflation more directly through real wage and mark-up determination in industry.

2 *Brazil's experience with inflation since 1960: the evidence and existing interpretations*

1 This point is taken up in a more specific way at various points throughout the study.
2 Here, as elsewhere in this study, the intention is not to provide a detailed chronological description of Brazil's inflation nor of its interaction with stabilisation policies in each subperiod of the approximately twenty years under review. Neither is it intended to present an essay on Brazil's overall macro-economic policy and performance in the same period. These goals have been admirably attained elsewhere see Bacha (1977, 1980, 1983), Malan and Bonelli (1977) and Wells (1977, 1979). The intention is instead to identify important underlying causes of the inflation and to examine the fundamental mechanisms of its propagation. Naturally, these questions are intimately linked to macro-economic policy and performance and many specific aspects of these are addressed at relevant points throughout the text.
3 The general price index (domestic supply) is a fixed weight composite index of the wholesale price index (domestic supply), which excludes prices of goods for

export, the Rio de Janeiro consumer price index and the Rio de Janeiro construction cost index. The weights applied are 0.6, 0.3 and 0.1 respectively.

4 *Ex ante* indexation denotes a process by which contracts are set so as to incorporate expected inflation up to the expiry date and is therefore not true indexation in the normal sense of the word whereas *ex post* indexation implies adjustment upon expiry of the contract in accordance with past inflation.

5 Aspects of the indexation mechanisms are discussed at relevant points throughout the text. For a description and appraisal of indexation in Brazil see Baer and Beckerman (1980) and Simonsen (1983).

6 The emphasis on 'immediate' contributors is crucial since some indices are likely to be important determinants of others. For instance, on the hypothesis that raw material price is a major determinant of manufacturing price, the picture that emerges from the decomposition tends to obscure the true importance of the former.

7 In order to decompose the general price index in an interesting way and over an extended period of time some approximations had to be made. While this index is fixed weight, the consumer and wholesale price indices from which it is constructed are themselves made up of indices with moving average weights. Therefore a long-run average of the actual weighting was applied. A second approximation is necessary because the wholesale manufacturing price index, which includes not only prices of goods for domestic consumption but also prices of export goods, is not strictly a component of the GPI (internal supply) although its make up is very close to that of the individual industrial prices that figure in the GPI (internal supply). Thirdly, as explained in chapter 3(3.5), before 1970 both the manufacturing and crude raw material price indices used here included prices of mining output and semi-processed raw materials respectively and are not therefore fully independent of one another. These approximations mean that the decomposition gives rise to a small, unexplained residual. None of the approximations made impair the usefulness of this exercise which does not depend upon an absolutely precise accounting of the movements in the aggregate inflation index.

8 The construction of the consumer miscellaneous price index is explained in appendix 4(A4.2).

9 The weights applied in the decomposition were: wholesale price of food 0.20, wholesale price of crude raw materials 0.09, wholesale price of manufactured goods 0.31, RJ consumer price of food 0.12, RJ consumer miscellaneous 0.18 and RJ construction cost 0.10.

10 A few of the studies of recent inflation in Brazil are best thought of as adopting an eclectic approach that draws upon cost-push, structuralist and monetarist explanations. These include Cline (1981), Lemgruber (1977) and Marques (1985).

11 See chapter 4(4.1.1), for a much fuller discussion of the Phillips curve.

12 See appendix 3 for a discussion of 'gap' variables and Okun's Law.

13 The adoption of the Phillips curve construct does not necessarily imply a monetarist view of long-run inflation. Cysne (1985) starts from the assumption of a cost based theory of inflation with mark-up pricing throughout the

economy. Nevertheless, in testing his model he makes the heroic assumption that all factors influencing pricing, bar wage costs and demand, can be treated as white noise and therefore subsumed within the error term.

14 The lagged dependent variable is probably best thought of as representing the workings of the lagged indexation scheme which imparted a strong inertial character to inflation. In as much as past inflation and future indexation plans were the major determinants of expectations, the monetarist insistence on the independent role of expectations as opposed to the influence of indexation is not wholly misplaced.

15 Some of these studies suffer from serial correlation in the error terms (note the values of the DW statistics in table 2.3) and there is evidence of marked parameter instability. See the convincing demonstration of this latter point in Lopes (1982) and Contador (1985).

16 Lopes (1982) cites evidence from the U.S. economy that a 1 per cent rise in the rate of unemployment produces, after one year, a fall of 0.25 per cent to 0.5 per cent in the rate of inflation. Assuming that by Okun's Law, a 1 per cent rise in the rate of unemployment is equal to a 2.5 per cent rise in the GDP gap, Brazilian commodity market Phillips curve studies suggest, rather implausibly, that a 1 per cent rise in the rate of unemployment is associated with a fall in inflation of 1.25 per cent to 2.5 per cent.

17 Although constructed using the trend through peaks method to proxy potential output, this measure differs from similarly derived series used in the Brazilian literature in that peaks are assumed to have occurred in 1961, 1976, 1980 and 1986. The usual measures assume a constant exponential growth rate of potential output with peaks in 1961 and 1974–6 only. These are not good proxies for capacity utilisation after 1980 when fixed capital investment fell sharply. The measure used here exhibits quite close correlation with a survey based indicator of capacity utilisation in the post-1980 period.

18 The soundness of the methodology used to construct the composite demand and supply shock variables is open to question. His empirical results are unconvincing and it is hard to escape the conclusion that this study represents an attempt to resurrect the Phillips curve by building in some, but only a partial, role for costs.

19 Lemgruber's assertion that domestic credit and the high-powered money growth had an important causal role in the inflation is surprising when viewed in relation to the structural model that he proposes. In the model, monetary variables affect inflation only indirectly through the medium of interest rates and the impact of the latter upon aggregate demand. Evidence from other sources suggests that interest rates have not been important determinants of private expenditure in Brazil (see chapter 7 for more details). Moreover, if monetary variables did have an inflationary impact through the channel proposed, we would expect to find a robust relationship between inflation and the aggregate demand proxy; the output gap. He does not find such a relationship.

20 Cline (1981) estimated an 'eclectic' single equation model to explain inflation over the period 1961–77. He found that the rate of change of $M1$, with a six month lag, was a significant determinant of inflation only when inflation lagged

one year was excluded from the regression. This suggests that the inertia created by past inflation rather than past money growth was a more important causal variable.

21 See Montoro Filho (1982) and IBRD (1984). During the 1970s and 1980s, even government securities became increasingly liquid and were effectively substitutes for money in certain types of transactions.

22 The Bank of Brazil (Banco do Brasil) is a hybrid organisation that as well as being an integral part of the monetary authorities is also a development and commercial bank. During the period under review, liabilities of the Bank consisted of deposits and of the 'conta do movimento'. The latter is effectively a free credit line from the Central Bank (Banco Central do Brasil), thus appearing on the asset side of the latter's balance sheet. The Bank of Brazil is not required to hold reserves at the Central Bank. Effectively, therefore, lending by the bank is financed by the liabilities of the Central Bank; hence the link between Bank of Brazil lending and expansion of high-powered money.

Cardoso (1977) found that $M1$ and inflation caused each other in the specific sense of Granger causality (referred to as G-causation). Contador (1978) came to the same conclusion but, more importantly, found that high-powered money G-caused inflation and not vice versa. However, his results suffer from the lack of an adequate measure of economic activity. In contrast, Carneiro Netto and Fraga Neto (1984), using a quarterly industrial production series to proxy overall output, concluded that causation between the price level and high-powered money was bidirectional. They also found that Bank of Brazil lending to the private sector G-caused industrial output but was not itself G-caused by either high-powered money, prices or output. Finally, Fraga Neto (1985) again found bidirectional causality between high-powered money and prices and also concluded that Bank of Brazil loans were G-caused by economic activity. When total credit to the private sector was substituted for Bank of Brazil loans, prices and credit G-caused high-powered money but high-powered money no longer G-caused prices. Credit G-caused output.

23 For a treatment of this issue see IBRD (1984) and Montoro Filho (1982).

24 The real value of total loans outstanding from the Bank of Brazil to the private sector increased more than four-fold between end 1970 and end 1977 before beginning a steady decline through 1983.

25 Whereas in 1965, currency and demand deposits made up 87 per cent of a broad measure of financial assets, this percentage had fallen to 45 per cent by 1972, 36 per cent by 1976 and 13 per cent by 1983. Currency and demand deposits are here compared with a basket of assets – not all of which existed in 1965 – that comprises time and savings deposits, bills of exchange, state and federal government indexed bonds (ORTNs and others), federal treasury bills (LTNs) and housing bonds. All these assets carried *ex post* or *ex ante* monetary correction.

26 See Wells (1979) for an account of the consistent failure to meet monetary targets during the period 1974–7.

27 Moreover, this policy, as with attempts to implement tight money, may have encouraged foreign borrowing because of its impact upon domestic interest rates. In this way it may have been counter-productive.

28 The interaction between financial assets, inflation and output is taken up again in chapters 7, 8 and 9.
29 See our discussion of this point in chapter 3(3.5).
30 The latter are promissory notes of firms with maturities usually of 180 or 360 days, countersigned by finance companies (financeiras), and sold at a deep discount to the general public.
31 Kafka (1967) also points to a role for profit-push inflation in 1964–5. This argument is formalised by A. Lara Resende (1979).
32 The role of corrective inflation is stressed particularly by Ellis (1969). The details are reviewed by A. Lara Resende (1982).
33 See chapter 4(4.2) for a detailed explanation of wage fixing arrangements.
34 Viewed in light of the model of chapter 1, policy-makers effectively reduced the wage adjustment coefficient (h). Policy experiments are performed in chapter 9 to assess the impact of changes in wage indexation parameters.
35 Mandatory wage adjustments were only applied in the private sector from 1965 onwards, see chapter 4 (4.2) for details.
36 The nature of the relationship between these variables is taken up in detail in chapter 4. There we argue that official wage policy was the major determinant of changes in average earnings along with trend real wage growth, as is suggested by the data series in figure 2.6 and as maintained by Fishlow (1973), Morley (1971) and other commentators.
37 In the context of the framework of chapter 1, a rise in labour productivity is equivalent to a fall in the coefficient (β) in the industrial price equation. This in turn causes (θ^*) to rise; making price stabilisation more easily attainable.
38 The validity of this assertion depends upon the pricing model hypothesised. If firms followed some form of 'normal cost' pricing (see chapter 3(3.3.2)), this anti-inflationary effect would not have been as pronounced. In chapter 3(3.4) various models are tested with the preferred one having the characteristics outlined here.
39 Marques (1985) for instance concludes that, on the basis of a visual comparison of fairly aggregate production data with a consumer food price series, agricultural supply did not play a significant role in inflation during the 1970s and early 1980s. As is shown below, our analysis leads to different conclusions.
40 These are: wheat, rice, maize, manioc, potatoes, peanuts, beans and bananas. Together these accounted for a 60 per cent share of the wholesale food price index in 1976. The construction of the index is explained in appendix 4.
41 Of course the National Accounts data are computed on a very different basis and are not therefore strictly comparable with our index. As we are interested only in major trends this complication can be ignored.
42 A similar index covering 13 domestic food crops is presented in IBRD (1982) for 1955–65 and 1966–80. This too shows a strong declining trend in output, particularly after 1974. The rates of change of output are not quite as low as indicated by our data but this is due principally to the inclusion of oranges, production of which boomed from the late 1960s onwards fuelled by the surge in exports of concentrated orange juice.
43 The econometric estimates performed in chapter 5(5.6) suggest an income elasticity of demand of 0.45.

44 It is not the place here to enquire into the reasons for the apparent decline in the traditional food sector. For one interpretation see Furtado (1981).
45 This issue is discussed further in chapter 5(5.2).
46 The increasing degree of indexation was reflected particularly in changes made to the wage adjustment scheme in 1974 that more fully protected real earnings (see Simonsen, 1980).
47 Details of the institutional arrangements governing the exchange rate are reviewed in chapter 6.
48 Malan and Bonelli (1977) and Marques (1985) are among those who play down the direct impact of the first oil shock while Cline (1981) and M. Lara Resende (1982) attribute rather more importance to this event.
49 See Bacha (1977), Malan and Bonelli (1977), Wells (1979) and Cline (1981). The framework of chapter 1, when expanded to include a foreign sector, is able to encompass explicitly this process – showing how a reserve accumulation and/or a public sector deficit leads to asset accumulation which in turn boosts private expenditure and demand. Even if a vigorous demand expansion does not have a strong direct inflationary impact in the markets for industrial goods and labour, it may set in motion an inflationary process through the food market.
50 See Simonsen (1980). The inflationary consequences of the simultaneous introduction of differentiated indexation based upon absolute wage and salary levels has bred some controversy (see Camargo, 1980 and Carvalho, 1981).
51 See chapter 3(3.3.5).
52 The rationale for this specification is discussed in chapter 6(6.1).
53 The analytical framework used in this study does not allow for an independent role for expectations and would need to be adapted to study the more recent inflationary experience.

3 *The manufacturing price index*

1 The distinction between price-maker and price-taker is made by Okun (1981) although the same dichotomy has been emphasised before by, for instance, Kalecki (1943), Hicks (1974) and Kaldor (1976).
2 Laidler and Parkin (1975) surveyed a number of industrial price studies which, they maintained, are tests of the price-taking hypothesis. These include; Rushdy and Lund (1967), McCallum (1970) and Solow (1969). However as noted by Sylos-Labini (1979) and Sawyer (1983), among others, it is open to question whether many of these studies constitute acceptable tests of the price-taking model. One of the main problems is the use of costs along with excess demand among the explanatory variables.
3 The available evidence on the structure of industry in Brazil lends no support to the view that atomistic competition between firms is the dominant tendency. On the contrary, it clearly points to aggregate levels of concentration that by the standard yardsticks (see Scherer, 1980, p. 67) reveal oligopoly as dominant. For evidence on industrial market structure in Brazil see Bonelli (1980), Braga and Mascolo (1982) and Holanda Filho (1983).
4 Means was another pioneer in this field. Using American data, he found pricing

behaviour in large segments of the economy to be at variance with the predictions of price-taking theories. A short account of his full findings appears in Means (1936).

5 Throughout this essay we refer to this type of pricing as 'cost-plus'. The term 'full-cost' is somewhat ambiguous, being used to refer to the process of marking up over direct costs as well as, occasionally, over broader definitions of cost.

6 One of the most thorough and influential surveys of business pricing to follow Hall and Hitch was Kaplan, *et al.* (1958).

7 For a recent contribution to, and review of, the debate concerning the full cost model versus traditional marginalist theories see Lee (1984a, 1984b).

8 Domberger (1983) and Sawyer (1983) derive their mark-up price equations from a model of oligopoly based upon the Cournot-Nash solution to oligopoly in which it is assumed that firms maximise profits independently of their rivals but consider profit maximising output decisions as given.

9 These include Hall and Hitch (1939), Kalecki (1943), Sylos-Labini (1969, 1974) and Sawyer (1983).

10 Studies that use this approach include, Eckstein and Fromm (1968), Schultze and Tryon (1965) and Coutts, Godley and Nordhaus (1978). Further slight differences exist between studies regarding the categorisation of certain other costs. For instance, Coutts, Godley and Nordhaus (1978) treat some services and indirect taxes as part of direct costs while these items are more usually included in overheads.

11 Nordhaus (1972) argues that firms treat capital costs (depreciation allowances adjusted for tax) just as they do other direct costs. Nadiri and Gupta (1977) test a price model for the U.S. that includes these costs. Hall and Hitch (1939) and Eckstein (1964) can be interpreted as full-cost models in this broad sense but this interpretation is open to debate.

12 Godley (1959) was the first to advance the hypothesis that firms marked up price over normal rather than actual costs. Neild (1963) first applied the normal cost principle in econometric work. He experimented with different normalisations but came down in favour of one based on trend growth in productivity. A similar approach is followed in Eckstein and Fromm (1968). Schultze and Tryon (1965) use a moving average of productivity rather than its trend growth.

13 Solow (1969), Rushdy and Lund (1967) and Nadiri and Gupta (1977), among others, preferred the concept of actual labour costs.

14 Coutts, Godley and Nordhaus (1978, p. 34) report that an examination of input–output tables relating to the U.K. industrial sector for successive years suggested that, at least at the aggregate levels considered in their analysis, long-run trends in raw material productivity were generally flat.

15 A similar categorisation is drawn in Coutts, Godley and Nordhaus (1978).

16 Examples of studies that come down in favour of this view are, Eckstein (1964), Rushdy and Lund (1967), Stigler and Kindahl (1970) and Tavlas (1984).

17 A counter-cyclical outcome is raised as a possibility by Kalecki (1943) and Sylos-Labini (1969). Some empirical evidence for the view is presented in Kaplan *et al.* (1958), Kalecki (1943), Means (1972) and Eckstein and Wyss (1972).

18 This is the position favoured by Neild (1963), Coutts, Godley and Nordhaus (1978) and Sawyer (1983) in analyses based on U.K. data and by Schultze and Tryon (1965) for the U.S.A. and Ros (1980) for Mexico.

19 See Sylos-Labini (1969, pp. 70–3) for a review of different views on probable changes in price elasticity of demand over the trade cycle.

20 This problem has been widely discussed in the literature. See for instance Rushdy and Lund (1967), Laidler and Parkin (1975) and Coutts, Godley and Nordhaus (1978).

21 See Nordhaus (1972) for a review of many of the demand variables customarily used and a commentary thereupon.

22 This point is brought home forcefully by Coutts, Godley and Nordhaus (1978).

23 Such a model is derived explicitly in Eckstein (1964).

24 Over the longer term, sustained changes in overhead costs, that have a general impact upon the industry rather than a firm specific impact, will tend to be passed on to price.

25 The seminal work is by Cavallo (1977, 1981). Also see Bruno (1979), Taylor (1981, 1983) and van Wijnbergen (1981, 1982, 1983).

26 Taylor (1983, p. 88) has shown that the nominal interest rate constitutes the relevant measure of interest charges in the price equation only if the wage rate, the price of raw materials and the interest rate remain unchanged in nominal terms for the duration of the production period. This would clearly be an unsatisfactory assumption to make in the context of a high inflation economy with extensive *de jure* and *de facto* indexation. In such cases, the real rate of interest is the correct measure of financial charges.

27 Given the essentially closed nature of the Brazilian economy and the existence of important barriers to most manufactured imports, the latter is a reasonable assumption. Moreover, the hypothesis that foreign competition has influenced price has been tested elsewhere (Considera, 1981) and found not to be supported by the data.

28 A number of studies have sought to test for a role for price controls in industrial pricing in Brazil. Dall'Acqua (1985) tests for the influence of wage and price controls in the 1964–8 period. He concludes that, while wage controls were effective at reducing prices, industrial price controls were not. Mata (1980) found that price controls had some impact in the early 1970s but that generally the influence of controls was very limited. Modiano (1985) and Considera (1983) attempt to incorporate the influence of controls in their price equations in a very rudimentary way through the use of dummy variables. They claim to find some role for controls.

29 These include Calabi (1982), Considera (1975, 1981, 1983) and Modiano (1983a, 1985).

30 We did experiment with a normalisation based on a three year moving average of productivity, however the results were not substantially different to those reported below using trend productivity.

31 This specification is a convenient one since, $\log\,[(1+R)/(1+\dot{P}^{G})] \approx R-\dot{P}^{G}$.

32 We do not consider the issue of possible incomplete transmission of changes in costs to price; a topic that is given certain prominence in Sylos-Labini (1984).

His own empirical results for Argentina suggest that in high inflation economies, the pass-through of costs to price is in fact complete whereas this may not always be the case in other, lower inflation contexts.

33 This observation appears to be borne out by a wide range of empirical price studies that use annual data. However, often one is unable to judge whether the lack of dynamics in a reported preferred specification results from an *a priori* restriction on the model or whether lags were properly tested for and subsequently rejected.

34 The inclusion of a lagged dependent variable among the explanatory terms can be interpreted as equivalent to the imposition of a geometrically declining lag structure on each of the explanatory terms via the well-known Koyck transformation.

35 In the Brazilian context, previous studies have made exclusive use of percentage rates of change models.

36 Nordhaus (1972, pp. 28–9), arguing from a neo-classical point of view, maintains that there is a slight theoretical preference for a constant elasticity specification for the price equation, assuming that the production process is better described by a Cobb-Douglas constant returns to scale function rather than by a linear additive function. On the assumptions that $MC = AC$ and that productive capital is fixed in the short run, he shows how a constant elasticity cost-plus type model can be derived from a Cobb-Douglas function.

37 See section 3.3.4.

38 Contaminated data are widely used in the literature. Official U.S. price indices, used in most econometric price studies of American industry, suffer from this same problem of double counting (see Nordhaus and Shoven, 1977). All existing price studies using Brazilian data make use of these contaminated series.

39 See chapter 2, figure 2.4 for a graphical exposition of interest rate data. For a fuller assessment of problems of availability and reliability of Brazilian interest rate data see Rezende Rocha (1983) and Syvrud (1972).

40 The research methodology used here is explained in appendix 2. Details of test procedures are set out there also.

41 See for instance Considera (1981). As noted in chapter 2, Modiano (1985) approaches this problem by including only imported non-petroleum raw material and imported petroleum prices along with labour costs in his price function. Calabi (1982) and Considera (1983) experiment with composite raw material terms constructed by applying fixed weights to various raw material prices.

42 Although not reported here, a fixed mark-up model in which both the interest rate and all demand terms were constrained to zero fitted the data poorly. Here too the errors were autocorrelated.

43 See chapter 2, figure 2.4. The real cost of consumer credit rose to over 60 per cent in 1981 and 30 per cent in 1966.

44 The hypothesis of financial costs as a determinant of industrial prices in Brazil has been much discussed. See for example A. Lara Resende (1979, pp. 72–85), Calabi (1982), Ramos (1981), Camargo and Landau (1983) and Tavares (1978, p. 132). However, we know of only one attempt to test the hypothesis in the

context of an econometric price study. Considera (1983) includes the nominal rate of change of the cost of credit in a rate of change equation for the price of output in the transport equipment subsector of Brazilian manufacturing. He finds that the interest rate is a significant explanatory variable but expresses scepticism about the results because of the fact that the nominal interest rate is highly correlated with other prices in the economy. The use by us of the real rate of interest is not only more plausible on *a priori* grounds but also means that the danger of spurious correlation with price variables is much less acute.

45 For simplicity's sake, we did not consider the possibility of simultaneous equation bias arising from joint determination of manufacturing and raw material prices or demand and manufacturing price. Although these are likely to be much less important phenomena, a more complete study would test for them as well.

We tested a number of instrument generating equations for earnings that included an *ad hoc* selection of variables which are predetermined in the model. We used the predictor from the equation that gave the best fit, in terms of SEE and R^2, as an instrument. The equation used was:

$$\begin{aligned}\ln W_t^{\mathrm{I}} = {} & -0.474 + 1.63 \ln W_{t-1}^{\mathrm{I}} - 0.632 \ln W_{t-2}^{\mathrm{I}} + 0.121 \ln P_t^{\mathrm{IMR}*} \\ & (-2.05) \quad (14.71) \qquad (-5.28) \qquad\qquad (2.01) \\ & +0.546 \ln r_t \qquad\qquad\qquad\qquad\qquad\qquad (2.18) \\ & (2.18) \\ R^2 = {} & 0.99 \quad \mathrm{SEE} = 0.061 \quad \mathrm{DW} = 1.83\end{aligned}$$

where ($P^{\mathrm{IMR}*}$) is the dollar price of imported raw materials. The predicted values for this equation were divided through by productivity to yield an instrument for (ULC^{A}).

46 It can be shown that OLS will overstate the true value of the coefficient of ULC if simultaneous equation bias is present. See Koutsoyiannis (1977, pp. 332–5).

47 Nordhaus (1972) stresses the importance of making such a check but notes the fact that this is seldom done in applied studies. Very often estimates bear no relation whatsoever to extraneous values.

48 The census gives no indication of the breakdown between domestic and foreign raw materials.

49 Considera (1981, p. 672) finds ULC coefficients ranging from 0.35 to 0.48. Modiano (1985, p. 12 and p. 17) presents estimates ranging from 0.55 to 0.65. Nordhaus (1972, pp. 36–40) finds that for a sample of U.S. pricing studies there was a similar tendency to understate raw material price shares and to overstate unit labour cost shares.

50 Modiano (1985), for all industry, and Considera (1983) for the transport materials subsector obtain similar results using models that are consistent with a normal labour cost hypothesis. Their estimation results exhibit autocorrelation, as do those obtained here.

51 As noted by Hendry *et al.* (1983), simple differencing imposes stringent restrictions on the model. The inclusion of such error correction mechanisms in a difference equation results in a much less restrictive model and one that both implements long-run proportionality and ensures that the dynamic equation reproduces in an equilibrium context the associated equilibrium theory.

52 A Chow test for parameter stability in equation (3.8b) does not allow us to reject stability.

53 With the exception of some specifications used by Modiano (1985), virtually all tests for a role for demand in price equations assume that the level of demand enters rates of change equations. As mentioned above, this is a difficult specification to justify by reference to theory, especially when the theoretical framework used is claimed to be one of oligopoly, as in the overwhelming bulk of empirical studies for Brazil. Only Considera (1983) in his study on a subsector of industry, tests for demand in conjunction with the interest rate.

Considera (1981) finds that the level of demand, as proxied by a variable similar to the ($CU2$) employed here, is insignificant in a variety of rates of change price equations. Calabi (1982) reaches the same conclusion using different demand proxies. Modiano (1985) finds tenuous evidence of a tendency for the mark-up over normal costs to rise (fall) continuously in the face of low (high) levels of demand. Not only are the statistical results poor but also, as he himself acknowledges to a degree, it is very difficult to rationalise such behaviour on theoretical grounds. Camargo and Landau (1983) claim to find support for counter-cyclical influence of demand upon the mark-up.

Calabi (1982) finds some evidence of a significant role for demand in a number of industrial subsectors, with counter-cyclical behaviour more often evident than pro-cyclical. The more concentrated subsectors exhibit clearer evidence of counter-cyclical pricing. Considera's (1983) findings suggest that the mark-up over normal costs in the transportation goods subsector rises continuously with a low level of demand and vice versa with high demand. Once again, the rationale is unclear.

54 An index of the implied mark-up is calculated by

$$M_t = [P^{WI}/(0.28ULC^A + 0.63P^{WR} + 0.08P^{IMR})]_t$$

where the weights applied to the cost coefficients are those estimated in equation (3.7f). If weights taken from the industrial census are used instead, the time path of the implied mark-up is not appreciably different.

4 *Average earnings in manufacturing industry*

1 Wren-Lewis (1982) introduced another somewhat different approach which attempts to model directly the demand and supply of labour rather than make use of the unemployment rate as a proxy for excess supply.

2 Throughout this paper we take 'expectations augmented Phillips curve' to mean the form of the Phillips relationship that explicitly incorporates an expectations variable irrespective of the value of its coefficient. Sometimes the term is used to denote only the case where $\beta_2 = 1$, but we call this the 'natural rate' or 'accelerationist' hypothesis.

3 Assuming that the long-run or natural rate of unemployment can be taken to be constant.

4 The microeconomic foundations of the model, under this assumption, are derived in Nickell (1984).

5 Sumner (1978) achieved better results by assuming that the natural rate of

unemployment rose continuously over the sample period; being functionally related to the ratio of earnings to actual or expected unemployment benefits. Artis and Miller (1978) criticised this approach as a 'mere *post hoc* rationalisation'.

6 Artis and Lewis (1985) reviewed *inter alia*, these latter two studies and were prompted to speak of the re-emergence of the Phillips curve.

7 The augmented Phillips relation is used to explain wage changes in the Data Resources Model (DRI), see Eckstein (1983) and in the MPS model (formerly Federal Reserve – MIT model), see Ando (1974).

8 See, for instance, Gordon (1970), Parkin (1970), Henry, Sawyer and Smith (1976) and Solow (1969).

9 Ormerod (1982) does this using a subsystem of the NIESR U.K. forecasting model.

10 Ormerod (1982) tested a real wage resistance model for the U.K. using expectations generated by this method as well as by first- and fourth-order autoregressions and by assuming perfect foresight. He concluded, '... there cannot be said to be any significant advantage in the use of rational as opposed to simpler, mechanistic methods of forming inflationary expectations' (p. 386).

11 See, for instance, Sargan (1980a), McCallum (1975), Ormerod (1982), Sumner and Ward (1983) and Artis *et al.* (1984). Eckstein (1983) finds support for a 'near-accelerationist' view using U.S. data. However, quite long lags are found to persist before wages adjust fully to price changes.

12 See Solow (1969), Gordon (1970) and Turnovsky and Wachter (1972).

13 Bhalla (1981) applied the model to a sample of thirty LDCs, Siri and Dominguez (1981) to two Central American countries, Bomberger and Makinen (1976) to sixteen Latin American countries, Hojman (1983) and Corbo (1974) to Chile, Lemgruber (1974, 1978), Contador (1977) and Reis Queiroz (1983) to Brazil.

14 In many cases, often because wage data are lacking, researchers resort to testing hypotheses that essentially concern the labour market by using overall price change data. This is equivalent to assuming that price changes equal changes in wages minus a constant change in productivity. For developing countries, particularly susceptible to price shocks from the foreign and agricultural sectors, this is a very strong assumption indeed and one that begs all the problems studied in the previous chapter on industrial price formation. Studies that adopt this approach include those reviewed in chapter 2 for Brazil and in Bomberger and Makinen (1976).

15 See for instance the results presented in Bomberger and Makinen (1976).

16 See for instance Hojman (1983), who fits an expectations augmented Phillips curve to Chilean quarterly wage data for 1974–9, Contador (1977) on Brazil and Bomberger and Makinen (1976) on sixteen Latin American economies.

17 If the target is considered in net after tax terms the model allows for the possibility that fiscal shocks, as much as price shocks, can set off a wage inflation.

18 See for example Henry (1981, p. 32), Sargan (1964, p. 43) and Artis (1981, p. 74).

19 This point is taken up in Henry (1981, p. 32).

20 See Sargan (1964) and references in Artis (1981).

21 Some authors prefer to consider the type of model described here as a hybrid

augmented Phillips curve-wage resistance model (see Artis *et al.*, 1984 and Artis and Lewis, 1985). From this perspective a 'pure' wage resistance model would allow no role for demand pressure.

22 Henry (1981, p. 31) claimed that this interpretation was not supported (for the U.K.) by evidence of time series behaviour of the unemployment rate and real wage.

23 Some recent U.K. studies that successfully employed the model include Henry (1981), Sargan (1980a), Artis and Miller (1978), Tavlas (1983) and Artis and Lewis (1985). Recently the model has been tested using quarterly data covering the period 1973–82 for France, Italy, Belgium, Germany, the Netherlands, as well as the United Kingdom (Artis *et al.*, 1984). A wage equation based on the target real wage model is employed in the NIESR model of the U.K. economy, see Britton (1983).

24 The retention ratio is included as an explanatory term by Ormerod (1982) and Artis *et al.* (1984). Sometimes demand variables other than the unemployment rate (i.e. vacancies) are also used.

25 van Wijnbergen (1982) successfully applied the model to a study of quarterly wage changes in South Korean manufacturing industry. Hojman (1983) uses a superficially similar model to explain wages in Chilean manufacturing although he adopts the neo-classical rationale for the inclusion of the lagged real wage, namely as a proxy for labour market excess demand.

26 The new wage adjustment system was first introduced for public sector employees during 1964.

27 Any increase above the compulsory adjustment could not however be passed on in price increases nor could the agreement be enforced in the Labour Courts.

28 Originally official wage adjustments were calculated quarterly, then later monthly, on the basis of inflation in the previous twelve months. Changes in inflation meant that adjustments varied over the course of a given year.

29 An algebraic statement of this original adjustment formula and subsequent formulae can be found in Simonsen (1983).

30 Following Lopes (1984) this can be shown to be true in the following manner. If (w^*) is the real wage at the beginning of the year and ($\dot{P}^{CG+}$) is the cumulative rate of inflation over the year, then $[w^*/(1+\dot{P}^{CG+})]$ represents the value of the real wage at the end of the year. The average real wage over the period, assuming constant inflation, can be represented by the geometric mean of the two values, that is

$$w^A=[w^*\cdot(w^*/(1+\dot{P}^{CG+})]^{1/2}=w^*/(1+\dot{P}^{CG+})^{1/2}$$

From this expression it is apparent that average real wages and the rate of inflation are inversely related.

31 This can be seen by generalising the expression derived in the previous note for the average real wage. Still assuming for simplicity a constant rate of inflation over the year, and letting (n) equal the number of adjustments per year, the value of the real wage just prior to readjustment can be written $[w^*/(1+\dot{P}^{CG+})^{1/n}]$. The average real wage over the year is therefore

$$w^A=w^*/(1+\dot{P}^{CG+})^{1/2n}$$

The higher the value of (n), the greater the average real wage.

32 Under the scheme introduced in 1979, workers earning up to the equivalent of three times the minimum wage were guaranteed an increase of at least 110 per cent of the cost of living. Those in the three to ten minimum wage bracket received 100 per cent indexation while higher wage and salary earners received progressively less. Between 1980 and the economic reforms of 1986, the indexation scale underwent several changes aimed at reducing the rise in average real wages implied by the initial formula. The latter ensured a rising average wage due to the fact that a large proportion of the workforce earned between one and three minimum wages.

33 From 1966 through 1984, a period in which compulsory wage adjustments were in place, earnings in manufacturing rose in real terms at a compound annual rate of 4.3 per cent compared with a −0.5 per cent for mandatory wage adjustments in real terms. From 1965 onwards, the minimum wage was adjusted at the same intervals and by similar amounts as compulsory adjustments imposed upon private sector wages, although no formal link existed (see chapter 2, especially figures 2.5 and 2.6).

34 See Drobny and Wells (1983) for some evidence from the construction industry.

35 Bacha and Taylor (1980) cite evidence that real unskilled wages actually fell over the period 1966–72, while skilled workers' wages rose by an annual average of 2.6 per cent in real terms and managerial wages by 8.1 per cent.

36 For evidence on this tendency see Tavares and Souza (1983).

37 This debate is well reviewed in Bacha and Taylor (1980).

38 Tavares and Souza (1983) use a model based on the concept of internal and external labour markets to explain the co-existence of sectoral differentials in skilled wages with a basic unskilled wage common to all industries. Firms recruit unskilled labour in the general or external market, paying a wage determined by official wage policy. This wage acts as a basis for the distributional structure of all wages. Large firms have an internal market which supplies most of their requirements for personnel to fill medium- and high-level positions. Given the dominance of large firms in many industries and the similar employment structures of each, internal labour markets can develop for specific industries. Tolosa (1978) proposes a model in the Lewis-Fei-Ranis tradition to explain dualism in the overall urban labour market.

39 Turner and Jackson (1970) found that LDCs in general exhibited much greater heterogeneity in the structure of manufacturing earnings than did industrialised countries. See Maia Gomes (1985b) for a discussion of the 'fallacy of average salary' problem. Because the series includes high and low wages and salaries it can sometimes throw up perverse results.

40 Current and twice lagged values of inflation are included in the specification to ensure as general a dynamic structure as possible for the maintained hypothesis. In the recent Brazilian literature (see for instance Modiano, 1983a and 1985) it has been common practice to posit a role only for current and once lagged inflation, based on a proposition derived from a simple theoretical model of the wage adjustment process due to Lopes and Bacha (1983). Not only does it seem unwise to impose *a priori* this restriction on the dynamic adjustment process but also, Lopes (1984) derives a more complex theoretical representation of the adjustment process in which, abstracting from productivity increments, adjust-

ments are a positive function of both current and one period lagged average cost of living inflation and of end period inflation in $t-1$ as well as a negative function of end of period inflation in $t-2$. Equation (4.10) can be thought of as a crude approximation to this system in which, given the absence of December to December prices in our model, average inflation in $t-1$ and $t-2$ are used to capture the influence of cumulative inflation in the same years.

41 Not only were the adjustment formulae themselves subject to numerous minor alterations over time but also average mandatory adjustments could be influenced by policy decisions concerning expected inflation and productivity increments.

42 It was outside the scope of the study to attempt to test for the role of skill differentials and the changing composition of industry in the growth of real earnings. These issues are, in any case, better suited to cross section rather than time series analysis.

43 Empirical support for the view that a major structural break occurred in 1965, as a consequence of the radical change in the institutional environment, was obtained by estimating the model using data for 1961 to 1984 and comparing these estimates with those for 1966–84. The model was unable to explain both sample periods.

44 Changes in the adjustment formula were such that the average private sector increase awarded fell from about 100 per cent of the change in the cost of living in January 1983 to around 86 per cent by year end.

45 As official cost of living adjustments, as distinct from cost of living plus productivity awards, were not, it would seem, on average sufficient to ensure 100 per cent indexation, it is possible that the model is picking up some slight independent influence of costs upon wages. As noted earlier, it can be very difficult to distinguish in econometric work the role of price expectations from that of official indexation.

46 Despite the difference in the coefficient estimate on the demand term, a Chow F test to compare parameter stability in equations (4.12c) and (4.12d) gave a value of 1.30(6,8). The null hypothesis of stability could not be rejected. We chose 1966–78 as the subsample for use in stability tests in order to see whether the models could explain, with the help of the shift dummy (DU7984), the post-1978 experience when indexation rules and labour policy in general underwent significant changes. Findings on model stability are not appreciably affected if alternative cut-off dates are chosen.

47 Predictions from the following equation, converted back into rates of change, were used as an instrument for current consumer price inflation

$$\begin{aligned} \ln P_t^{CG} = &-0.91 + 0.60 \ln P_{t-1}^{CG} - 0.44 \ln P_{t-2}^{CG} - 1.01 \ln r_t^{I*} \\ &(-0.91) \quad (1.80) \qquad (-4.37) \qquad (-4.79) \\ &+ 0.84 \ln P_{t-1}^{WI} + 0.23 m_t \\ &\quad (3.15) \qquad\quad (3.51) \end{aligned}$$

$$\bar{R}^2 = 0.99 \qquad \text{SEE} = 0.044 \qquad \text{DW} = 2.06$$

where (m) is the unit food subsidy rate, a major exogenous determinant of consumer food price.

48 Camargo (1984) and Lopes (1984) each estimate rate of change equations for the real wage. They both find that a GDP gap variable, used as a proxy for demand, is a significant determinant of the real wage – although its quantitative impact is not great – along with the acceleration of current or lagged price inflation. However, Camargo finds no evidence of a role for demand when a proxy based on survey data on capacity utilisation is used instead of the GDP gap. He concludes that, '. . . if there exists some link between the rate of change of the real salary and the level of unemployment, it is quite tenuous' (1984, p.156).

49 The same problems of specification persist if the dummy variables are excluded and also when the model is estimated using the sample employed by Modiano; 1966–82. Modiano uses $(1-GDPCU)$ i.e. the output gap, as a demand proxy.

50 As we argue in appendix 3, the GDP output gap is less likely to be a good proxy for demand than manufacturing capacity utilisation because of the influence upon it of agricultural supply factors.

5 *The price of food and food supply*

1 A measure of this consensus is that economists who reject marginalist theories as a basis for the explanation of price and output determination in modern industry are generally agreed on the basic characterisation of agricultural markets. See for instance Kalecki (1943), Kaldor (1976) and Sylos-Labini (1984).

2 A comprehensive survey of the literature on agricultural pricing appears in Tomek and Robinson (1977). A shorter review is found in Heien (1977).

3 We know of no substantial econometric studies of agricultural or food price determination in Brazil in recent decades. Assis (1983) and Modiano (1985) both incorporate very basic single equation models for these prices in their more general macromodels. There is little discussion of the rationale for these although, in both cases, the equations can be interpreted as reduced form equations derived from a competitive market model. As regards studies that are somewhat related, Sayad (1981) discusses how food price variability interacts with overall inflation. Barros and Graham (1978) give some consideration to food price and supply. Finally, Accarini (1982) was concerned with price differentials in Brazilian agricultural markets.

4 The other principal agricultural price index available is the wholesale agricultural price index which includes prices of all major commodities produced, whether for export or domestic consumption. Insufficient data are available on producer food prices to allow their use in the econometric analysis although, on methodological grounds, these rather than wholesale prices should be used in the production equation of the model. Producer price data, for a small selection of commodities, exist only from 1966 and no aggregate is computed for domestic foodstuffs prices, nor can one easily be derived from the disaggregated series.

5 When total output minus exports but including coffee was experimented with as a proxy for food production, the results achieved were poor.

6 For a good review of government agricultural policy in Brazil during the 1960s and 1970s see IBRD (1982).

7 See Heien (1977, pp. 130–1) and references therein for some examples. Price studies based on annual data for the U.S. suggest that agricultural markets do generally clear within one year. This led Heien (1977, p. 130), to conclude that when annual models are used, disequilibria can often be ignored.

8 Equilibrium models experimented with failed completely to provide an adequate characterisation of the price determination process, see section 5.6 below.

9 The notion that demand depends upon relative as opposed to nominal price derives from the homogeneity assumption of demand theory. The assumption is that, when all prices and incomes increase or decrease by the same percentage, demand remains unchanged. In other words, the sum of own and cross price elasticity and of income elasticity for a particular commodity is equal to zero.

10 Population, like real income, is a shift variable, growth in which can be expected to cause an outward displacement of the demand schedule. Rather than include population as a separate explanatory variable in the demand equation, it is customary to impose the restriction of homogeneity in degree one of demand with respect to population by deflating demand and income by the population variable. However, we choose to use this more general specification as it allows the model to be solved more easily for price. As we show below, the homogeneity restriction is tested and subsequently imposed when it has been shown to be data compatible.

11 Total food imports are difficult to isolate. However, wheat was by far the major component of this total.

12 This is quite a simple, although adequate, production model. In the literature, models are sometimes specified which include such additional variables as measures of climatic conditions, relative production costs, additional government policy variables and prices of alternative crops.

13 This hypothesis is shared by the authors of IBRD (1982).

14 Under certain conditions regarding the parameter values, price and quantity will tend towards equilibrium by way of a particular cyclical path. A theoretical explanation for this process is provided by the cobweb model which has been widely applied in agricultural market studies. The seminal statement of the model was by Ezekiel (1938). Waugh (1964a) considers a generalisation of the basic model.

15 Simultaneity may also arise on a third account as real income is in part determined by prices and quantities sold. The general tendency in agricultural price studies has been to ignore the bias involved in treating income as predetermined by arguing that it is likely to be very small, particularly when the demand equation specified refers to an individual commodity whose retail value is small relative to total income (see Foote, 1958, pp. 50–1 and Tomek and Robinson, 1977, p. 337). However if, as in this study, we are concerned with the demand for a composite good the value of which is high relative to income, the simultaneous equation bias may be substantial, see Girshick and Haavelmo (1947, p. 88). In LDCs, where a large proportion of income is spent on food, this bias may be all the more acute. In estimating the price equations below, we checked for simultaneous equation bias in the OLS estimates using a Wu-Hausman test and by performing an IV estimate.

16 The inclusion of a lagged dependent variable in the output equation can be interpreted in more ways than one. Current production can be viewed as being modified from the previous year's output in response to changes in relative price or real credit. Inertia and resource fixity may prevent even a large change in price or credit from leading to a complete re-thinking of planned production decisions. Nerlove (1956) introduced a lagged dependent variable resulting from the transformation of an equation containing a geometrically declining lag on price, where the latter was used to represent expected price in the current period.

17 The predicted values from the following equation were used as an instrument for current relative wholesale price

$$(P^{WF}/P^{CG})_t = \underset{(-3.28)}{-58.1} + \underset{(4.39)}{0.95}\,(P^{WF}/P^{CG})_{t-1} - \underset{(-1.10)}{0.04}\,(P^{WF}/P^{CG})_{t-2} + \underset{(1.78)}{0.64}\,(P^{WF}/P^{CG})_{t-3}$$

$R^2 = 0.91 \qquad \text{SEE} = 9.73 \qquad \text{DW} = 1.89$

18 A Wu-Hausman test was performed on equation (5.6a), yielding a t statistic of 1.60 with 17 degrees of freedom. The null hypothesis of orthogonality of the residuals could not therefore be rejected at the 5 per cent significance level.

19 Average elasticities were calculated in the standard way using the formula

$$\eta = \hat{b} \cdot \bar{X}/\bar{Y}$$

where $(\hat{b})$ is the relevant estimated coefficient from equation (5.6c) and $(\bar{X})$ and $(\bar{Y})$ are the average values over the sample period of the corresponding explanatory and dependent variables. Being linear, the model exhibits the feature that as output rises over time, the elasticities fall. This is not a particularly desirable property but, as reported below, a constant elasticity specification did not perform well.

20 See the discussion in Foote (1958, pp. 37–9) and in Waugh (1964b, p. 28) regarding the choice of functional form. Harlow (1962), and many studies quoted in Heien (1977), use linear specifications for demand and supply functions.

21 A simple rule of thumb states that the fit of the linear model is better than that of the log-linear version if

$$\text{SEE}_{(\text{linear})} < \text{SEE}_{(\text{log-linear})} \times \bar{Y}$$

where $(\bar{Y})$ is the geometric mean of the dependent variable and SEE the standard error of the regression. In this case $\text{SEE}_{(\text{linear})} = 0.48$ and $\text{SEE}_{(\text{log-linear})} \times \bar{Y} = 0.57$.

22 The anti-logs of the predicted values from the following equation, deflated by population, were used as an instrument for (y_t^{DC})

$$\ln y_t^{DC} = \underset{(-3.59)}{-1.91} + \underset{(4.72)}{0.94}\ln y_{t-1}^{DC} - \underset{(-2.73)}{0.38}\ln y_{t-2}^{DC} + \underset{(1.38)}{0.21}\ln g + \underset{(1.73)}{0.18}\ln y_t^{US}$$

$R^2 = 0.99 \qquad \text{SEE} = 0.044 \qquad \text{DW} = 1.85$

where (g) is real expenditure on goods and services by general government and (y^{US}) is real U.S. GNP. Predicted values from the following equation were used as an instrument for (m)

$$m_t = -0.22 + 0.57 m_{t-1} + 0.20\, m_{t-2} + 0.48\, m_{t-3}$$
$$(-1.60)\ (2.23) \qquad (1.64) \qquad (1.66)$$

$R^2 = 0.84 \qquad \text{SEE} = 0.054 \qquad \text{DW} = 1.74$

23 A 10 per cent fall in supply relative to demand leads to a 4.3 per cent rise in relative prices and to a 2.6 per cent decrease in demand. Thus, only one quarter of the disequilibrium is eliminated in the initial period. Allowing for a 1.1 per cent rise in production in the second period and a further fall in demand, there is still excess demand of about 7 per cent at the end of period two.

6 *The Cruzeiro/U.S. dollar exchange rate*

1 PPP is said to prevail when the exchange rate between two currencies is such that the purchasing power of each in its home market is equivalent.

2 The exact time path of the real exchange rate differs, of course, depending upon the choice of internal and external price indices used in the calculation. Since the operation of the crawling peg was based upon discretionary policy decisions one can only speculate as to which official or unofficial indices guided policy-makers. It is generally believed, however, that wholesale prices in the U.S.A. and Brazil played this guiding role.

3 While the real cruzeiro/U.S. dollar exchange rate underwent a cumulative depreciation of approximately 90 per cent between December 1978 and December 1983, the real depreciation of the cruzeiro against a basket of the currencies of Brazil's major trading partners over this same five year period was much less, being in the order of 15 per cent.

4 Modiano (1985) and Assis (1983) use exchange rate models of this variety. If the coefficients on the domestic and U.S. inflation rates are equal to one and minus one respectively, this model approximately reproduces purchasing power parity. However, using this formulation, an acceleration in domestic inflation in fact leads, *ceteris paribus*, to a rise in the real exchange rate. The greater the acceleration of inflation, the more pronounced is this effect.

5 Too few data points are available to attempt to model more fully the authorities' policy reaction function in the post-1966 period. Even if the degrees of freedom constraint could be overcome, by for instance using quarterly data, it is still unclear whether an econometric model could be developed that would be capable of explaining the deviations that did occur from strict purchasing power parity. The dominance of the informal purchasing power indexation rule, the plethora of additional factors that apparently influenced parity changes – often with long lags – and the size of the maxi-devaluations would all combine to make the search for an explanation in terms of a few economic variables difficult, if not impossible. Bacha (1979) examined the Brazilian crawling peg system up

to 1976 and could find no obvious link between the effective exchange rate and either the current account deficit or domestic versus foreign interest rate differentials.

6 The same procedure could be followed using equation (6.2) to derive a testable model in log levels. Very similar empirical results were obtained with this specification and it was not thought necessary to present them here. There is a slight preference for the changes model as exchange rate policy appears to have been based not on absolute price levels but rather on inflation differentials.

7 Several instrument generating equations were experimented with, the one finally chosen being that with the highest SEE. As an instrument for $(\Delta \ln P_t^{WG})$ the predicted values from the following equation were used

$$\Delta \ln P_t^{WG} = \underset{(-3.18)}{-0.21} \underset{(2.73)}{-1.18} \Delta \log P_{t-2}^{WG} + \underset{(2.33)}{0.66} \Delta \ln P_{t-3}^{WG}$$

$$+ \underset{(2.03)}{1.18} \Delta \ln W_{t-1}^{I} + \underset{(-2.65)}{0.81} \Delta \ln P_{t-1}^{WI} + \underset{(1.87)}{0.35} \Delta \ln P_t^{IMR*}$$

$$R^2 = 0.86 \qquad SEE = 0.100 \qquad DW = 2.18$$

where (W^I) is an index (1970 = 100) of average earnings in manufacturing, (P^{WI}) is an index (1970 = 100) of wholesale prices of manufactured goods and (P^{IMR*}) is an index (1970 = 100) of the dollar wholesale price of imported raw materials.

8 The wholesale manufacturing price index does not exactly correspond to the sum of manufacturing goods prices in the overall wholesale price index due to the fact that the former includes some prices of export goods.

7 *A macroeconomic model for Brazil*

1 See the discussion of these macromodels in section 7.3.3.

2 Behrman and Klein (1970) and Taylor, *et al.* (1980) both model consumption in Brazil as a function not of aggregate private sector income but rather of sectoral incomes. Behrman and Klein modelled the pre-1964 period when some national accounts data were available on factor incomes. Taylor, *et al.* generate data starting from base year estimates. No data are available to permit time series estimation over our sample period although, were such data available, the model would clearly be enriched by the ability to analyse the interactions between inflation, income distribution and stabilisation policies.

3 The inclusion of a lagged dependent variable does however carry the unusual implication that past values of wealth affect current consumption.

4 Summary OLS estimation results for this model, using annual data for 1960–83, are given below

$$(c/N)_t = \underset{(-1.77)}{-3.92} + \underset{(9.83)}{0.43} (y^D/N)_t + \underset{(4.47)}{0.18}$$

$$\times \{[WE_{t-1} + (0.93 \cdot \dot{P}_t^G \cdot B_{t-1}) - (\dot{P}_t^{CG} \cdot H_{t-1})]/(N \cdot P_t^{CG})\}$$

$$+ \underset{(8.77)}{0.47} (c/N)_{t-1} \underset{(-4.0)}{-12.03} DU75$$

$$R^2 = 0.99 \qquad SEE = 2.54 \qquad DW = 1.86$$

5 Jul (1977) uses a similar model but with the addition of capital goods imports among the explanatory terms to capture the impact of the balance of payments constraint on investment. Because the long-run elasticity of investment with respect to income is less than unity, the model implies that actual and desired capital/output ratios fall over time. This tendency will be accentuated since some gross investment is required simply to compensate for depreciation of the existing capital stock. An OLS estimate of the model using annual data for 1961–83 yielded

$$i_t^{F} = \exp(-0.53 + 0.66 \ln y_t + 0.29 \ln le_t^{PT})$$
$$(-2.07)\ (10.59)\qquad (8.69)$$

$R^2 = 0.99$ SEE $= 0.051$ DW $= 1.66$

6 We make use of the stock of credit rather than the change in the stock, or flow, as is often done. This reflects the fact that investment decisions are influenced by a stream of credits received over time rather than by credit conceded in a single period.

7 See chapter 5 for fuller details on the food subsidy term.

8 The value of total national accounts subsidies in 1970 was CR$1.5 billion, therefore, we are assuming that food subsidies equalled 27 per cent of the total.

9 We ignore the complications that result from the fact that in the 1970s and early 1980s, some federal bonds (ORTNs) were indexed to changes in the cruzeiro/dollar exchange rate rather than to domestic inflation.

10 1980 was an exceptional year in that indexation was cut back to approximately one half the rate of inflation.

11 An interesting extension to the model would be to include subsidised credit explicitly. This would, however, require overcoming some problems of data availability and would also necessitate a fuller modelling of the financial system.

12 Contador (1984) uses this model estimated with data for 1955–80. Upon re-estimating with the sample 1961–83, it was found necessary to include a dummy variable to capture the upwards shift in exports that occurred after 1980. This upwards shift was due to a concerted export drive combined with reduced domestic consumption of exportables due to the recession at home. An OLS estimate yielded

$$\ln x_t^{G} = \exp\{-9.56 + 1.60 \ln y_t^{US} + 0.54 \ln[(z^{E} \cdot P^{EX*} \cdot E)/P^{G}]_t\}$$
$$(-9.48)\ (11.90)\qquad (4.66)$$
$$+0.42\, DU8183$$
$$(5.67)$$

$R^2 = 0.97$ SEE $= 0.105$ DW $= 1.70$

The estimated income elasticity of export demand is fairly high at 1.6, while price elasticity is low at 0.54. The model is somewhat suspect in that no income response lags are present.

13 Re-estimating Abreu and Horta's model using, like they do, a Cochrane–Orcutt

first-order estimator but with an extended sample for 1961–83 yielded

$$im_t^{NWP} = \exp\{-3.83 + 1.20 \ln y_t - 0.71 \ln[(z^I \cdot P^{IMNP*} \cdot E)/P^{WG}]_t$$
$$(-5.66)\ (9.48)\qquad (-2.51)$$

$$+ 2.05 \ln GDPG_t\} + 0.20DU74$$
$$(4.49)\qquad (2.39)$$

$$R^2 = 0.98 \qquad SEE = 0.101 \qquad DW = 1.62$$

The parameters of the re-estimated model are close to those reported in the original work with the exception of income elasticity. They obtain an estimate of 0.95 in contrast to the 1.2 found here.

14 Assis (1983) proposed this model. Re-estimating using a Cochrane–Orcutt first-order estimator instead of OLS as in Assis and annual data for 1961–83 gave

$$im_t^P = \exp\{-5.47 + 1.09 \ln y_t - 0.192 \ln[(P^{IMP*} \cdot E)/P^{WG}]_t$$
$$(-4.05)\ (4.21)\qquad (-2.62)$$

$$+ 0.287 \ln im_{t-1}^P\}$$
$$(1.64)$$

$$R^2 = 0.98 \qquad SEE = 0.083 \qquad DW = 2.12$$

These results are fairly close to those reported by Assis. The model shows petrol imports to be highly price inelastic (long-run elasticity of 0.27) while income elastic: elasticity of 1.48 in the long run.

15 Including coffee and non-food raw materials with secondary and tertiary output is clearly a dubious procedure to follow but it is beyond the scope of this study to model the production of each separately.

16 Jul (1977) and Assis (1983) both adopt this procedure.

17 Very briefly, the rationale is as follows. From an input/output model of current inter-industry flows and final demands, an expression for gross sectoral output can be obtained. Assuming that value added in each sector is proportional to gross output in the same sector, the former can be expressed as a function of the elements of GDP demanded by each sector. In the absence of disaggregated data on these demands, they are replaced selectively by GDP elements that are thought to be closely related to the particular sectoral demands. The technique is most appropriate at a high level of disaggregation. However, like other modellers of the Brazilian economy, we are constrained to use it here by the lack of other feasible means to build up an alternative to the expenditure measure of GDP.

18 Similar equations were used by Jul (1977) and Assis (1983) although both broke output down into secondary and tertiary sectors. Summary OLS estimation results using data for 1961–83 are given below

$$q_t^{NF} = -2.58 + 0.70\,(c + c^G)_t + 0.68(i^F + i^G)_t + 1.09x_t$$
$$(-1.47)\ (19.45)\qquad (12.2)\qquad (6.40)$$

$$R^2 = 0.99 \qquad SEE = 1.74 \qquad DW = 1.82$$

The average elasticities implied by this equation are 0.69 for consumption, 0.21

for investment and 0.12 for exports. These are similar to the findings of Jul (1977) and Assis (1983). The low elasticity on investment suggests a leakage of investment spending into imports. The elasticity of export demand is much too low. The data would not accept the restriction of an elasticity closer to unity.

8 *Model validation and evaluation*

1 The historical value for the rate of depreciation in 1966 was used in the simulation exercises in place of a solution value since the exchange rate equation was estimated using data for 1967–84 only.

2 Theil (1961) showed that (U) could be decomposed into three component parts, each of which yields information on the sources of simulation error. The three 'proportions of inequality' are defined by

$$U^m = \frac{(\bar{v}^s - \bar{v})^2}{1/n\Sigma(v_t^s - v_t)^2} \quad U^s = \frac{(\sigma_s - \sigma)^2}{1/n\Sigma(v_t^s - v_t)^2} \quad U^c = \frac{2(1-\rho)\sigma_s\sigma}{1/n\Sigma(v_t^s - v_t)^2}$$

where (ρ) is the correlation coefficient between the simulated and historical series and (σ_s) and (σ) are the standard deviations of the series. (U^m), (U^s) and (U^c) are termed the bias, variance and covariance proportions respectively. Since it can be shown algebraically that

$$1/n\Sigma(v_t^s - v_t)^2 = (\bar{v}^s - \bar{v})^2 + (\sigma_s - \sigma)^2 + 2(1-\rho)\sigma_s\sigma$$

it follows that: $U^m + U^s + U^c = 1$.

3 It is of course possible that the model does exhibit oscillatory or unstable behaviour but that the period of oscillation is longer than the simulation period or that the rate of unstable divergence may be so slow as to be imperceptible within this time frame.

4 The food shock differs slightly from the other two shocks in that the counterfactual change engineered does not represent an equal percentage change in each time period. A constant percentage change could not sensibly be applied to the standard model with endogenous food. Even though for the purposes of shocking the system, food output was de-trended for population growth, the historical series still rises slightly over time. This means that the percentage impact of a constant CR\$1.57 billion reduction in food output, while equal to 10 per cent in 1966, is somewhat less in percentage terms in 1983. In the standard model with endogenous food, the shock was engineered by reducing the value of the constant in the expression for food output, having first converted this into *per capita* terms.

5 In this type of exercise it is customary to make use of the concepts of dynamic multipliers and dynamic elasticities. A dynamic multiplier is defined by

$$\Omega = (v_t^{sh} - v_t)/\Delta X_t$$

where (v) is any endogenous variable and (X) an exogenous variable to which a shock is applied. If the change in (X) takes the form of a constant percentage change then a dynamic elasticity is readily calculated

$$\varepsilon = (X/v)_t \cdot [(v_t^{sh} - v_t)/(X_t^{sh} - X_t)] = \%\Delta v_t / \%\Delta X_t$$

In tables 8.1 through 8.6, the measures of the response of GDP and the consumer price level to the shocks correspond to dynamic multipliers (multiplied by ten). However, in recording the response of other variables to the shocks, multipliers or elasticities could not be used uniformly as they would have been difficult to interpret or nonsensical in many cases. For simplicity, we continue to refer to these as dynamic elasticities.

6 As the model is non-linear, its response to a shock will not be independent of the size of the shock. However, the extent of the re-scaling performed here is not sufficient to invalidate the exercises.

7 It is the same mechanism that forms part of Modiano's (1985) linkages between demand and prices.

8 Since the food sector – by the approximate accounting used here – contributes 10.4 per cent to 1966 GDP (expenditure measure), the latter should fall by at least 1.04 per cent ($0.1 \cdot 0.104 = 0.014$) in the first period of the shock in order to maintain consistency between the model's two measures of GDP. In fact, the fall registered is only 0.89 per cent, pointing to some misspecification of either the links between supply and demand in the model or of sectoral outputs that show up in the statistical discrepancy linking GDP (output) and GDP (expenditure).

9 *Policy experiments*

1 For an acceleration of inflation to reduce real earnings it is a sufficient condition that the speed of adjustment of nominal earnings to changes in prices be reduced so that less adjustment occurs in the first period and more in subsequent periods. It is not necessary as well for the sum of the adjustment coefficients to be reduced below unity. This result was shown analytically in chapter 4(4.2), when discussing Brazil's 1979 wage indexation changes. Here, a slow down in adjustment is combined with a partial de-indexation in order to achieve outcomes sufficiently distinct so as to be amenable to visual differentiation.

2 The magnitude of the rise in real earnings after period 10 does however once again signal an overshooting tendency in the model that may be destabilising.

3 As discussed in chapter 7(7.2.1), the non-existence of national accounts data on factor incomes made it impossible to build up private disposable income from this perspective.

4 A more precise evaluation of the contribution to overall inflation and real earnings of wage policy changes during these two episodes would require that a more complex experiment be set up. Even then, however, the model is not properly equipped to provide a realistic quantitative appraisal of the impact of these policy changes.

5 The 1979 maxi-devaluation occurred in the same year as the introduction of semi-annual wage adjustment and 'super-indexation' of some wages and salaries.

Bibliography

Abreu, Marcelo de Paiva and Horta, Maria Helena T. T. (1982), 'Demanda de Importações no Brasil, 1960–1980: Estimações Agregadas e Desagregadas por Categoria de Uso e Projeções para 1982', *Textos para Discussão Interna*, No. 48, Rio de Janeiro: IPEA/INPES.

Accarini, José Honório (1982), 'Agricultural commodity prices in Brazil: empirical evidence', *Brazilian Economic Studies*, 6.

Ando, A. (1974), 'Some aspects of stabilization policies, the monetarist controversy, and the MPS model', *International Economic Review*, 15(3).

Ando, A. and Modigliani, F. (1963), 'The "life-cycle" hypothesis of savings: aggregate implications and tests', *American Economic Review*, 53(1).

Arestis, Philip and Hadjimatheou, George (1982), *Introducing Macroeconomic Modelling: An Econometric Study of the United Kingdom*, London: Macmillan.

Arida, Persio (1982), 'Reajuste salarial e inflação', *Pesquisa e Planejamento Econômico*, 12(2).

Arida, Persio and Lara-Resende, A. (1985), 'Inertial inflation and monetary reform: Brazil', in Williamson, John (ed.).

Artis, M. J. (1981), 'Is there a wage equation?', in Courakis, Anthony S. (ed.), *Inflation, Depression and Economic Policy in the West*, London: Mansell.

Artis, M. J., Farmelo, C., Murfin, A. and Ormerod, P. (1984), 'Price expectations and wage inflation in Western Europe', *Discussion Paper No. 42*, Department of Economics, University of Manchester.

Artis, M. J. and Lewis, M. K. (1985), 'Inflation in the United Kingdom', in Argy, V. E. and Nevile, J. W. (eds.), *Inflation and Unemployment: Theory, Experience and Policy Making*, London: George Allen & Unwin.

Artis, M. J. and Miller, M. H. (1978), 'Inflation and real wages', *Discussion Paper No. 5*, Department of Economics, University of Manchester.

Assis, Milton P. (1981), *Um model macroeconométrico de política a curto prazo para o Brasil*, Monografia No. 32, Rio de Janeiro: IPEA/INPES.

(1983), 'A estrutura e o mecanismo de transmissão de um modelo macroeconométrico para o Brasil (MEB)', *Revista Brasileira de Economia*, 37(4).

Bacha, Edmar L. (1977), 'Issues and evidence on recent Brazilian economic growth', *World Development*, 5(1–2).

(1979), 'Notes on the Brazilian experience with minidevaluations, 1968–1976', *Journal of Development Economics*, 6(4).

(1980), 'Selected issues in post-1964 Brazilian economic growth', in Taylor *et al.*

(1983), 'Vicissitudes of recent stabilization attempts in Brazil and the IMF alternative', in Williamson, John (ed.), *IMF Conditionality*, Cambridge, Mass.: Institute for International Economics/MIT Press.

Bacha, Edmar L. and Taylor, Lance (1980), 'Brazilian income distribution in the 1960s: "facts", model results, and the controversy', in Taylor *et al.*

Baer, Werner and Beckerman, Paul (1980), 'The trouble with index-linking: reflections on the recent Brazilian experience', *World Development*, 8(9).

Baer, Werner and Kerstenetzky, Issac (eds.) (1964), *Inflation and Growth in Latin America*, New Haven: Yale University Press.

(1964), 'Some observations on the Brazilian inflation', in Baer and Kerstenetzky (eds.).

Banco Central do Brasil (various), *Boletim do Banco Central do Brasil*, Brasília.

Barros, José Roberto M. de and Graham, Douglas H. (1978), 'A agricultura brasileira e o problema da produção de alimentos', *Pesquisa e Planejamento Econômico*, 8(3).

Baumann Neves, Renato (1978), 'A utilização da capacidade produtiva na indústria brasileira – 1955/75', *Pesquisa e Planejamento Econômico*. 8(2).

Behrman, Jere and Klein, L. R. (1970), 'Econometric growth models for the developing economy', in Eltis, W. A., Scott, M. FG. and Wolfe, J. N. (eds.), *Induction, Growth and Trade: Essays in Honour of Sir Roy Harrod*, Oxford: Clarendon Press.

Bhalla, S. S. (1981), 'The transmission of inflation into developing countries', in Cline and associates.

Blinder, Alan S. and Solow, Robert M. (1973), 'Does fiscal policy matter?', *Journal of Public Economics*, 2(4).

Bomberger, W. A. and Makinen, G. E. (1976), 'Inflation, unemployment, and expectations in Latin America: some simple tests', *Southern Economic Journal*, 43(2).

Bonelli, Regis (1980), 'Concentração industrial no Brasil: indicadores da evolução recente', *Pesquisa e Planejamento Econômico*, 10(3).

Braga, Helson C. and Mascolo, João L. (1982), 'Mesuração da concentração industrial no Brasil', *Pesquisa e Planejamento Econômico*, 12(2).

Branson, William H. (1976), 'The dual roles of the government budget and the balance of payments in the movement from the short-run to the long-run', *Quarterly Journal of Economics*, 40(3).

Britton, Andrew (ed.) (1983), *Employment, Output and Inflation: The National Institute Model of the British Economy*, London: Heinemann.

Bruno, Michael (1979), 'Stabilization and stagflation in a semi-industrialized economy', in Dornbusch, Rudiger and Frenkel, Jacob A. (eds.), *International Economic Policy: Theory and Evidence*, Baltimore and London: Johns Hopkins University Press.

Calabi, Andrea Sandro (1982), 'Price Formation in Brazilian Industry', unpublished Ph.D. Thesis, University of California at Berkeley.

Camargo, José Marcio (1980), 'A nova política salarial, distribuição de rendas e inflação', *Pesquisa e Planejamento Econômico*, 10(3).

(1984), 'Salário real e indexação salarial no Brasil: 1969/81', *Pesquisa e Planejamento Econômico*, 14(1).

Camargo, José Marcio and Landau, Elena (1983), 'Variações de demanda, estrutura de custos e margem bruta de lucros no Brasil: 1974/81', *Pesquisa e Planejamento Econômico*, 13(3).

Cambridge Economic Policy Group (1983), 'CEPG Model Processing System MPS Version 1.2', *Mimeo*, Department of Applied Economics, University of Cambridge.

Canavese, A. J. (1980), 'A hipótese estrutural na teoria da inflação', *Estudos Econômicos*, 10(3).

Cardoso, Eliana A. (1977), 'Moeda, renda e inflação: algumas evidências da economia brasileira', *Pesquisa e Planejamento Econômico*, 7(2).

(1979), 'Inflation, growth and the real exchange rate: essays on economic history in Brazil', unpublished Ph.D. Thesis, M.I.T.

(1981), 'Food supply and inflation', *Journal of Development Economics*, 8(3).

Carneiro Leão, A. S., Silva, C. R. da, Giestas, E. and Nobrega, J. (1973), 'Matriz de insumo-produto do Brasil', *Revista Brasileira de Economia*, 27(3).

Carneiro Netto, Dionísio Dias and Fraga Neto, Armínio (1984), 'Variáveis de crédito e endogeneidade dos agregados monetários: nota sobre a evidência empírica nos anos 70', *Pesquisa e Planejamento Econômico*, 14(1).

Carvalho, Lívio de (1981), 'A nova política salarial, distribuição de rendas e inflação: um comentário', *Pesquisa e Planejamento Econômico*, 11(3).

Cavallo, Domingo F. (1977), 'Stagflationary effects of monetarist stabilization policies in economies with persistent inflation', unpublished Ph.D. Thesis, Harvard University.

(1981), 'Stagflationary effects of monetarist stabilization policies in economies with persistent inflation', in Flanders, M. June and Razin, Assaf (eds.), *Development in an Inflationary World*, New York: Academic Press.

Challen, D. W. and Hagger, A. J. (1983), *Macroeconometric Systems: Construction, Validation and Applications*, London: Macmillan.

Chichilnisky, Graciela and Taylor, L. (1980), 'Agriculture and the rest of the economy: macroconnections and policy restraints', *American Journal of Agricultural Economics*, 62(2).

Chow, Gregory C. (1960), 'Tests of equality between sets of coefficients in two linear regressions', *Econometrica*, 28(3).

Christ, Carl F. (1967), 'A short-run aggregate-demand model of the interdependence and effects of monetary and fiscal policies with Keynesian and classical interest elasticities', *American Economic Review*, 57(2).

Christiano, L. J. (1981), 'A survey of measures of capacity utilisation', *IMF Staff Papers*, 28(1).

Cline, William R. (1981), 'Brazil's aggressive response to external shocks', in Cline and associates.

Cline, William R. and associates (1981), *World Inflation and the Developing Countries*, Washington D.C.: The Brookings Institute.

Considera, Claudio Monteiro (1975). 'Estrutura de Mercado e Formação de Preços na Indústria Brasileira – 1969/74', unpublished Master's Thesis, Universidade de Brasília.

(1981), 'Preços, *mark up* e distribuição funcional da renda na indústria de transformação: dinâmica de longo e de curto prazo – 1959/80', *Pesquisa e Planejamento Econômico*, 11(3).

(1983), 'Comportamento oligopolista e controle de preços industriais: o caso do gênero material de transporte – 1969/82', *Pesquisa e Planejamento Econômico*, 13(1).

Contador, Claudio R. (1977), 'Crescimento econômico e o combate à inflação', *Revista Brasileira de Economia*, 31(1).

(1978), 'A exogeneidade da oferta de moeda no Brasil', *Pesquisa e Planejamento Econômico*, 8(2).

(1982), 'Sobre as causas da recente aceleração inflacionária: comentário', *Pesquisa e Planejamento Econômico*, 12(2).

(1984), 'Um modelo macroeconométrico com choques de oferta', *Revista Brasileira de Economia*, 38(3).

(1985), 'Reflexões sobre o dilema entre inflação e crescimento econômico na decada de 80', *Pesquisa e Planejamento Econômico*, 15(1).

Corbo, Vittorio Lioi (1974), *Inflation in Developing Countries: An Econometric Study of Chilean Inflation*, Amsterdam: North-Holland.

Correa do Lago, Luiz Aranha, Costa, Margaret Hanson, Batista, Paulo Nogueira Jr and Ryff, Tito Bruno Bandeira (1984), *Uma Proposta de Política Anti-inflacionária para o Brasil* (versão preliminar), Instituto Brasileiro de Economia, Fundação Getulio Vargas, Rio de Janeiro.

Council of Economic Advisors (1970), 'Realising the economy's potential', in Smith and Teigen (eds.).

Coutts, K. J., Godley, W. and Nordhaus, W. (1978), *Industrial Pricing in the United Kingdom*, Cambridge University Press.

Coutts, K. J., Tarling, Roger and Wilkinson, Frank (1976), 'Costs and prices, 1974–76', *Cambridge Economic Policy Review*, 2.

Cripps, Francis and Godley, Wynn (1976), 'A formal analysis of the Cambridge Economic Policy Group Model', *Economica*, 43(172).

Cysne, R. Penha (1985), 'A relação de Phillips no Brasil: 1964–66 × 1980–84', *Revista Brasileira de Economia*, 39(4).

Dall'Acqua, F. Maida (1985), 'Impactos anti-inflacionários dos controles de salários e preços 1964/68', *Pesquisa e Planejamento Econômico*, 15(2).

Domberger, Simon (1983), *Industrial Structure, Pricing and Inflation*, Oxford: Martin Robertson.

Dornbusch, Rudiger (1985), 'Comments, Brazil' (comment on Arida and Lara Resende (1985)), in Williamson, John (ed.).

Drobny, Andres and Wells, John (1982), 'A distribuição da renda e o salário mínimo no Brasil: uma revisão crítica da literatura existente', *Pesquisa e Planejamento Econômico*, 12(3).

(1983), 'Wages, minimum wages, and income distribution in Brazil: results from the construction industry', *Journal of Development Economics*, 13(3).

Eckstein, O. (1964), 'A theory of the wage-price process in modern industry', *Review of Economic Studies*, 31(4).

(1968), 'Money wage determination revisited', *Review of Economic Studies*, 35(2).

(1983), *The DRI Model of the U.S. Economy*, New York: McGraw-Hill.

Eckstein, O. (ed.) (1972), *The Econometrics of Price Determination Conference*, Board of Governors of the Federal Reserve System, Washington D.C.

Eckstein, O. and Fromm, Gary (1968), 'The price equation', *American Economic Review*, 58(5).

Eckstein, O. and Wyss, David (1972), 'Industry price equations', in Eckstein (ed.).

Ellis, Howard S. (1969), 'Corrective inflation in Brazil, 1964–66', in Ellis, Howard S. (ed.), *The Economy of Brazil*, Berkeley: University of California Press.

Ezekiel, Mordecai (1938), 'The cobweb theorem', *Quarterly Journal of Economics*, 52(2).

Fishlow, Albert (1973), 'Some reflections on post-1964 Brazilian economic policy', in Stepan, Alfred (ed.), *Authoritarian Brazil: Origins, Policies, and Future*, New Haven: Yale University Press.

Foote, Richard J. (1958), *Analytical Tools for Studying Demand and Price Structures*, Agricultural Handbook No. 146, U.S.D.A., Washington D.C.

Fraga Neto, Arminio (1985), 'Indexation and Inflation in Brazil', *Texto para discussão*, No. 96, Departamento de Economia, Pontifícia Universidade Católica do Rio de Janeiro.

Friedman, M. (1968), 'The role of monetary policy', *American Economic Review* 58(1).

Fundação Getulio Vargas (various), *Conjuntura Econômica*, Rio de Janeiro.

Furtado, Celso (1981), *O Brasil Pós-'Milagre'*, 6th edition, Rio de Janeiro: Paz e Terra.

Girshick, M. A. and Haavelmo, Trygve (1947), 'Statistical analysis of the demand for food: examples of simultaneous estimation of structural equations', *Econometrica*, 15(2).

Godley, W. A. H. (1959), 'Costs, prices and demand in the short run', in Surrey, M. J. C. (ed.) (1976), *Macroeconomic Themes: Edited Readings in Macroeconomics with Commentaries*, London: Oxford University Press.

Godley, W. A. H. and Nordhaus, W. D. (1972), 'Pricing in the trade cycle', *Economic Journal*, 82(327).

Goldfeld, S. M. and Quandt, R. E. (1965), 'Some tests for homoscedasticity', *Journal of the American Statistical Association*, 60(310).

Gordon, Robert J. (1970), 'The recent acceleration of inflation and its lessons for the future', *Brookings Papers*, 1.

Granger, C. W. J. (1969), 'Investigating causal relationships by econometric methods and cross spectral methods', *Econometrica*, 3.

Grubb, D., Jackman, R. and Layard, R. (1982), 'Causes of the current stagflation', *Review of Economic Studies*, 49(5).

Hall, R. L. and Hitch, C. J. (1939), 'Price theory and business behaviour', *Oxford Economic Papers*, 2.

Harlow, Arthur A. (1962), *Factors Affecting the Price and Supply of Hogs*, Technical Bulletin No. 1274, U.S.D.A., Washington D.C.

Hausman, J. A. (1978), 'Specification tests in econometrics', *Econometrica*, 46(6).

Heien, Dale (1977), 'Price determination processes for agricultural sector models', *American Journal of Agricultural Economics*, 59(1).

Hendry, David F. (1979), 'Predictive failure and econometric modelling in macroeconomics: the transactions demand for money', in Ormerod, Paul (ed.) (1979), *Economic Modelling: Current Issues and Problems in Macro Economic Modelling in the U.K. and U.S.*, London: Heinemann.

(1980), 'Econometrics – alchemy or science?', *Economica*, 47(188).

Hendry, David F., Pagan, Adrian R. and Sargan, J. Denis (1983), 'Dynamic specification', in Griliches, Zvi and Intriligator, Michael D. (eds.), *Handbook of Econometrics*, Volume 1, Amsterdam: North-Holland.

Hendry, David F. and Richard, Jean-François (1982), On the formulation of empirical models in dynamic econometrics', *Journal of Econometrics*, 20(1).

Hendry, David F. and Mizon, G. E. (1978), 'Serial correlation as a convenient simplification, not a nuisance: a comment on a study of the demand for money by the Bank of England', *Economic Journal*, 88(351).

Hendry, David F. and Wallis, Kenneth F. (eds.) (1984), *Econometrics and Quantitative Economics*, Oxford: Basil Blackwell.

Henry, S. G. B. (1981), 'Incomes policy and aggregate pay', in Fallick, J. L. and Elliott, R. F. (eds.), *Incomes Policies, Inflation and Relative Pay*, London: George Allen & Unwin.

Henry, S. G. B., Sawyer, M. C. and Smith, P. (1976), 'Models of inflation in the United Kingdom: an evaluation', *National Institute Economic Review*, 77.

Hicks, John (1974), *The Crisis in Keynesian Economics*, Oxford: Basil Blackwell.

Hojman, David E. (1983), 'Wages, unemployment and expectations in developing countries: the labour market and the augmented Phillips curve for Chile', *Journal of Economic Studies*, 10(1).

Holanda Filho, Sérgio Buarque de (1983), *Estrutura industrial no Brasil: Concentração e diversificação*, Serie PNPE–7, Rio de Janeiro: IPEA/INPES.

Holden, Kenneth and Peel, David A. (1979), 'The augmented Phillips curve: some empirical results for Italy, Japan and the U.K.', *Economic Studies Quarterly*, 30(1).

Horta, Maria Helena (1981), 'Atribuições das autoridades monetárias no Brasil e formulação do orçamento monetário', *Textos para discussao interna*, No. 36, Rio de Janeiro: IPEA/INPES.

IBGE (Instituto Brasileiro de Geografia e Economia) (various), *Anuário Estatístico do Brasil*, Rio de Janeiro.

(1975), *Censo Industrial de 1970*, Rio de Janeiro.

IBRD (The World Bank) (1982), *Brazil: A Review of Agricultural Policies*, A World Bank Country Study, Washington D.C.

(1984), *Brazil: Financial Systems Review*, A World Bank Country Study, Washington D.C.

Jackson, D. A. S., Turner, H. A. and Wilkinson, Frank (1975), *Do Trade Unions Cause Inflation*?, 2nd edition, Cambridge University Press.

Jul, Ana Maria (1977), 'A Macroeconometric Forecasting Model for Brazil', unpublished Ph.D. Thesis, University of Pennsylvania.

Kafka, Alexandre (1967), 'The Brazilian Stabilization Program, 1964–66', *The Journal of Political Economy*, 75(4).

Kahil, Raouf (1973), *Inflation and Economic Development in Brazil: 1946–63*, Oxford: Clarendon Press.

Kaldor, N. (1976), 'Inflation and recession in the world economy', *Economic Journal*, 86(344).

Kalecki, M. (1943), 'Costs and prices', in Kalecki, M. (1971), *Selected Essays on the Dynamics of the Capitalist Economy*, Cambridge University Press.

(1955), 'The problem of financing of economic development', *The Indian Economic Review*, 2(3).

Kanbur, S. M. Ravi and Vines, David (1986), 'North-south interaction and commod control', *Journal of Development Economics*, 23(2).

Kaplan, A. D. N., Dirlam, J. B. and Lanzilotti, R. F. (1958), *Pricing in Big Business – A Case Approach*, Washington D.C.: The Brookings Institute.

Klein, L. R. and Summers, Roberts (1966), *The Wharton Index of Capacity Utilization*, Wharton School of Finance and Commerce, Philadelphia.

Koutsoyiannis, A. (1977), *Theory of Econometrics*, 2nd edition, London: Macmillan.

Laidler, D. E. W. and Parkin, J. M. (1975), 'Inflation – a survey', *Economic Journal*, 85(340).

Lara Resende, Andre Pinheiro de (1979), 'Inflation, Growth and Oligopolistic Pricing in a Semi-Industrialized Economy: The Case of Brazil', unpublished Ph.D. Thesis, MIT.

(1982), 'A política brasileira de estabilização: 1963/68, *Pesquisa e Planejamento Econômico*, 12(3).

Lara Resende, Andre Pinheiro de and Lopes, F. L. (1981), 'Sobre as causas da recente aceleração inflacionária', *Pesquisa e Planejamento Econômico*, 11(3).

Lara Resende, M. de Moura (1982), 'Energy prices and the post oil/energy crisis Brazilian inflation: an input/output study', unpublished Ph.D. thesis, Yale University.

Leamer, Edward E. (1983), 'Let's take the con out of econometrics', *American Economic Review*, 73(1).

Lee, F. S. (1984a), 'Full cost pricing: a new wine in a new bottle', *Australian Economic Papers*, June.

(1984b), 'Whatever happened to the full-cost principle (USA)?', in Wiles and Routh (eds.).

Lemgruber, A. C. (1974), 'Inflação: o modelo de realimentação e o modelo de aceleração', *Revista Brasileira de Economia*, 28(3).

(1977), 'External effects on the Brazilian inflation', in Krause, Lawrence B. and Salant, Walter S. (eds), *Worldwide Inflation: Theory and Recent Experience*, Washington D.C.: The Brookings Institute.

(1978), *Inflação, Moeda e Modelos Macroeconômicos: O Caso do Brasil*, Rio de Janeiro: Fundação Getulio Vargas.

(1980), 'Real output – inflation trade-offs, monetary growth and rational expectations in Brazil – 1950/79', *Anais do II Encontro Brasileiro de Econometria*, Novo Friburgo.

Lewis, W. A. (1964), 'Closing remarks', in Baer and Kerstenetzky (eds.).

Lipsey, Richard G. (1960), 'The relation between unemployment and the rate of change of money wage rates in the United Kingdom, 1862–1957: a further analysis', *Economica*, 27(105).

London Business School (1982), *London Business School Quarterly Model of the U.K. Economy*, Centre for Economic Forecasting, London.

Lopes, F. L. (1982), 'Inflação e nível de atividade no Brasil: un estudo econométrico', *Pesquisa e Planejamento Econômico*, 12(3).

(1984), 'Política salarial e a dinâmica do salário nominal', *Mimeo*, Pontifícia Universidade Católica do Rio de Janeiro.

(1986), *Choque Heterodoxo: Combate a Inflação e Reforma Monetária*, Rio de Janeiro: Editora Campus.

Lopes, F. L. and Bacha, Edmar L. (1983), 'Inflation, growth and wage policy: a Brazilian perspective', *Journal of Development Economics*, 13(1–2).

Lucas, R. (1976), 'Econometric policy evaluation: a critique', *Journal of Monetary Economics*, Supplementary Series, 1.

Maia Gomes, Gustavo (1985a), 'Monetaristas, neo-estruturalistas e a inflação brasileira em 1985', *Revista da ANPEC*, December.

(1985b), 'O programa brasileiro de estabilização: 1980/84', *Pesquisa e Planejamento Econômico*, 15(2).

Malan, P. S. and Bonelli, R. (1977), 'The Brazilian economy in the seventies: old and new developments', *World Development*, 5(1–2).

Marques, M. S. Bastos (1985), 'A aceleração inflacionária no Brasil: 1973–83', *Revista Brasileira de Economia*, 39(4).

Mata, M. da (1980), 'Controle de preços na economia brasileira: aspectos institucionais e resultados', *Pesquisa e Planejamento Econômico*, 10(3).

McAleer, Michael, Pagan, Adrian R. and Volker, Paul A. (1985), 'What will take the con out of econometrics?', *American Economic Review*, 75(3).

McCallum, B. T. (1970), 'The effects of demand on prices in British manufacturing industry: another view', *Review of Economic Studies*, 37(1).

(1975), 'Rational expectations and the natural rate hypothesis: some evidence for the United Kingdom', *The Manchester School*, 43(1).

McCarthy, D. F. (1982), 'Brazil-general equilibrium model', *World Bank Staff Working Papers*, Washington D.C.: The World Bank.

Meade, J. E. (1981), 'Note on the inflationary implications of the wage-fixing assumptions of the Cambridge Economic Policy Group', *Oxford Economic Papers*, 33(1).

Means, Gardiner C. (1936), 'Notes on inflexible prices', *American Economic Review* (Supplement), 26(1).

(1972), 'The administered price thesis reconfirmed', *American Economic Review*, 62(3).

Meinken, K. W. (1955), *The Demand and Price Structure for Wheat*, Technical Bulletin No. 1136, U.S.D.A., Washington D.C.

Mizon, Graham E. (1984), 'The encompassing approach in econometrics', in Hendry and Wallis (eds.).

Modiano, E. M. (1983a), 'A dinâmica de salários e preços na economia brasileira: 1966/82', *Pesquisa e Planejamento Econômico*, 13(1).

(1983b), 'Conseqüências macroeconómicas da restrição externa de 1983: simulações com um modelo econométrico para a economia brasileira', *Revista Brasileira de Economia*, 37(3).

(1985), 'Salários, preços e câmbio: os multiplicadores dos choques numa economia indexada', *Pesquisa e Planejamento Econômico*, 15(1).

Modigliani, Franco (1958), 'New developments on the oligopoly front', *Journal of Political Economy*, 66(3).

Modigliani, Franco and Padoa-Schioppa, Tommaso (1978), 'The management of an open economy with "100% plus" wage indexation', *Essays in international finance*, no. 130, Princeton University.

Montoro Filho, André Franco (1982), *Moeda e sistema financeiro no Brasil*, Serie PNPE – 5, Rio de Janeiro: IPEA/INPES.

Morley, Samuel A. (1971), 'Inflation and stagnation in Brazil', *Economic Development and Cultural Change*, 19(2).

Musalem, Alberto Roque (1982), 'Salário real, produtividade, progresso tecnológico, emprego e preço relativo dos manufaturados no Brasil', *Pesquisa e Planejamento Econômico*, 12(1).

Muth, John F. (1961), 'Rational expectations and the theory of price movements', *Econometrica*, 29(3).

Nadiri, M. I. and Gupta, V. (1977), 'Price and wage behavior in the U.S. aggregate economy and in manufacturing industries', in Popkin (ed.).

Nakamura, A. and Nakamura, M. (1981), 'On the relationship among several specification error tests presented by Wu, Durbin and Hausman', *Econometrica*, 49(6).

Neild, R. R. (1963), 'Pricing and employment in the trade cycle', *Occasional Paper XXI*, National Institute (NIESR), Cambridge University Press.

Nerlove, M. (1956), 'Estimates of the elasticities of supply of selected agricultural commodities', *Journal of Farm Economics*, 38.

Nickell, Stephen J. (1984), 'The modelling of wages and employment', in Hendry and Wallis (eds.).

Nordhaus, William D. (1972), 'Recent developments in price dynamics', in Eckstein (ed.).

Nordhaus, William D. and Shoven, John B. (1977), 'A technique for analyzing and decomposing inflation', in Popkin (ed.).

Noyola, Juan (1956), 'El desarrollo económico y la inflación en Mexico y otros países latinoamericanos', *Investigación económica*, Mexico, 16(4).

Okun, Arthur M. (1962), 'Potential GNP: its measurement and significance', *Proceedings of the Business and Economics Statistics Section of the American Statistical Association*, reprinted in Smith and Teigen (eds.).

(1981), *Prices and Quantities: A Macroeconomic Analysis*. Washington, D.C.: The Brookings Institute.

Olivera, Julio H. G. (1964), 'On structural inflation and Latin-American structuralism', *Oxford Economic Papers*, 16(3).

(1967a), 'Aspectos dinámicos de la inflación estructural', *Desarrollo Económico*, 7(27).

(1967b), 'Money, prices and fiscal lags: a note on the dynamics of inflation', *Banca Nazionale del Lavoro Quarterly Review*, 20(82).

Ormerod, Paul (1982), 'Rational and non-rational expectations of inflation in wage equations for the United Kingdom', *Economica*, 49(196).

Ott, David J. and Ott, Attiat F. (1965), 'A budget balance and equilibrium income', *Journal of Finance*, 20(1).

Pagan, Adrian (1984), 'Econometric issues in the analysis of regressions with generated regressors', *International Economic Review*, 25(1).

Pagan, Adrian and Hall, A. D. (1983), 'Diagnostic tests as residual analysis', *Econometric Reviews*, 2(2).

Parkin, Michael (1970), 'Incomes policy: some further remarks on the rate of change of money wages', *Economica*, 37.

(1975), 'The causes of inflation: recent contributions and current controversies', in Parkin, Michael and Nobay, A. R. (eds.), *Current Economic Problems*, Cambridge University Press.

(1978), 'Alternative explanations of U.K. inflation: a survey', in Parkin and Sumner (eds.).

Parkin, Michael and Sumner, Michael T. (eds.) (1978), *Inflation in the United Kingdom*, Manchester University Press.

Parkin, Michael, Sumner, Michael T. and Ward, Robert (1976), 'The effects of excess demand, generalized expectations and wage-price controls on wage inflation in the U.K.', in Brunner, Karl and Meltzer, Allan H. (eds.), *The Economics of Wage and Price Controls*, Amsterdam: North-Holland.

Parkin, Vincent N. (1983), 'Economic liberalism in Chile, 1973–82: a model for growth and development or a recipe for stagnation and impoverishment?', *Cambridge Journal of Economics*, 7(2).

Pesaran, M. H. and Evans, R. A. (1984), 'Inflation, capital gains and U.K. personal savings: 1953–1981', *Economic Journal*, 94(374).

Pesaran, M. H., Smith, R. P. and Yeo, J. S. (1985), 'Testing for structural stability and predictive failure: a review', *The Manchester School*, 53(3).

Phelps, Edmund S. (1968), 'Money-wage dynamics and labor-market equilibrium', *Journal of Political Economy*, 76(4).

Phillips, A. W. (1958), 'The relation between unemployment and the rate of change of money wage rates in the United Kingdom, 1861–1957', *Economica*, 25(100).

Pinto, Aníbal (1968), 'Raíces estructurales de la inflación en América Latina', *El Trimestre Económico*, 35(1).

Popkin, Joel (ed.) (1977), *Analysis of Inflation: 1965–74*, Studies in Income and Wealth Vol. 42, Cambridge, Mass.: NBER/Ballinger.

Prebisch, R. (1964), *Towards a New Trade Policy for Development*, Report by the Secretary-General of UNCTAD, United Nations.

Ramos, Raimundo Nonato Mendonca (1981), 'The Problem of Financing Economic Development: The Case of Brazil's External Debt in the 1970s', unpublished Ph.D. Thesis, University of Illinois (Urbana-Champaign).

Rangel, Ignacio (1981), *A Inflação Brasileira*, 4th edition, São Paulo: editora brasiliense.

Reis Queiroz, Carlos Alberto (1983), 'Monetary policy in the context of price indexation: the Brazilian case', *Brazilian Economic Studies*, 7.

Rezende Rocha, R. de (1983), 'Juros e inflação: Uma análise da equação de Fisher para o Brasil', unpublished Doctoral Thesis, EPGE/IBE, Fundação Getulio Vargas, Rio de Janeiro.

Ros, Jaime (1980), 'Pricing in the Mexican manufacturing sector', *Cambridge Journal of Economics*, 4(3).

Rowthorn, Bob (1980), 'Conflict, inflation and money', in *Capitalism, Conflict and Inflation*, London: Lawrence and Wishart.

Rushdy, F. and Lund, P. J. (1967), 'The effects of demand on prices in British manufacturing industry', *Review of Economic Studies*, 34(4).

Sahota, G. S. (1975), *Brazilian Economic Policy: An Optimal Control Theory Analysis*, New York: Praeger Publishers.

Sargan, J. D. (1964), 'Wages and prices in the United Kingdom: a study in econometric methodology', in Hart, P. E., Mills, G. and Whitaker, J. K. (eds.), *Econometric Analysis for National Economic Planning*, London: Butterworth (for Colston Research Society).

(1971), 'A study of wages and prices in the United Kingdom, 1949–68', in Johnson, H. G. and Nobay, A. R. (eds.), *The Current Inflation*, London: Macmillan.

(1980a), 'A model of wage-price inflation', *Review of Economic Studies*, 47(1).

(1980b), 'The consumer price equation in the post war British economy: an exercise in equation specification testing', *Review of Economic Studies*, 47(1).

Sawyer, Malcolm C. (1983), *Business Pricing and Inflation*, London: Macmillan.

Sayad, João (1981), 'Abastecimento urbano e inflação', *Pesquisa e Planejamento Econômico*, 11(3).

Scherer, F. M. (1980), *Industrial Market Structure and Economic Performance*, 2nd edition, Chicago: Rand-McNally.

Schultze, C. L. and Tryon, J. L. (1965), 'Prices and wages', in Duesenberry, J. S., *The Brookings Quarterly Econometric Model of the United States*, Chicago: Rand-McNally.

Seers, Dudley (1962), 'A theory of inflation and growth in under-developed economies based on the experience of Latin America', *Oxford Economic Papers*, 14(2).

Simonsen, Mario Henrique (1970), *Inflação, gradualismo e tratamento de choque*, Rio de Janeiro: APEC Editora.

(1980), 'Inflation and anti-inflationary policies in Brazil', presented at the Conference on World Inflation and Inflation in Brazil at the Fundação Getulio Vargas, published in (1984), *Brazilian Economic Studies*, 8.

(1983), 'Indexation: current theory and the Brazilian experience', in Dornbusch, Rudiger and Simonsen, Mario Henrique (eds.), *Inflation, Debt and Indexation*, Cambridge, Mass.: The MIT Press.

Sims, C. A. (1972), 'Money, income and causality', *American Economic Review*, 62(4).

Siri, Gabriel and Dominguez, Luis Raúl (1981), 'Central American accommodation to external disruption', in Cline and associates.

Smith, W. L. and Teigen, R. (eds.) (1970), *Readings in Money, National Income and Stabilization Policy*, Illinois: R. D. Irwin.

Solow, R. M. (1969), *Price Expectations and the Behaviour of the Price Level*, Manchester University Press.

Souza, J. A. and Monteiro, J. V. (1974), 'Models of the Brazilian economy', in Ruggles, N. D. (ed.), *The Role of the Computer in Economic and Social Research in Latin America*, New York: NBER.

Souza, Juarez de (1982), 'Inflation in Brazil: 1974–1980', unpublished Ph.D. Thesis, University of Illinois (Urbana – Champaign).

Srinivasan, T. G., Parkin, Vincent and Vines, David (1989), 'Food subsidies and inflation in developing countries: a bridge between structuralism and monetarism', *Discussion Paper Series No. 334*, London: Centre for Economic Policy Research.

Steindal, J. (1976), *Maturity and Stagnation in American Capitalism*, New York: Monthly Review Press.

Stigler, G. J. and Kindahl, J. K. (1970), *The Behavior of Industrial Prices*, New York: NBER.

Sumner, Michael T. (1978), 'Wage determination', in Parkin and Sumner (eds.).

Sumner, Michael T. and Ward, R. (1983), 'The reappearing Phillips curve', in Greenhalgh, C. A., Layard, P. R. G. and Oswald, A. J. (eds), *The Causes of Unemployment*, Oxford: Clarendon Press.

Sunkel, Osvaldo (1958), 'La inflación chilena: un enfoque heterodoxo', *El Trimestre Económico*, 25(4), also published in English as: (1960), 'Inflation in Chile: an unorthodox approach', *International Economic Papers*, 10.

Sweezy, Paul M. (1939), 'Demand under conditions of oligopoly', *Journal of Political Economy*, 47(4).

Sylos-Labini, Paolo (1969), *Oligopoly and Technical Progress* (revised edition), Cambridge, Mass.: Harvard University Press.

(1979), 'Industrial pricing in the United Kingdom' (review article), *Cambridge Journal of Economics*, 3(2).

(1984), *The Forces of Economic Growth and Decline*, Cambridge, Mass.: MIT Press.

Syvrud, D. (1972), 'Estrutura e política de juros no Brasil – 1960/70', *Revista Brasileira de Economia*, 26(1).

Tavares, Maria de Conceição (1978), 'Ciclo e crise – o movimento recente da industrialização brasileira', unpublished Thesis, Universidade Federal do Rio de Janeiro.

Tavares, Maria de Conceição and Souza, Paulo Renato (1983), 'Employment and wages in industry: the case of Brazil', in Urquidi, V. L. R. and Trejo, S. (eds.), *Human Resources, Employment and Development, Vol. 4 Latin America*, International Economic Association, London: Macmillan.

Tavlas, George S. (1983), 'A model of the inflationary process in six major O.E.C.D. economies: empirical results and policy implications', *Journal of Policy Modeling*, 5(1).

(1984), 'The price equation and excess demand: a reappraisal', *Applied Economics*, 16(6).

Taylor, L. (1979), *Macro Models for Developing Countries*, New York: McGraw-Hill.

(1981), 'IS/LM in the tropics: diagrammatics of the new structuralist macro critique', in Cline, William R. and Weintraub, Sidney (eds.), *Economic Stabilization in the Developing Countries*, Washington D.C.: The Brookings Institute.

(1983), *Structuralist Macroeconomics*, New York: Basic Books.

Taylor, L., Bacha, Edmar L., Cardoso, Eliana A. and Lysy, Frank J. (1980), *Models of Growth and Distribution for Brazil*, New York: Oxford University Press.

Theil, H. (1961), *Economic Forecasts and Policy*, 2nd edition, Amsterdam: North-Holland.

Tinbergen, J. (1955), *On the Theory of Economic Policy*, Amsterdam: North-Holland.

Tolosa, Hamilton C. (1978), 'Dualism in the urban labour market', *Brazilian Economic Studies*, 4.

Tomek, William G. and Robinson, Kenneth L. (1977), 'Agricultural price analysis and outlook', in Martin L. R. (ed.), *A Survey of Agricultural Economics Literature*, Vol. 1, Minneapolis: University of Minnesota Press.

(1981), *Agricultural Product Prices*, 2nd edition, Ithaca, New York: Cornell University Press.

Turner, H. A. and Jackson, D. A. S. (1970), 'On the determination of the general wage level – a world analysis; or "*unlimited labour forever*"', *The Economic Journal*, 80(320).

Turnovsky, S. J. (1977), *Macroeconomic analysis and stabilization policy*, Cambridge University Press.

Turnovsky, S. J. and Wachter, Michael L. (1972). 'A test of the 'expectations hypothesis' using directly observed wage and price expectations', *Review of Economics and Statistics*, 54(1).

van Wijnbergen, S. J. (1981), 'Short-run macroeconomic adjustment policies in South Korea: a quantitative analysis', *World Bank Staff Working Papers No. 510*, Washington D.C.: IBRD.

(1982), 'Stagflationary effects of monetary stabilization policies: a quantitative analysis of South Korea', *Journal of Development Economics*, 10(2).

(1983), 'Credit policy, inflation and growth in a financially repressed economy', *Journal of Development Economics*, 13(1–2).

Wachter, Susan M. (1976), *Latin American Inflation*, Lexington, Mass.: Lexington Books, D. C. Heath and Co.

Waugh, Frederick V. (1964a), 'Cobweb models', *Journal of Farm Economics*, 46(4).

(1964b), *Demand and Price Analysis: Some Examples from Agriculture*, Technical Bulletin No. 1316, Economic Research Service, U.S.D.A., Washington D.C.

Wallis, K. F. (ed.) (1984), *Models of the U.K. Economy: A Review*, Oxford University Press.

Wells, John R. (1977), 'Growth and Fluctuations in the Brazilian Manufacturing Sector during the 1960s', unpublished Ph.D. Thesis, University of Cambridge.

(1979), 'Brazil and the post 1973 crisis in the international economy', in Thorp, Rosemary and Whitehead, Laurence (eds.), *Inflation and Stabilisation in Latin America*, London: Macmillan.

Wiles, Peter (1984), 'Whatever happened to the full-cost principle (UK)?', in Wiles and Routh (eds.).

Wiles, Peter and Routh, Guy (eds.) (1984), *Economics in Disarray*, Oxford: Basil Blackwell.

Williamson, John (ed.) (1985), *Inflation and Indexation – Argentina, Brazil and Israel*, Washington D.C.: Institute for International Economics.

Wren-Lewis, Simon (1982). 'A model of private sector earnings behaviour', *H.M. Treasury Working Paper No.* 23, London.

Wu, D-Min (1973), 'Alternative tests of independence between stochastic regressors and disturbances', *Econometrica*, 41(4).

Zottman, L. (1978), *Inflação no Brasil: 1947/67*, Estudos para o Planejamento No. 18, Brasília: IPEA/IPLAN.

Index

For EU product safety concerns, contact us at Calle de José Abascal, 56–1°, 28003 Madrid, Spain or eugpsr@cambridge.org.

www.ingramcontent.com/pod-product-compliance
Ingram Content Group UK Ltd.
Pitfield, Milton Keynes, MK11 3LW, UK
UKHW042211180425
457623UK00011B/159

* 9 7 8 0 5 2 1 1 3 4 1 2 5 *